YOTSUBA&!

1

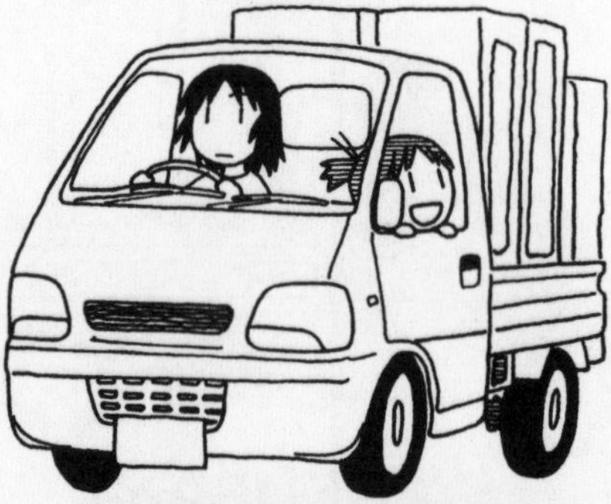

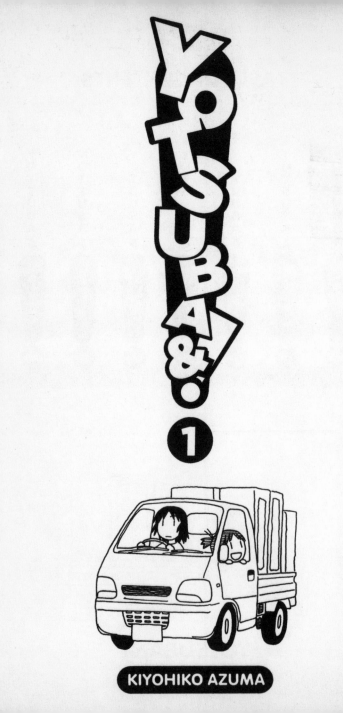

KIYOHIKO AZUMA

TABLE OF CONTENTS

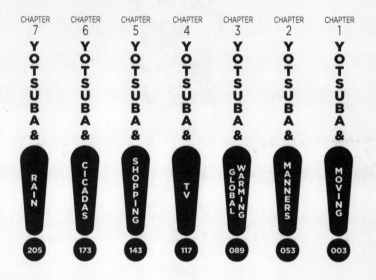

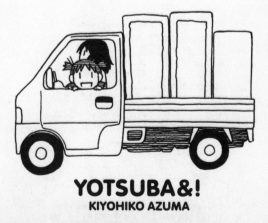

YOTSUBA&!
KIYOHIKO AZUMA

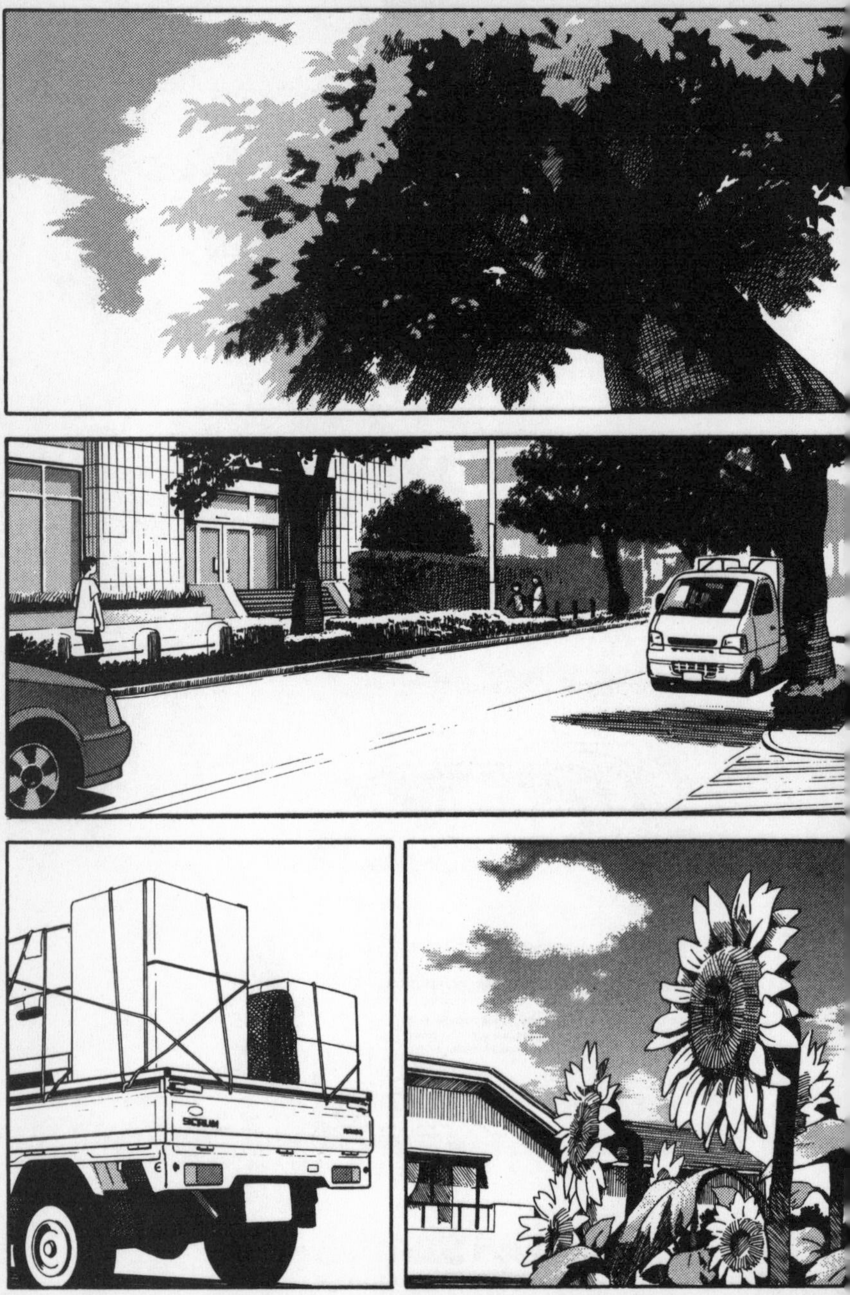
SCRUM

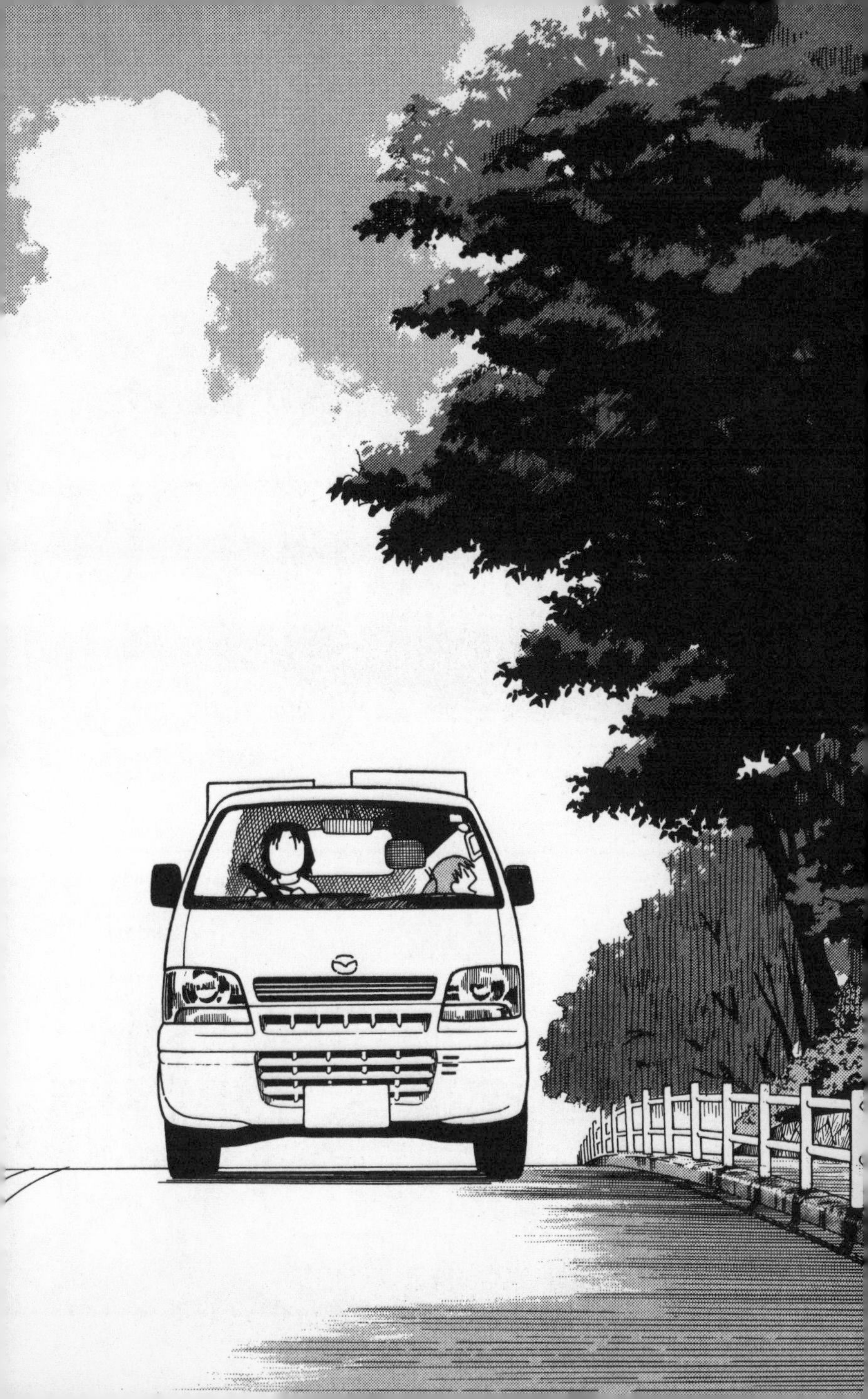

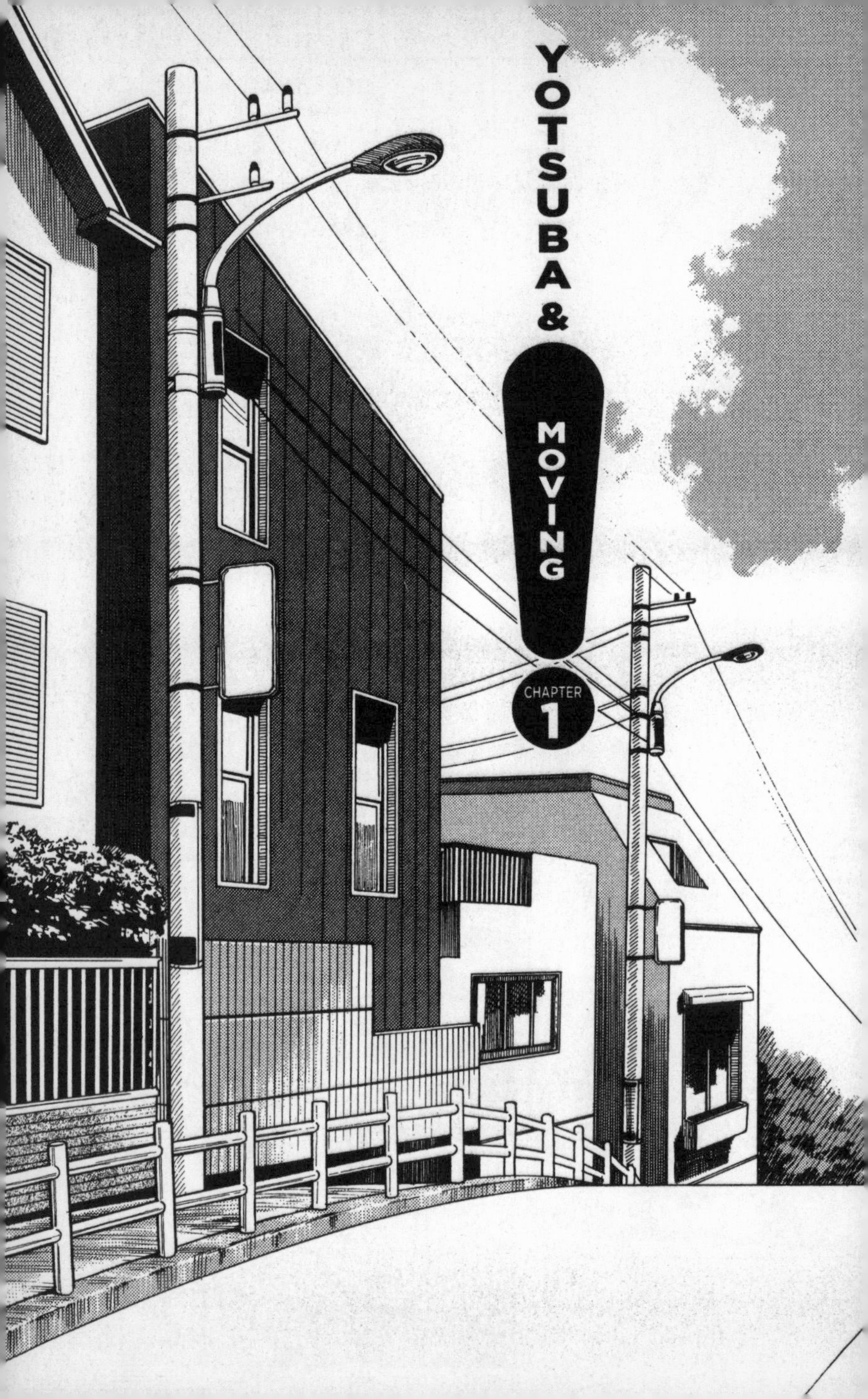
YOTSUBA &
MOVING
!
CHAPTER
1

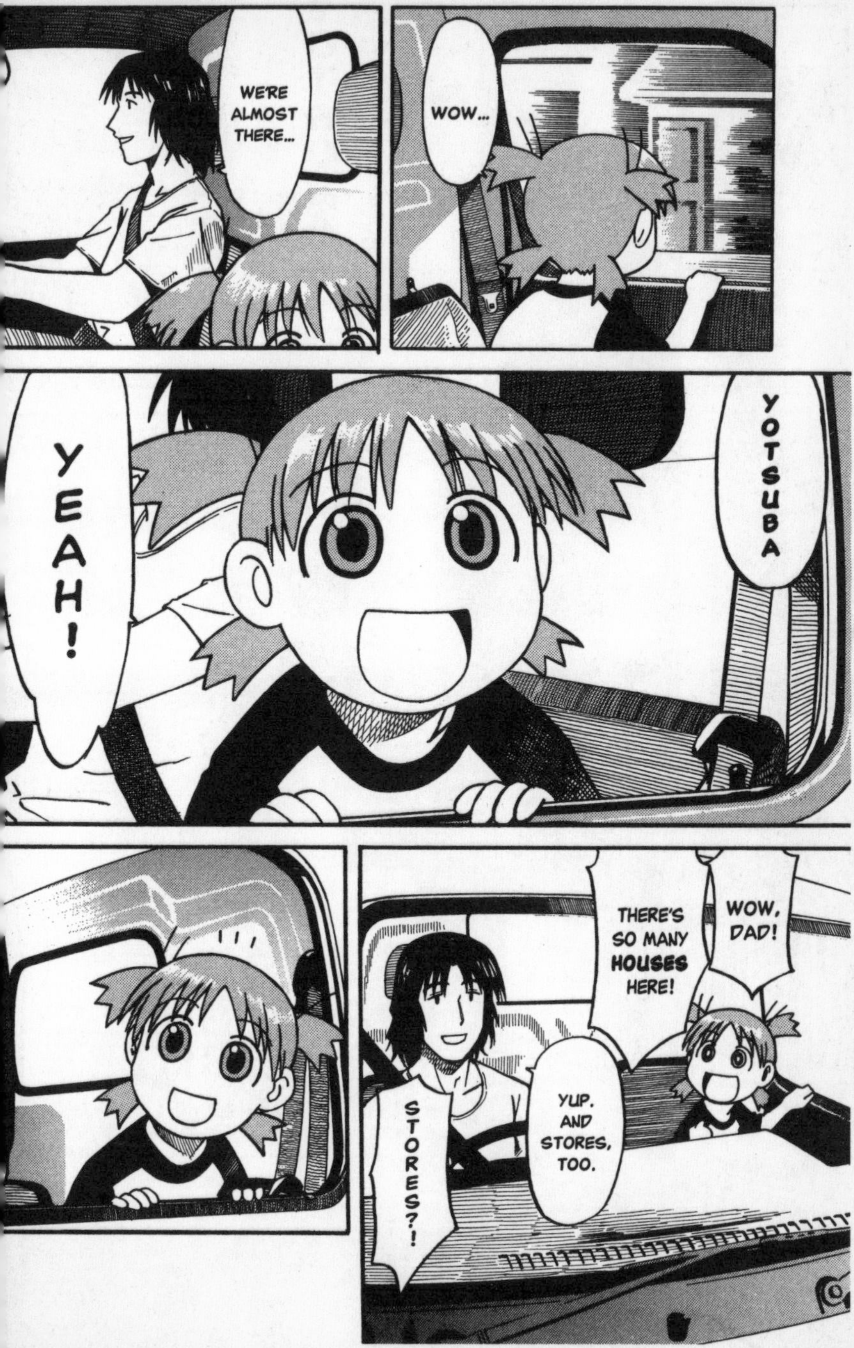
WOW...
WE'RE ALMOST THERE...
YOTSUBA
YEAH!
WOW, DAD!
THERE'S SO MANY HOUSES HERE!
YUP. AND STORES, TOO.
STORES?!

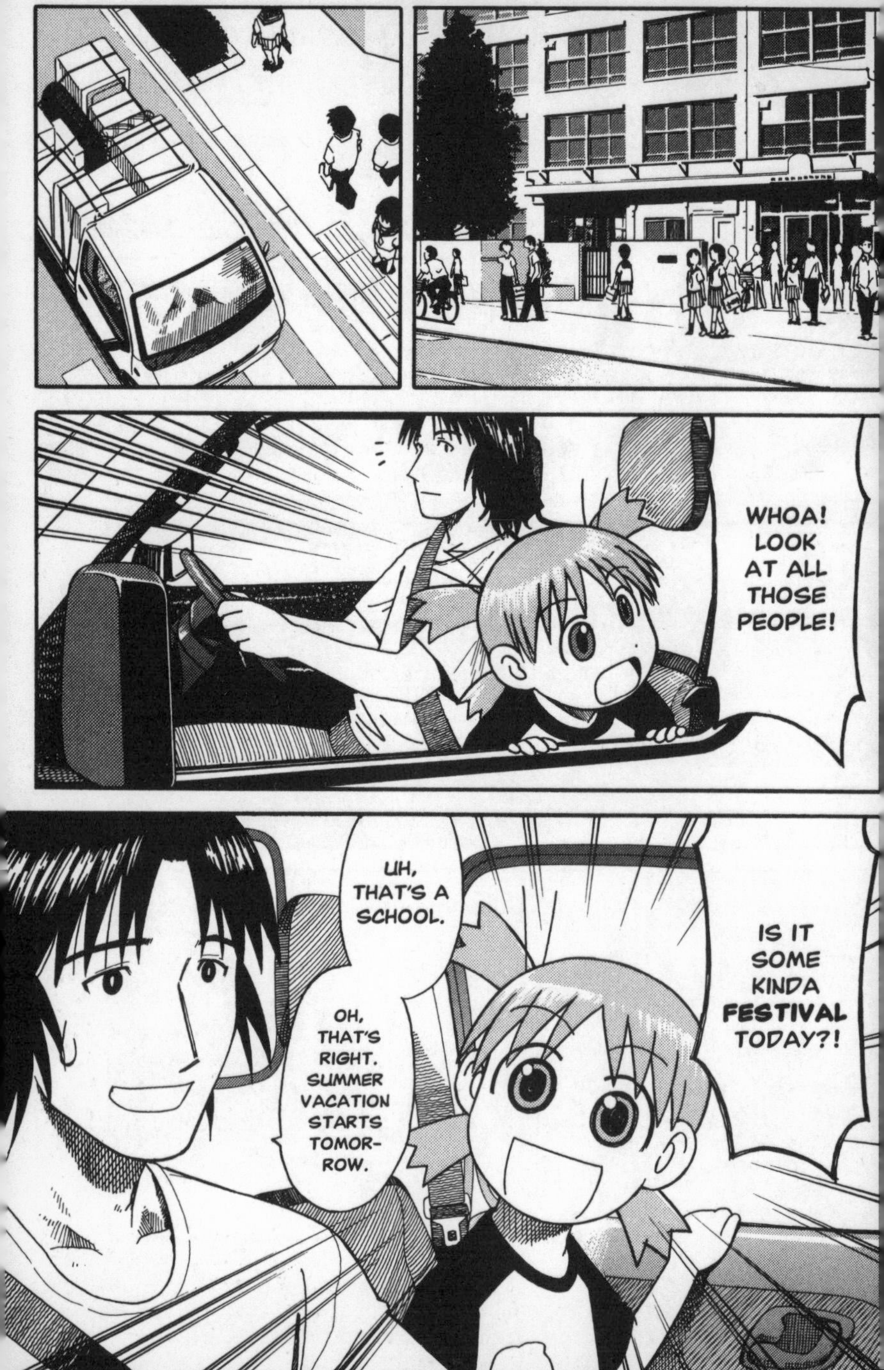
WHOA! LOOK AT ALL THOSE PEOPLE!
IS IT SOME KINDA FESTIVAL TODAY?!
UH, THAT'S A SCHOOL.
OH, THAT'S RIGHT. SUMMER VACATION STARTS TOMOR-ROW.

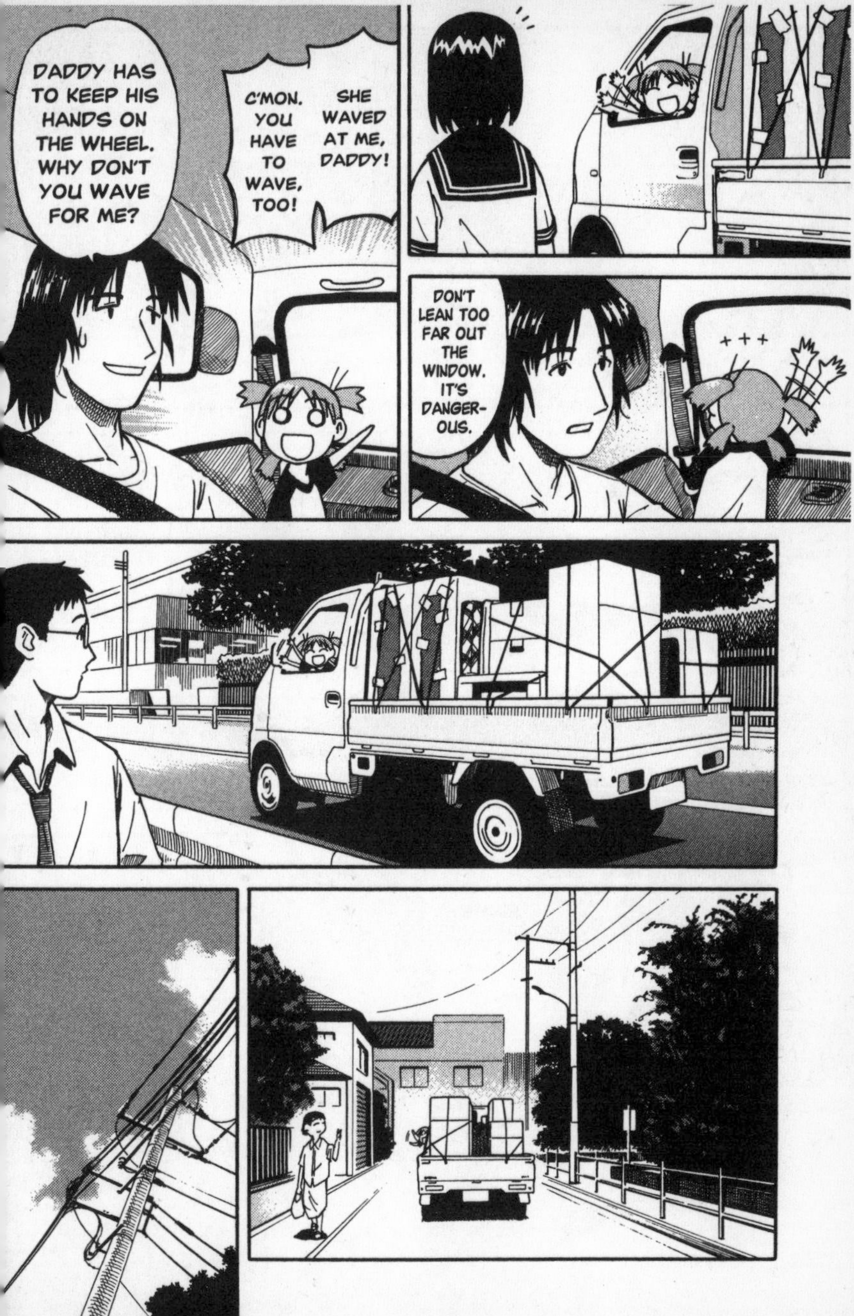
DON'T LEAN TOO FAR OUT THE WINDOW. IT'S DANGER-OUS.
SHE WAVED AT ME, DADDY!
C'MON. YOU HAVE TO WAVE, TOO!
DADDY HAS TO KEEP HIS HANDS ON THE WHEEL. WHY DON'T YOU WAVE FOR ME?

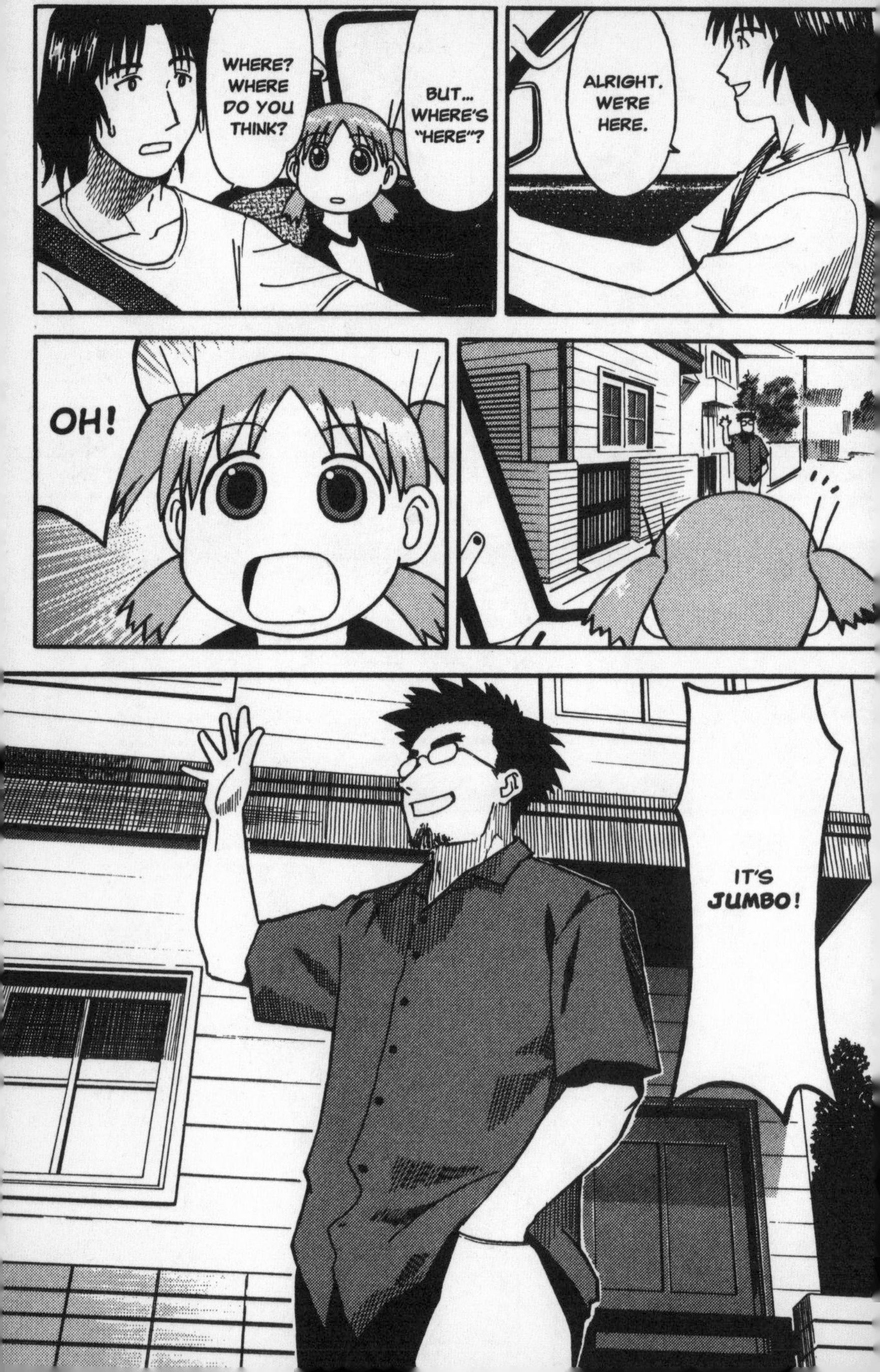
ALRIGHT. WE'RE HERE.
BUT... WHERE'S "HERE"?
WHERE? WHERE DO YOU THINK?
OH!
IT'S JUMBO!

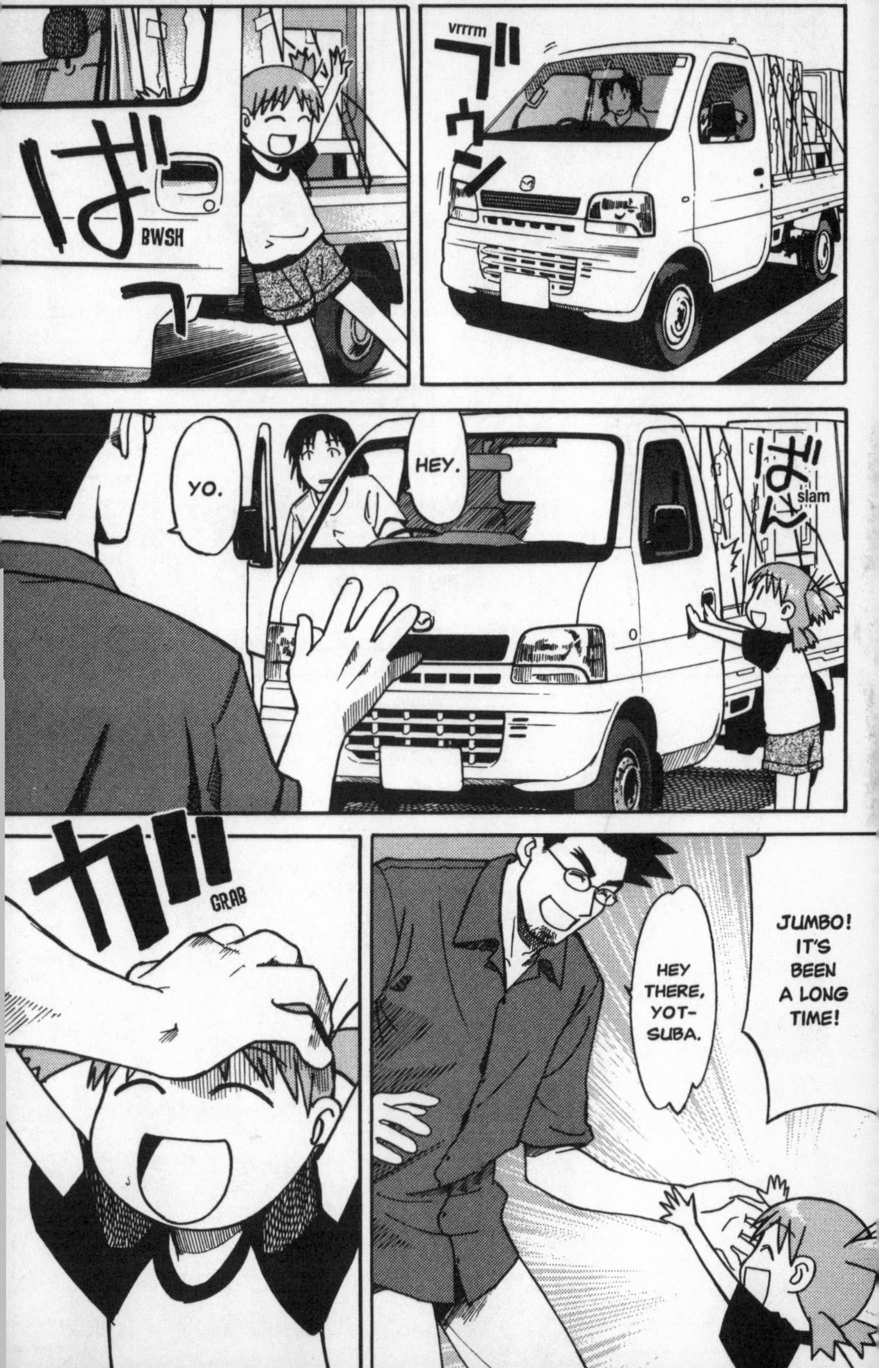
ブウン
vrrrm
ばっ
BWSH
ばん
slam
HEY.
YO.
JUMBO! IT'S BEEN A LONG TIME!
HEY THERE, YOT-SUBA.
GRAB

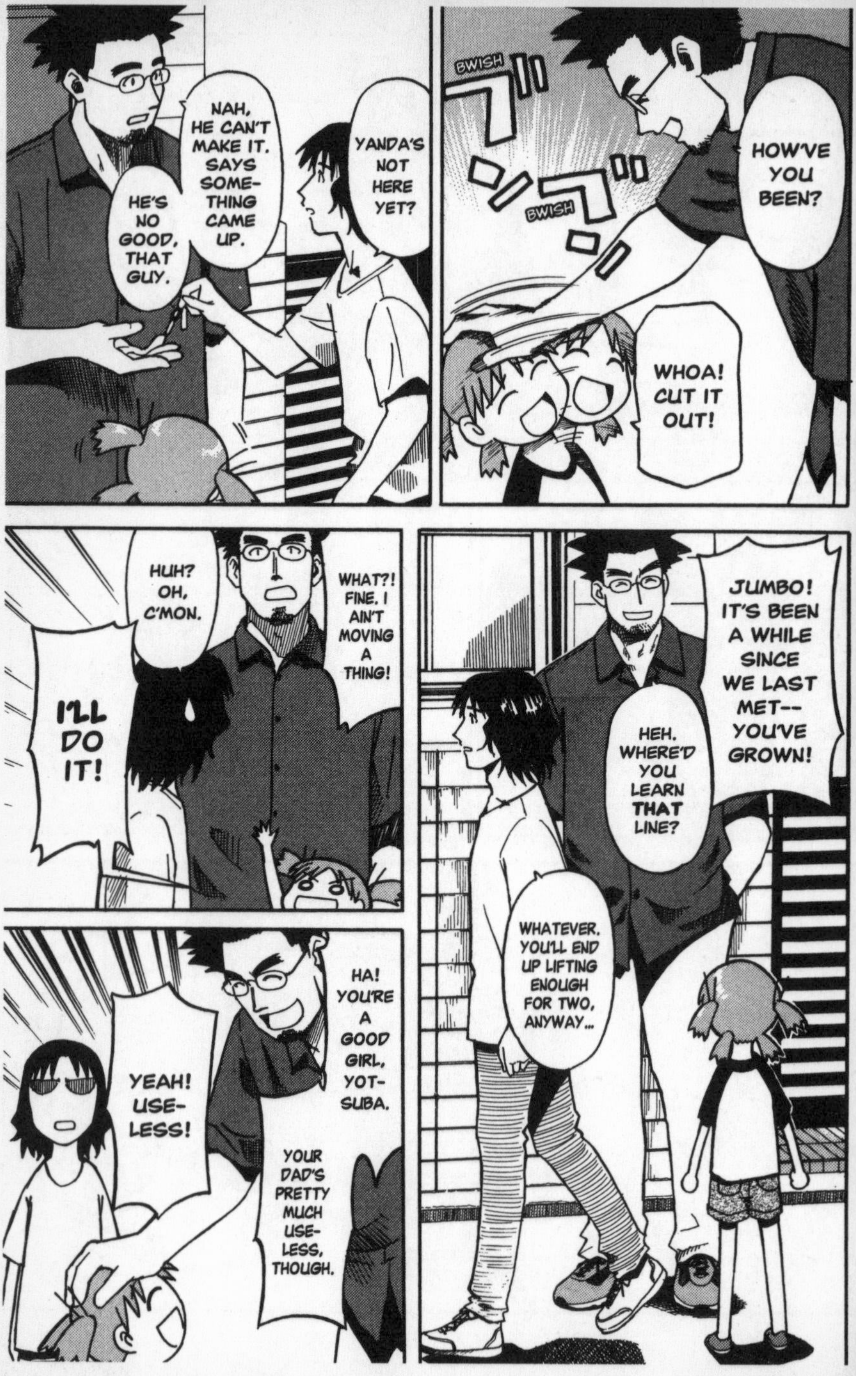
BWISH
BWISH
HOW'VE YOU BEEN?
WHOA! CUT IT OUT!
YANDA'S NOT HERE YET?
NAH, HE CAN'T MAKE IT. SAYS SOMETHING CAME UP.
HE'S NO GOOD, THAT GUY.
JUMBO! IT'S BEEN A WHILE SINCE WE LAST MET-- YOU'VE GROWN!
HEH. WHERE'D YOU LEARN THAT LINE?
WHATEVER. YOU'LL END UP LIFTING ENOUGH FOR TWO, ANYWAY...
WHAT?! FINE. I AIN'T MOVING A THING!
HUH? OH, C'MON.
I'LL DO IT!
HA! YOU'RE A GOOD GIRL, YOTSUBA.
YEAH! USELESS!
YOUR DAD'S PRETTY MUCH USELESS, THOUGH.

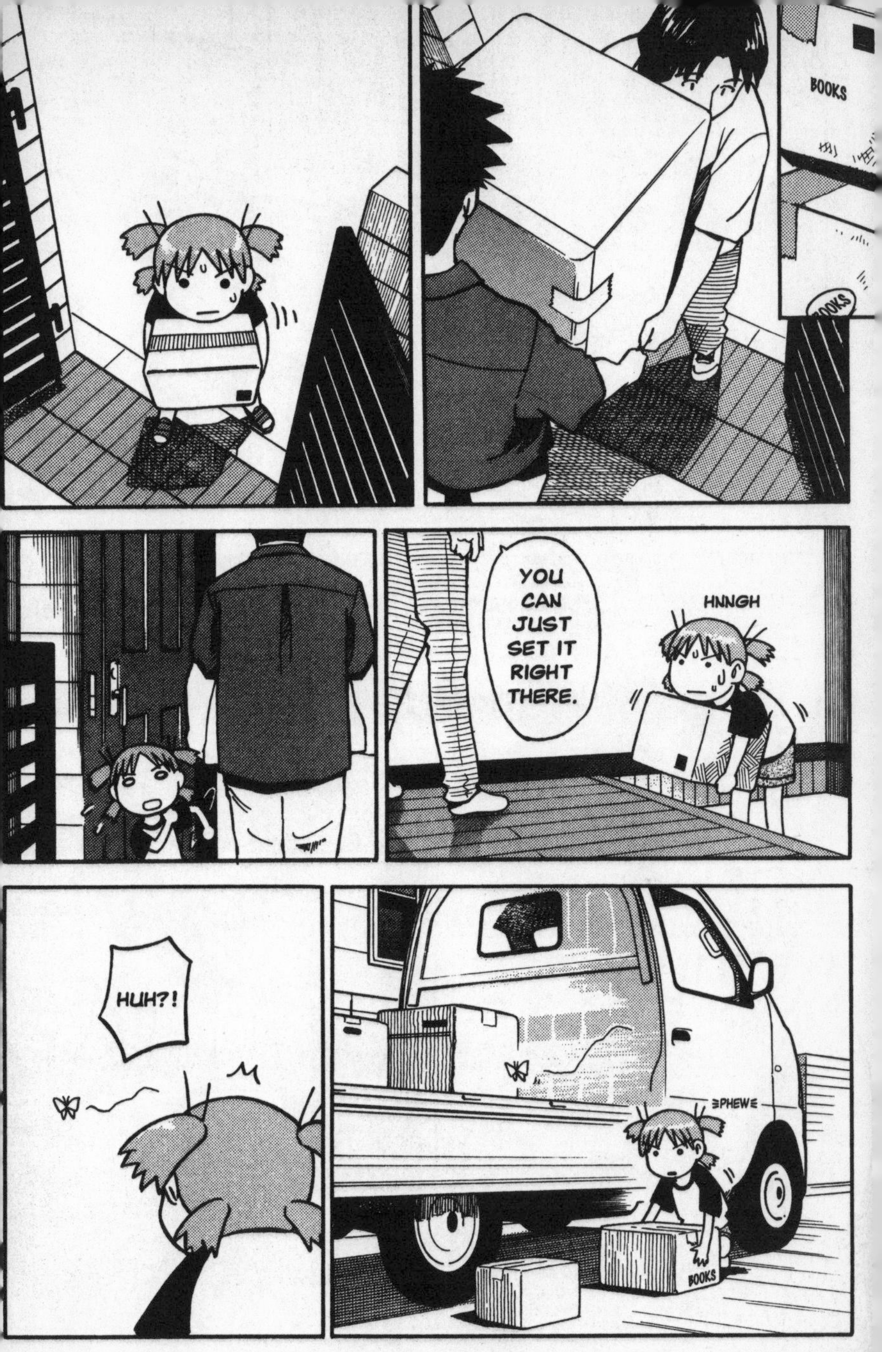
BOOKS
BOOKS
YOU CAN JUST SET IT RIGHT THERE.
HNNGH
PHEW
BOOKS
HUH?!

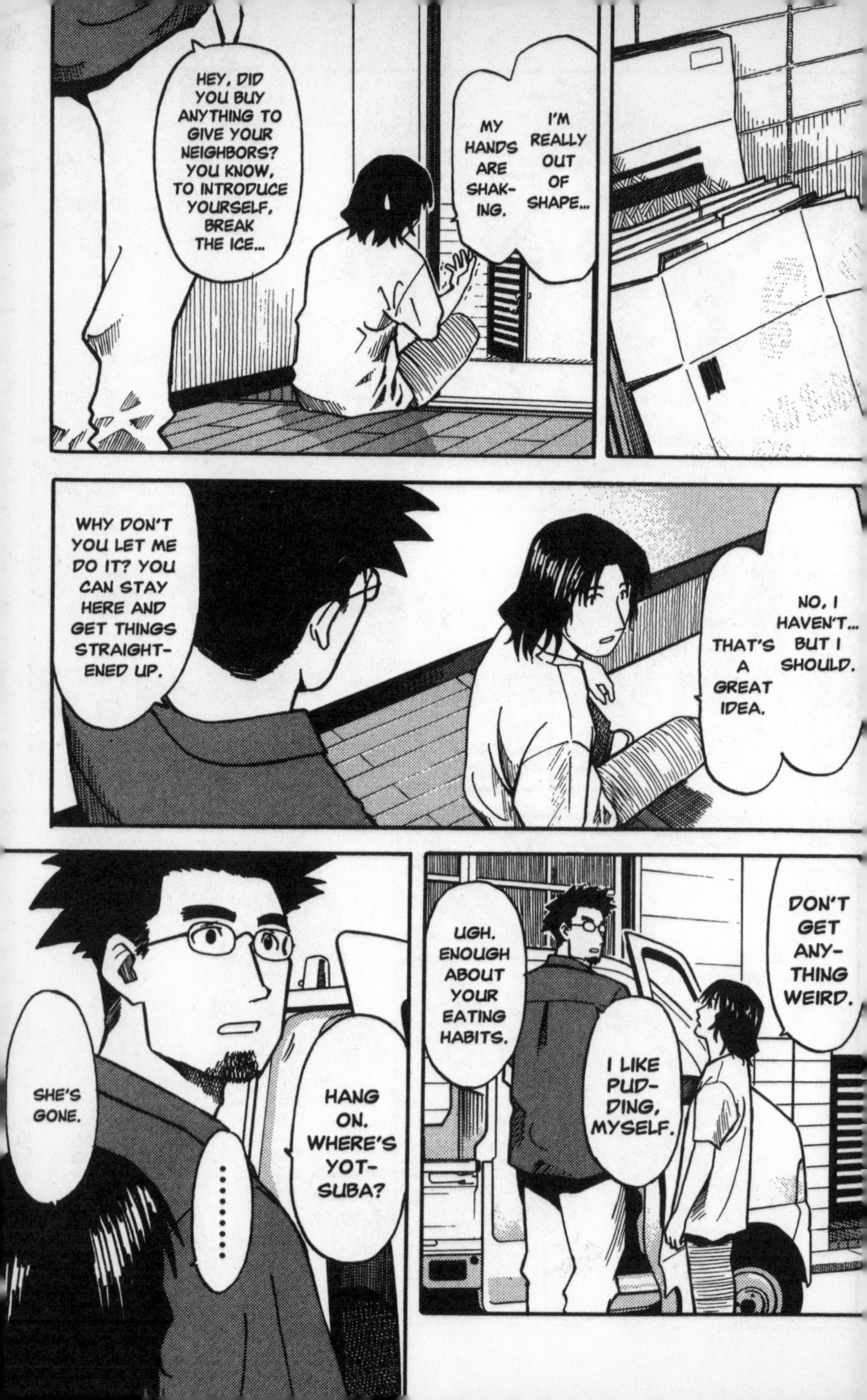
I'M REALLY OUT OF SHAPE...
MY HANDS ARE SHAKING.
HEY, DID YOU BUY ANYTHING TO GIVE YOUR NEIGHBORS? YOU KNOW, TO INTRODUCE YOURSELF, BREAK THE ICE...
NO, I HAVEN'T... BUT I SHOULD.
THAT'S A GREAT IDEA.
WHY DON'T YOU LET ME DO IT? YOU CAN STAY HERE AND GET THINGS STRAIGHTENED UP.
DON'T GET ANYTHING WEIRD.
I LIKE PUDDING, MYSELF.
UGH. ENOUGH ABOUT YOUR EATING HABITS.
HANG ON. WHERE'S YOTSUBA?
......
SHE'S GONE.

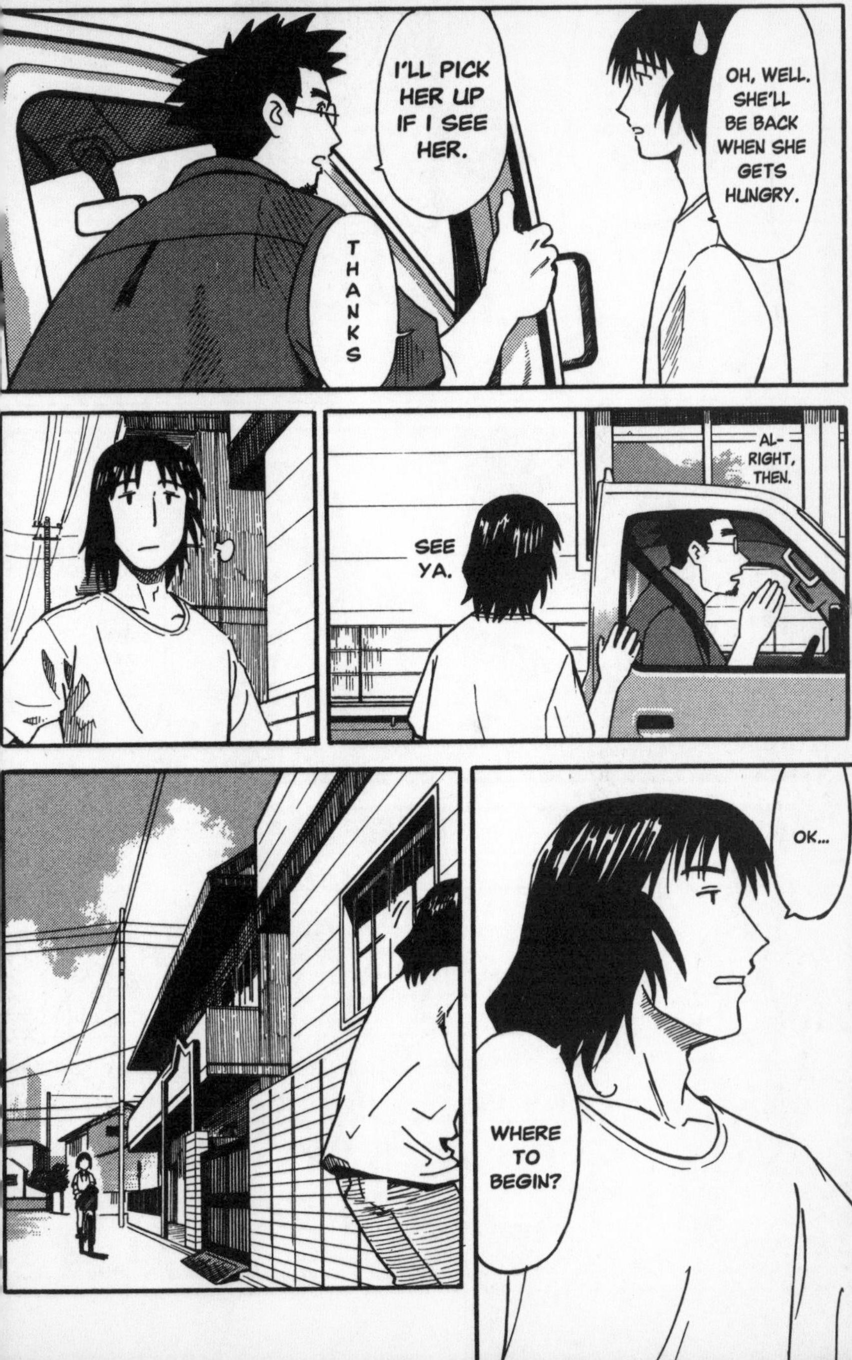
OH, WELL. SHE'LL BE BACK WHEN SHE GETS HUNGRY.
I'LL PICK HER UP IF I SEE HER.
THANKS
AL-RIGHT, THEN.
SEE YA.
OK...
WHERE TO BEGIN?

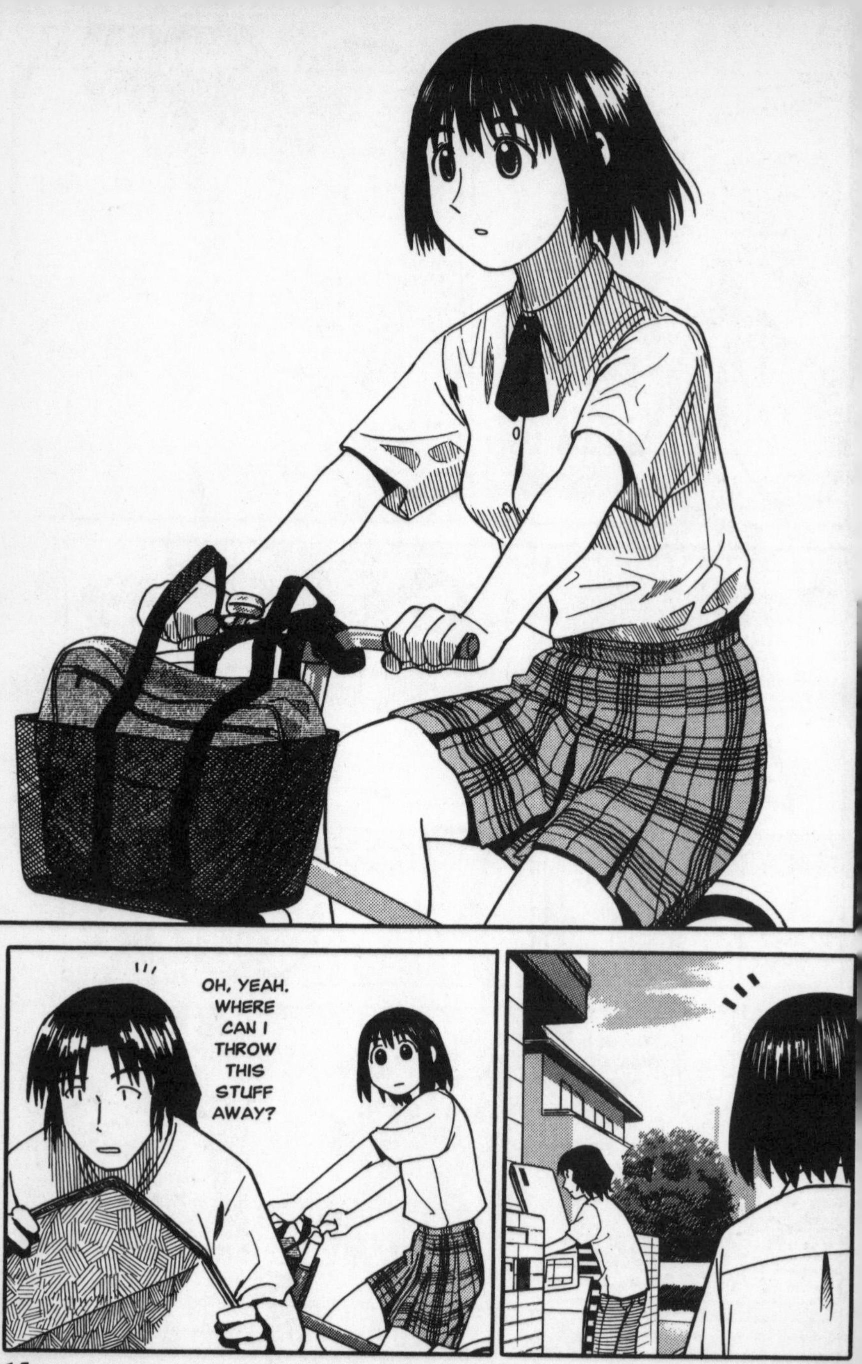
OH, YEAH. WHERE CAN I THROW THIS STUFF AWAY?

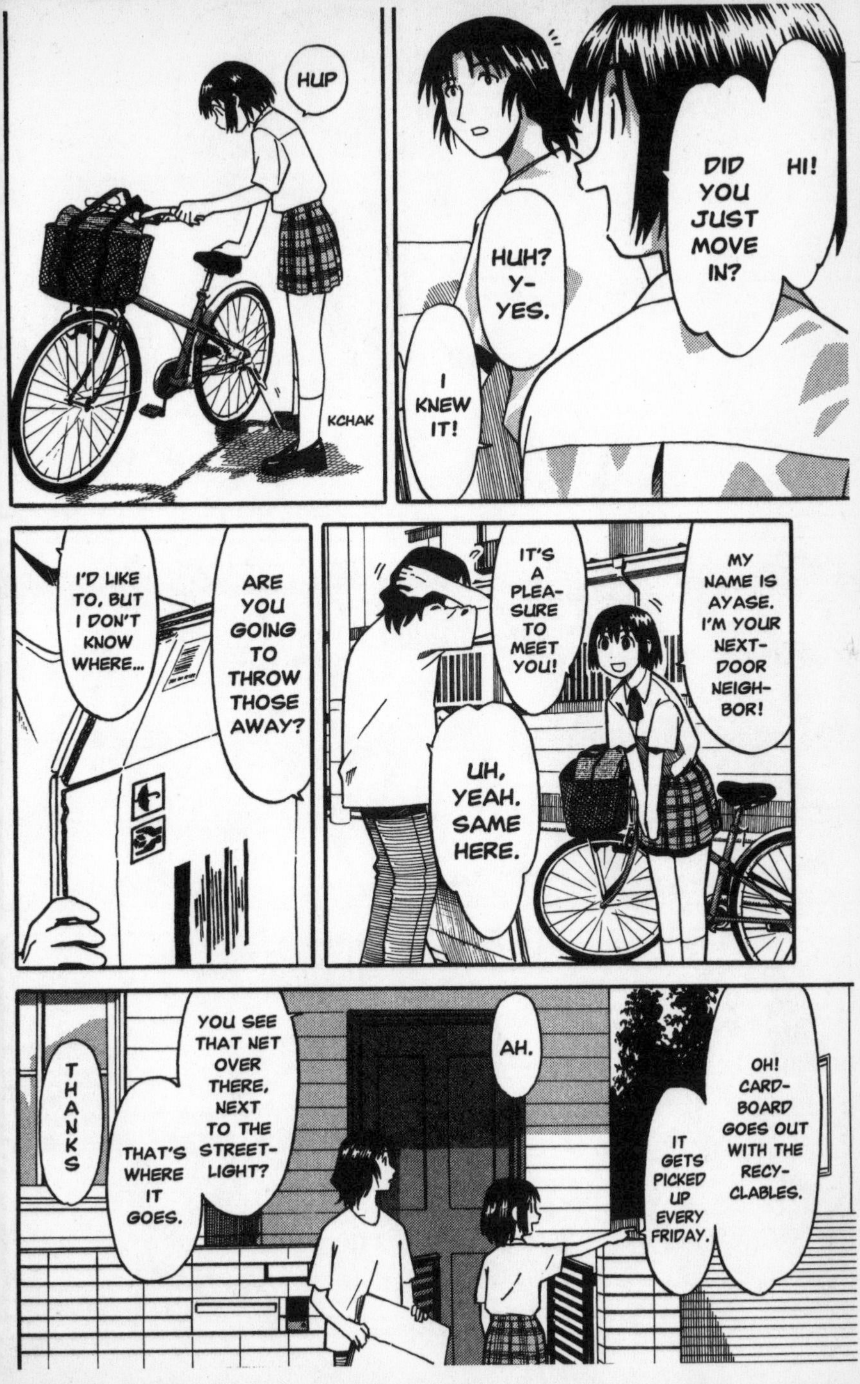
HI!
DID YOU JUST MOVE IN?
HUH? Y-YES.
I KNEW IT!
HUP
KCHAK
MY NAME IS AYASE. I'M YOUR NEXT-DOOR NEIGHBOR!
IT'S A PLEASURE TO MEET YOU!
UH, YEAH. SAME HERE.
ARE YOU GOING TO THROW THOSE AWAY?
I'D LIKE TO, BUT I DON'T KNOW WHERE...
OH! CARDBOARD GOES OUT WITH THE RECYCLABLES.
IT GETS PICKED UP EVERY FRIDAY.
AH.
YOU SEE THAT NET OVER THERE, NEXT TO THE STREETLIGHT?
THAT'S WHERE IT GOES.
THANKS

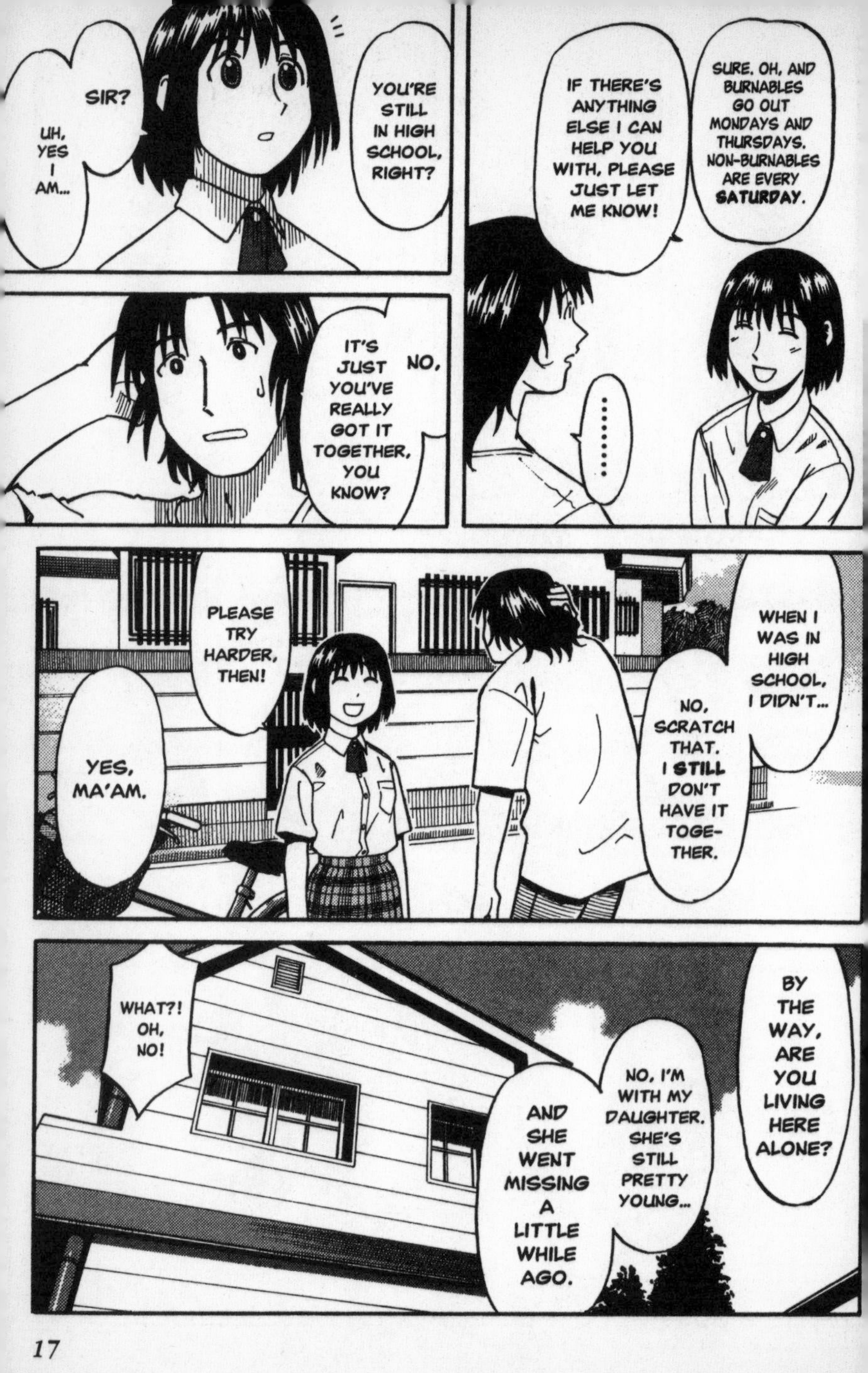
SURE. OH, AND BURNABLES GO OUT MONDAYS AND THURSDAYS. NON-BURNABLES ARE EVERY **SATURDAY**.
IF THERE'S ANYTHING ELSE I CAN HELP YOU WITH, PLEASE JUST LET ME KNOW!
....
YOU'RE STILL IN HIGH SCHOOL, RIGHT?
SIR? UH, YES I AM...
NO,
IT'S JUST YOU'VE REALLY GOT IT TOGETHER, YOU KNOW?
WHEN I WAS IN HIGH SCHOOL, I DIDN'T...
NO, SCRATCH THAT. I **STILL** DON'T HAVE IT TOGE-THER.
PLEASE TRY HARDER, THEN!
YES, MA'AM.
BY THE WAY, ARE YOU LIVING HERE ALONE?
NO, I'M WITH MY DAUGHTER. SHE'S STILL PRETTY YOUNG...
AND SHE WENT MISSING A LITTLE WHILE AGO.
WHAT?! OH, NO!

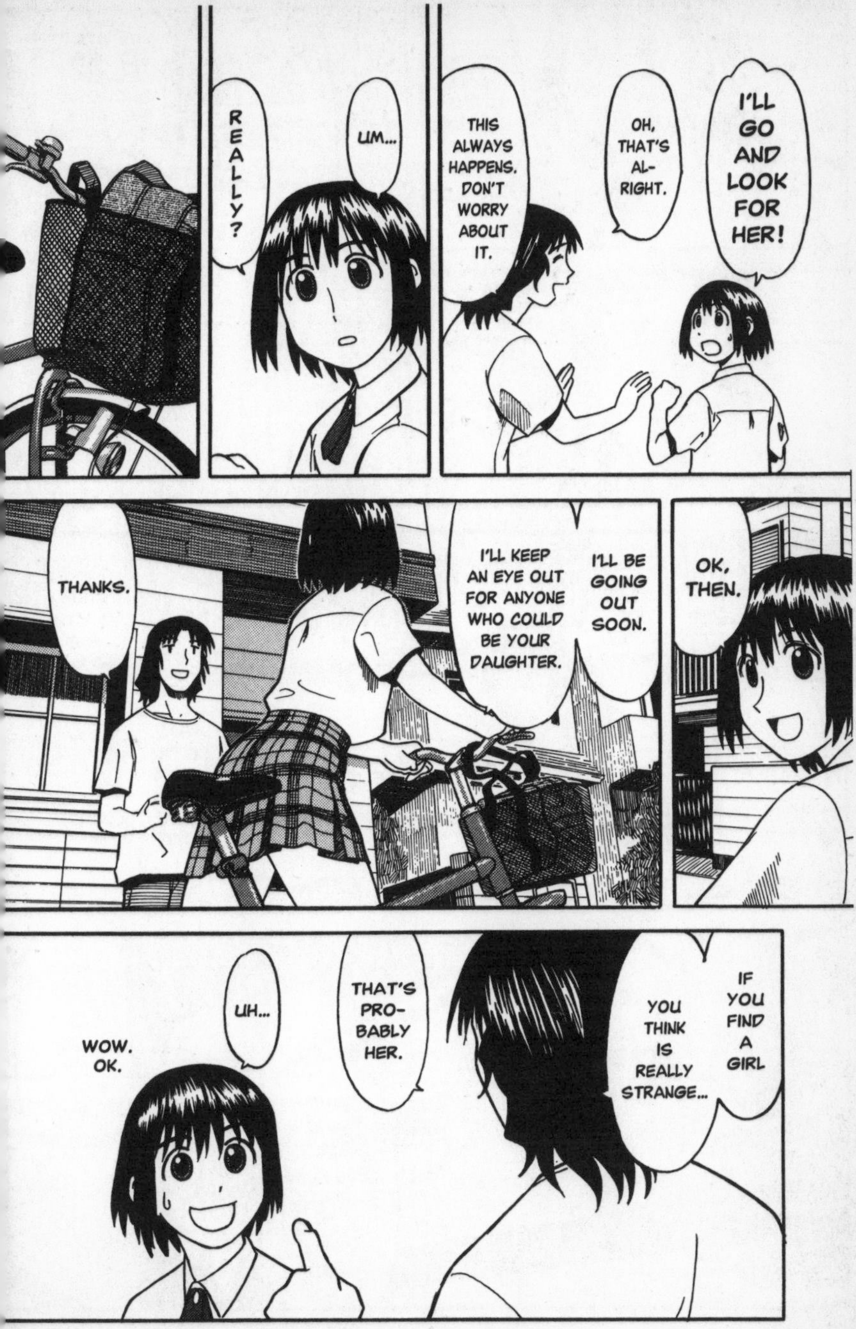
I'LL GO AND LOOK FOR HER!
OH, THAT'S AL-RIGHT.
THIS ALWAYS HAPPENS. DON'T WORRY ABOUT IT.
UM...
REALLY?
OK, THEN.
I'LL BE GOING OUT SOON.
I'LL KEEP AN EYE OUT FOR ANYONE WHO COULD BE YOUR DAUGHTER.
THANKS.
IF YOU FIND A GIRL
YOU THINK IS REALLY STRANGE...
THAT'S PRO-BABLY HER.
UH...
WOW. OK.

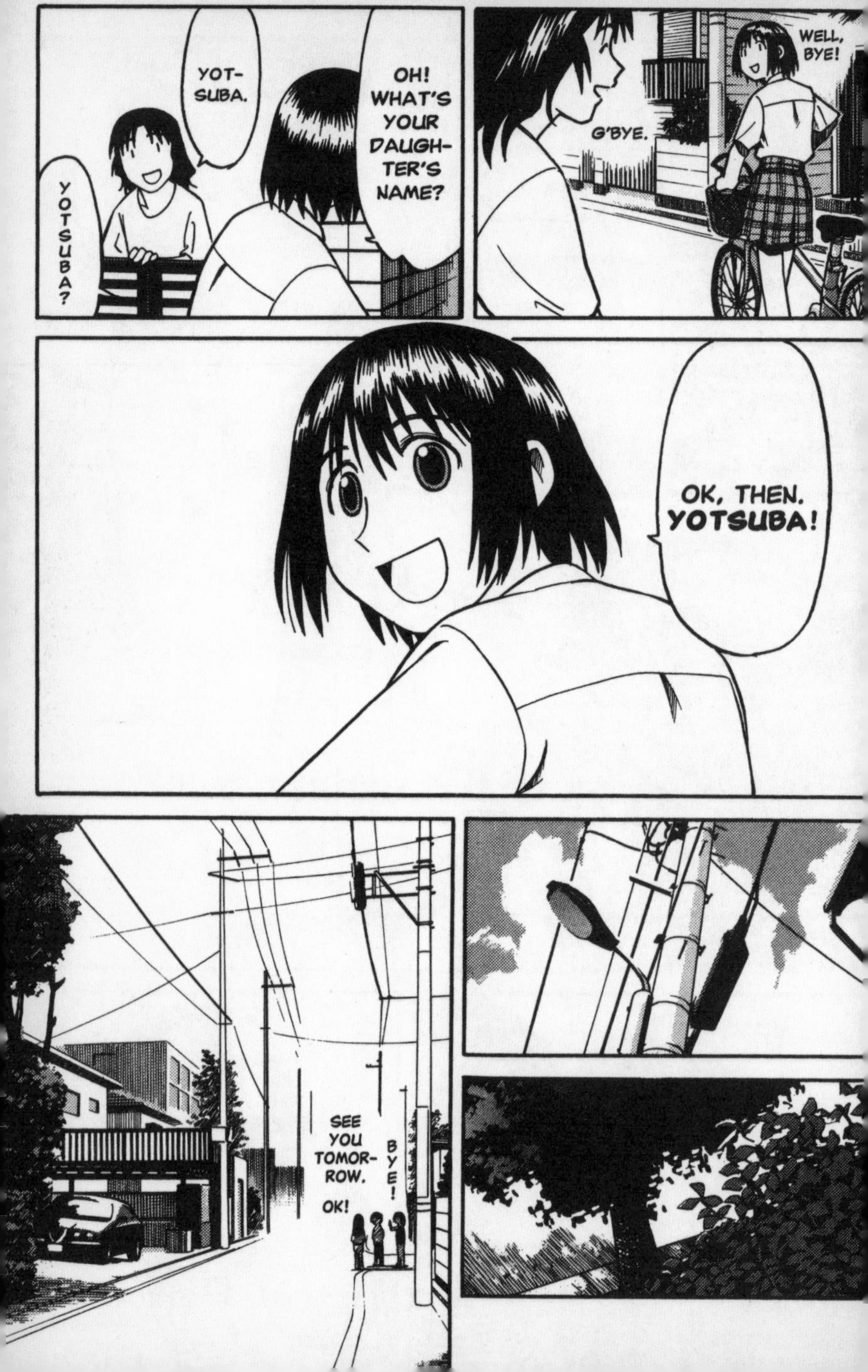
WELL, BYE!
G'BYE.
OH! WHAT'S YOUR DAUGH-TER'S NAME?
YOT-SUBA.
YOTSUBA?
OK, THEN. YOTSUBA!
SEE YOU TOMOR-ROW.
BYE!
OK!

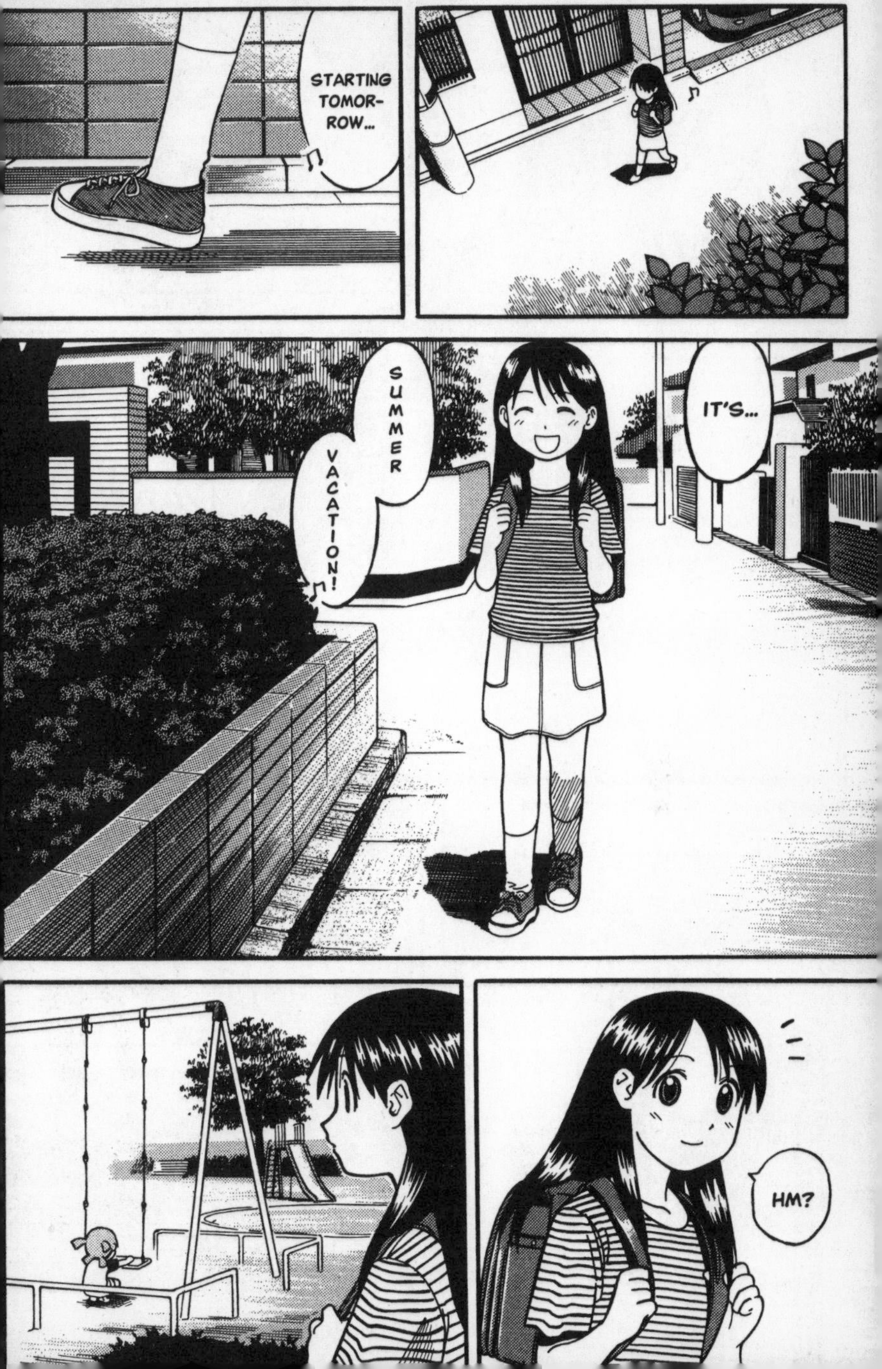
STARTING TOMOR-ROW...
IT'S...
SUMMER VACATION!
HM?

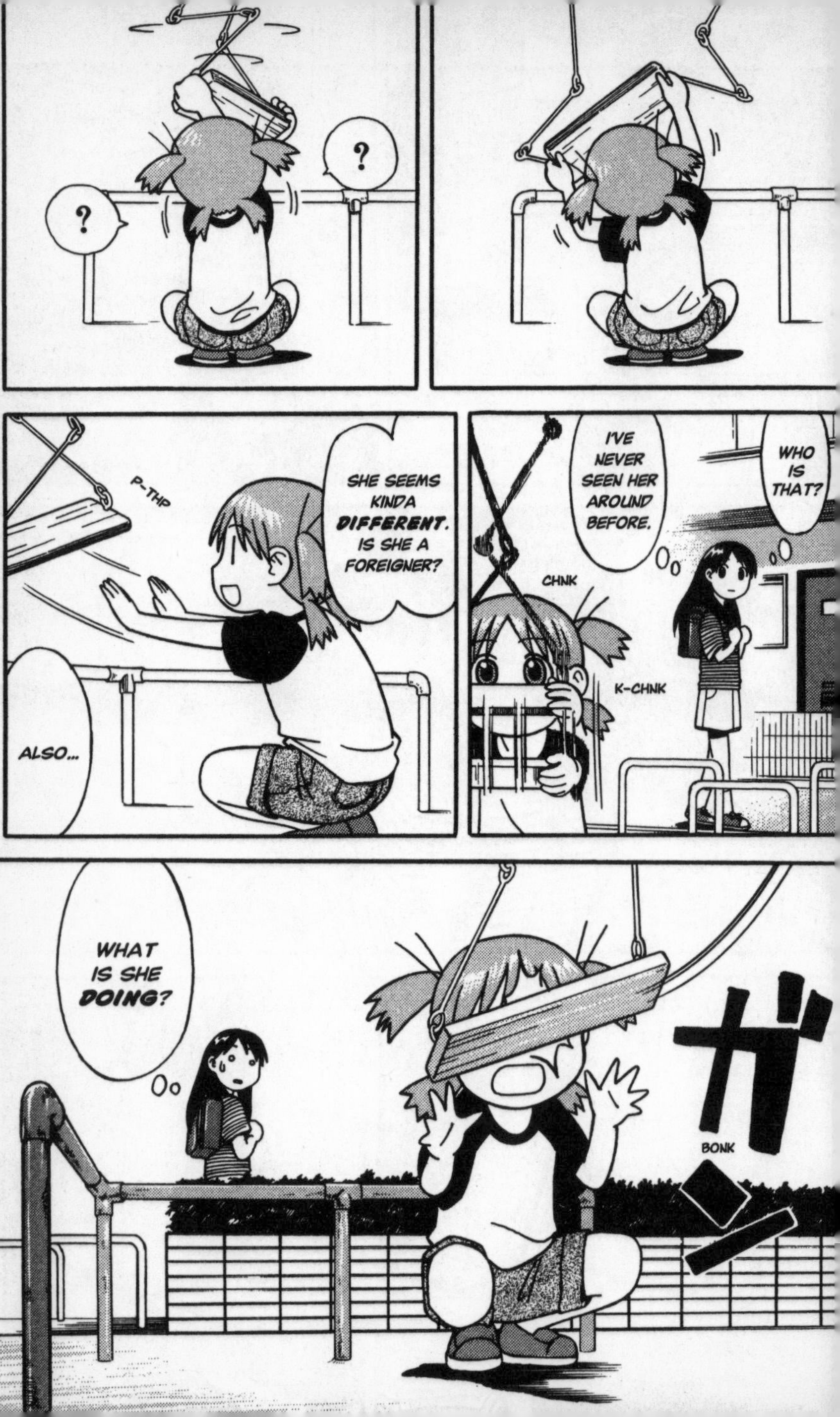
?
?
WHO IS THAT?
I'VE NEVER SEEN HER AROUND BEFORE.
CHNK
K-CHNK
SHE SEEMS KINDA DIFFERENT. IS SHE A FOREIGNER?
P-THP
ALSO...
WHAT IS SHE DOING?
ガン
BONK

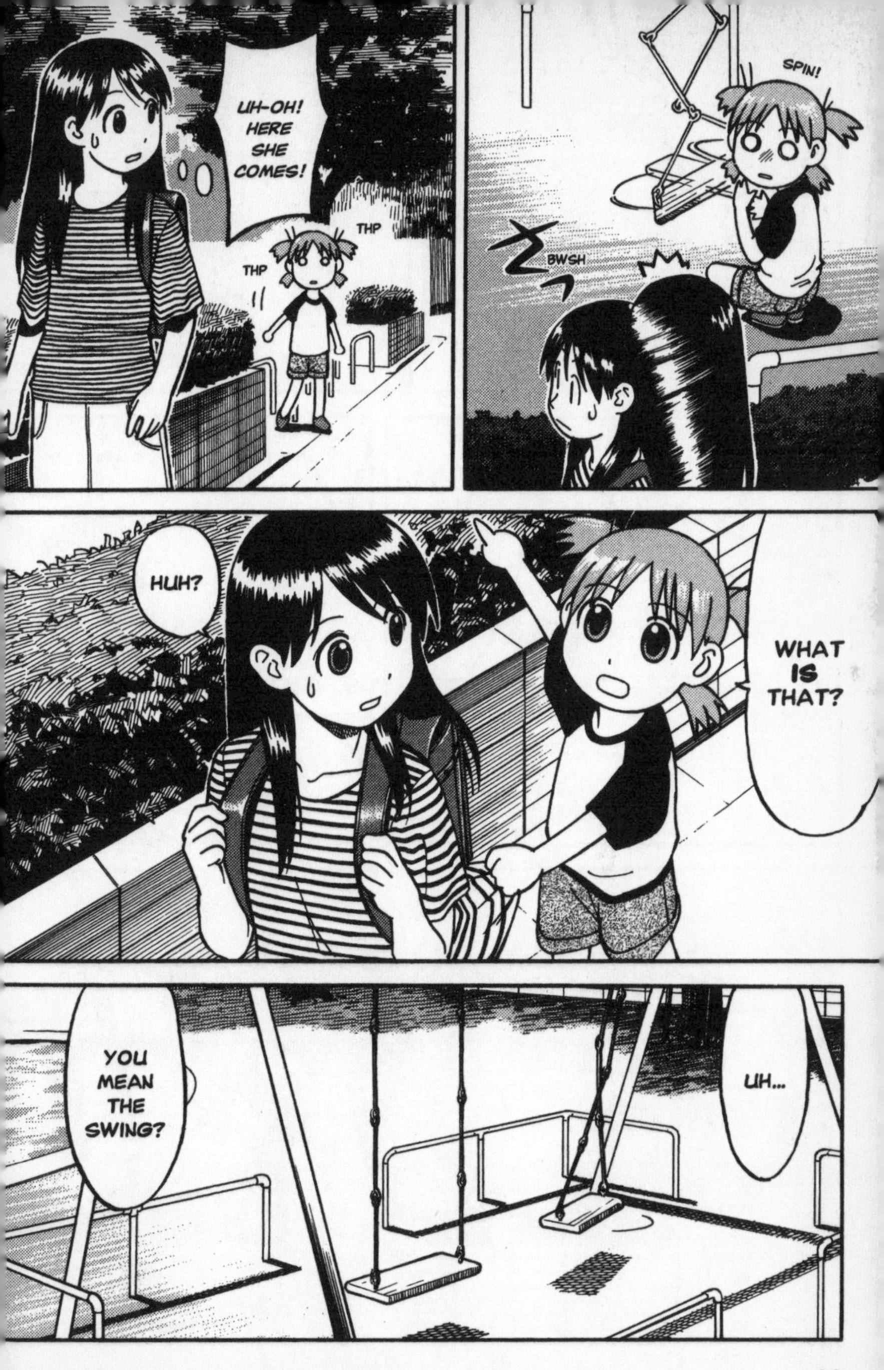
SPIN!
BWSH
UH-OH! HERE SHE COMES!
THP
THP
WHAT IS THAT?
HUH?
UH...
YOU MEAN THE SWING?

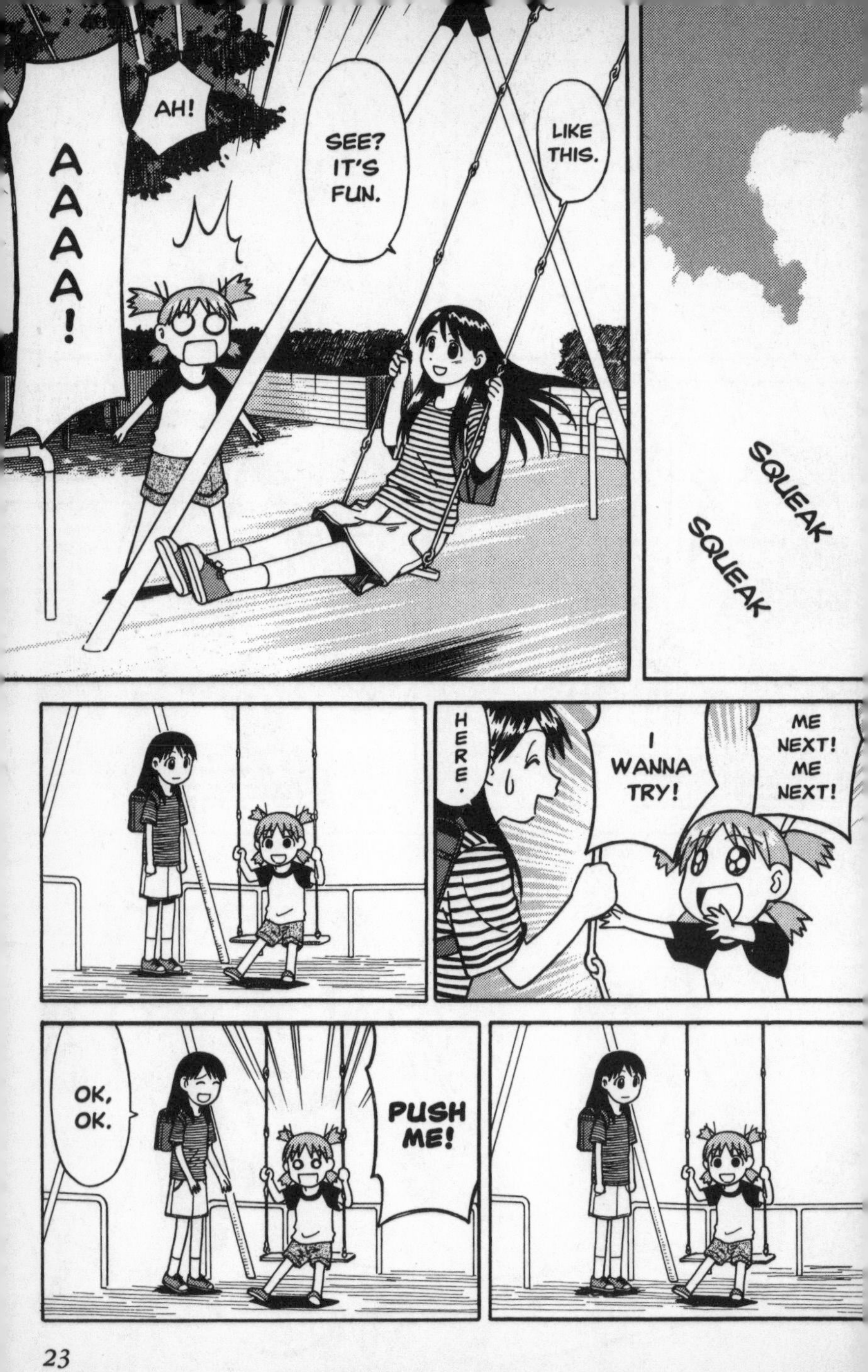
SQUEAK
SQUEAK
LIKE THIS.
SEE? IT'S FUN.
AH!
AAAA!
ME NEXT! ME NEXT!
I WANNA TRY!
HERE.
PUSH ME!
OK, OK.

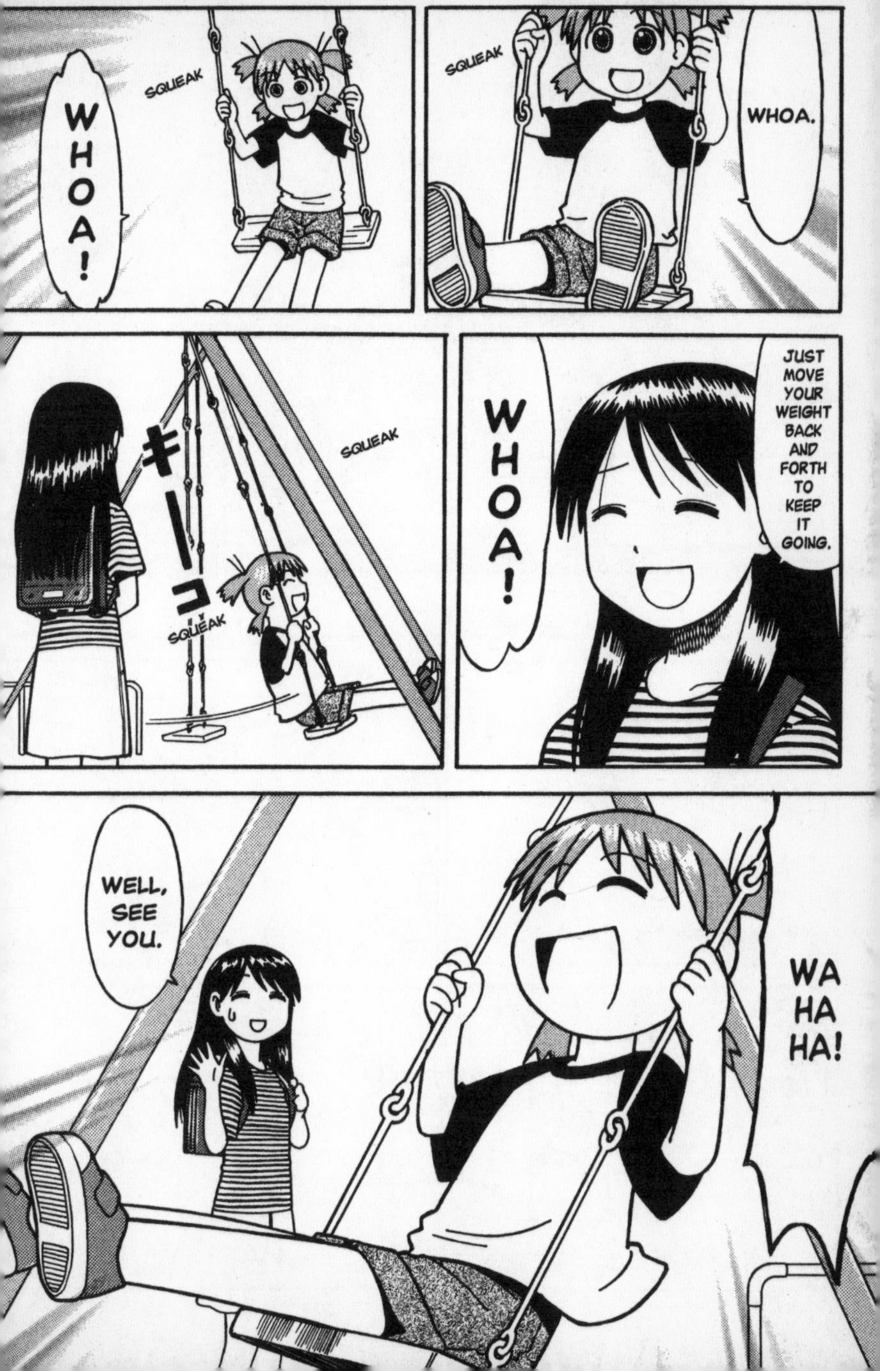
SQUEAK
WHOA.
SQUEAK
WHOA!
JUST MOVE YOUR WEIGHT BACK AND FORTH TO KEEP IT GOING.
WHOA!
SQUEAK
キーコ
SQUEAK
WA HA HA!
WELL, SEE YOU.

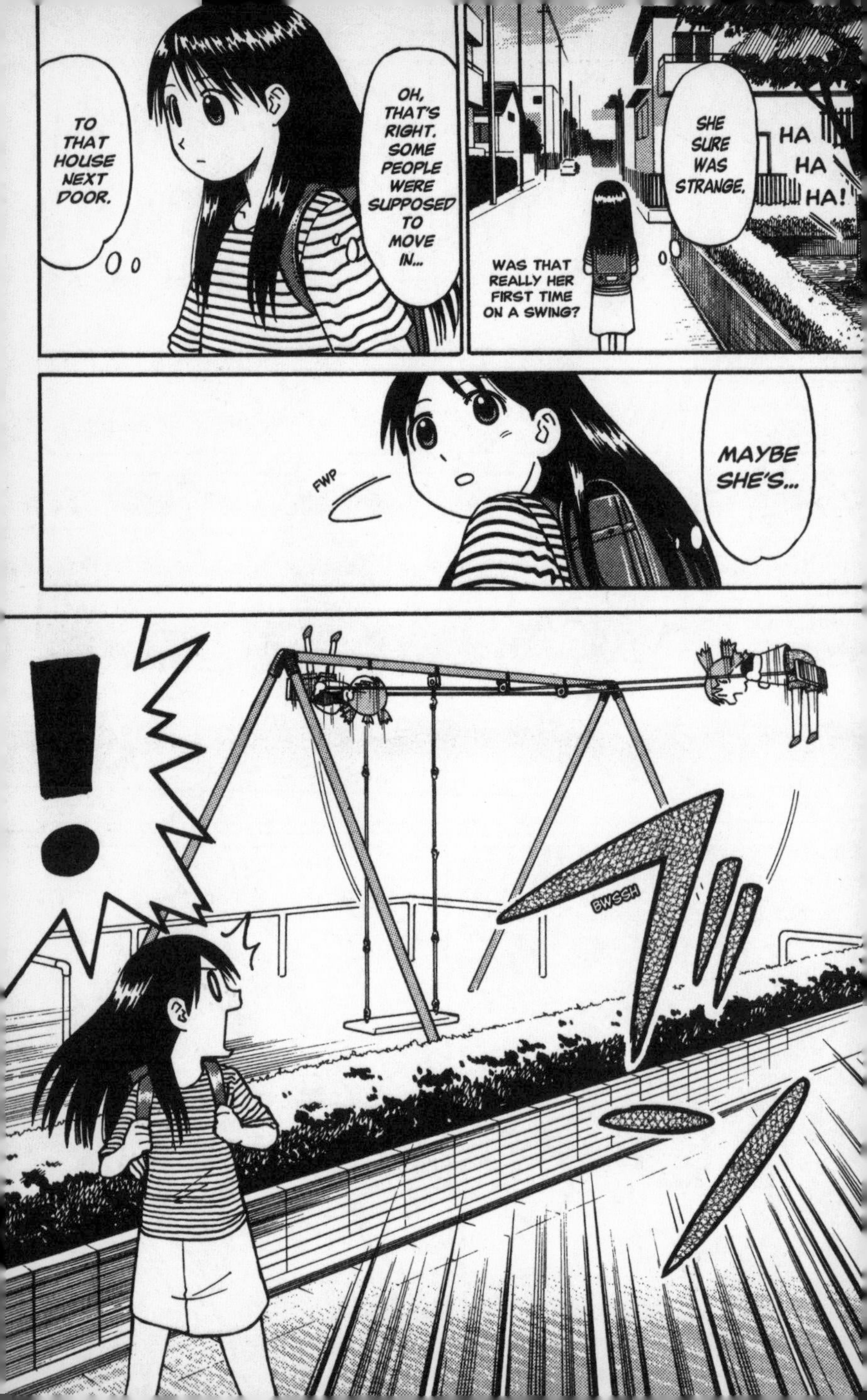
HA HA HA!
SHE SURE WAS STRANGE.
WAS THAT REALLY HER FIRST TIME ON A SWING?
OH, THAT'S RIGHT. SOME PEOPLE WERE SUPPOSED TO MOVE IN...
TO THAT HOUSE NEXT DOOR.
MAYBE SHE'S...
FWP
BWSSH
!

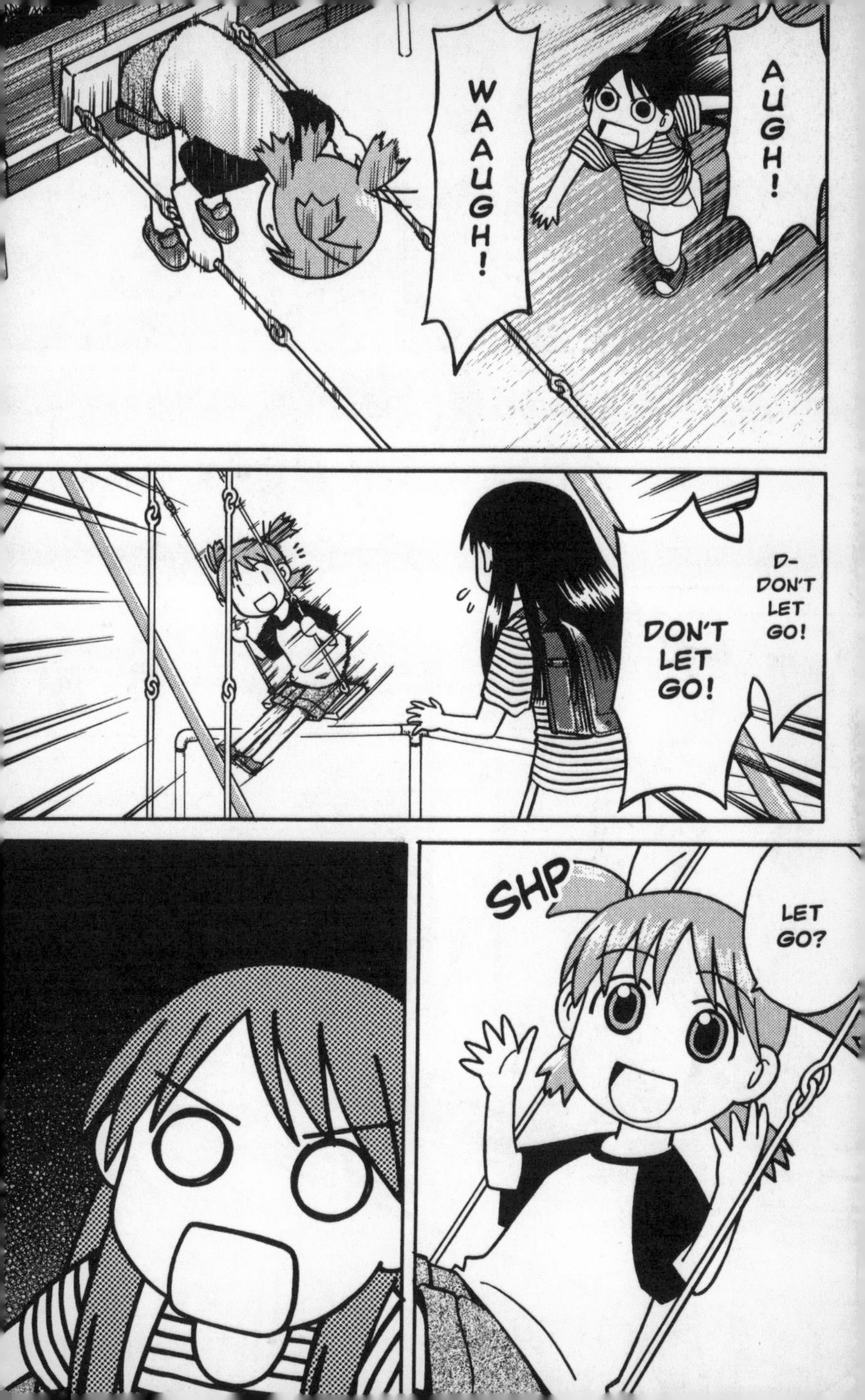
AUGH!
WAAAUGH!
D- DON'T LET GO!
DON'T LET GO!
LET GO?
SHP

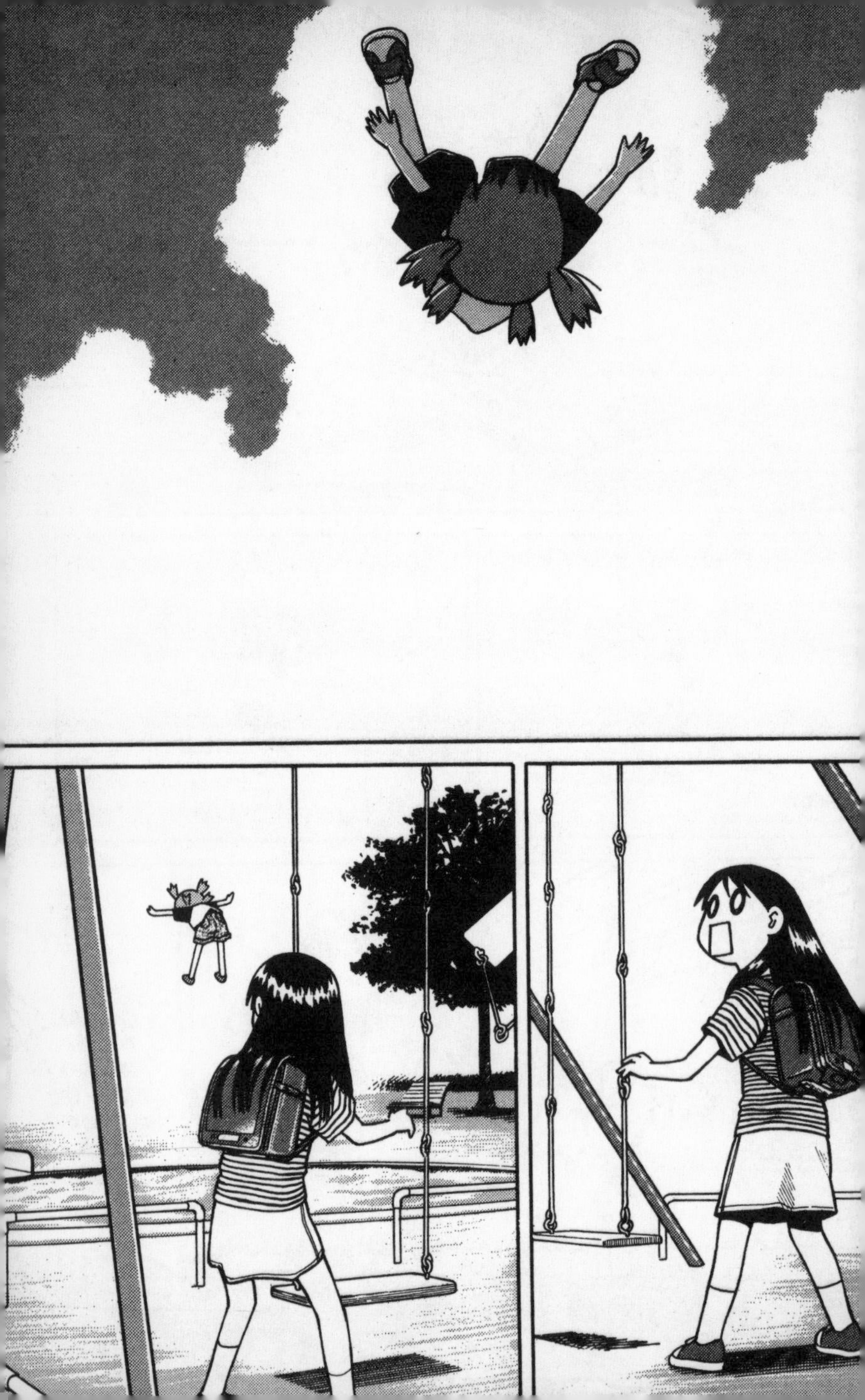

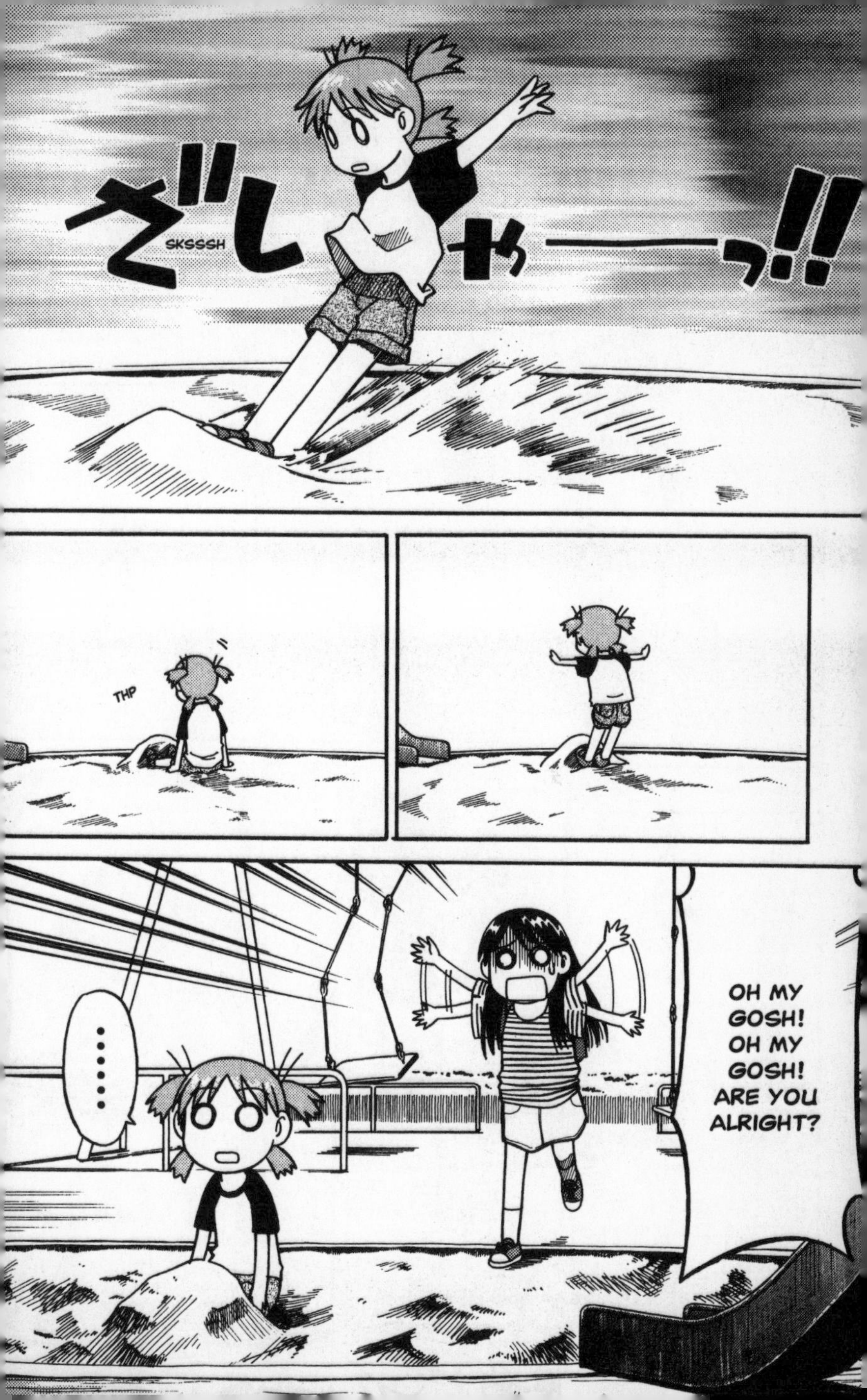
ざしゃーーーっ!!
SKSSSH
THP
OH MY GOSH! OH MY GOSH! ARE YOU ALRIGHT?
......

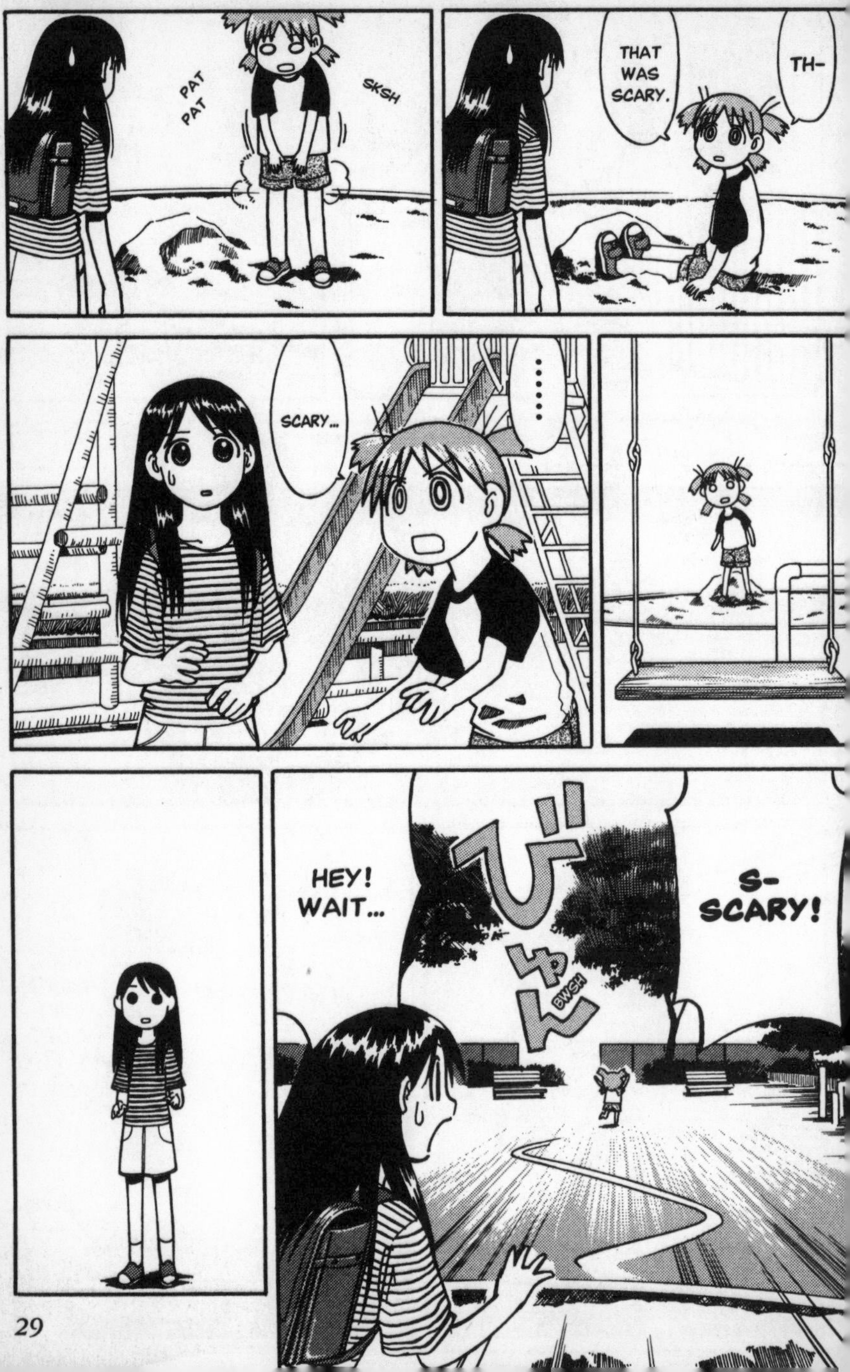
TH-
THAT WAS SCARY.
SKSH
PAT PAT
......
SCARY...
S- SCARY!
びゅん
BWSH
HEY! WAIT...

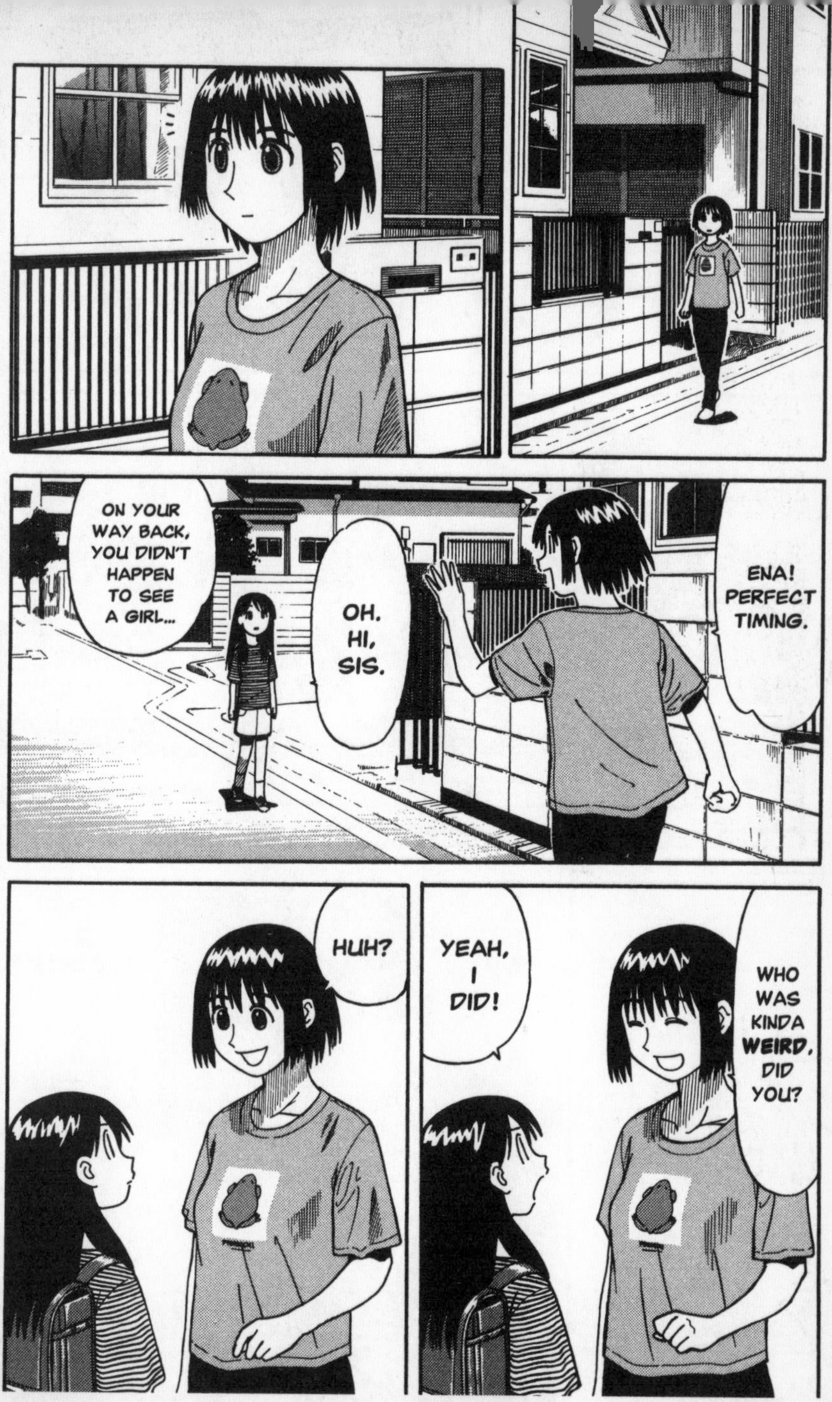
ENA! PERFECT TIMING.
OH. HI, SIS.
ON YOUR WAY BACK, YOU DIDN'T HAPPEN TO SEE A GIRL...
WHO WAS KINDA **WEIRD**, DID YOU?
YEAH, I DID!
HUH?

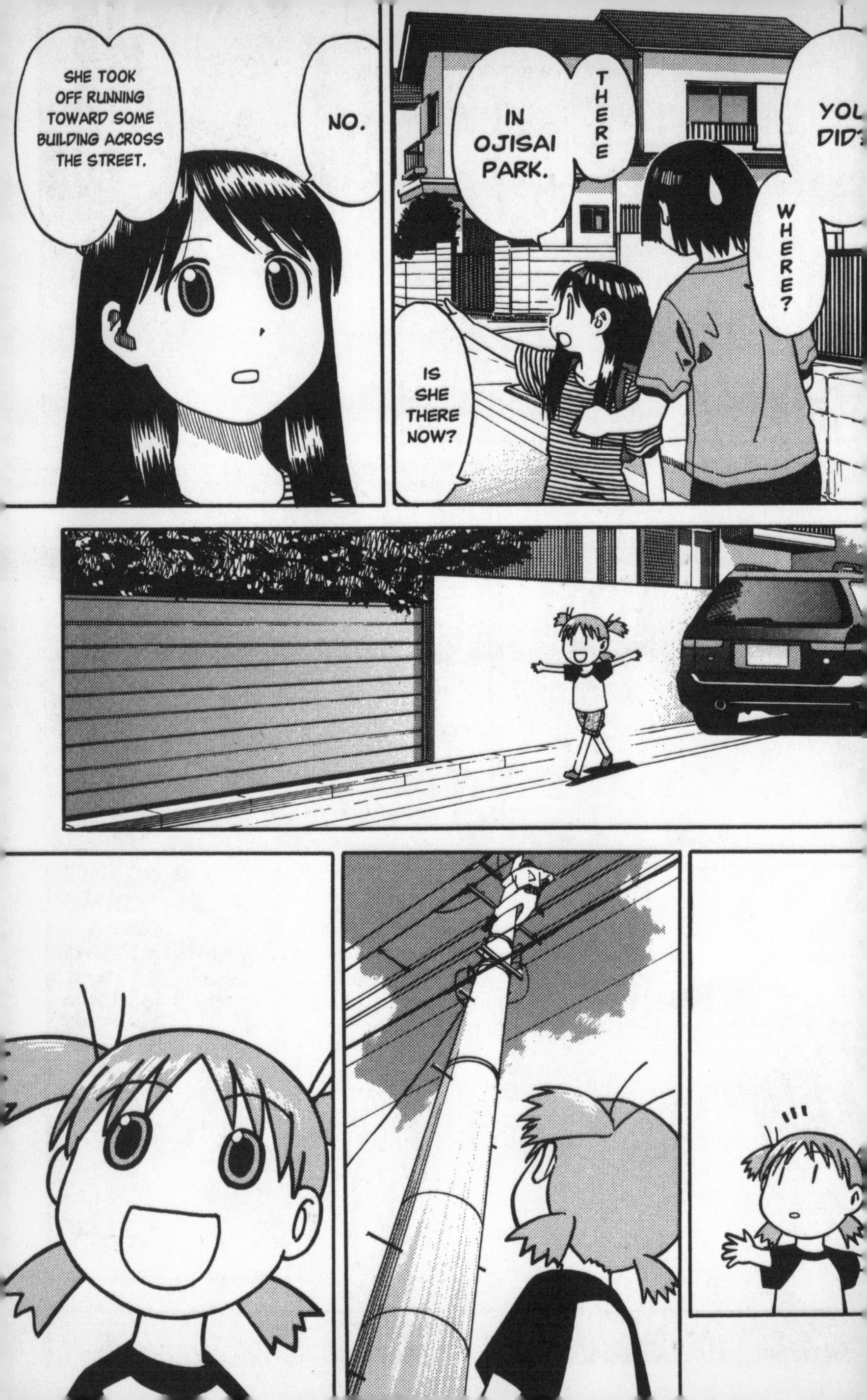
YOU DID?
WHERE?
THERE
IN OJISAI PARK.
IS SHE THERE NOW?
NO.
SHE TOOK OFF RUNNING TOWARD SOME BUILDING ACROSS THE STREET.

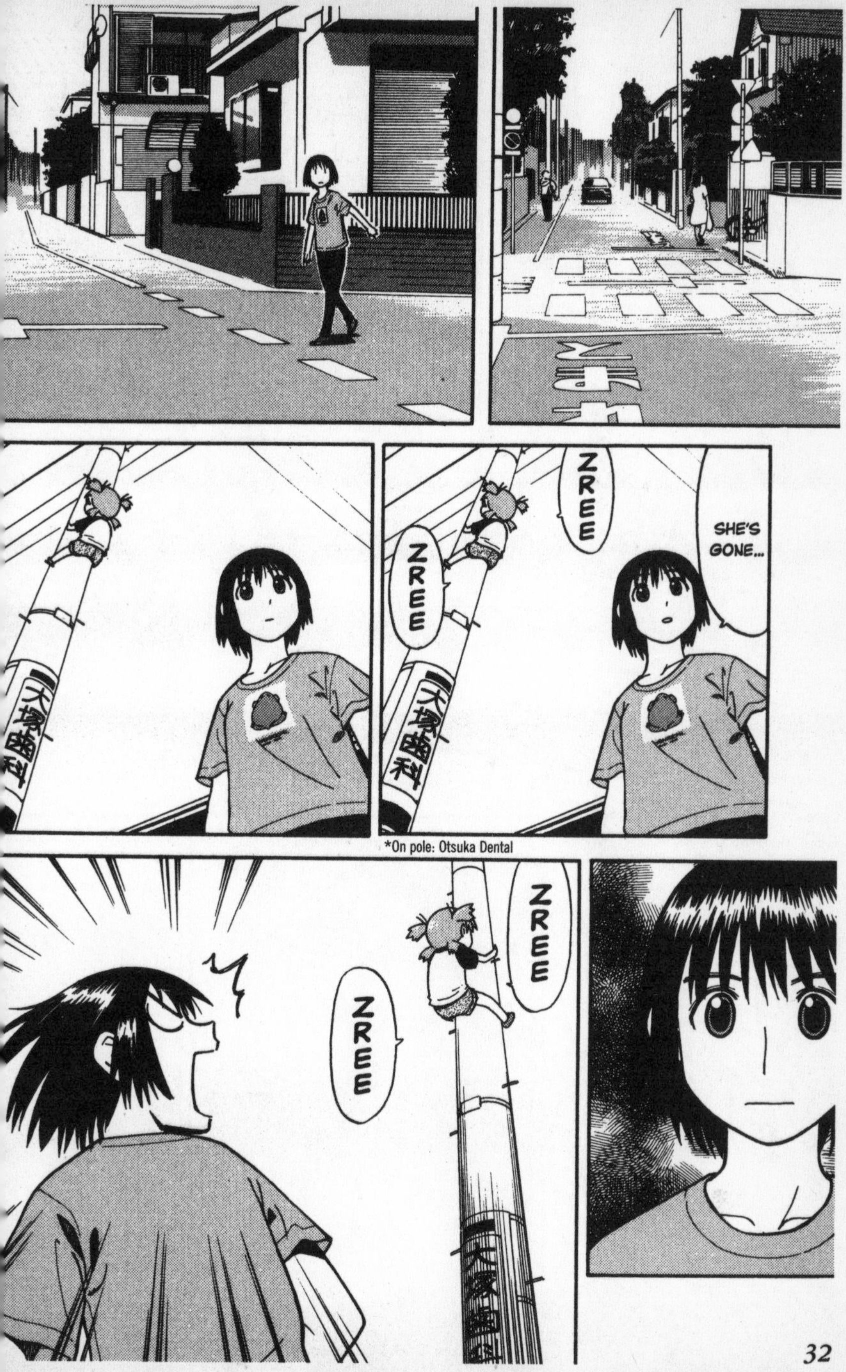
SHE'S GONE...
ZREE
ZREE
大塚歯科
ZREE
ZREE
*On pole: Otsuka Dental

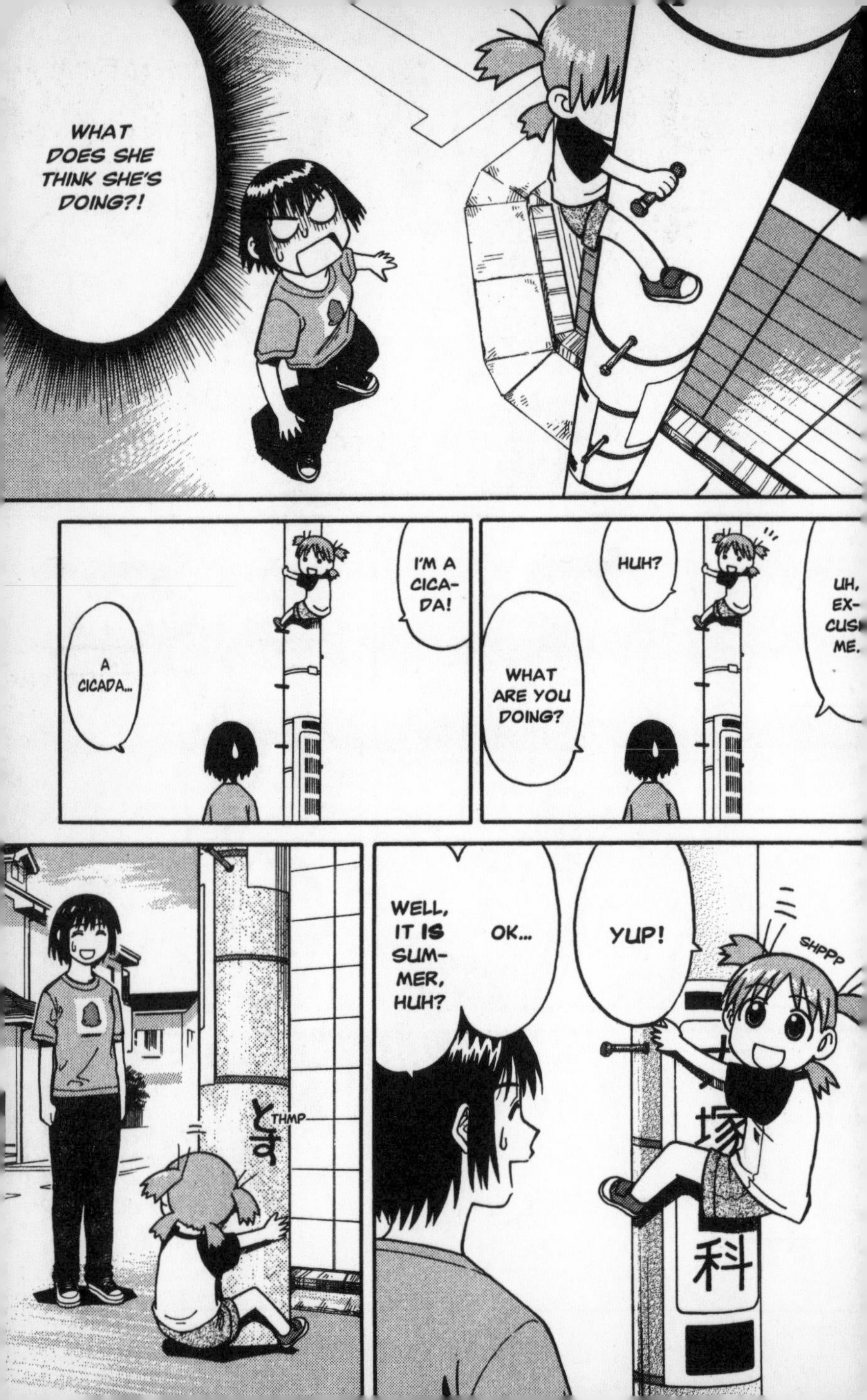
WHAT DOES SHE THINK SHE'S DOING?!
UH, EX-CUSE ME.
HUH?
WHAT ARE YOU DOING?
I'M A CICADA!
A CICADA...
YUP!
SHPPP
OK...
WELL, IT IS SUMMER, HUH?
とす
THMP

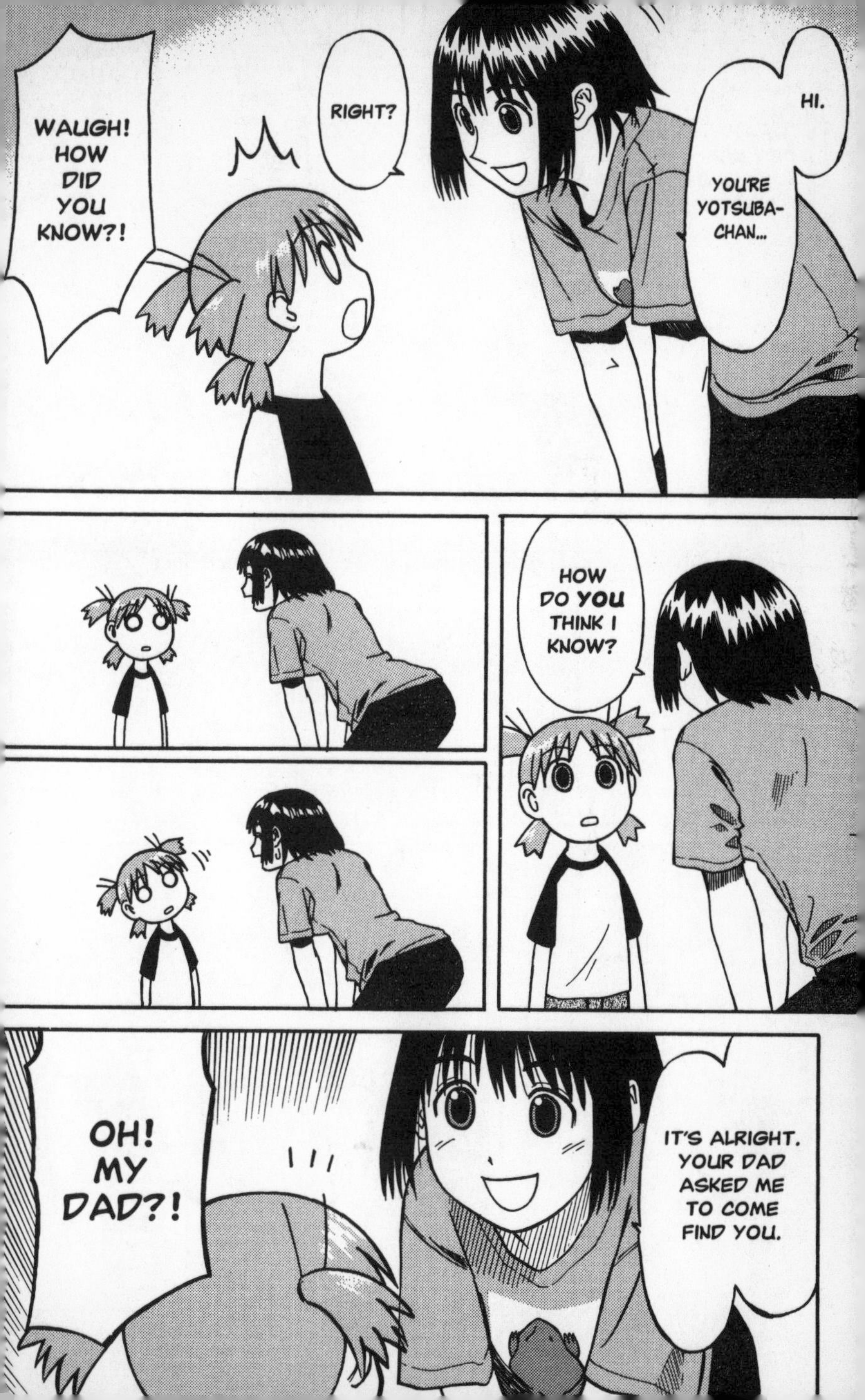
HI. YOU'RE YOTSUBA-CHAN...
RIGHT?
WAUGH! HOW DID YOU KNOW?!
HOW DO YOU THINK I KNOW?
IT'S ALRIGHT. YOUR DAD ASKED ME TO COME FIND YOU.
OH! MY DAD?!

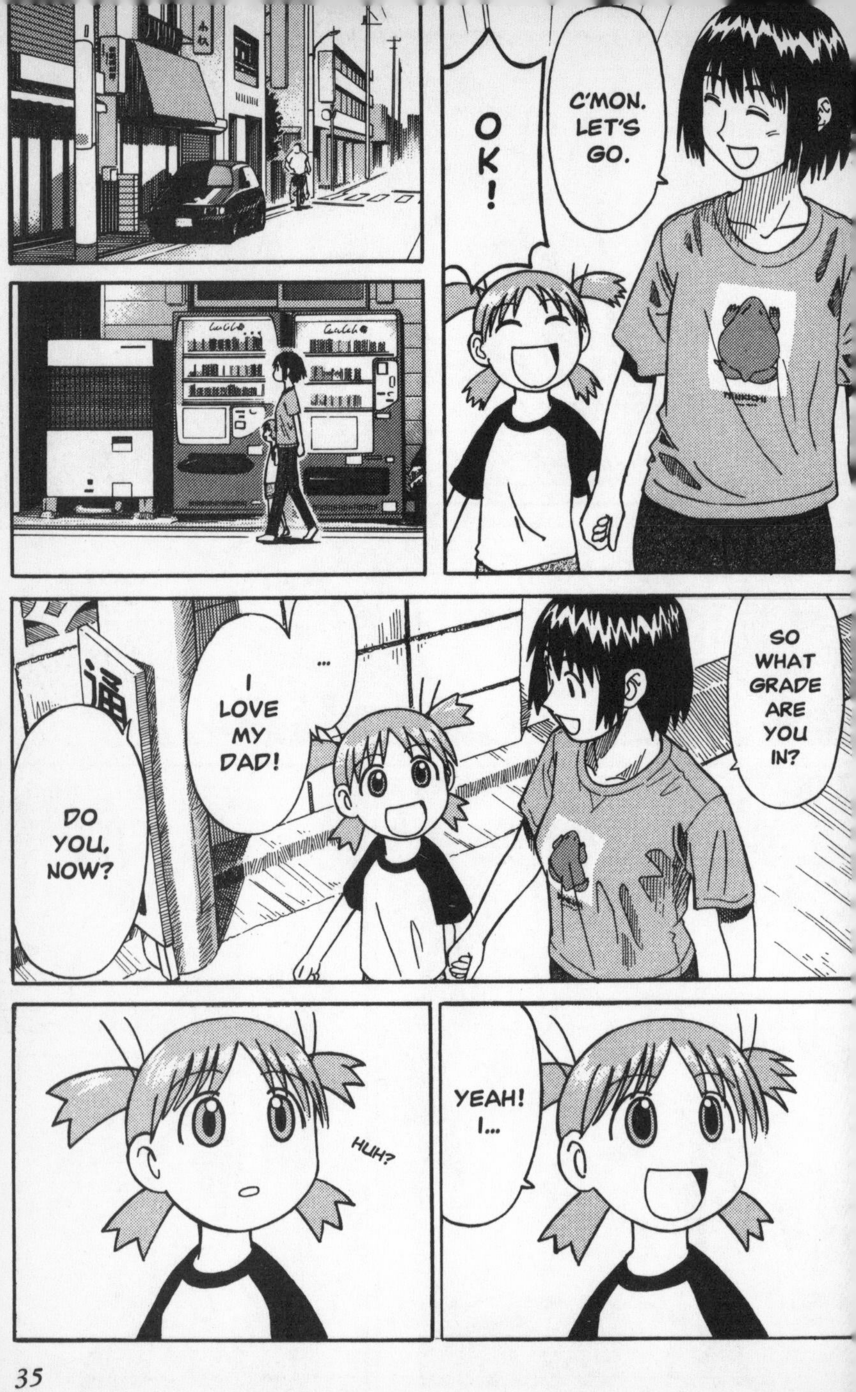
C'MON. LET'S GO.
OK!
SO WHAT GRADE ARE YOU IN?
...
I LOVE MY DAD!
DO YOU, NOW?
YEAH! I...
HUH?

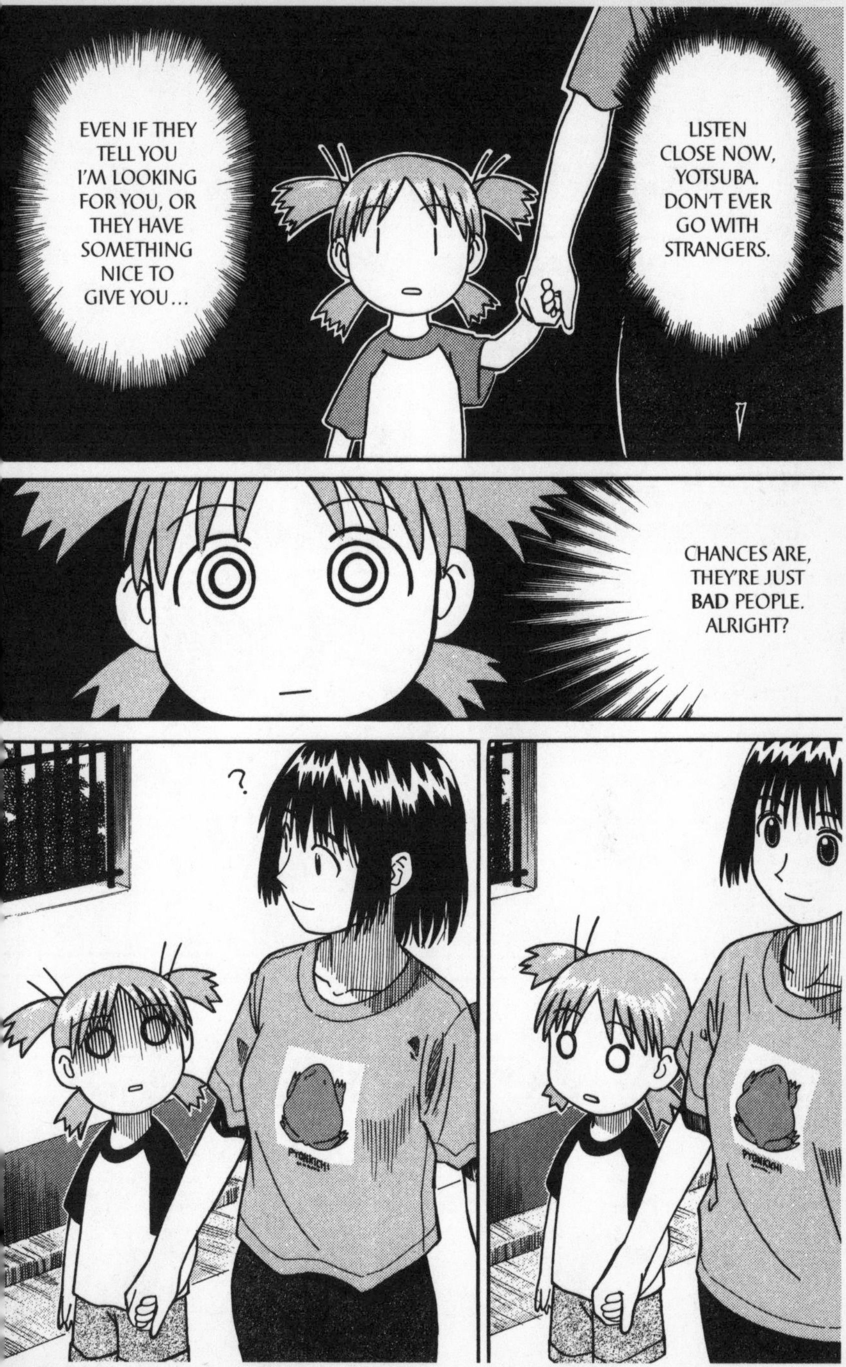
LISTEN CLOSE NOW, YOTSUBA. DON'T EVER GO WITH STRANGERS.
EVEN IF THEY TELL YOU I'M LOOKING FOR YOU, OR THEY HAVE SOMETHING NICE TO GIVE YOU...
CHANCES ARE, THEY'RE JUST **BAD** PEOPLE. ALRIGHT?
?

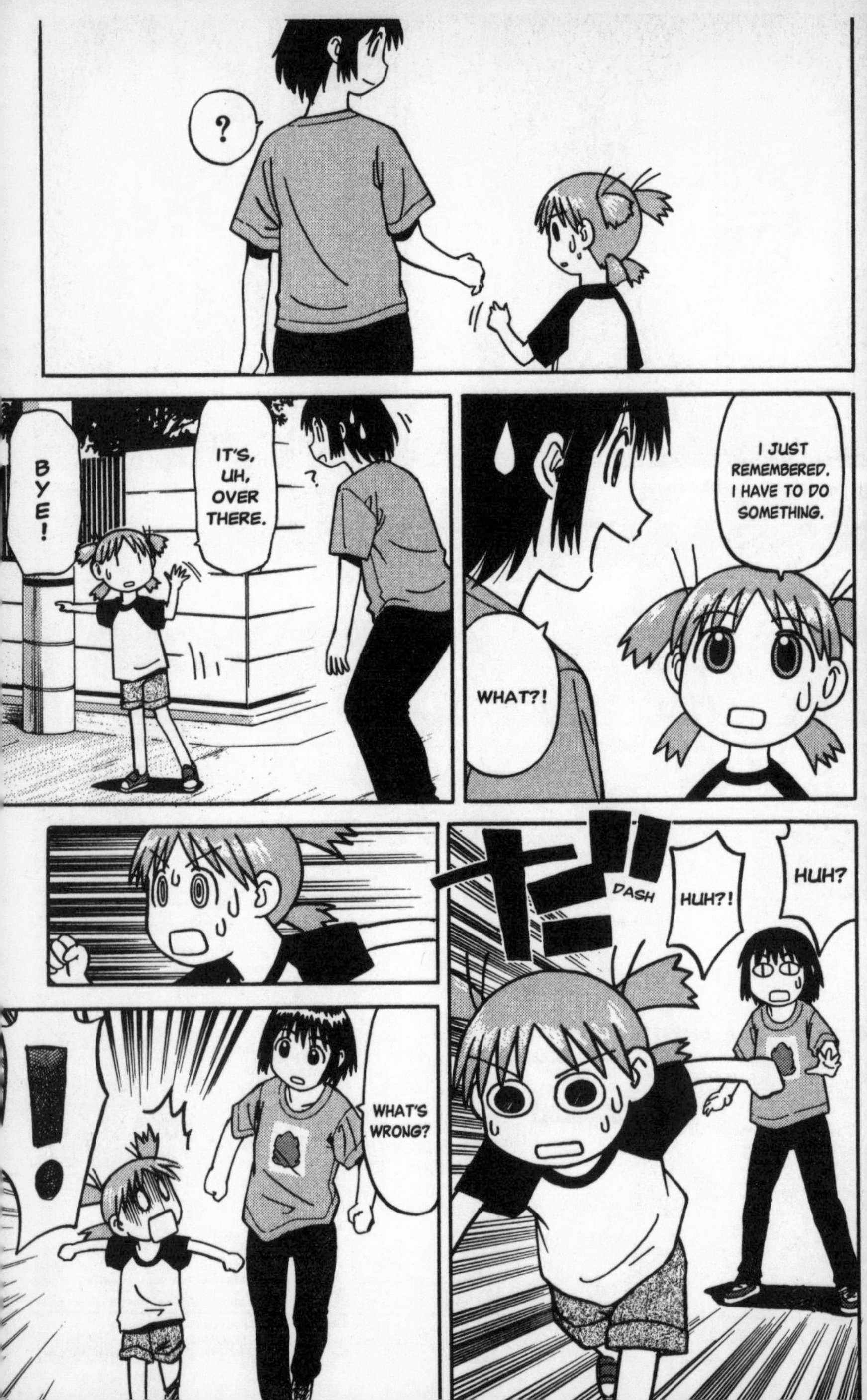
?
I JUST REMEMBERED. I HAVE TO DO SOMETHING.
WHAT?!
IT'S, UH, OVER THERE.
BYE!
HUH?
HUH?!
DASH
WHAT'S WRONG?
!

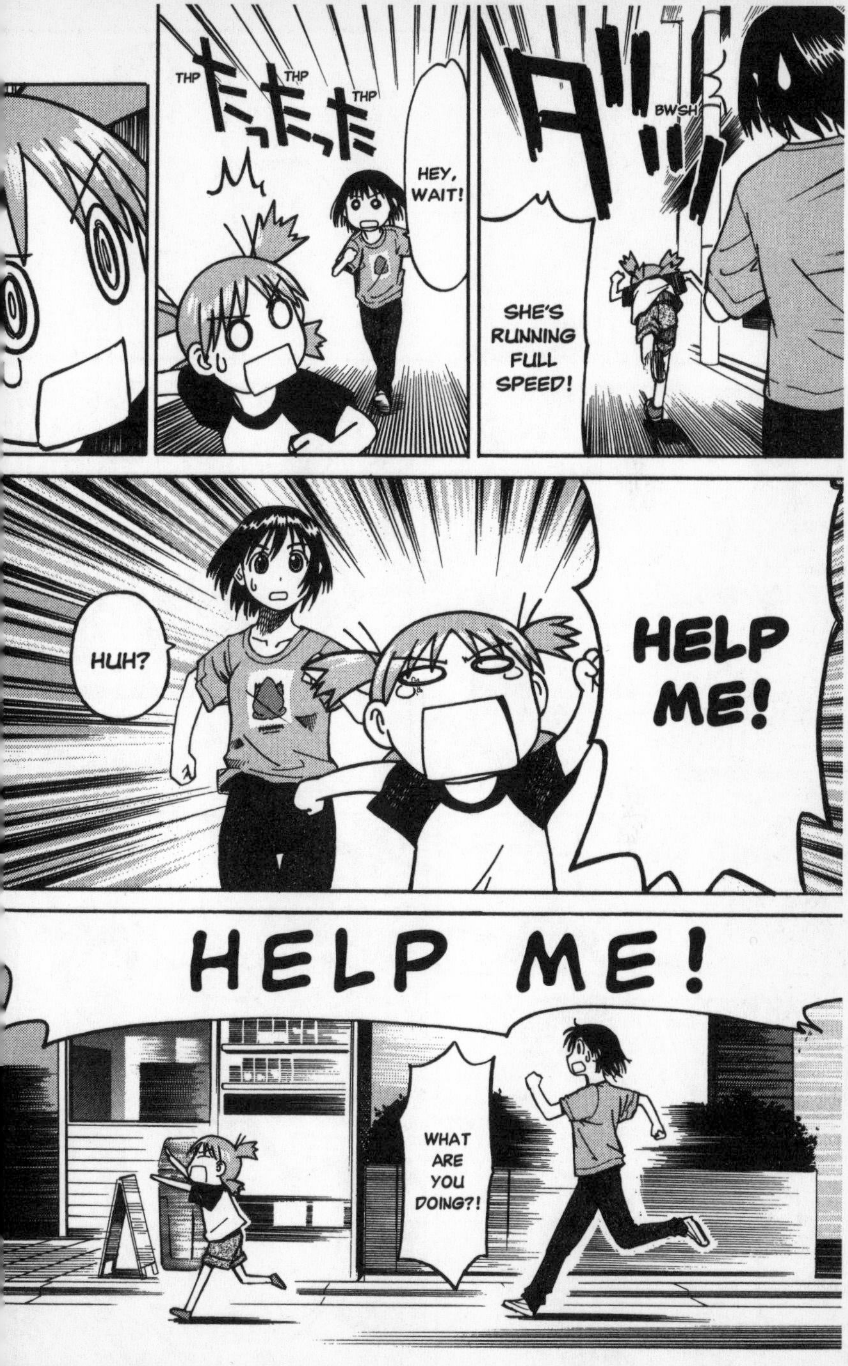
BWSH
ダッ
SHE'S RUNNING FULL SPEED!
THP THP THP
たったった
HEY, WAIT!
HELP ME!
HUH?
HELP ME!
WHAT ARE YOU DOING?!

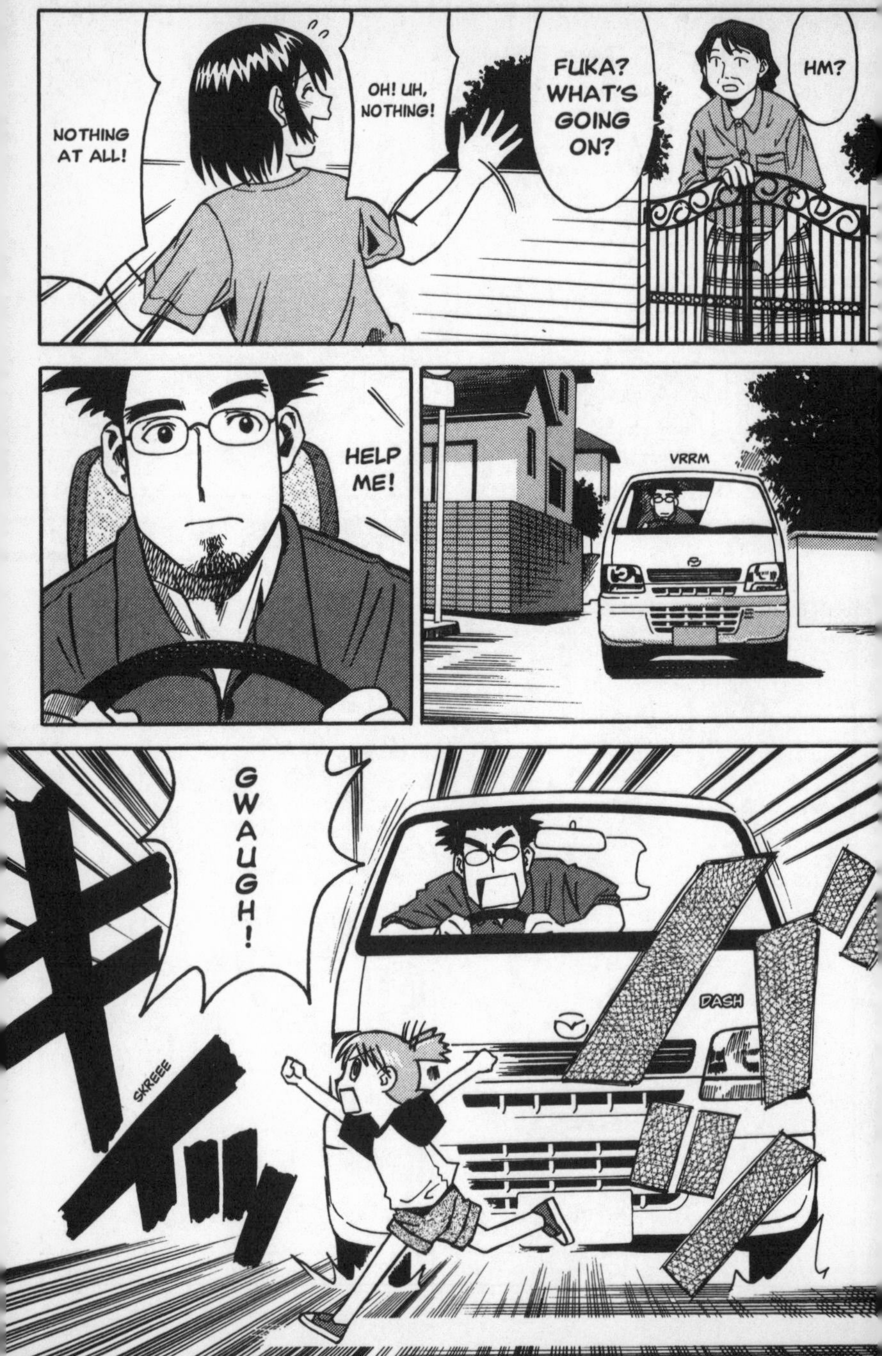
HM?
FUKA? WHAT'S GOING ON?
OH! UH, NOTHING!
NOTHING AT ALL!
VRRM
HELP ME!
GWAUGH!
DASH
SKREEE

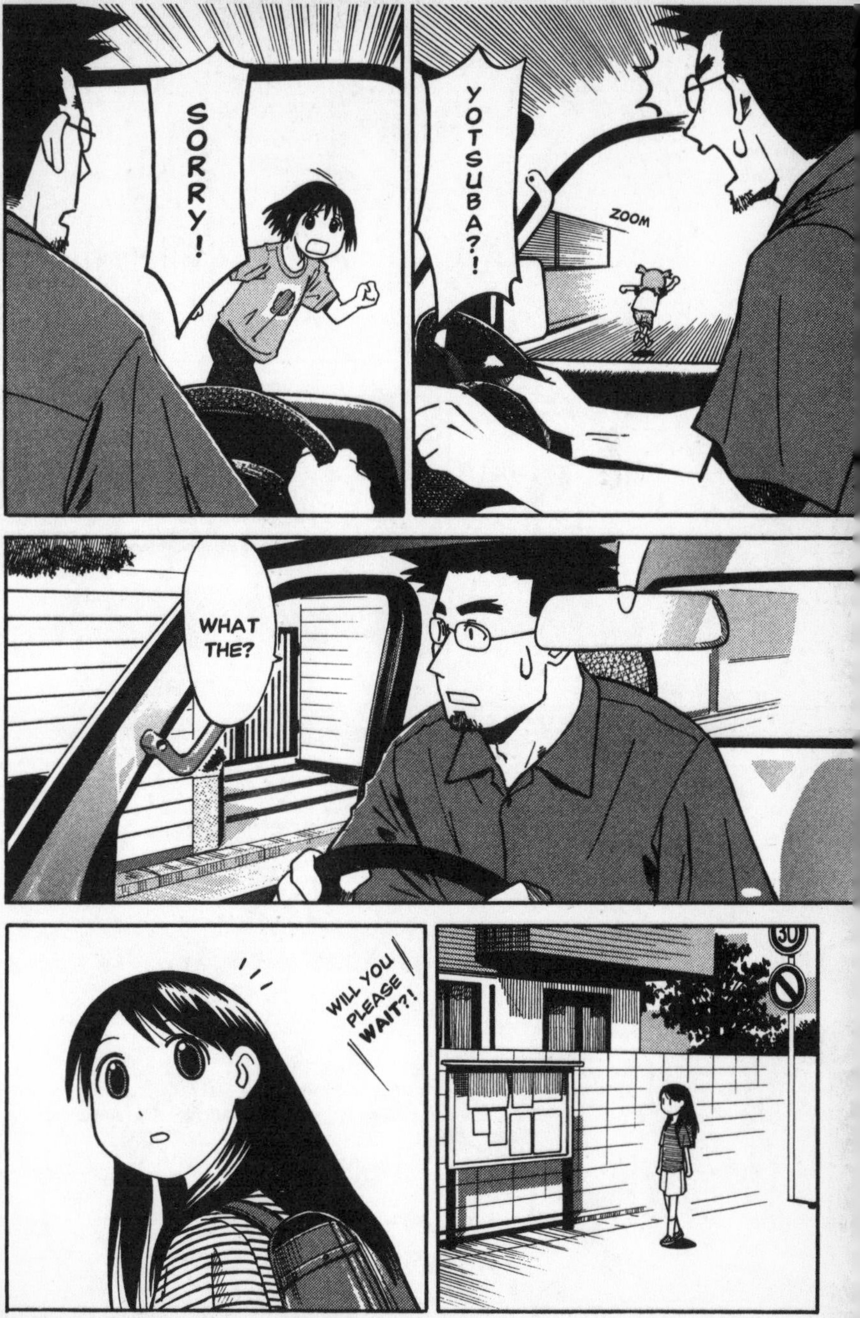
YOTSUBA?!
ZOOM
SORRY!
WHAT THE?
WILL YOU PLEASE WAIT?!

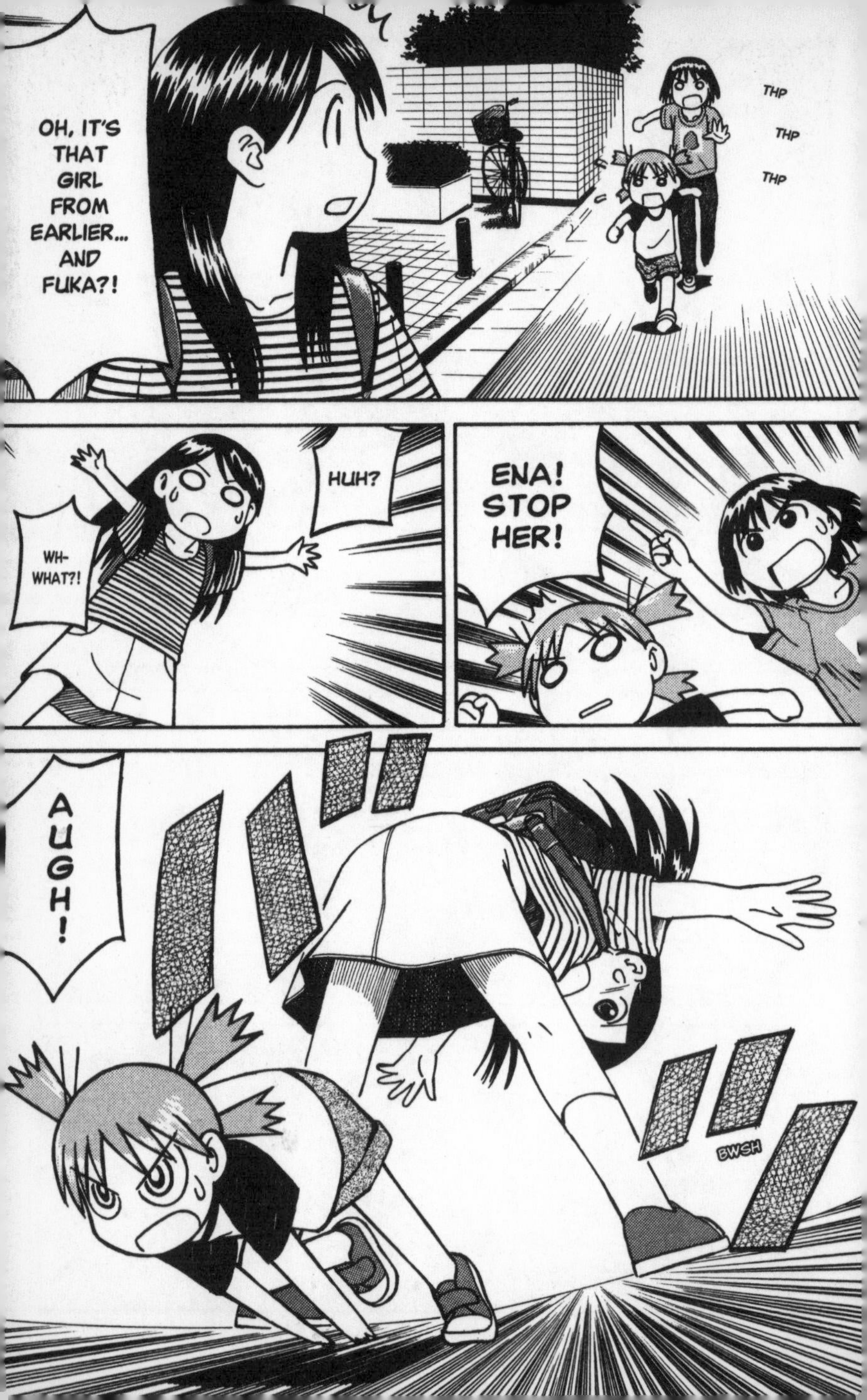
THP
THP
THP
OH, IT'S THAT GIRL FROM EARLIER... AND FUKA?!
ENA! STOP HER!
HUH?
WH-WHAT?!
AUGH!
BWSH

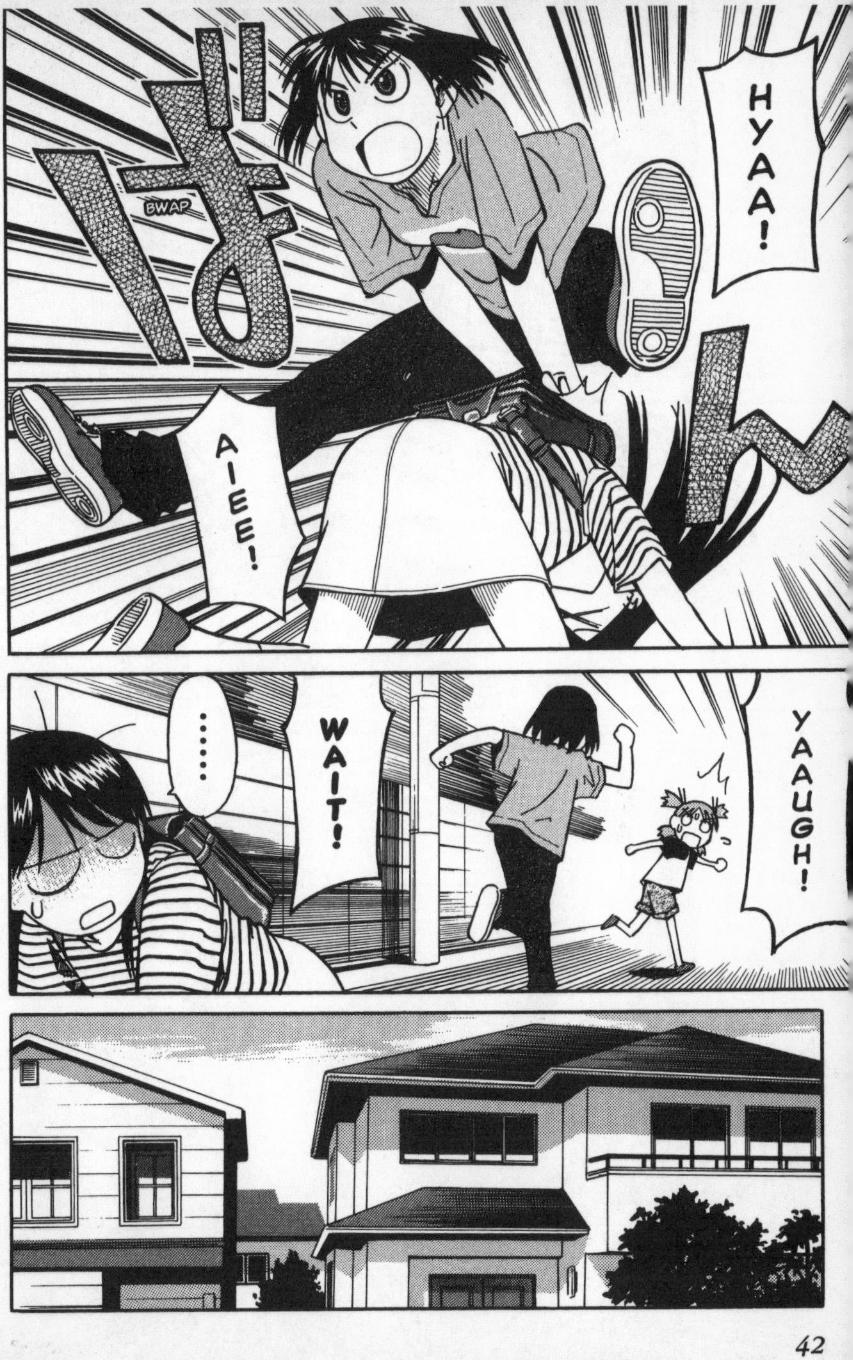
HYAAA!
BWAP
AIEEE!
YAAUGH!
WAIT!
......

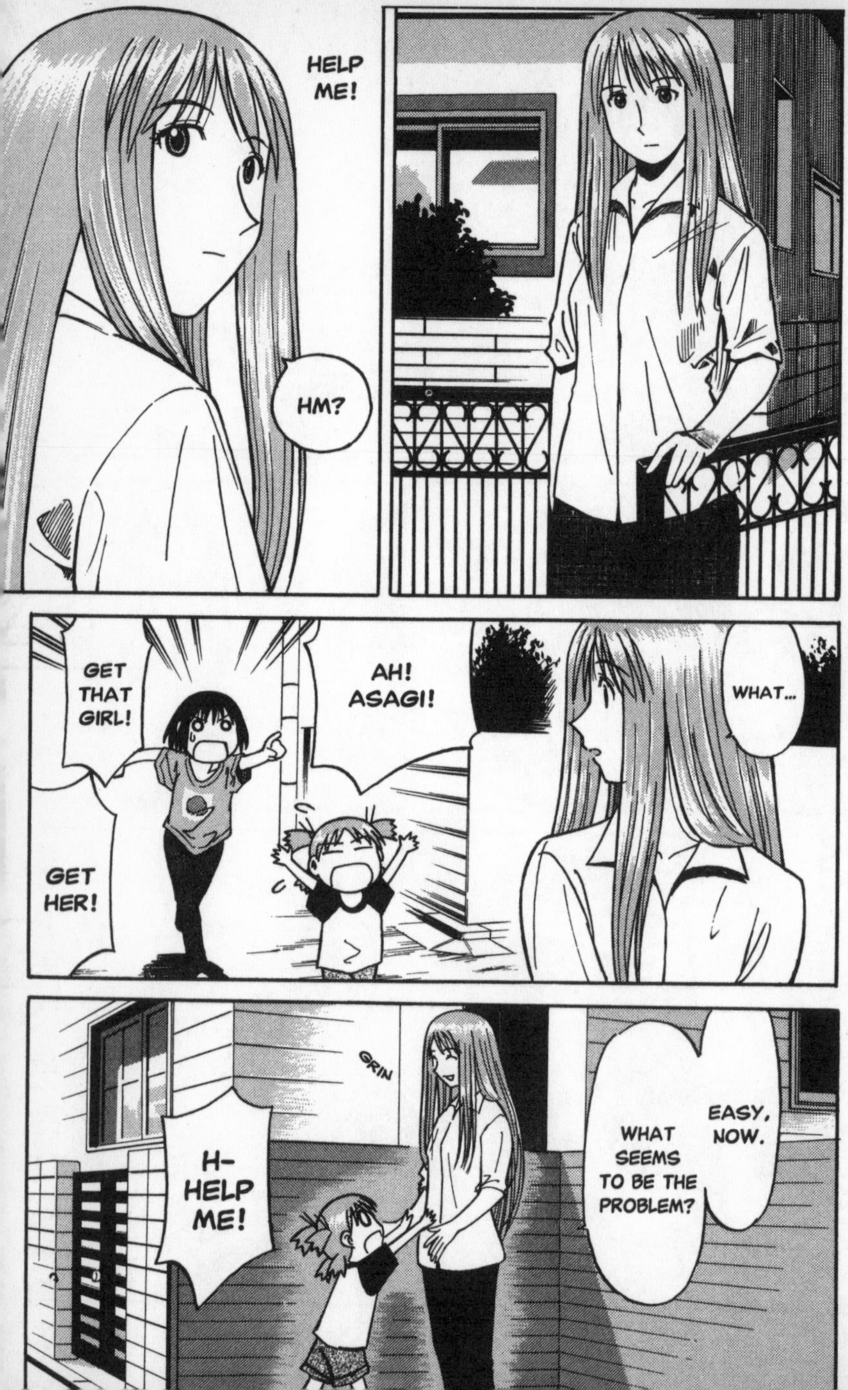
HELP ME!
HM?
WHAT...
AH! ASAGI!
GET THAT GIRL!
GET HER!
EASY, NOW.
WHAT SEEMS TO BE THE PROBLEM?
GRIN
H- HELP ME!

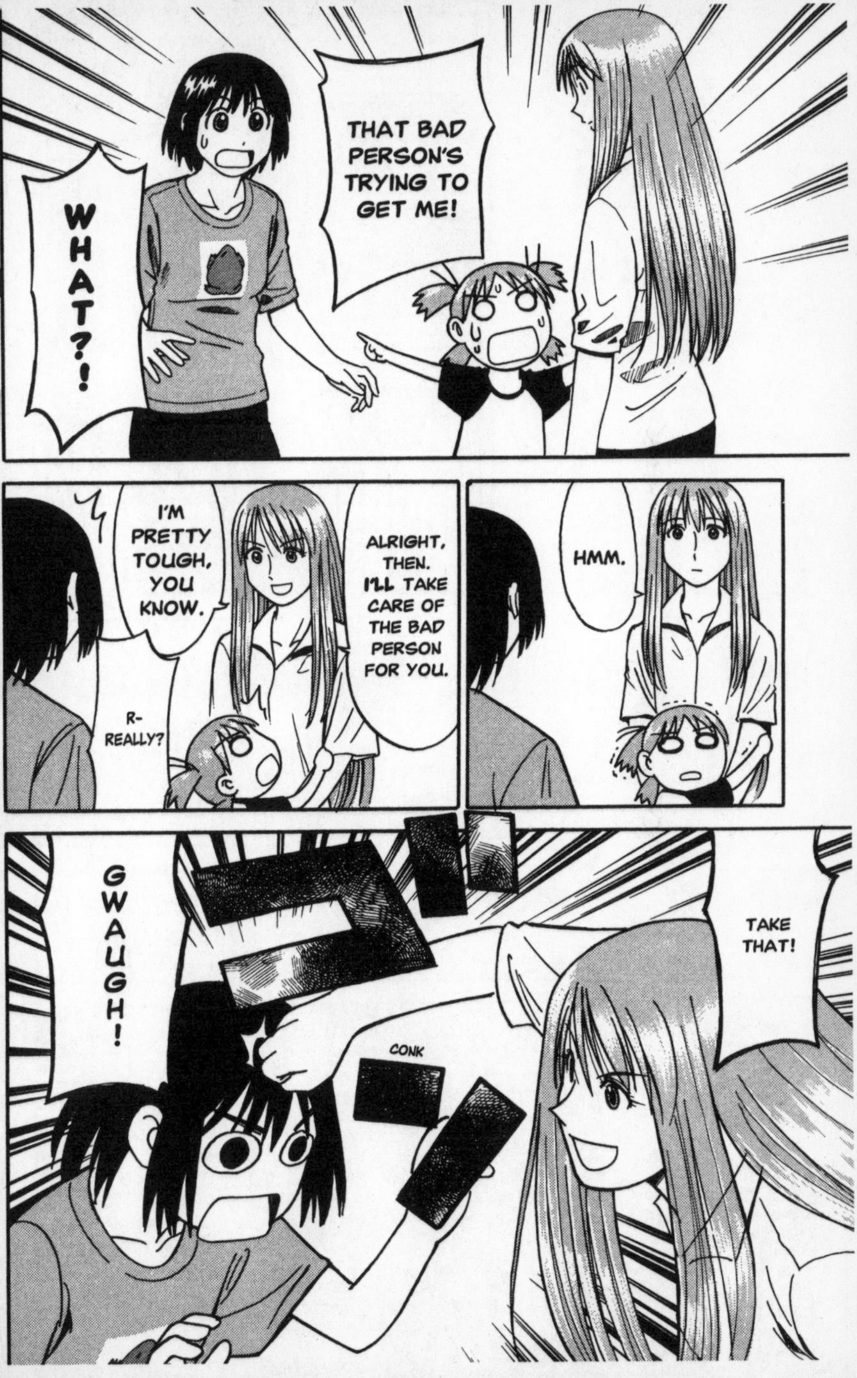
THAT BAD PERSON'S TRYING TO GET ME!
WHAT?!
HMM.
ALRIGHT, THEN. I'LL TAKE CARE OF THE BAD PERSON FOR YOU.
I'M PRETTY TOUGH, YOU KNOW.
R-REALLY?
TAKE THAT!
CONK
GWAUGH!

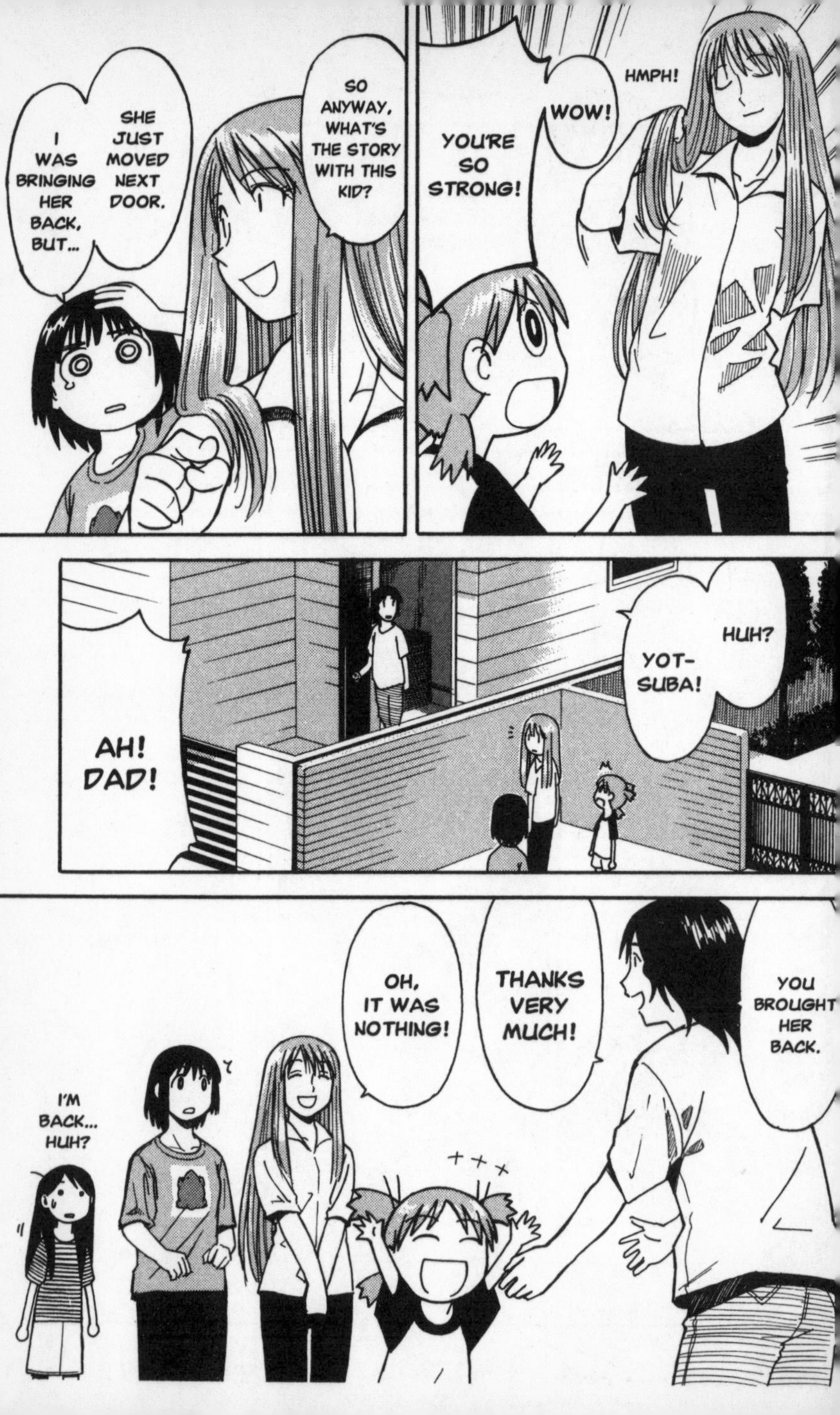
HMPH!
WOW!
YOU'RE SO STRONG!
SO ANYWAY, WHAT'S THE STORY WITH THIS KID?
SHE JUST MOVED NEXT DOOR.
I WAS BRINGING HER BACK, BUT...
HUH?
YOT-SUBA!
AH! DAD!
YOU BROUGHT HER BACK.
THANKS VERY MUCH!
OH, IT WAS NOTHING!
I'M BACK... HUH?

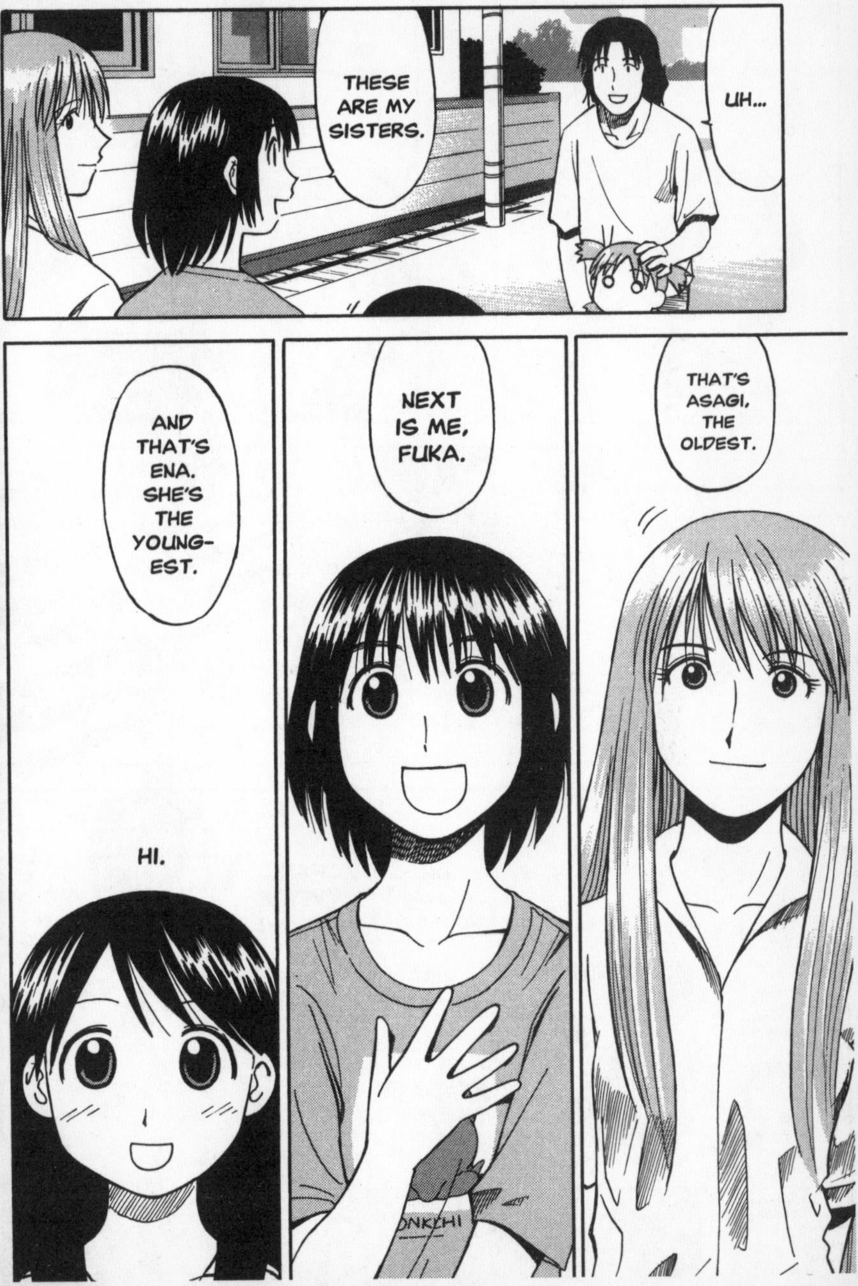
UH...
THESE ARE MY SISTERS.
THAT'S ASAGI, THE OLDEST.
NEXT IS ME, FUKA.
AND THAT'S ENA. SHE'S THE YOUNG-EST.
HI.

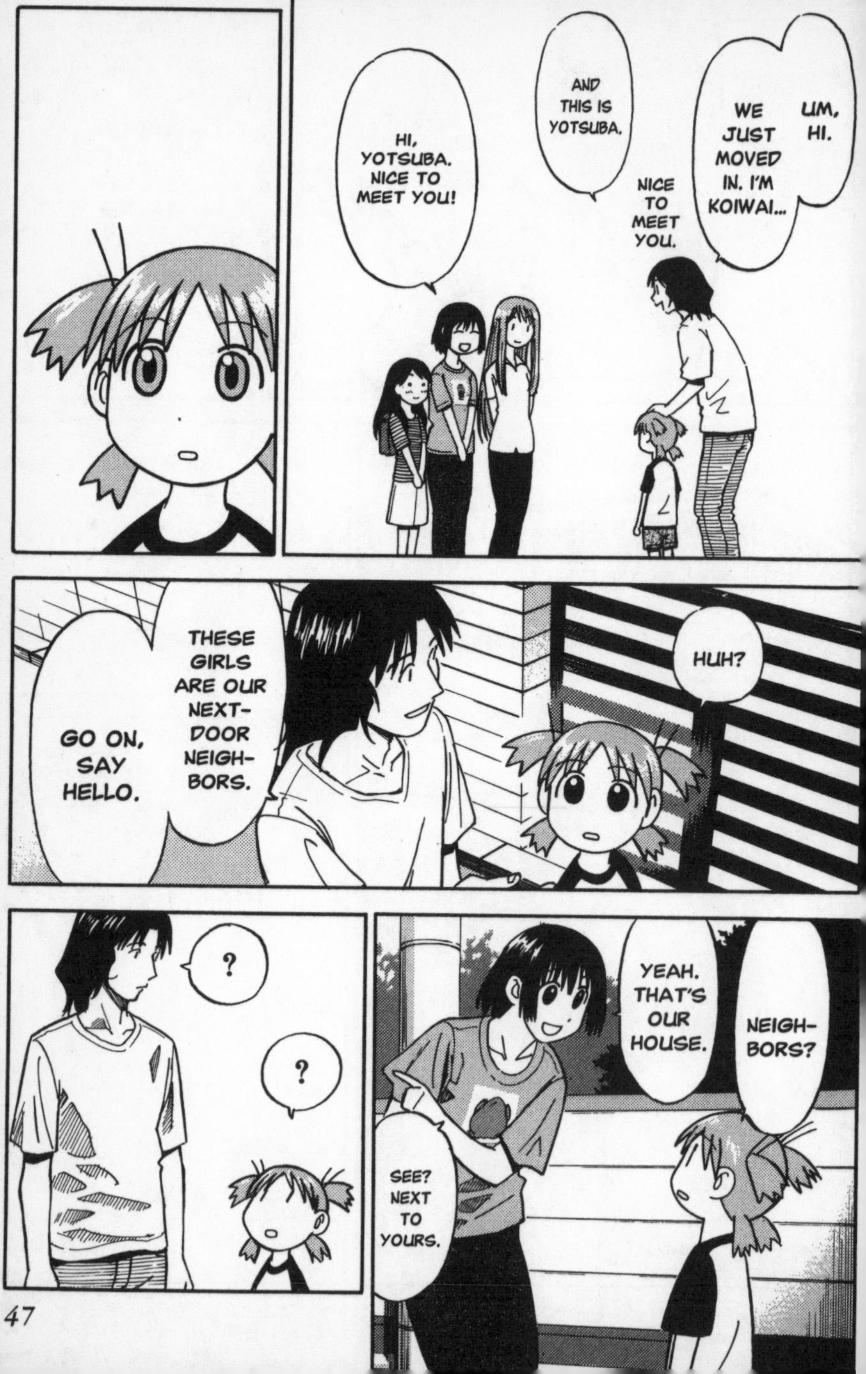
UM, HI.
WE JUST MOVED IN. I'M KOIWAI...
NICE TO MEET YOU.
AND THIS IS YOTSUBA.
HI, YOTSUBA. NICE TO MEET YOU!
HUH?
THESE GIRLS ARE OUR NEXT-DOOR NEIGHBORS.
GO ON, SAY HELLO.
NEIGHBORS?
YEAH. THAT'S OUR HOUSE.
SEE? NEXT TO YOURS.
?
?

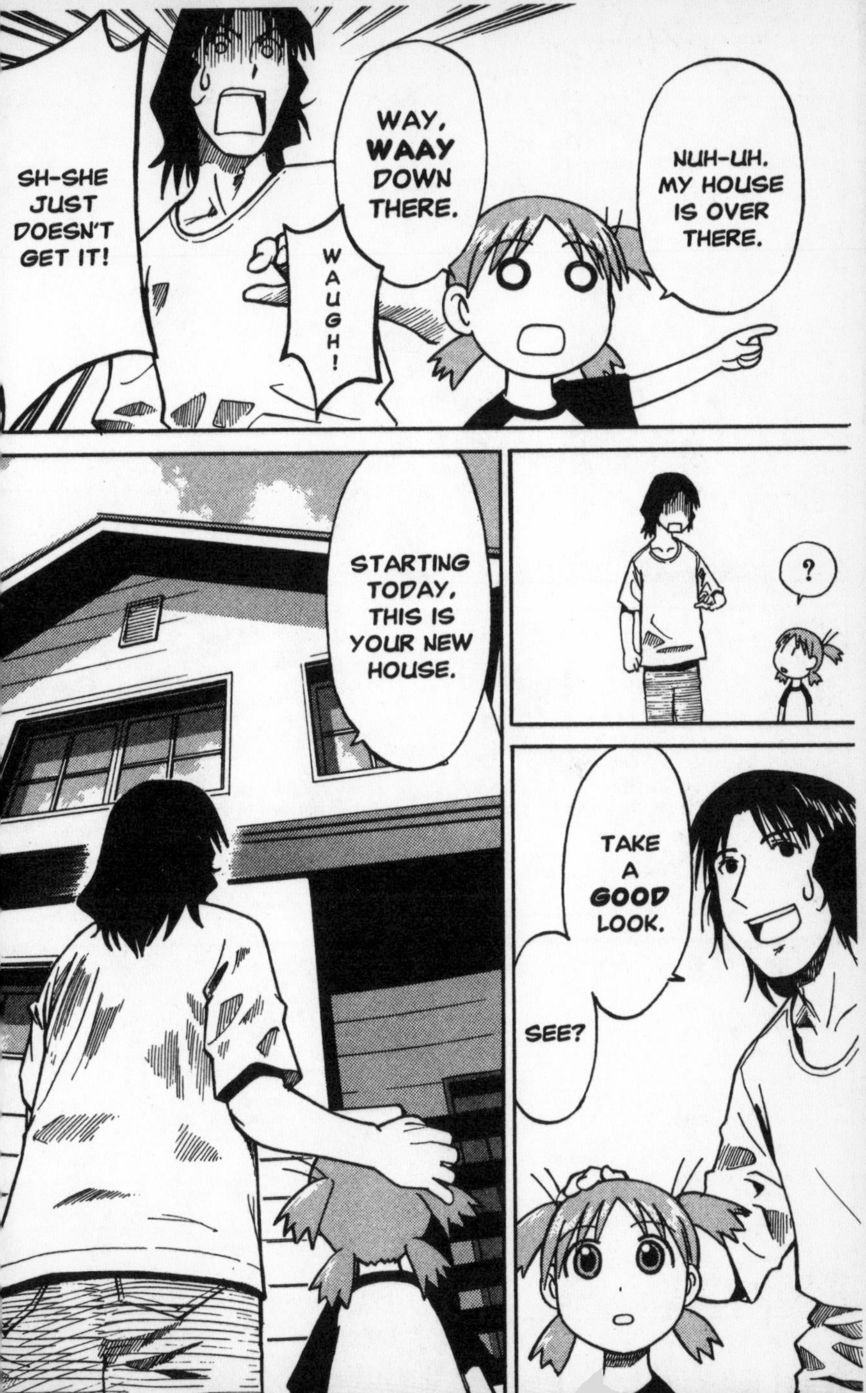
NUH-UH. MY HOUSE IS OVER THERE.
WAY, WAAAY DOWN THERE.
WAUGH!
SH-SHE JUST DOESN'T GET IT!
?
TAKE A GOOD LOOK.
SEE?
STARTING TODAY, THIS IS YOUR NEW HOUSE.

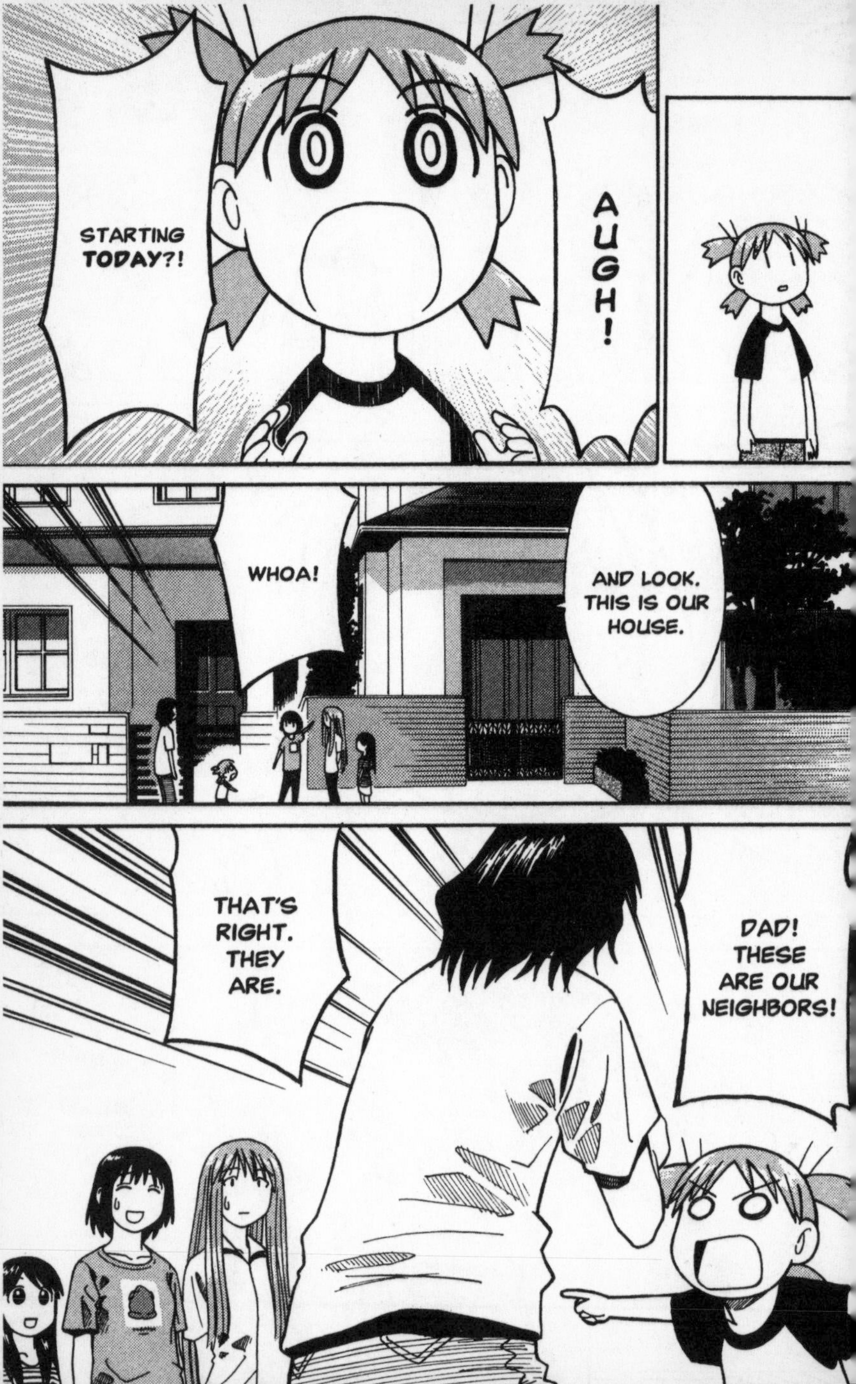
AUGH!
STARTING TODAY?!
AND LOOK. THIS IS OUR HOUSE.
WHOA!
DAD! THESE ARE OUR NEIGHBORS!
THAT'S RIGHT. THEY ARE.

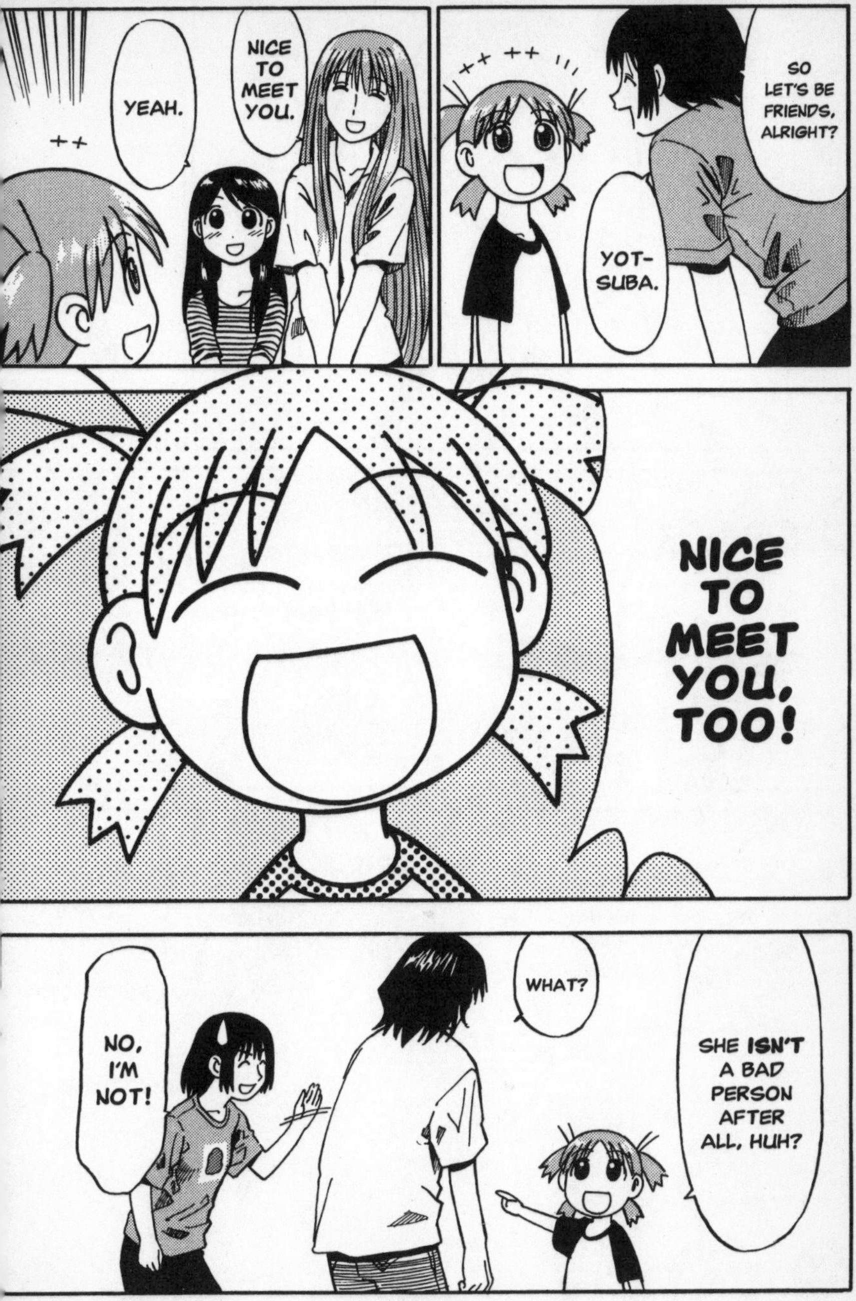
SO LET'S BE FRIENDS, ALRIGHT?
YOT-SUBA.
NICE TO MEET YOU.
YEAH.
NICE TO MEET YOU, TOO!
SHE **ISN'T** A BAD PERSON AFTER ALL, HUH?
WHAT?
NO, I'M NOT!

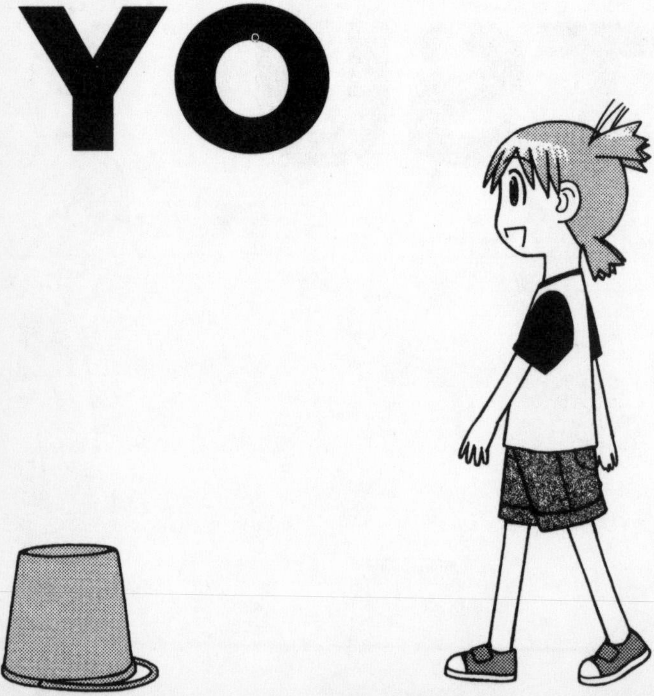
YO

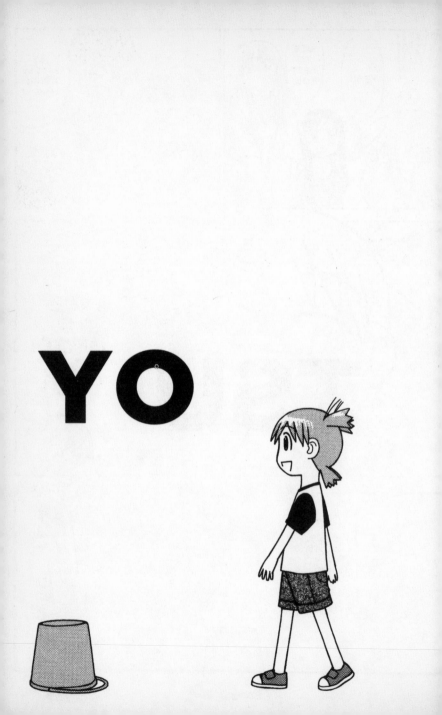

TSU

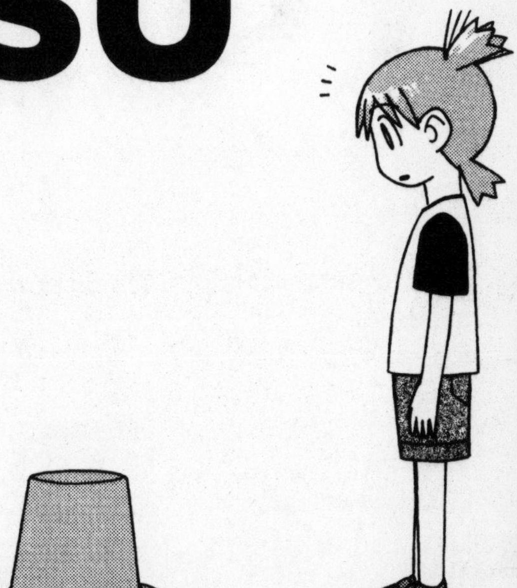

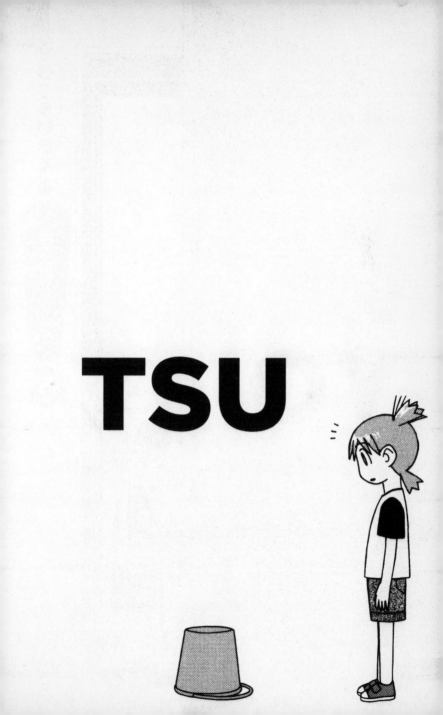

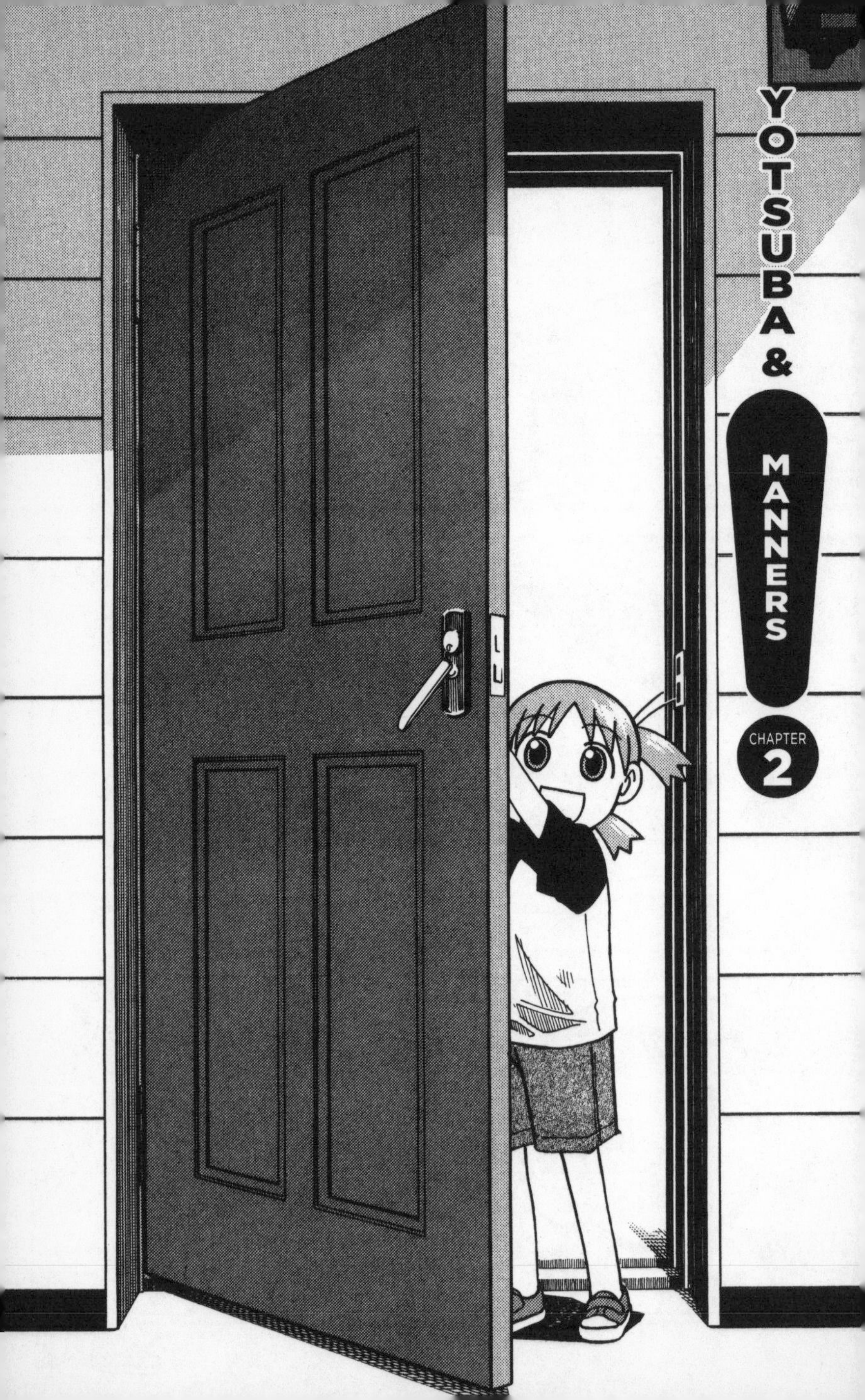
YOTSUBA &
MANNERS
!
CHAPTER 2

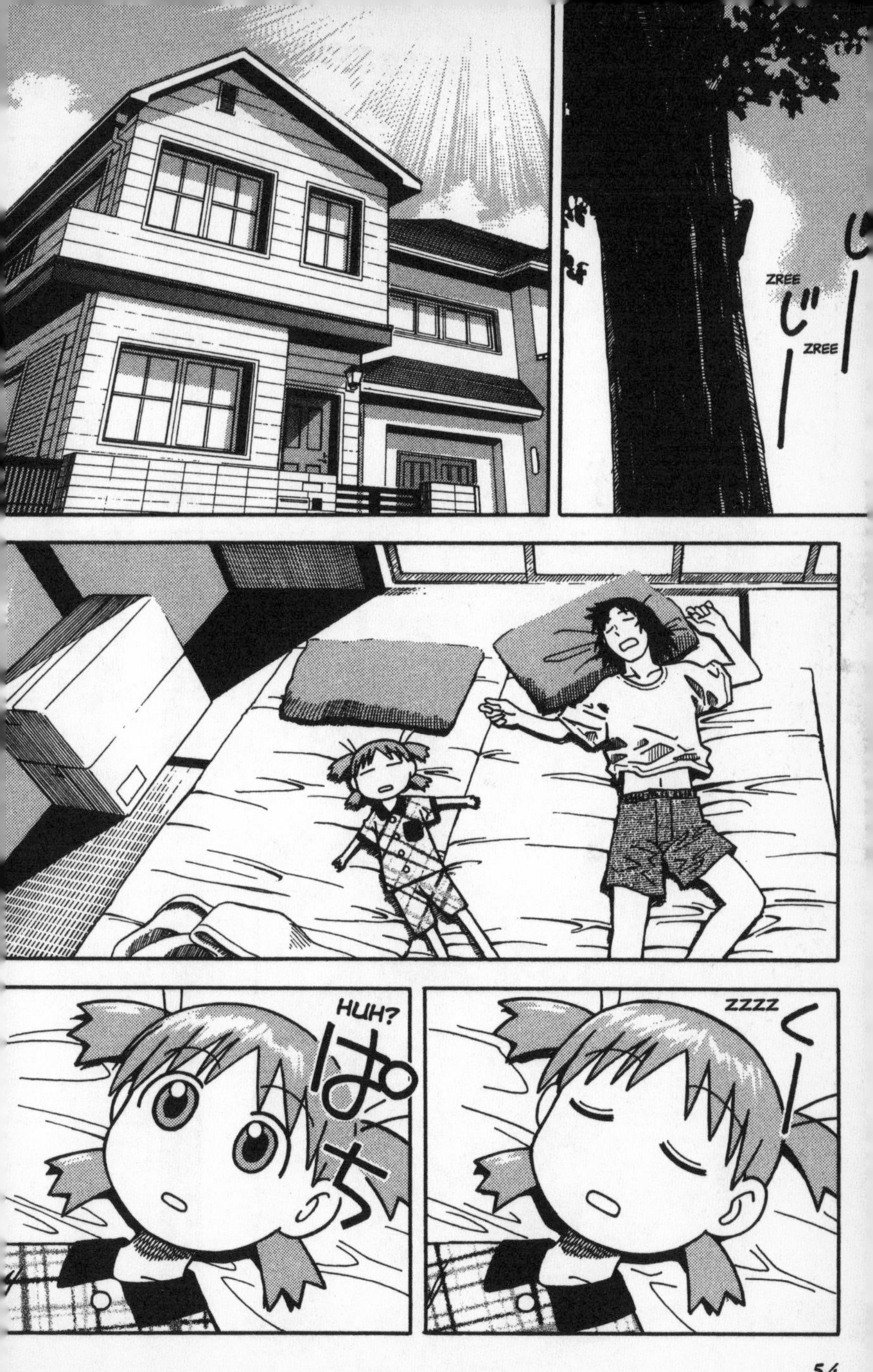

じー
ZREE
じー
ZREE
ZZZZ
くー
HUH?
ぱち

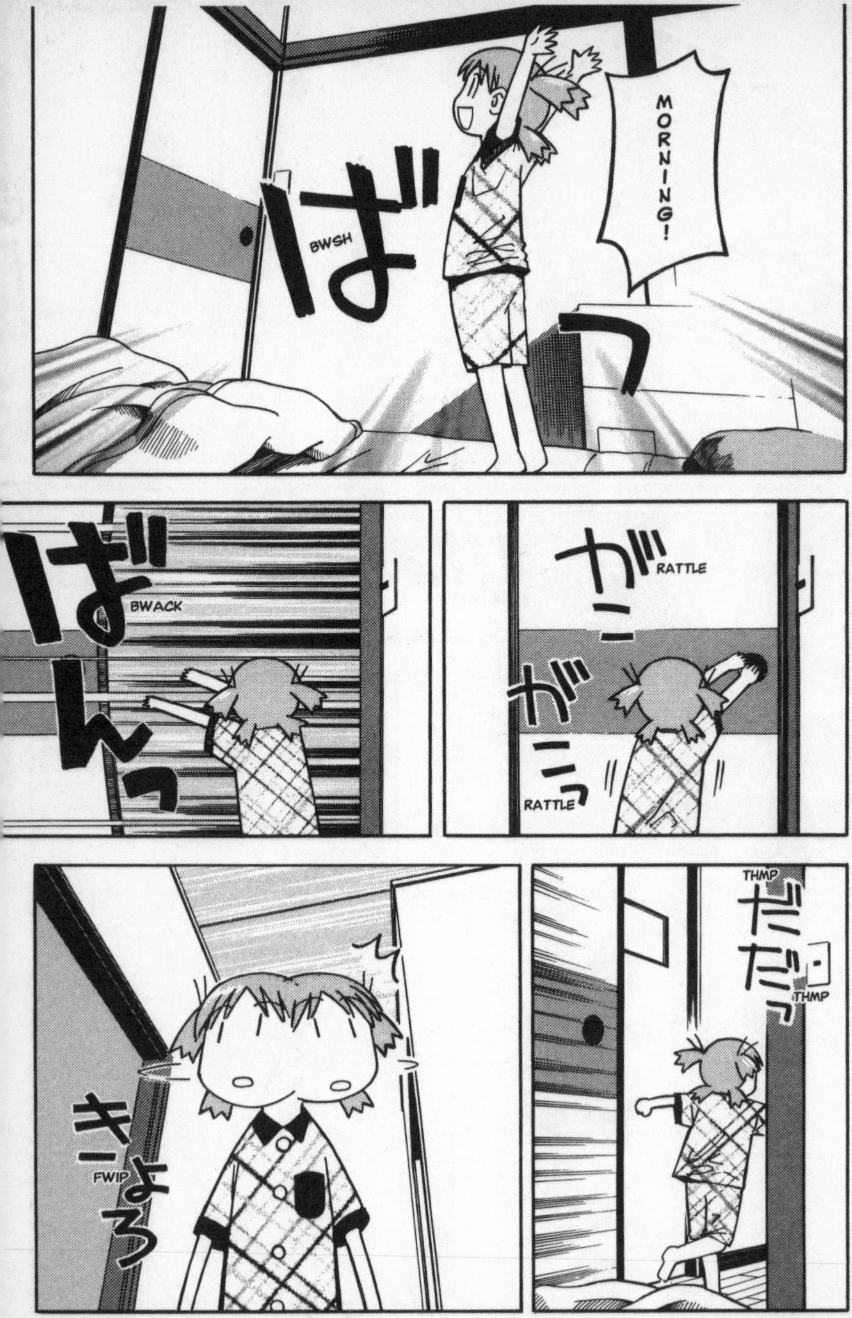
MORNING!
ばっ
BWSH
がこ
RATTLE
がこっ
RATTLE
ばんっ
BWACK
だだっ
THMP
THMP
きょろ
FWIP

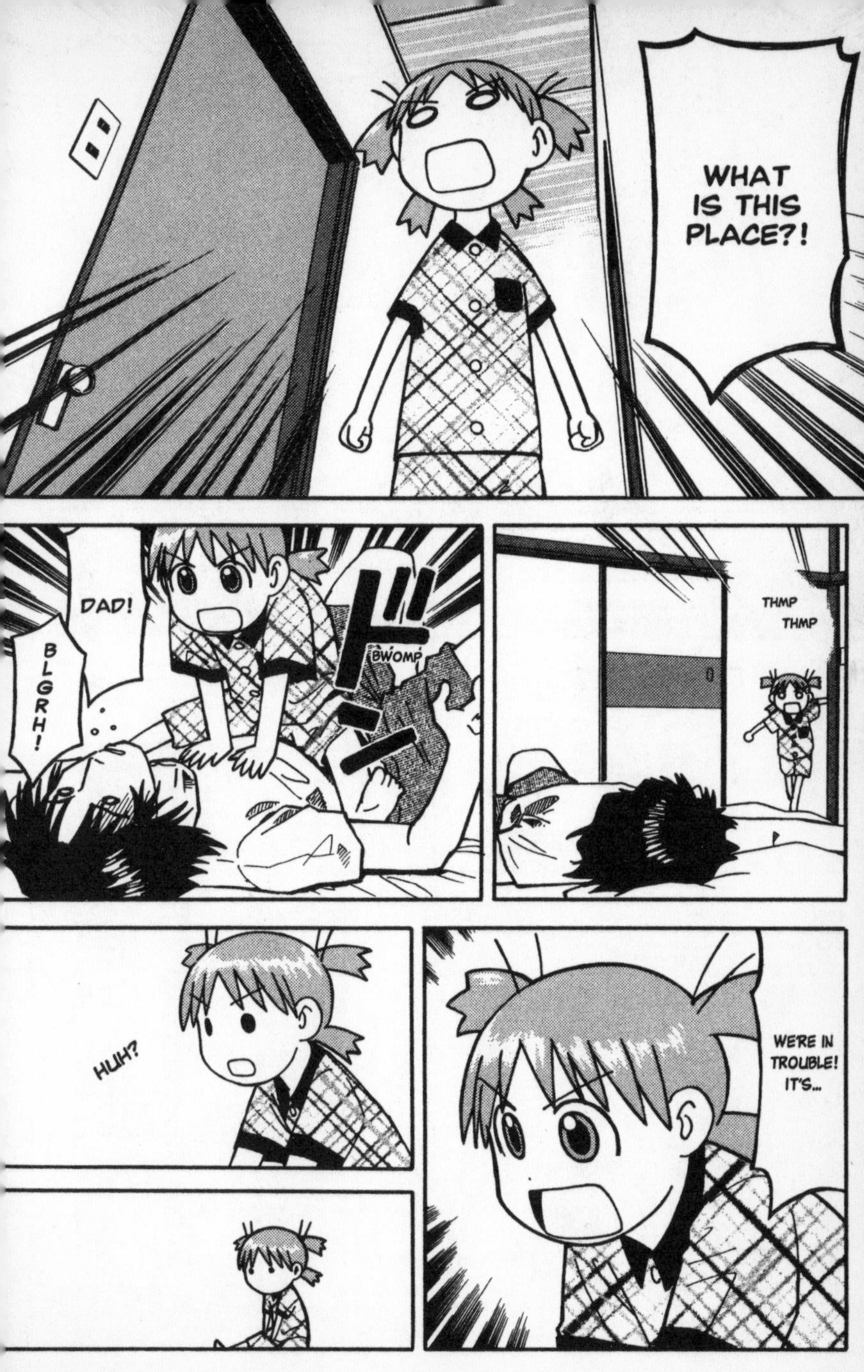
WHAT IS THIS PLACE?!
THMP
THMP
BWOMP
DAD!
BLGRH!
WE'RE IN TROUBLE! IT'S...
HUH?

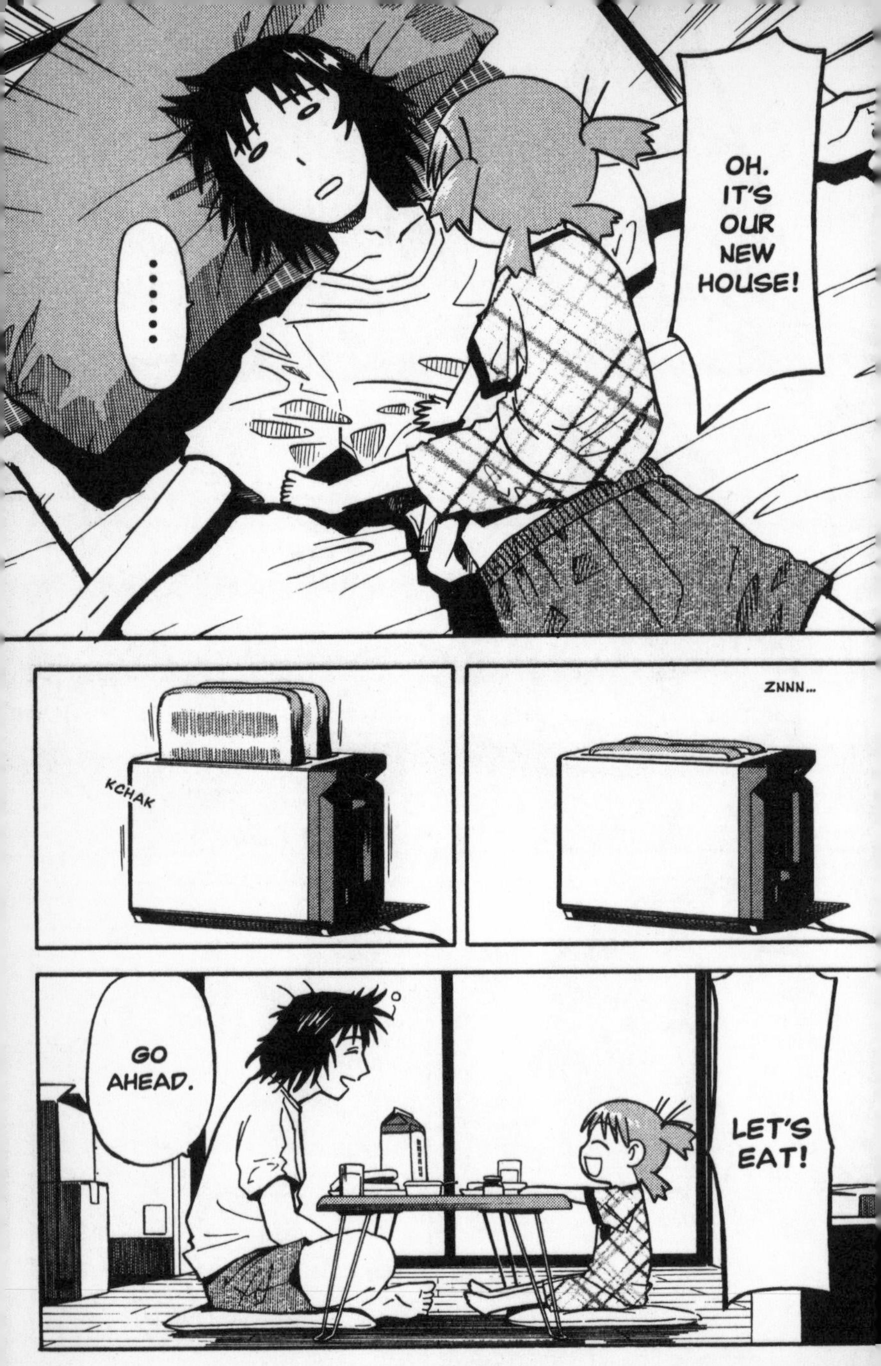
OH. IT'S OUR NEW HOUSE!
......
ZNNN...
KCHAK
LET'S EAT!
GO AHEAD.

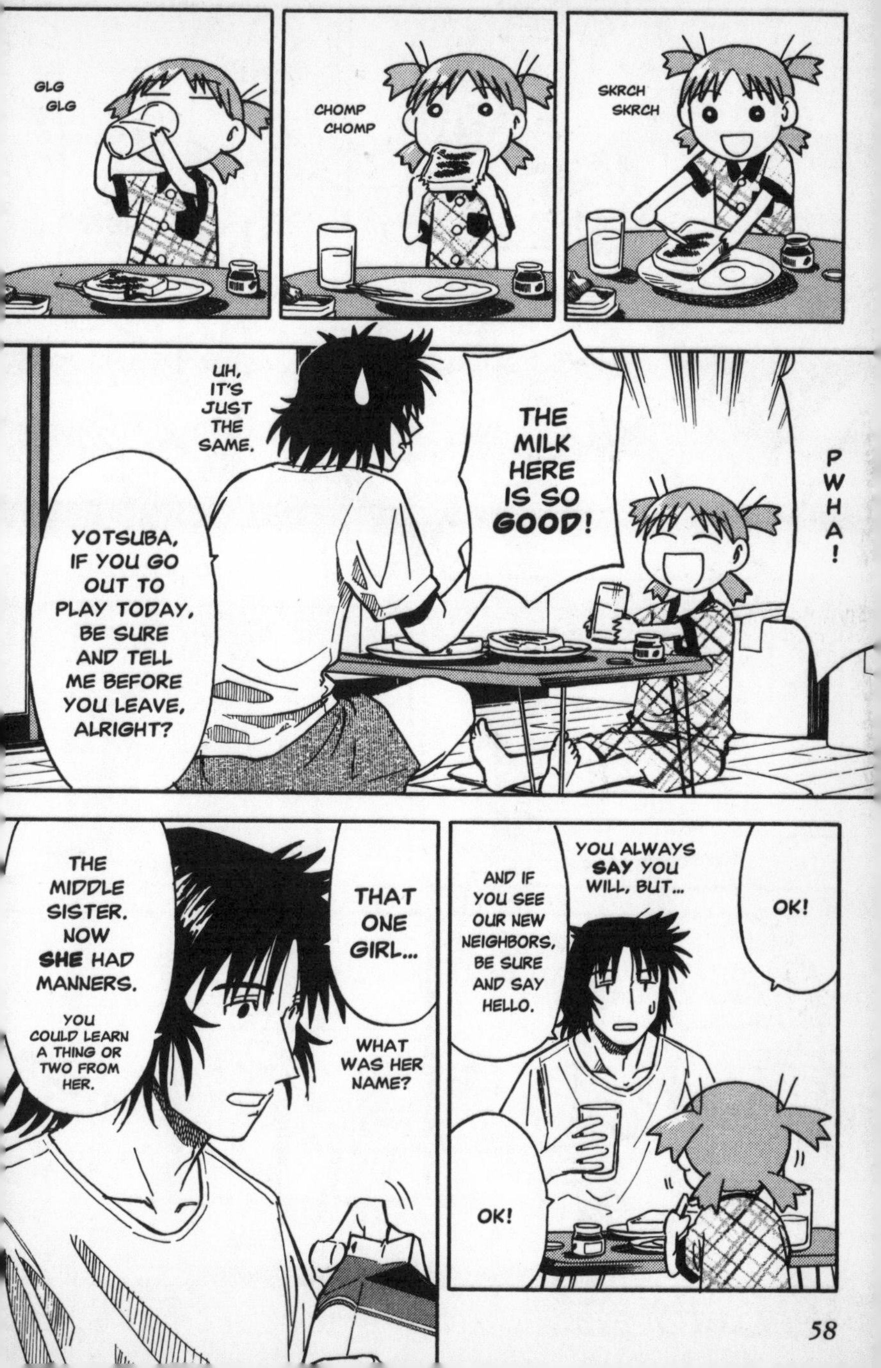
SKRCH SKRCH
CHOMP CHOMP
GLG GLG
PWHA!
THE MILK HERE IS SO GOOD!
UH, IT'S JUST THE SAME.
YOTSUBA, IF YOU GO OUT TO PLAY TODAY, BE SURE AND TELL ME BEFORE YOU LEAVE, ALRIGHT?
OK!
YOU ALWAYS SAY YOU WILL, BUT...
AND IF YOU SEE OUR NEW NEIGHBORS, BE SURE AND SAY HELLO.
OK!
THAT ONE GIRL...
WHAT WAS HER NAME?
THE MIDDLE SISTER. NOW SHE HAD MANNERS.
YOU COULD LEARN A THING OR TWO FROM HER.

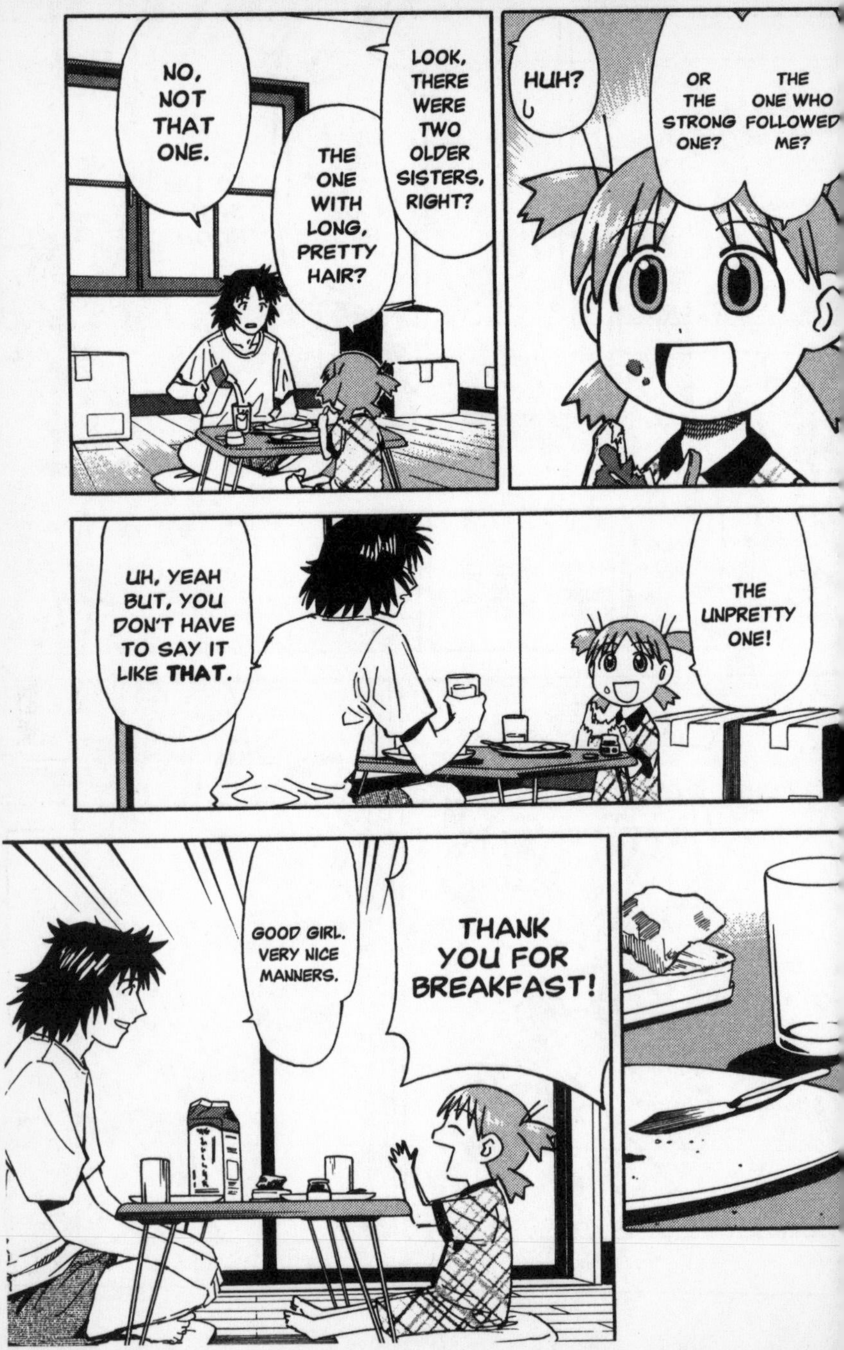
THE ONE WHO FOLLOWED ME?
OR THE STRONG ONE?
HUH?
LOOK, THERE WERE TWO OLDER SISTERS, RIGHT?
THE ONE WITH LONG, PRETTY HAIR?
NO, NOT THAT ONE.
THE UNPRETTY ONE!
UH, YEAH BUT, YOU DON'T HAVE TO SAY IT LIKE THAT.
THANK YOU FOR BREAKFAST!
GOOD GIRL. VERY NICE MANNERS.

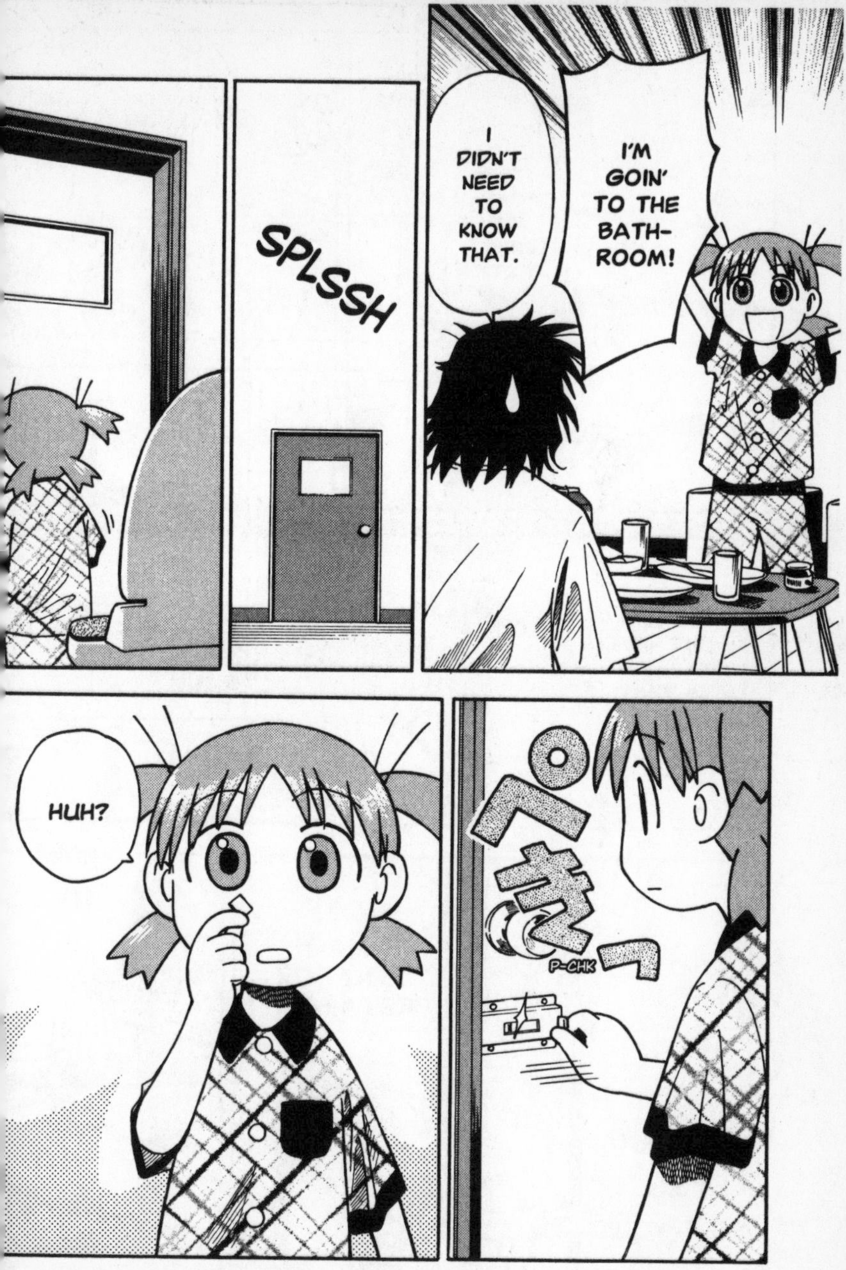
I'M GOIN' TO THE BATH-ROOM!
I DIDN'T NEED TO KNOW THAT.
SPLSSH
ぺきっ
P-CHK
HUH?

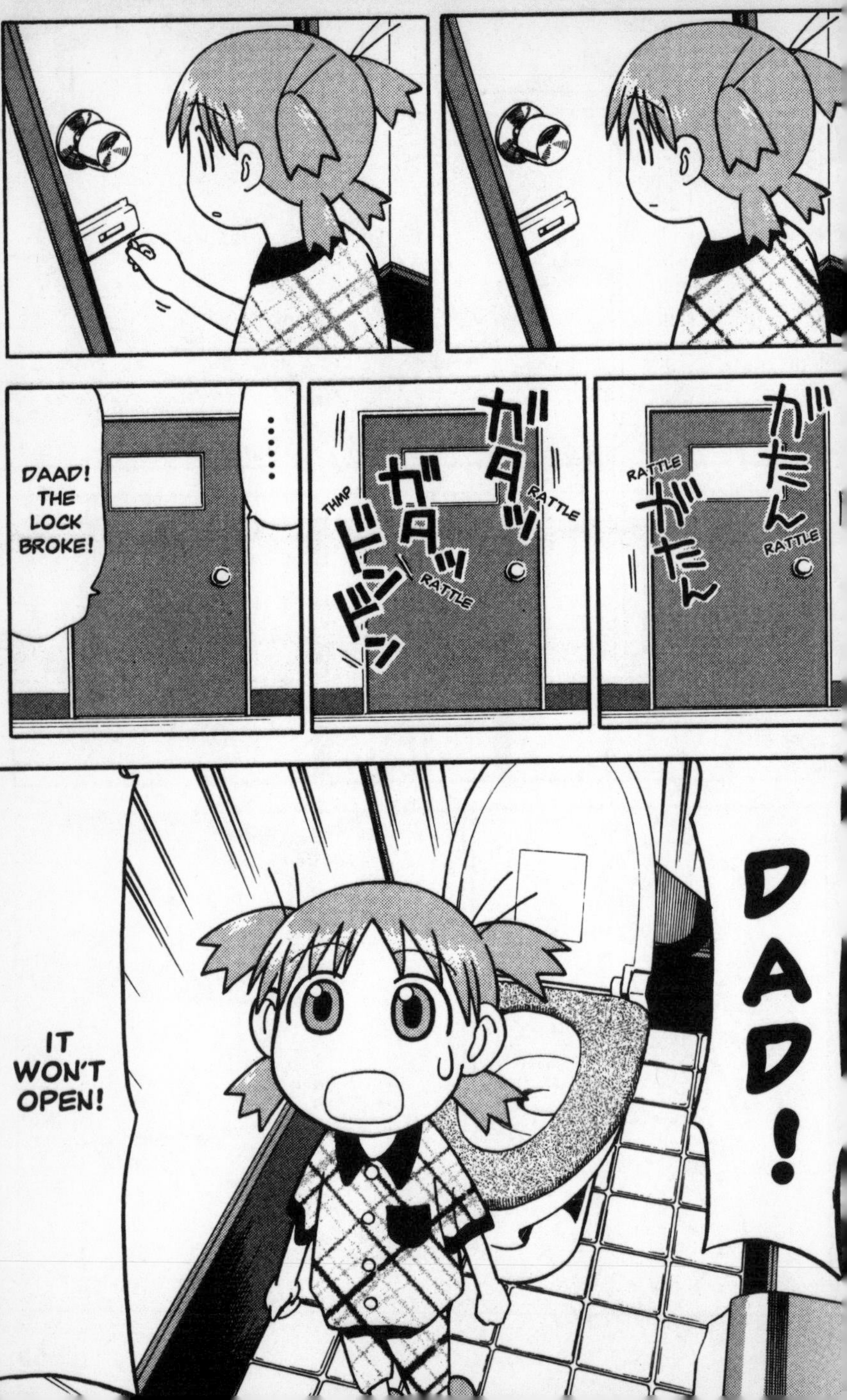
がたん
RATTLE
がたん
RATTLE
ガタッ
RATTLE
ガタッ
RATTLE
ドンドン
THMP
......
DAAD! THE LOCK BROKE!
DAD!
IT WON'T OPEN!

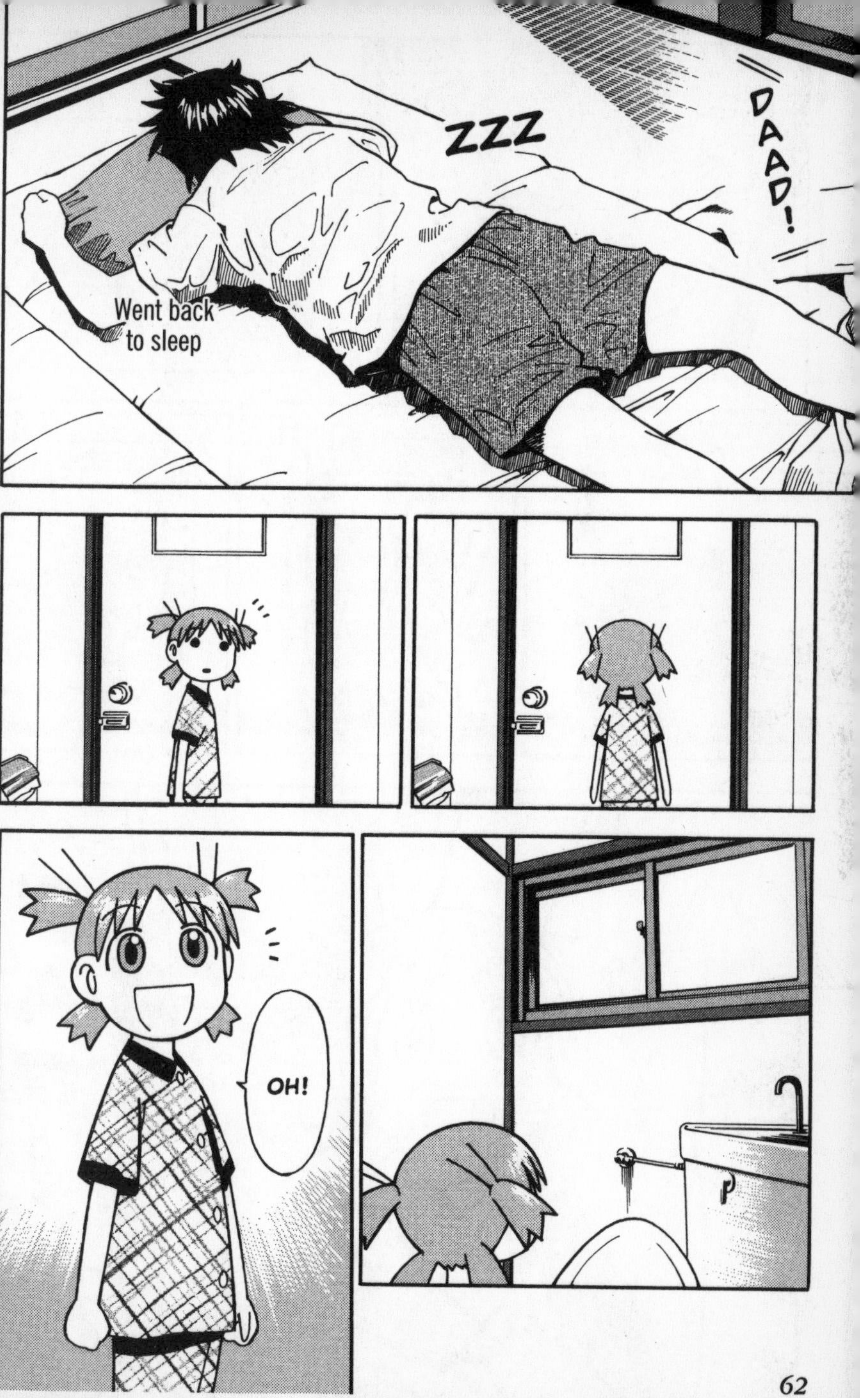
DAAD!
ZZZ
Went back to sleep
OH!

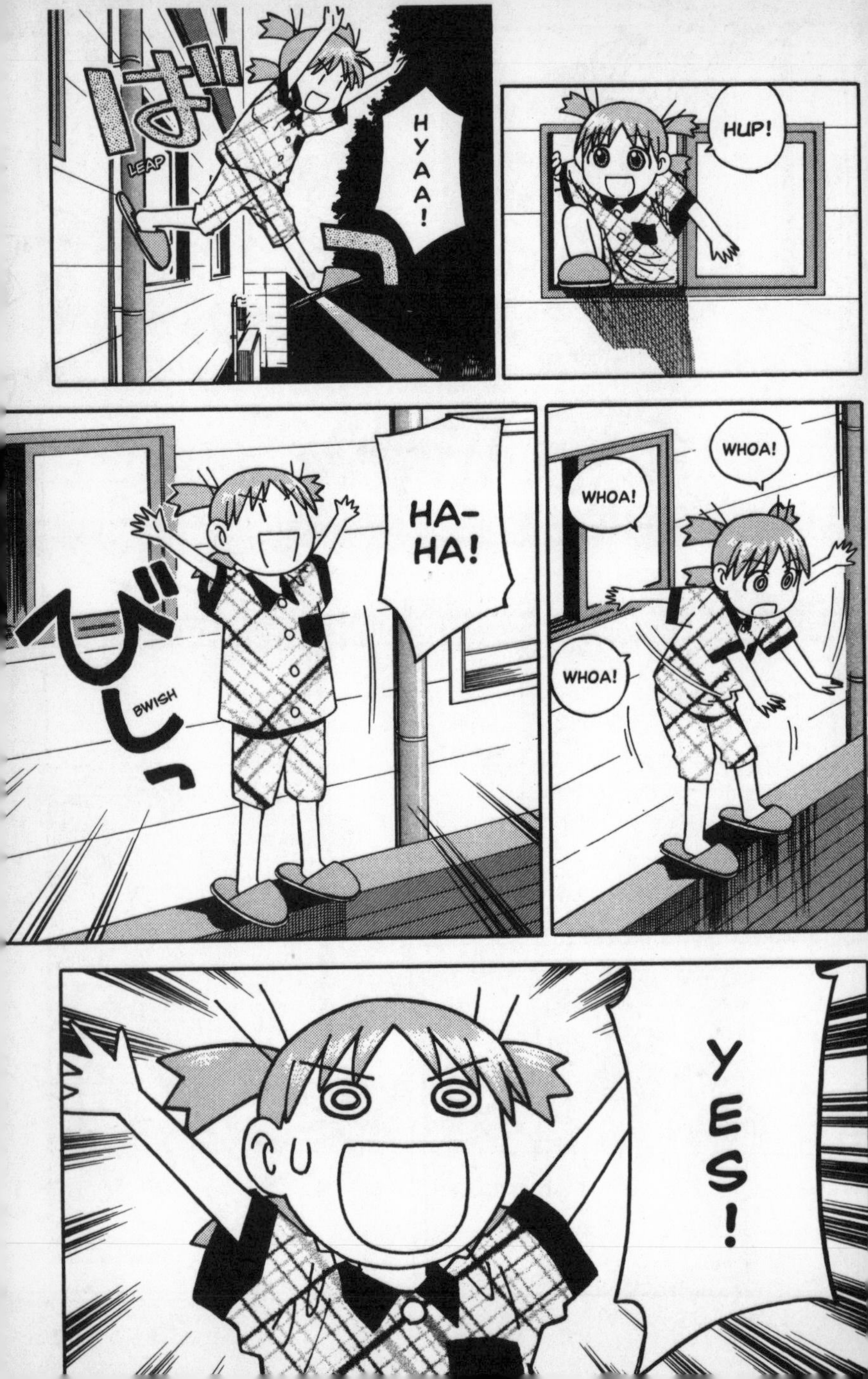
HUP!
LEAP
HYAA!
WHOA!
WHOA!
WHOA!
HA-HA!
びしっ
BWISH
YES!

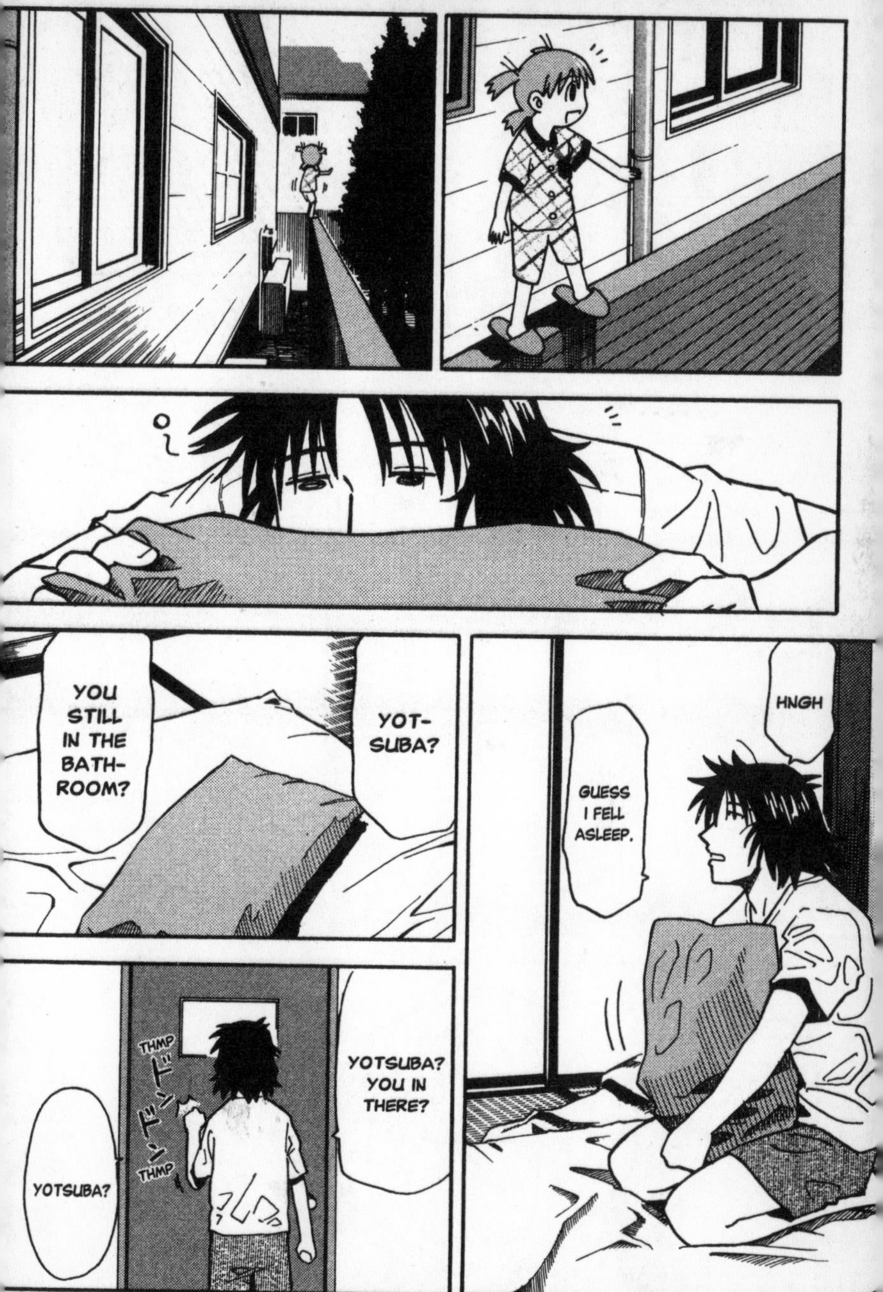
HNGH
GUESS I FELL ASLEEP.
YOT-SUBA?
YOU STILL IN THE BATH-ROOM?
YOTSUBA? YOU IN THERE?
THMP
THMP
YOTSUBA?

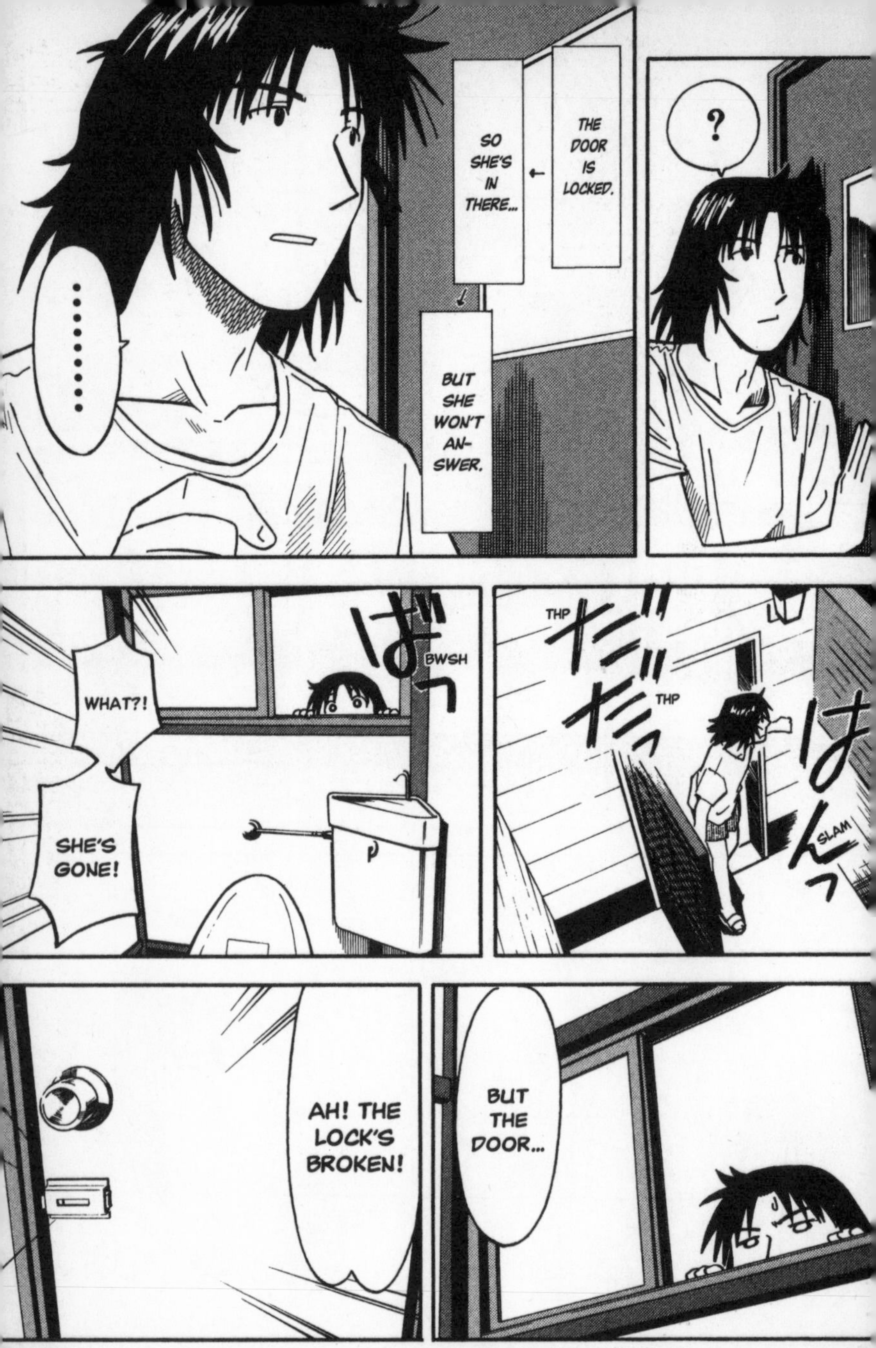
?
THE DOOR IS LOCKED.
SO SHE'S IN THERE...
BUT SHE WON'T AN-SWER.
......
だだっ
THP
THP
はんっ
SLAM
ばっ
BWSH
WHAT?!
SHE'S GONE!
BUT THE DOOR...
AH! THE LOCK'S BROKEN!

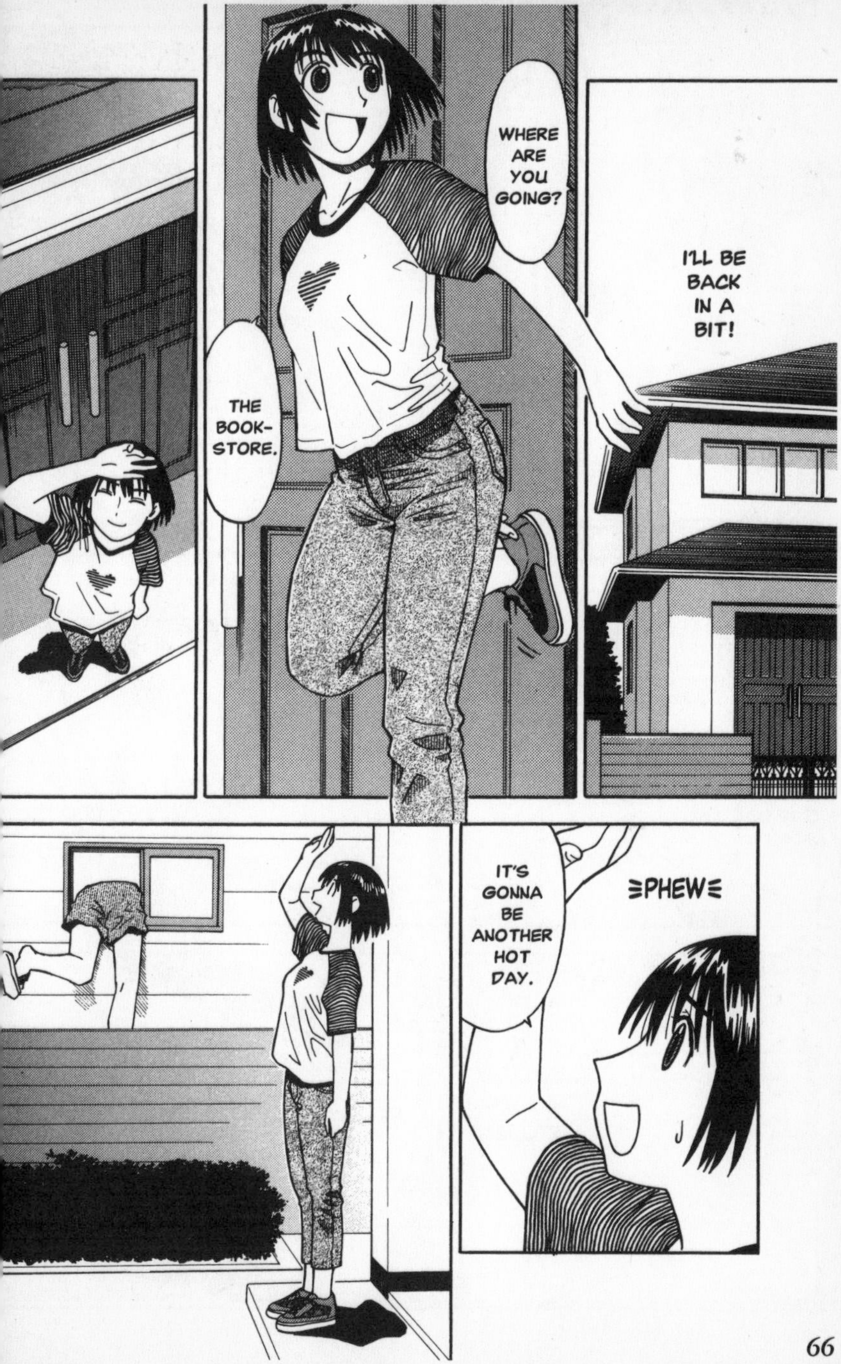
I'LL BE BACK IN A BIT!
WHERE ARE YOU GOING?
THE BOOK-STORE.
≡PHEW≡
IT'S GONNA BE ANOTHER HOT DAY.

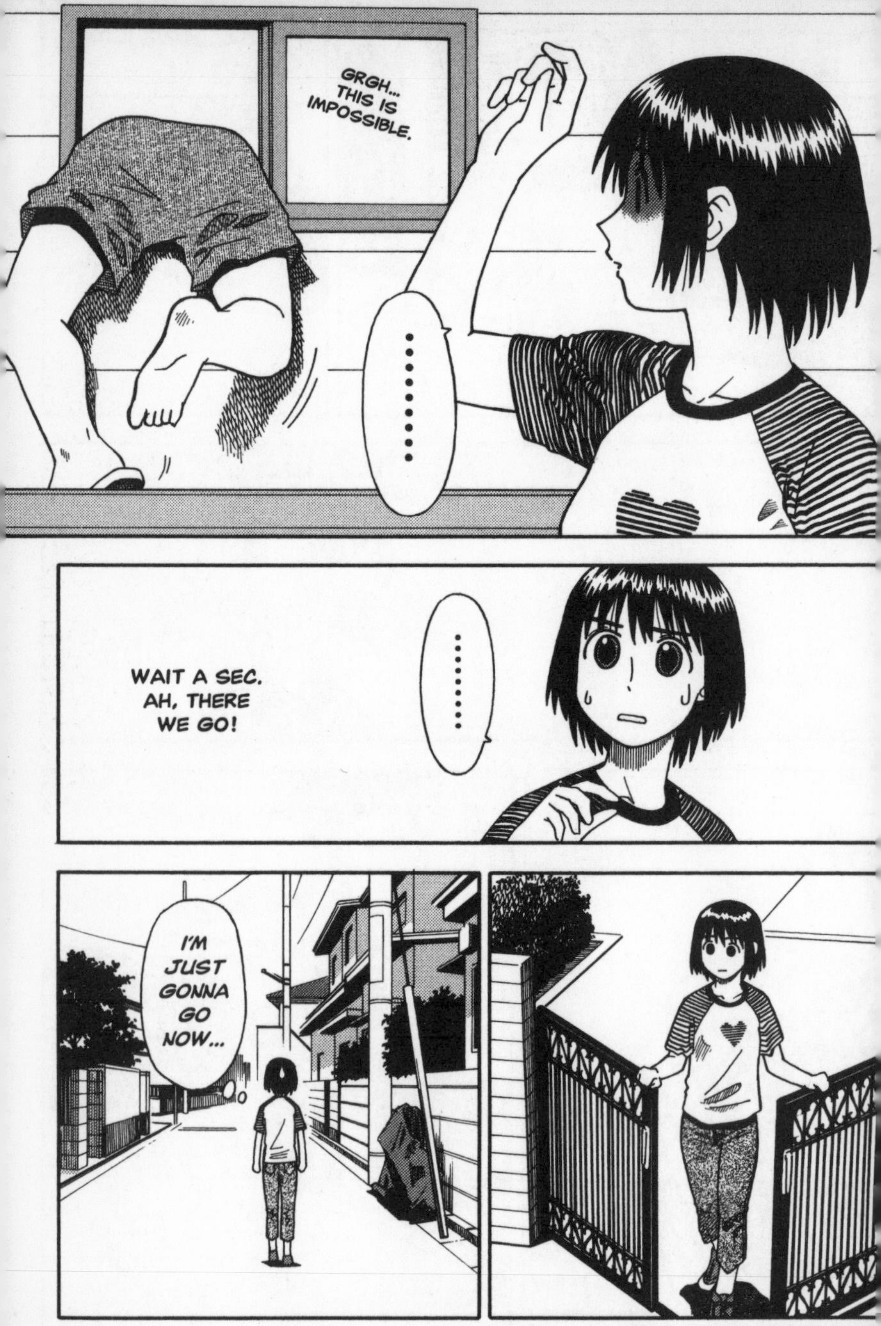
GRGH... THIS IS IMPOSSIBLE.
....
....
WAIT A SEC. AH, THERE WE GO!
I'M JUST GONNA GO NOW...

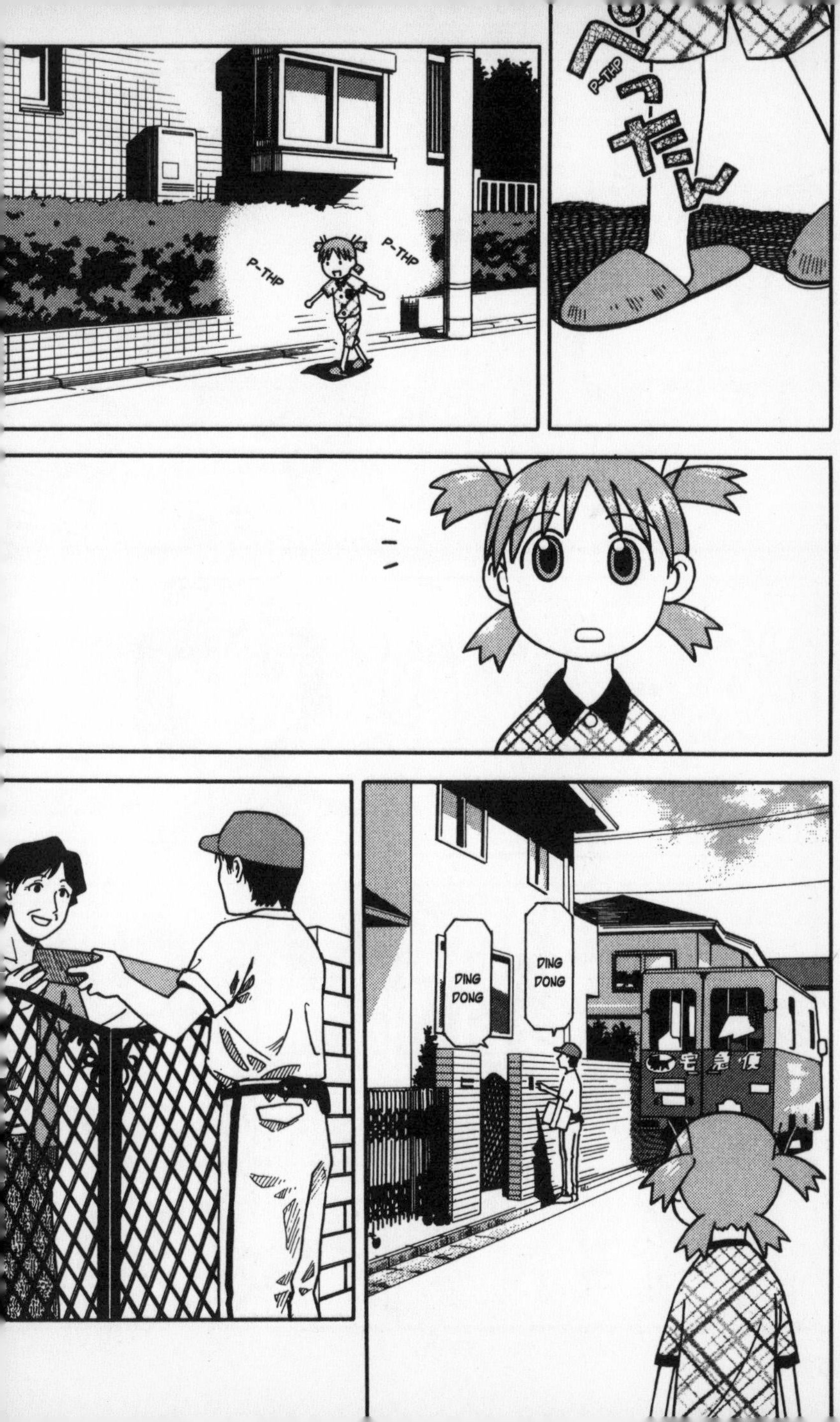
ぺったん
P-THP
P-THP
P-THP
DING DONG
DING DONG
宅急便

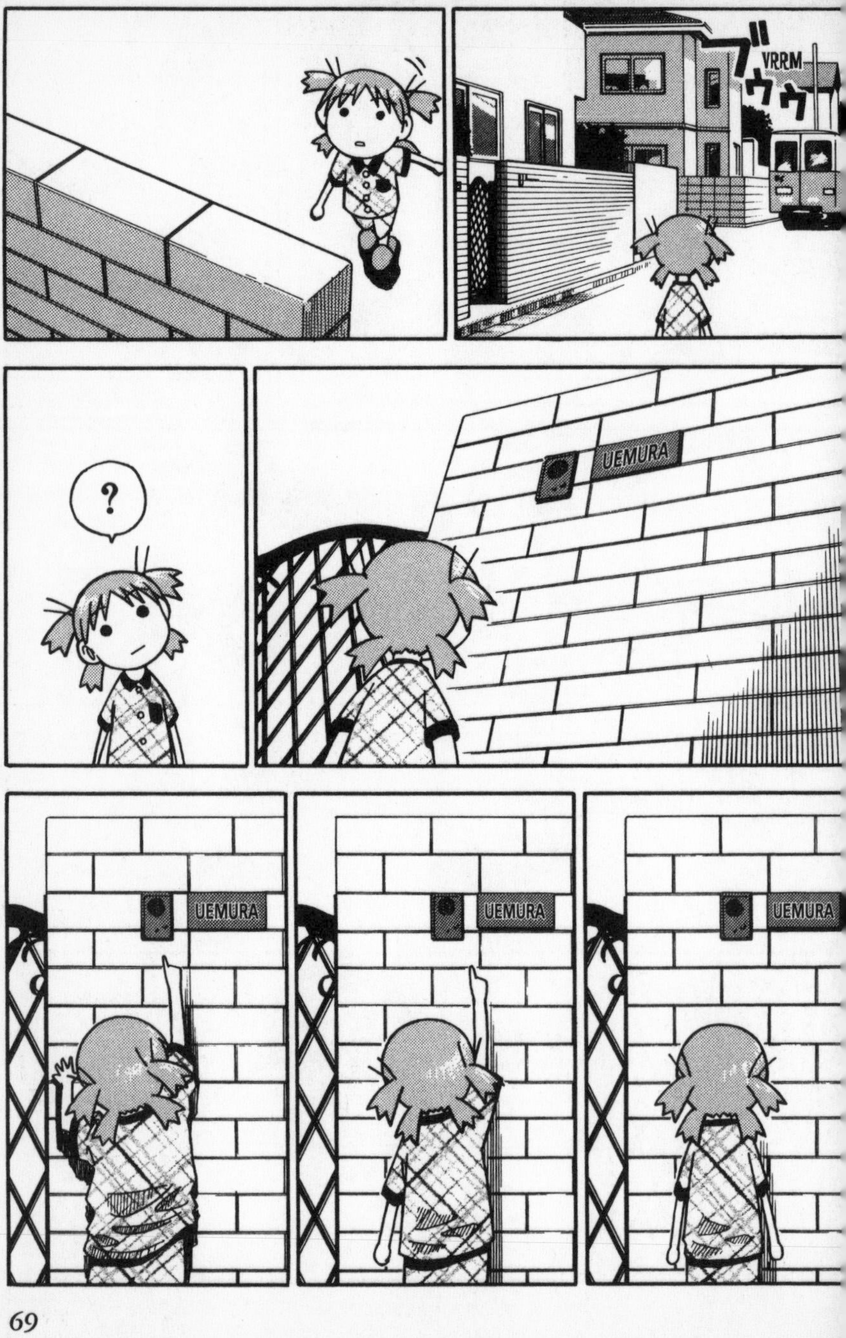
ブウウ
VRRM
UEMURA
?
UEMURA
UEMURA
UEMURA

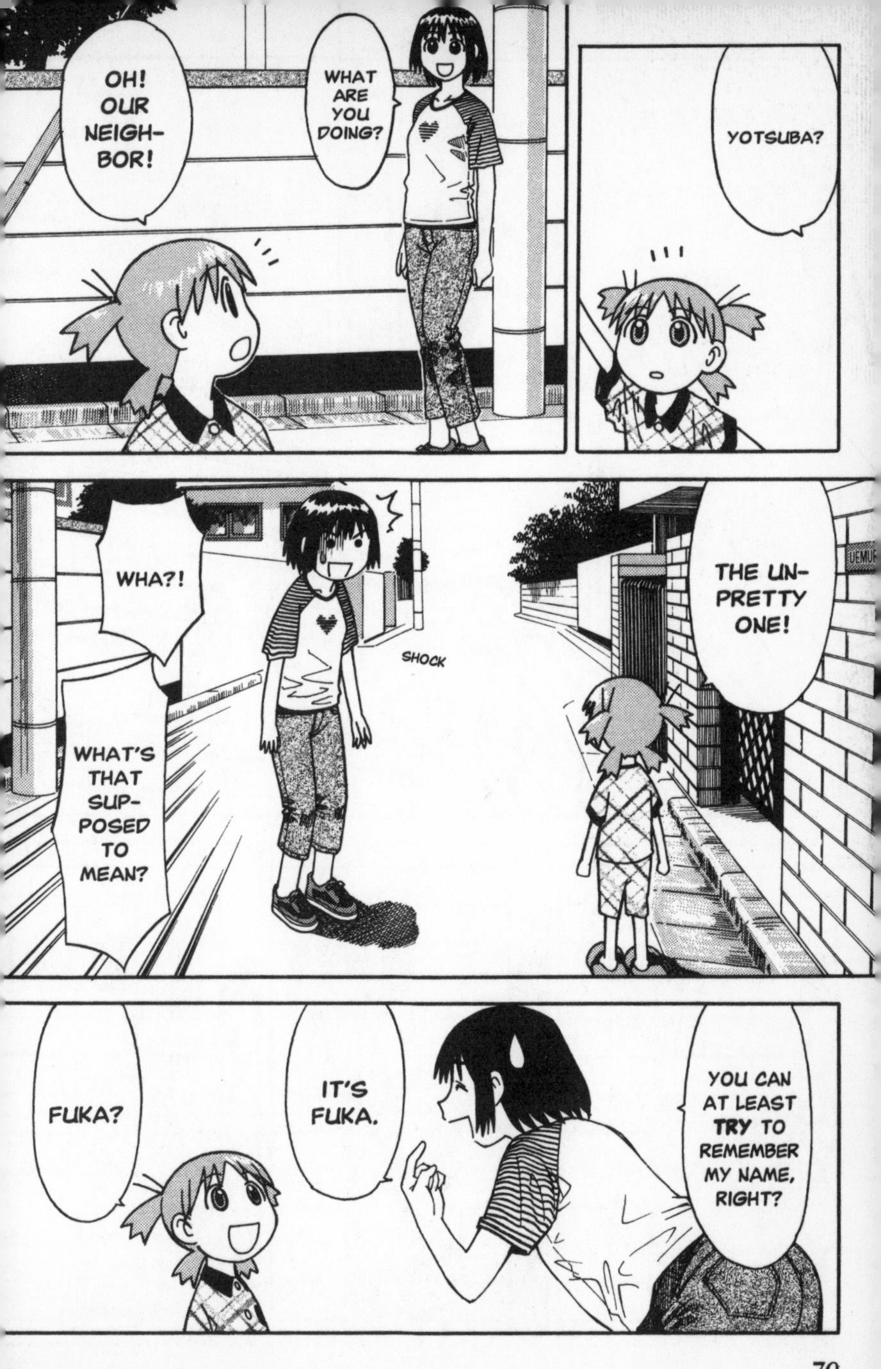
YOTSUBA?
WHAT ARE YOU DOING?
OH! OUR NEIGHBOR!
THE UN-PRETTY ONE!
SHOCK
WHA?!
WHAT'S THAT SUPPOSED TO MEAN?
YOU CAN AT LEAST **TRY** TO REMEMBER MY NAME, RIGHT?
IT'S FUKA.
FUKA?

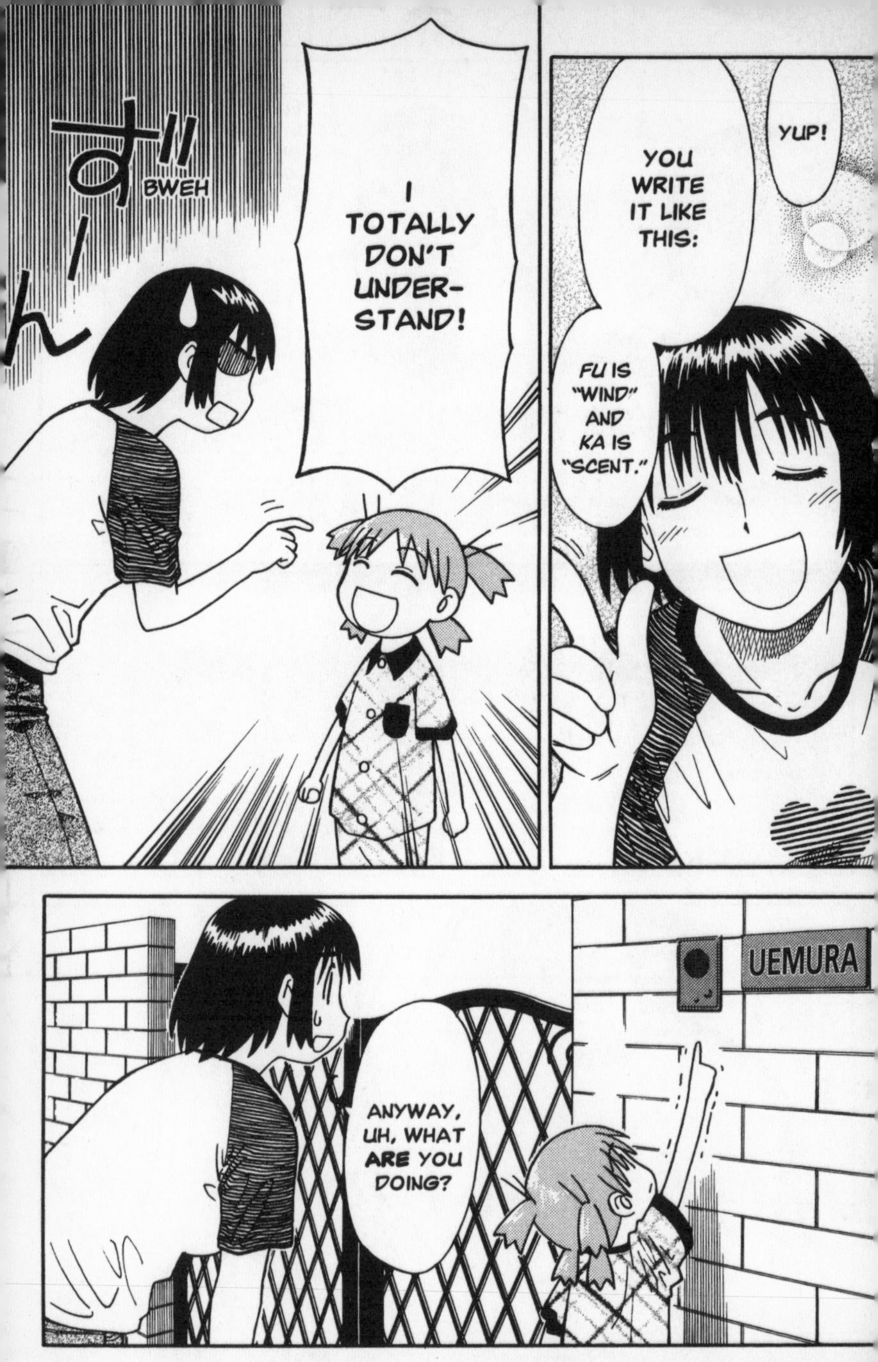
YUP!
YOU WRITE IT LIKE THIS:
FU IS "WIND" AND KA IS "SCENT."
I TOTALLY DON'T UNDER-STAND!
すーん
BWEH
UEMURA
ANYWAY, UH, WHAT **ARE** YOU DOING?

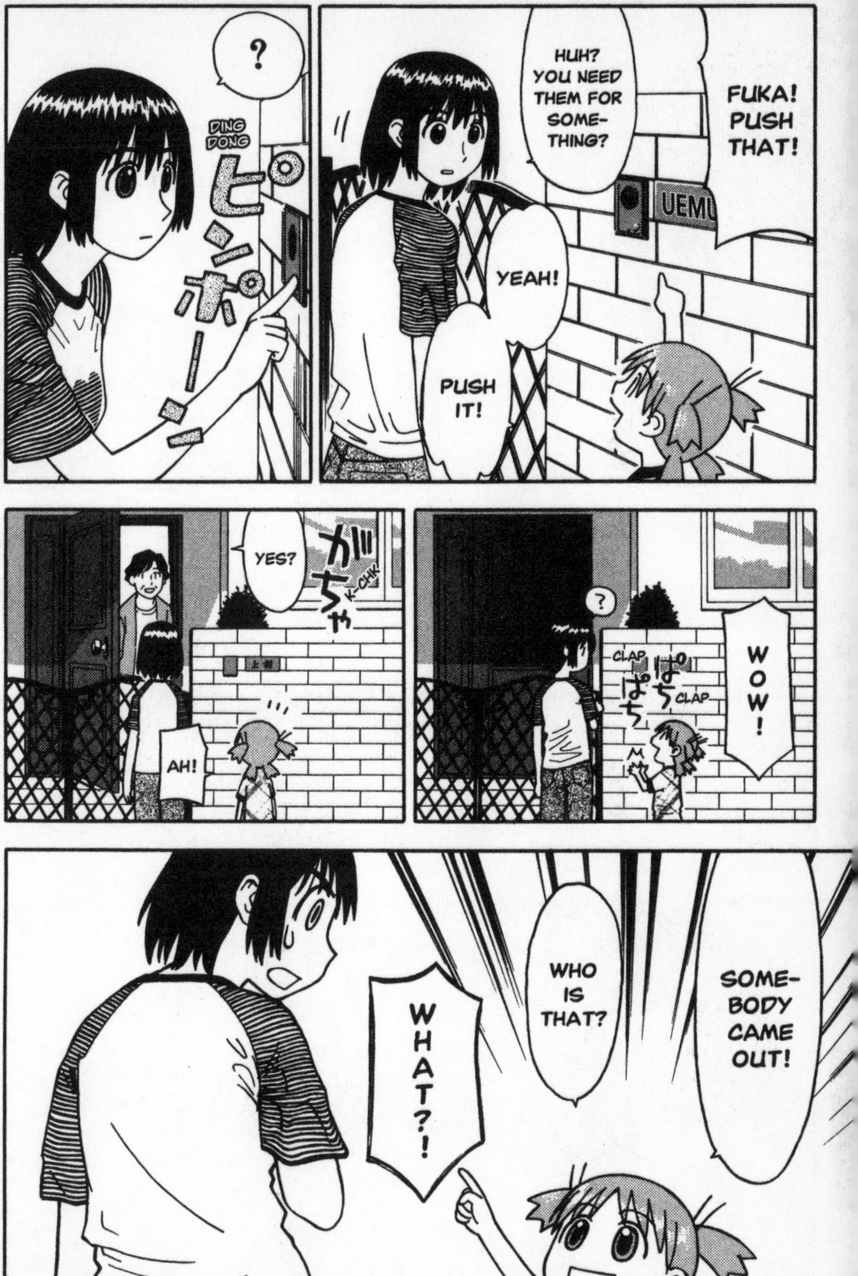
FUKA! PUSH THAT!
HUH? YOU NEED THEM FOR SOME-THING?
UEMU
YEAH!
PUSH IT!
?
DING DONG
ピンポーン
?
CLAP ぱち ぱち CLAP
WOW!
YES?
がちゃ K-CHK
AH!
SOME-BODY CAME OUT!
WHO IS THAT?
WHAT?!

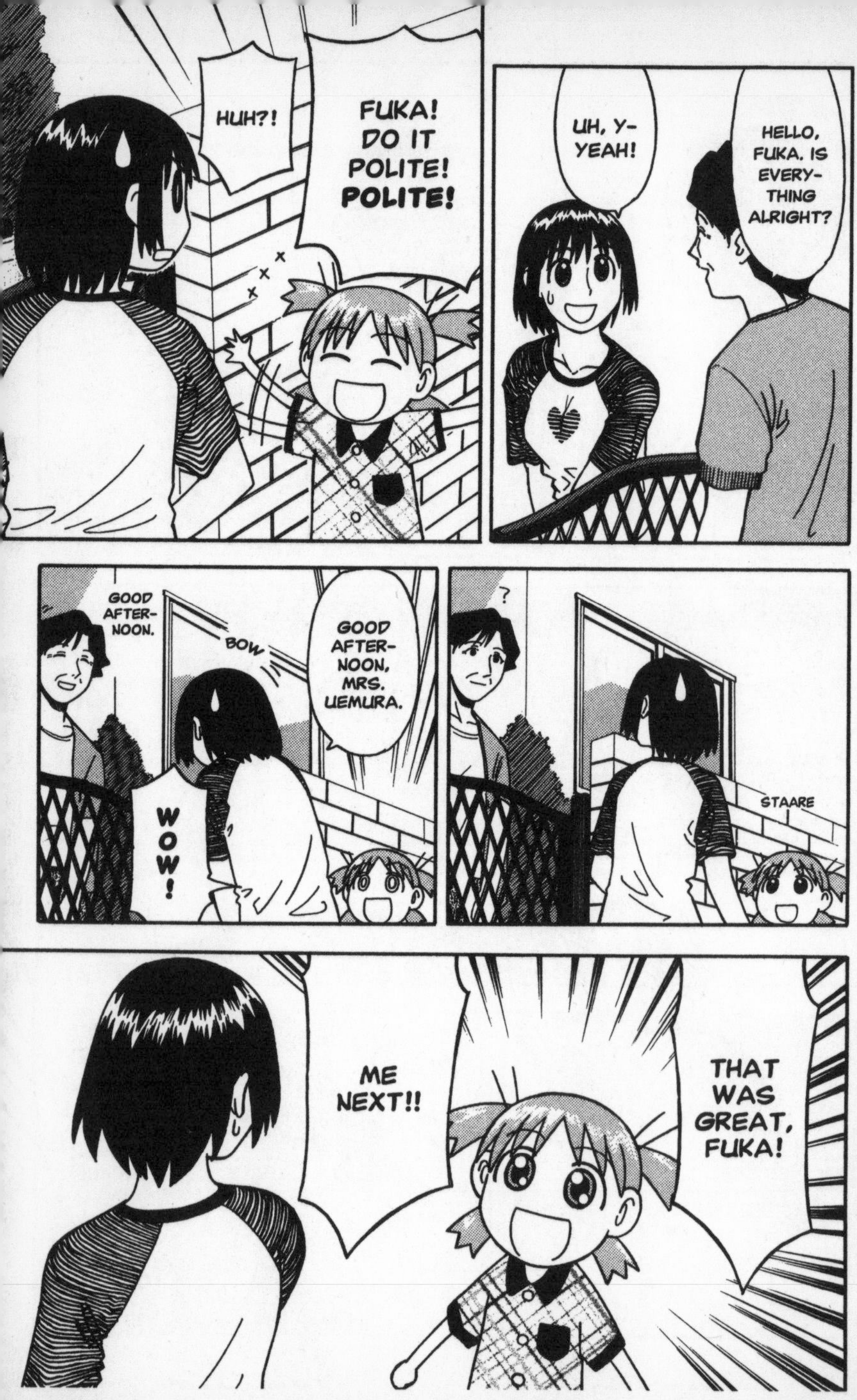
HELLO, FUKA. IS EVERYTHING ALRIGHT?
UH, Y-YEAH!
FUKA! DO IT POLITE! POLITE!
HUH?!
?
STAARE
GOOD AFTERNOON, MRS. UEMURA.
BOW
GOOD AFTERNOON.
WOW!
THAT WAS GREAT, FUKA!
ME NEXT!!

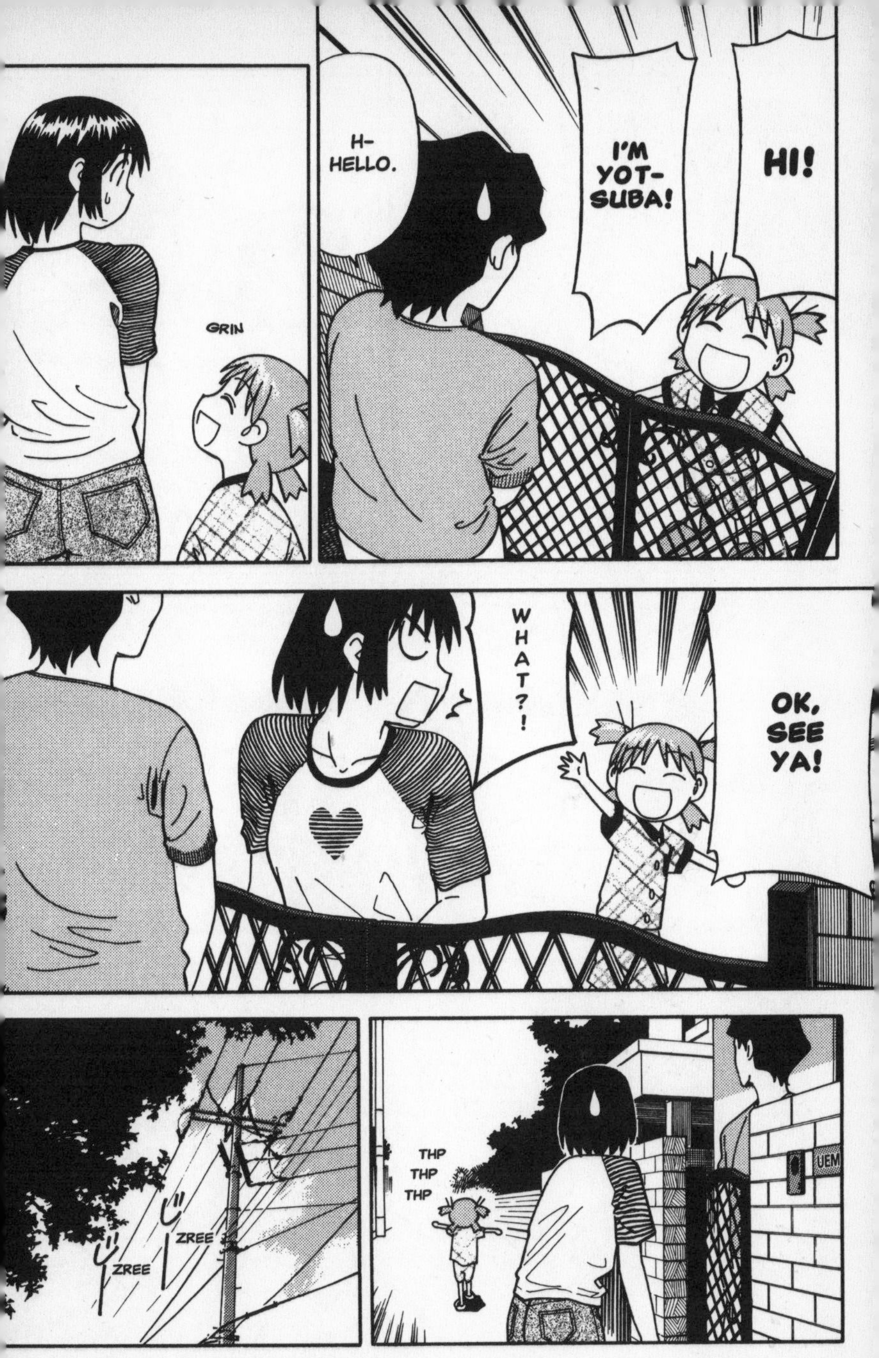
HI!
I'M YOT-SUBA!
H- HELLO.
GRIN
OK, SEE YA!
WHAT?!
UEM
THP THP THP
ZREE
ZREE

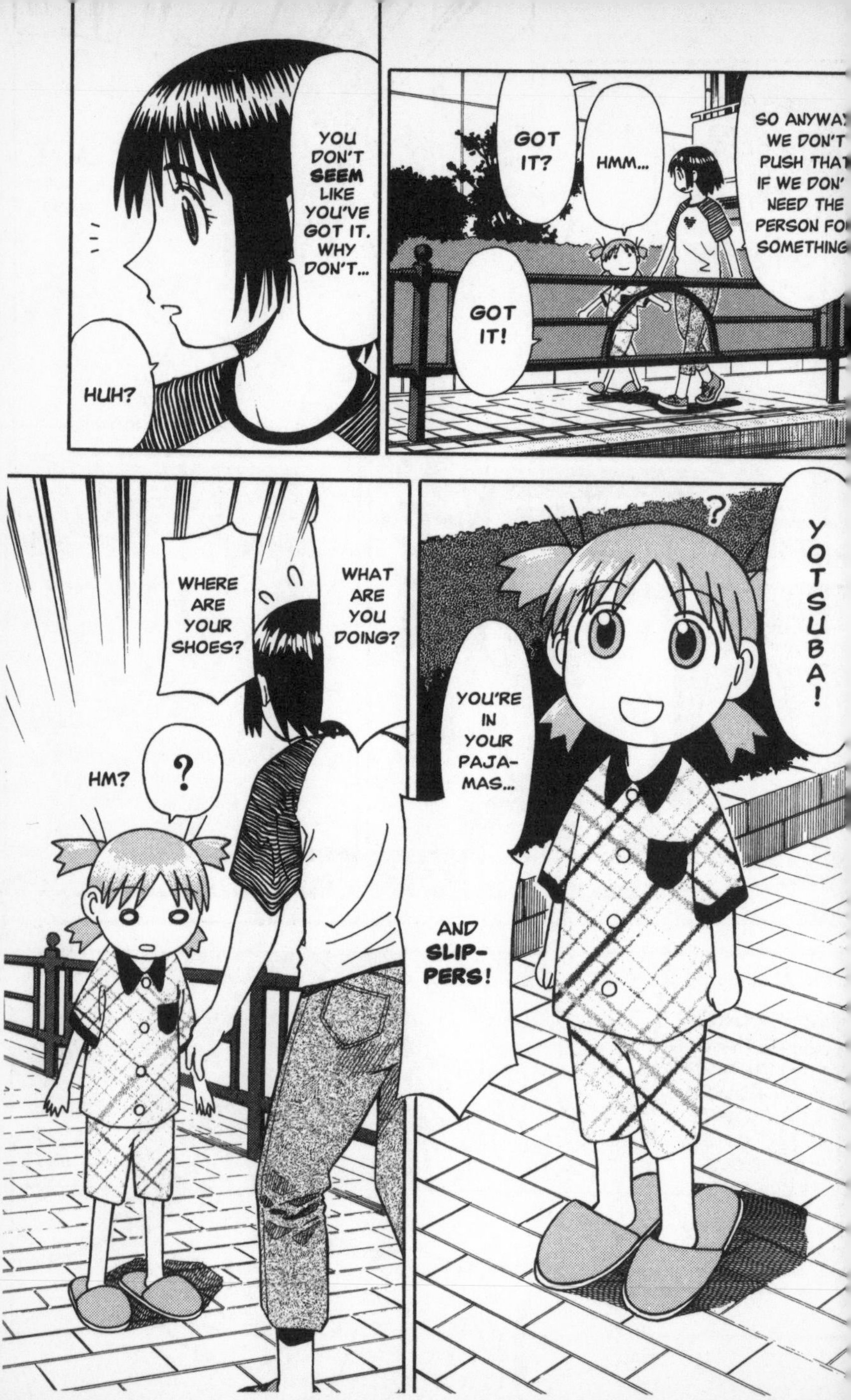
SO ANYWA WE DON'T PUSH THAT IF WE DON' NEED THE PERSON FO SOMETHING
HMM...
GOT IT?
GOT IT!
YOU DON'T SEEM LIKE YOU'VE GOT IT. WHY DON'T...
HUH?
YOTSUBA!
YOU'RE IN YOUR PAJAMAS...
AND SLIPPERS!
WHAT ARE YOU DOING?
WHERE ARE YOUR SHOES?
?
HM?

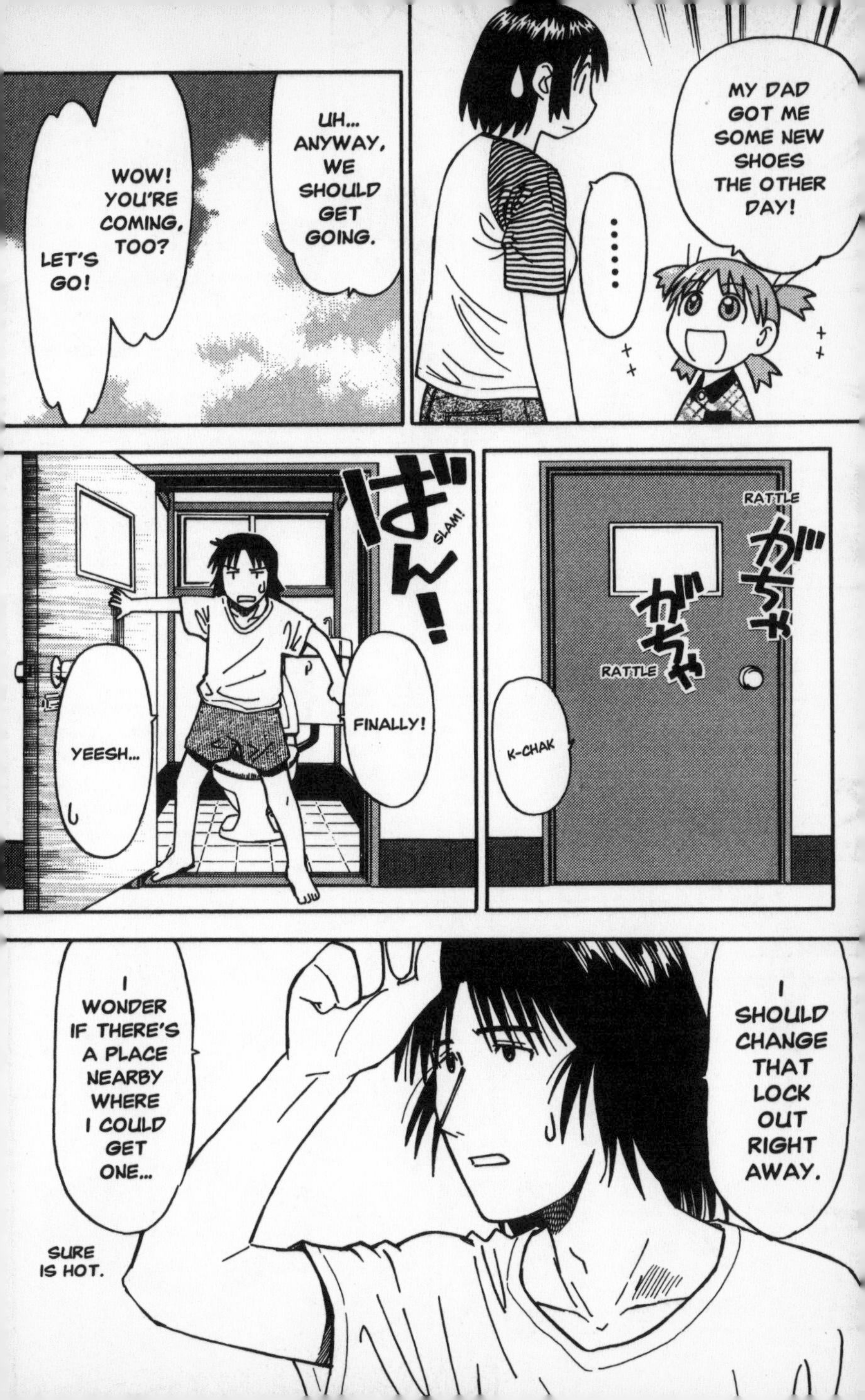
MY DAD GOT ME SOME NEW SHOES THE OTHER DAY!
......
UH... ANYWAY, WE SHOULD GET GOING.
WOW! YOU'RE COMING, TOO?
LET'S GO!
RATTLE
がちゃ
RATTLE
がちゃ
K-CHAK
ばん!
SLAM!
FINALLY!
YEESH...
I SHOULD CHANGE THAT LOCK OUT RIGHT AWAY.
I WONDER IF THERE'S A PLACE NEARBY WHERE I COULD GET ONE...
SURE IS HOT.

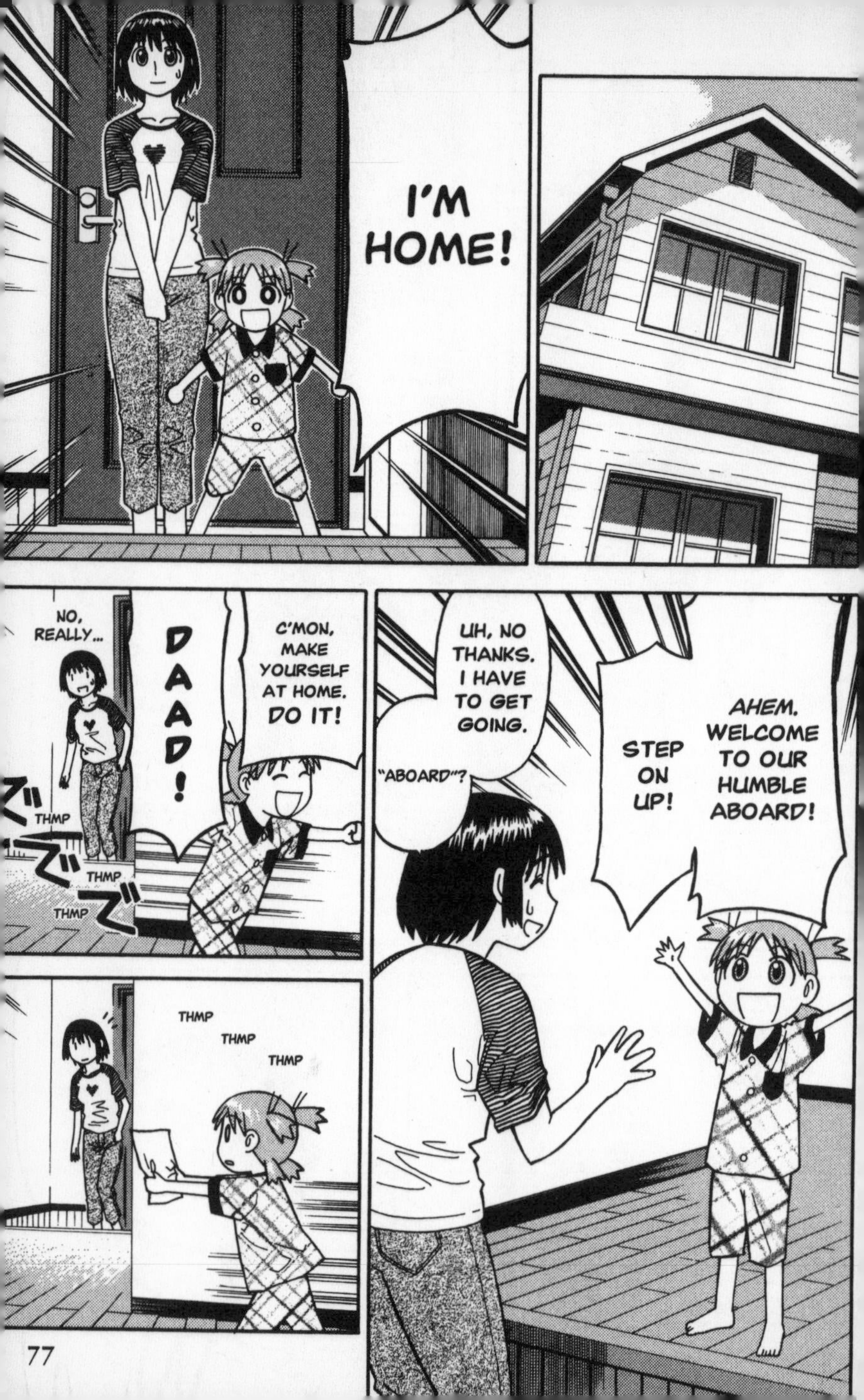
I'M HOME!
AHEM. WELCOME TO OUR HUMBLE ABOARD!
STEP ON UP!
UH, NO THANKS. I HAVE TO GET GOING.
"ABOARD"?
C'MON, MAKE YOURSELF AT HOME. DO IT!
DAAAD!
NO, REALLY...
THMP
THMP
THMP
THMP
THMP
THMP

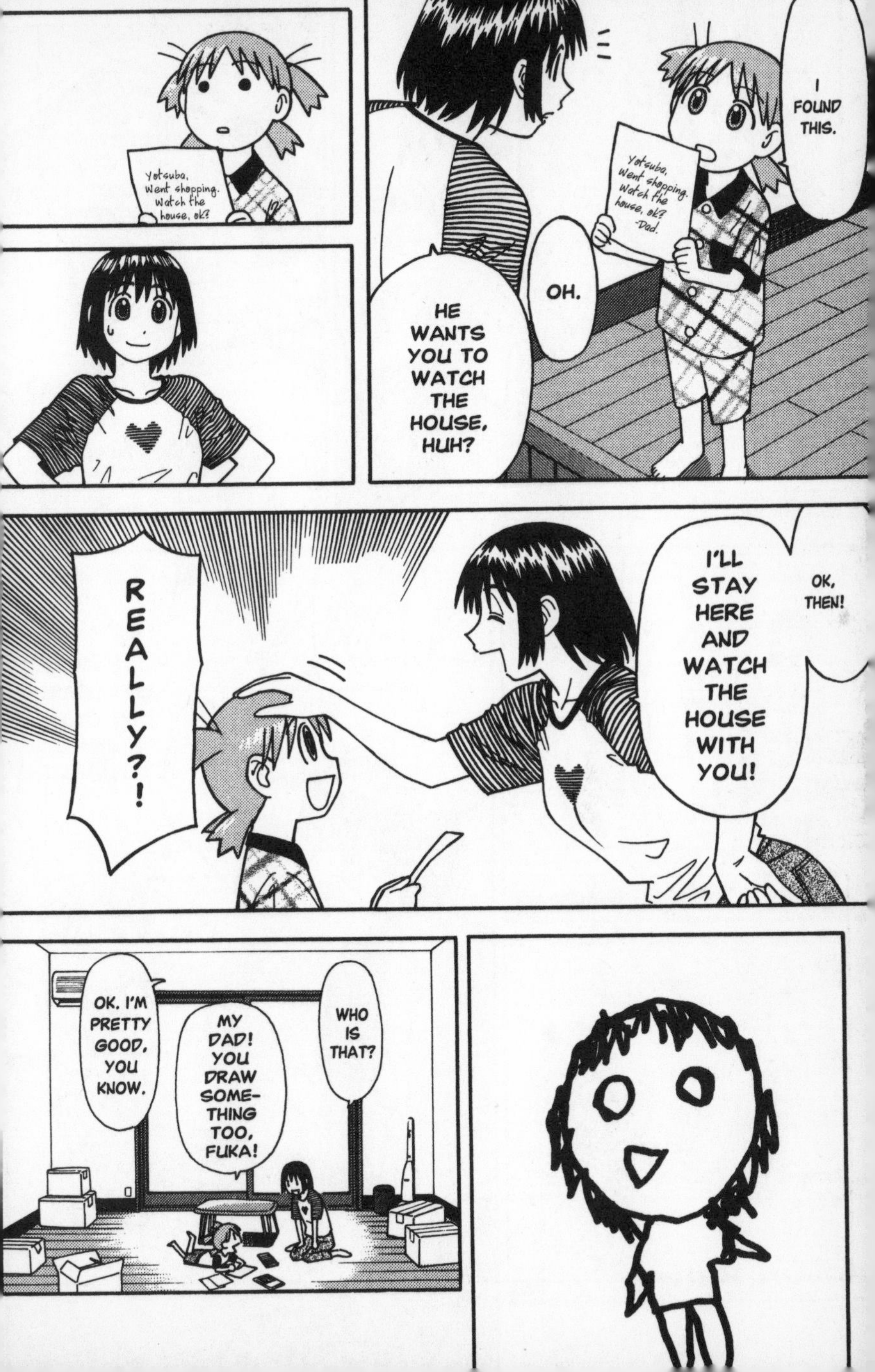
I FOUND THIS.
Yotsuba, Went shopping. Watch the house, ok? -Dad.
OH.
HE WANTS YOU TO WATCH THE HOUSE, HUH?
Yotsuba, Went shopping. Watch the house, ok?
OK, THEN!
I'LL STAY HERE AND WATCH THE HOUSE WITH YOU!
REALLY?!
WHO IS THAT?
MY DAD! YOU DRAW SOMETHING TOO, FUKA!
OK. I'M PRETTY GOOD, YOU KNOW.

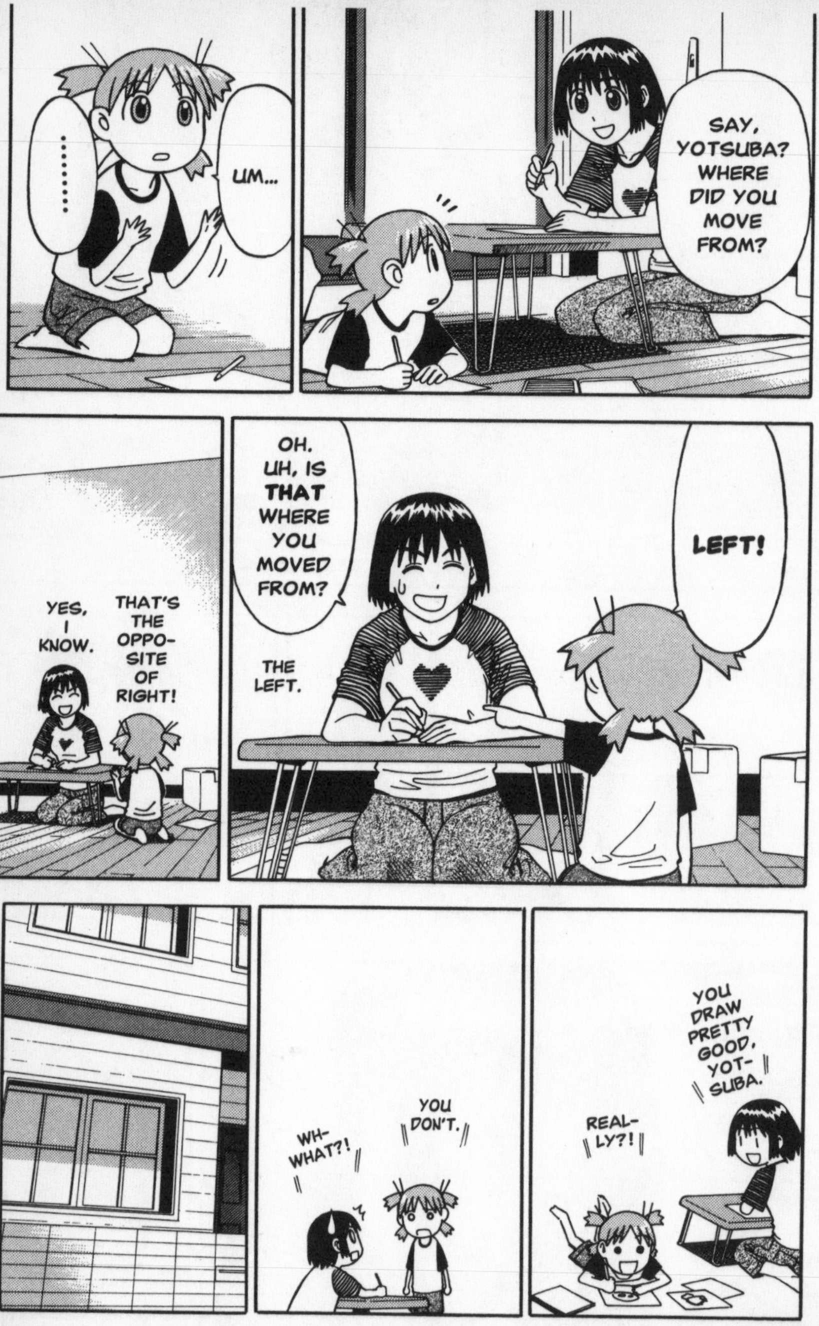
SAY, YOTSUBA? WHERE DID YOU MOVE FROM?
UM...
......
LEFT!
OH. UH, IS **THAT** WHERE YOU MOVED FROM?
THE LEFT.
THAT'S THE OPPO-SITE OF RIGHT!
YES, I KNOW.
YOU DRAW PRETTY GOOD, YOT-SUBA.
REAL-LY?!
YOU DON'T.
WH-WHAT?!

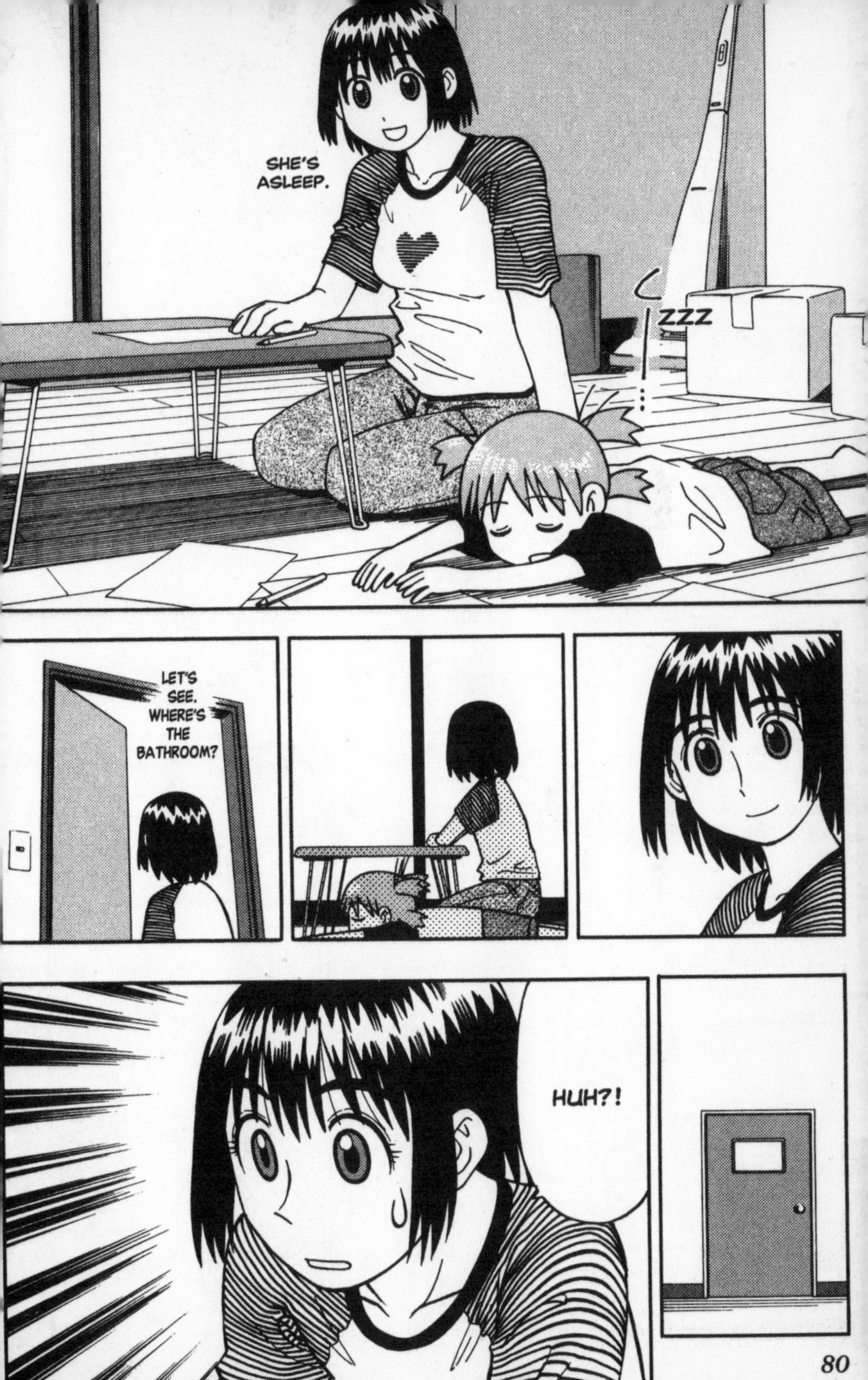
SHE'S ASLEEP.
ZZZ
LET'S SEE. WHERE'S THE BATHROOM?
HUH?!

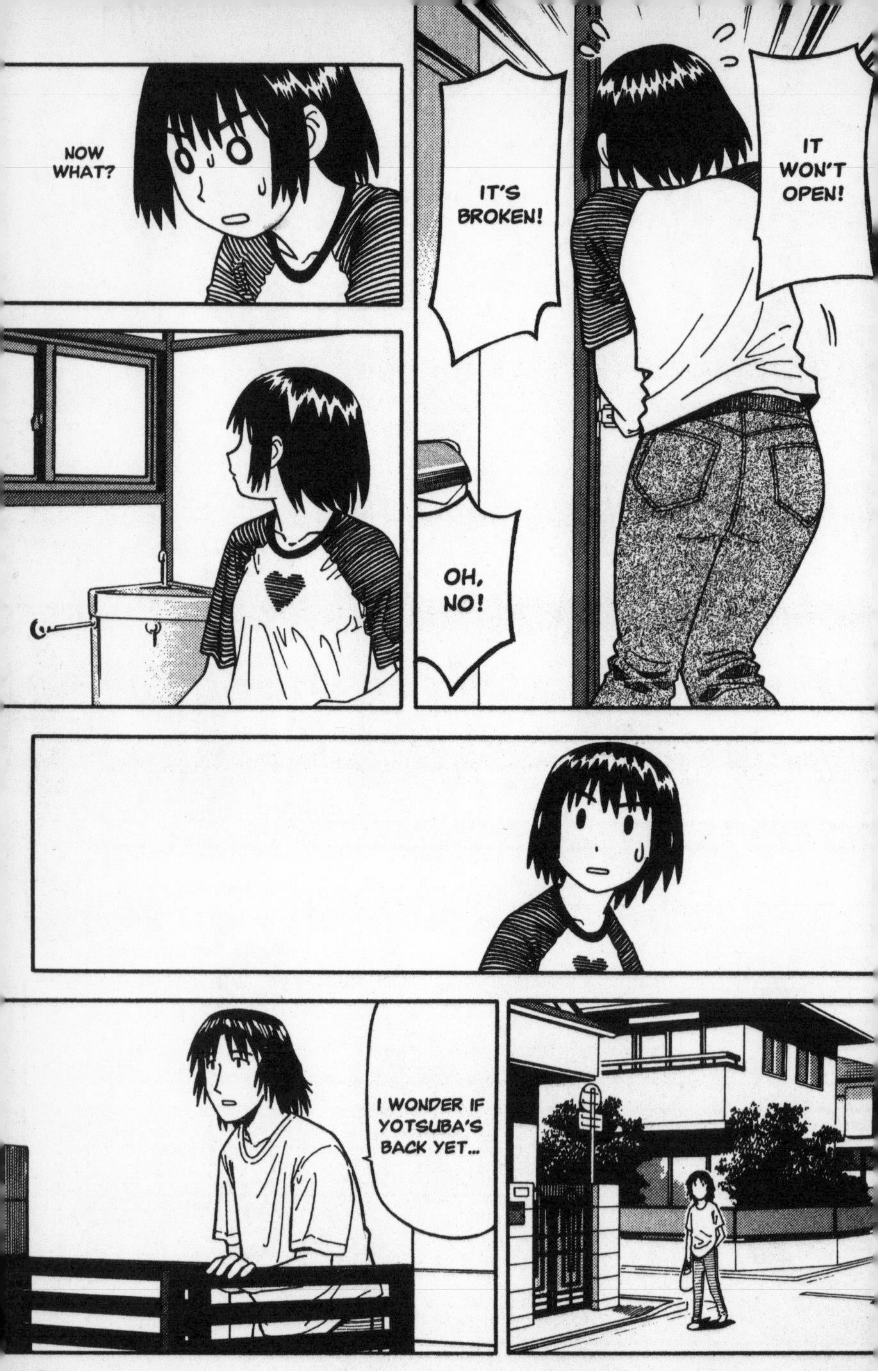
IT WON'T OPEN!
IT'S BROKEN!
OH, NO!
NOW WHAT?
I WONDER IF YOTSUBA'S BACK YET...

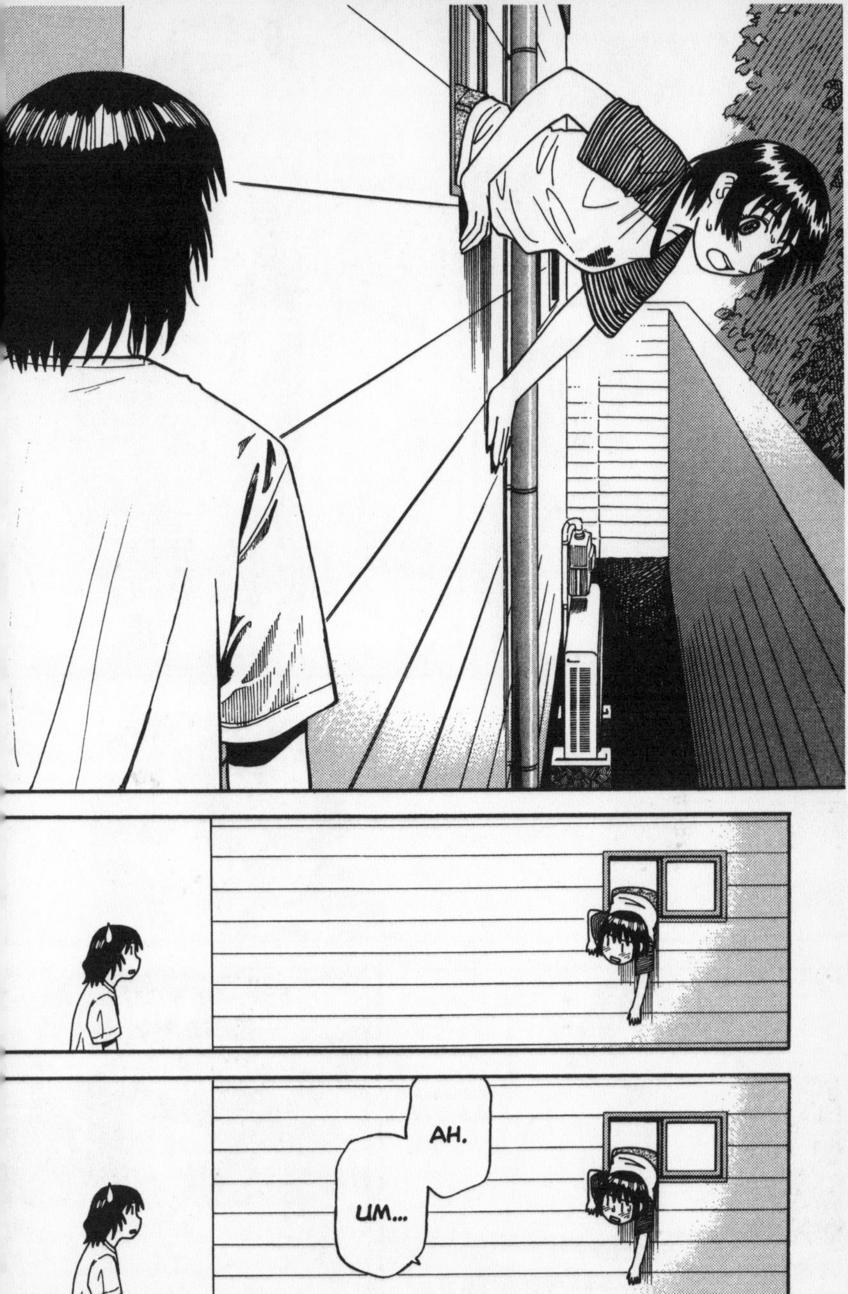
AH.
UM...

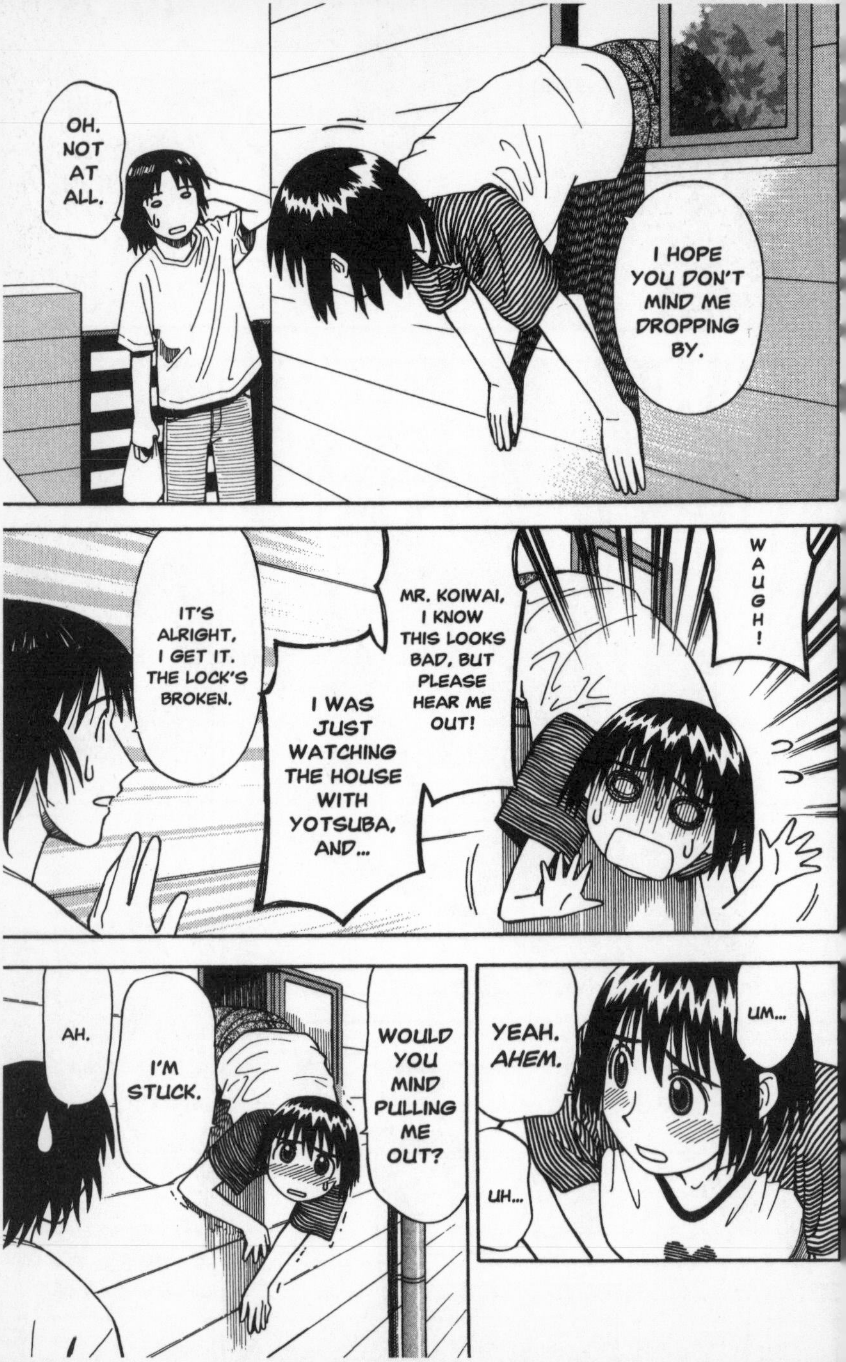
I HOPE YOU DON'T MIND ME DROPPING BY.
OH. NOT AT ALL.
WAUGH!
MR. KOIWAI, I KNOW THIS LOOKS BAD, BUT PLEASE HEAR ME OUT!
I WAS JUST WATCHING THE HOUSE WITH YOTSUBA, AND...
IT'S ALRIGHT, I GET IT. THE LOCK'S BROKEN.
UM...
YEAH. AHEM.
UH...
WOULD YOU MIND PULLING ME OUT?
I'M STUCK.
AH.

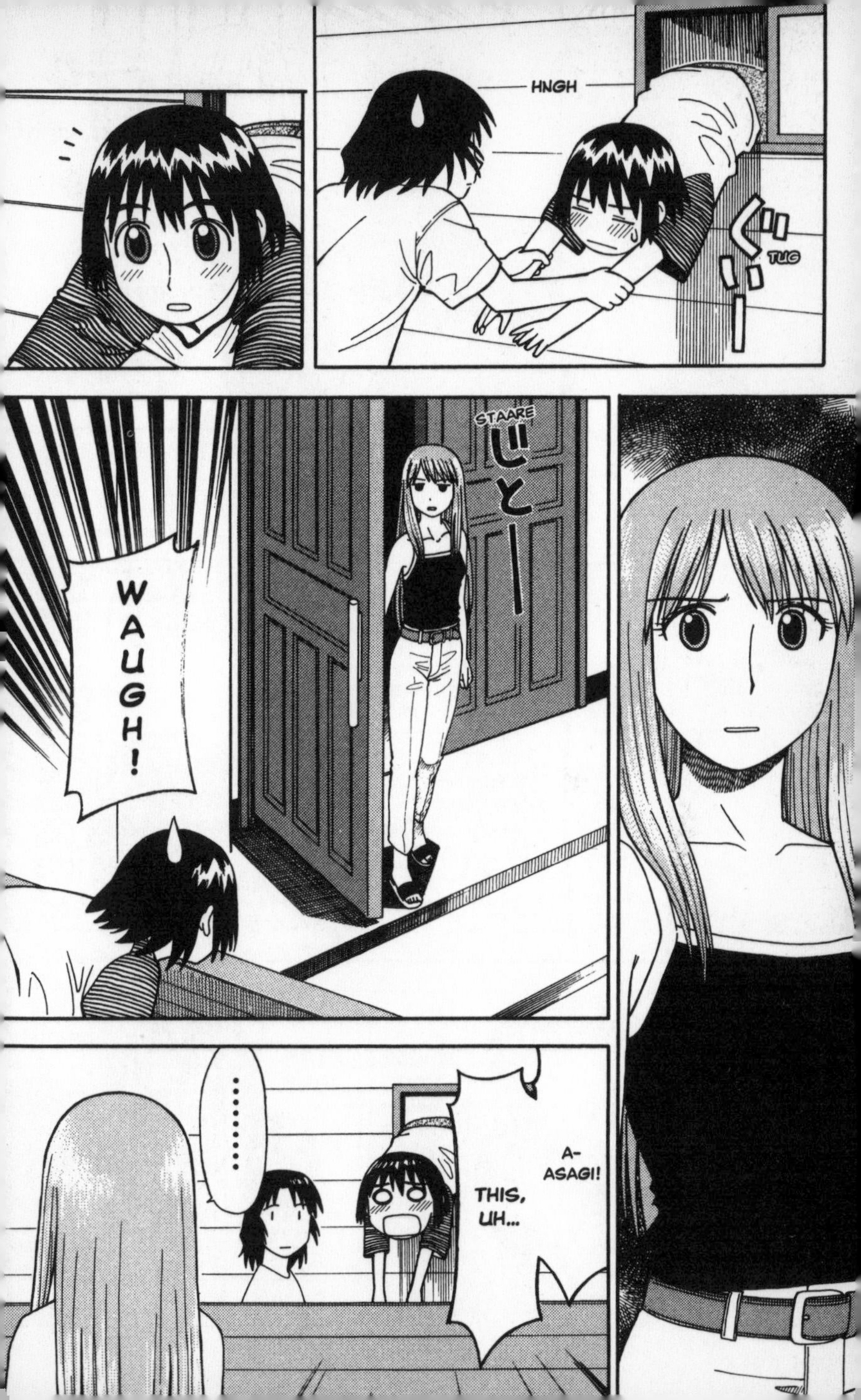
HNGH
ぐい
TUG
STAARE
じとー
WAUGH!
A- ASAGI! THIS, UH...
......

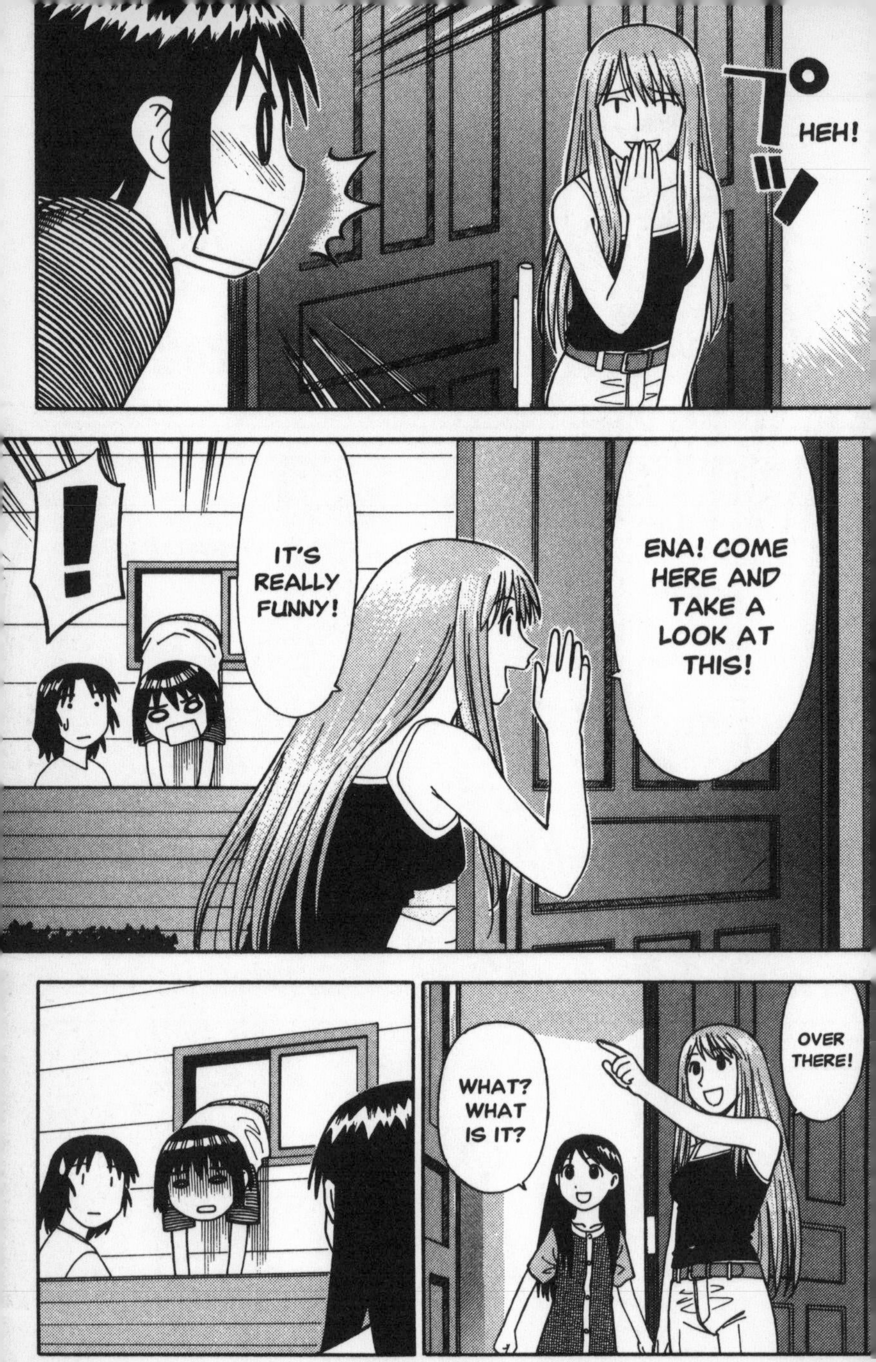
HEH!
ENA! COME HERE AND TAKE A LOOK AT THIS!
IT'S REALLY FUNNY!
!
OVER THERE!
WHAT? WHAT IS IT?

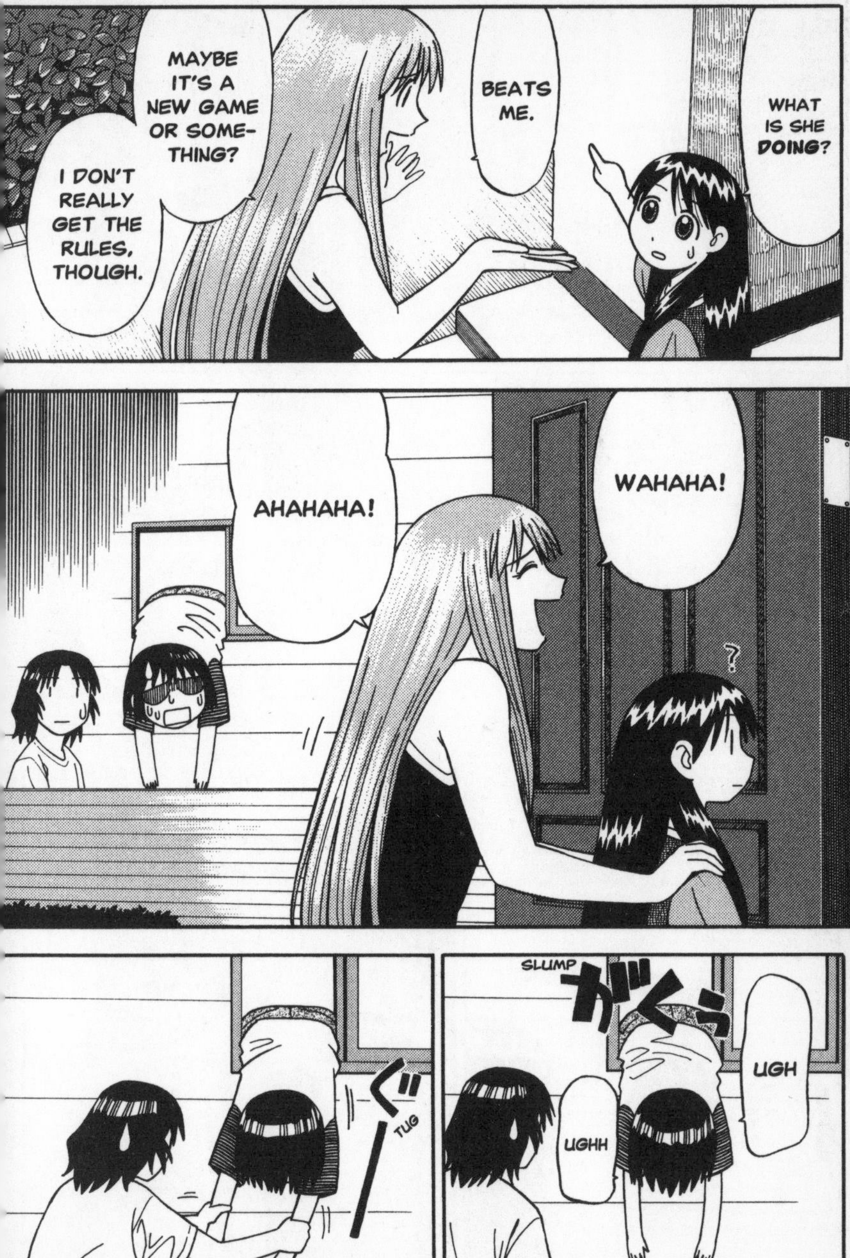
WHAT IS SHE DOING?
BEATS ME.
MAYBE IT'S A NEW GAME OR SOME-THING?
I DON'T REALLY GET THE RULES, THOUGH.
WAHAHA!
AHAHAHA!
?
SLUMP
UGH
UGHH
TUG

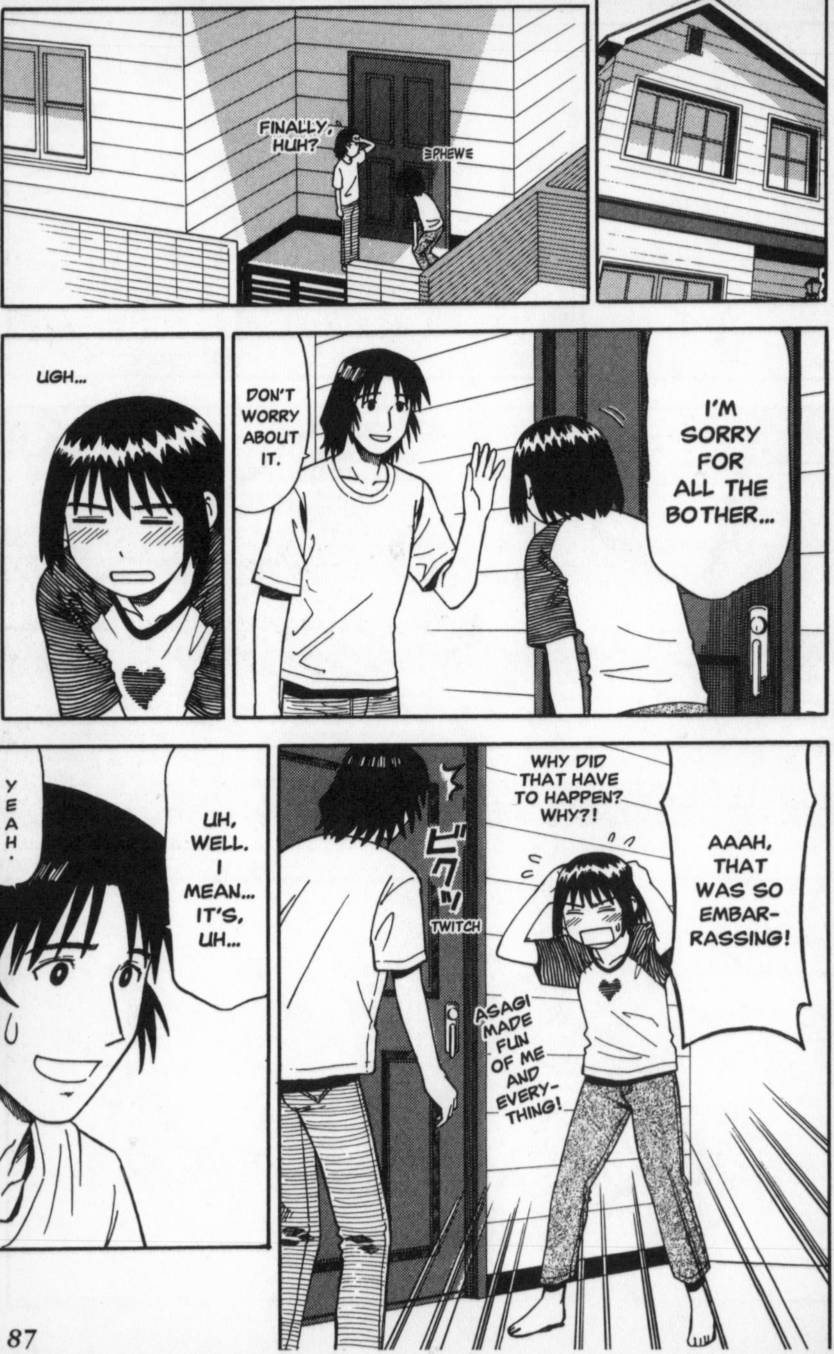
PHEW
FINALLY, HUH?
I'M SORRY FOR ALL THE BOTHER...
DON'T WORRY ABOUT IT.
UGH...
AAAH, THAT WAS SO EMBARRASSING!
WHY DID THAT HAVE TO HAPPEN? WHY?!
ASAGI MADE FUN OF ME AND EVERYTHING!
ビクッ
TWITCH
UH, WELL. I MEAN... IT'S, UH...
YEAH.

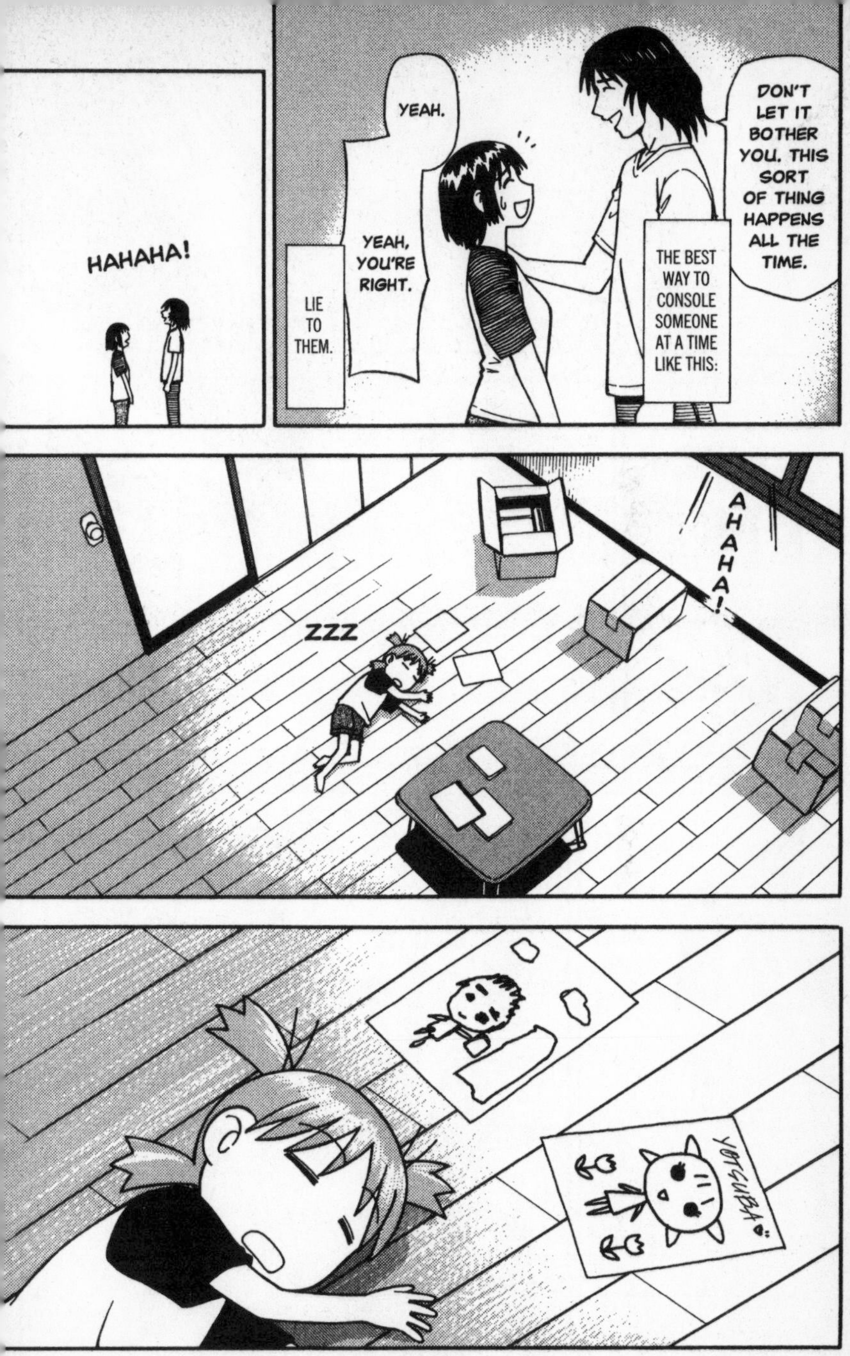
DON'T LET IT BOTHER YOU. THIS SORT OF THING HAPPENS ALL THE TIME.
THE BEST WAY TO CONSOLE SOMEONE AT A TIME LIKE THIS:
YEAH.
YEAH, YOU'RE RIGHT.
LIE TO THEM.
HAHAHA!
AHAHAHA!
ZZZ
YOTSUBA

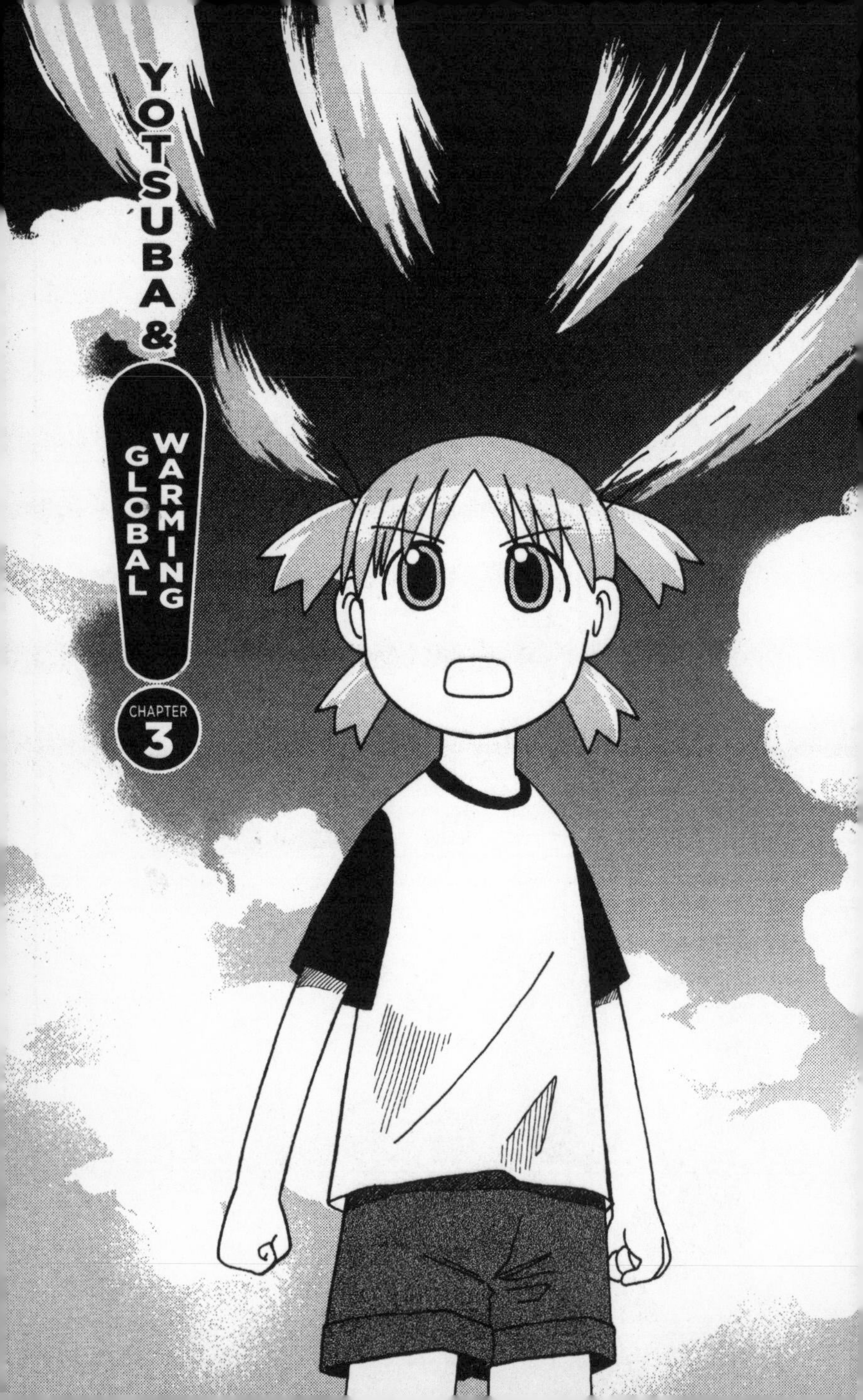
YOTSUBA &
GLOBAL WARMING
CHAPTER 3

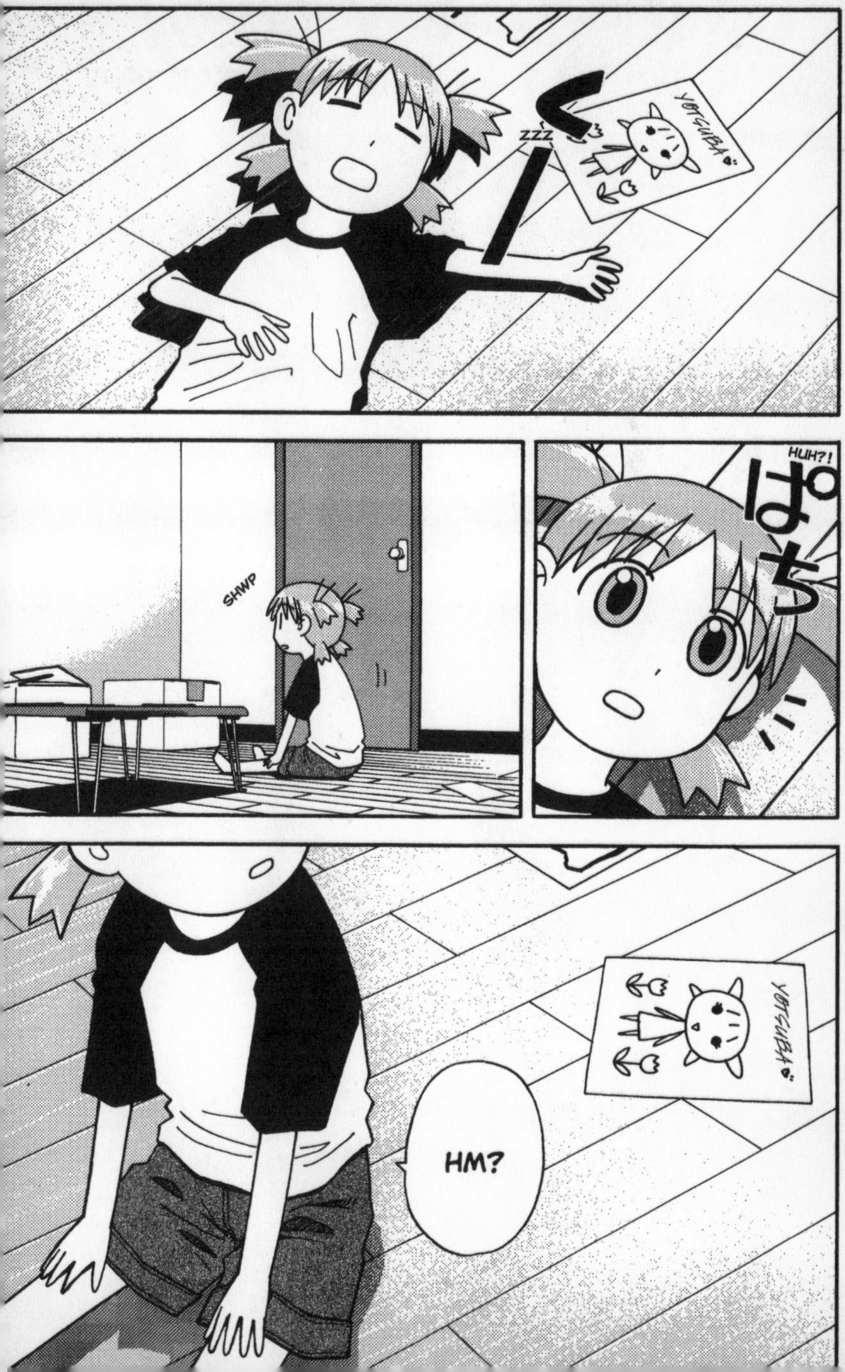

くー
ZZZ
YOTSUBA
HUH?!
ぱち
SHWP
YOTSUBA
HM?

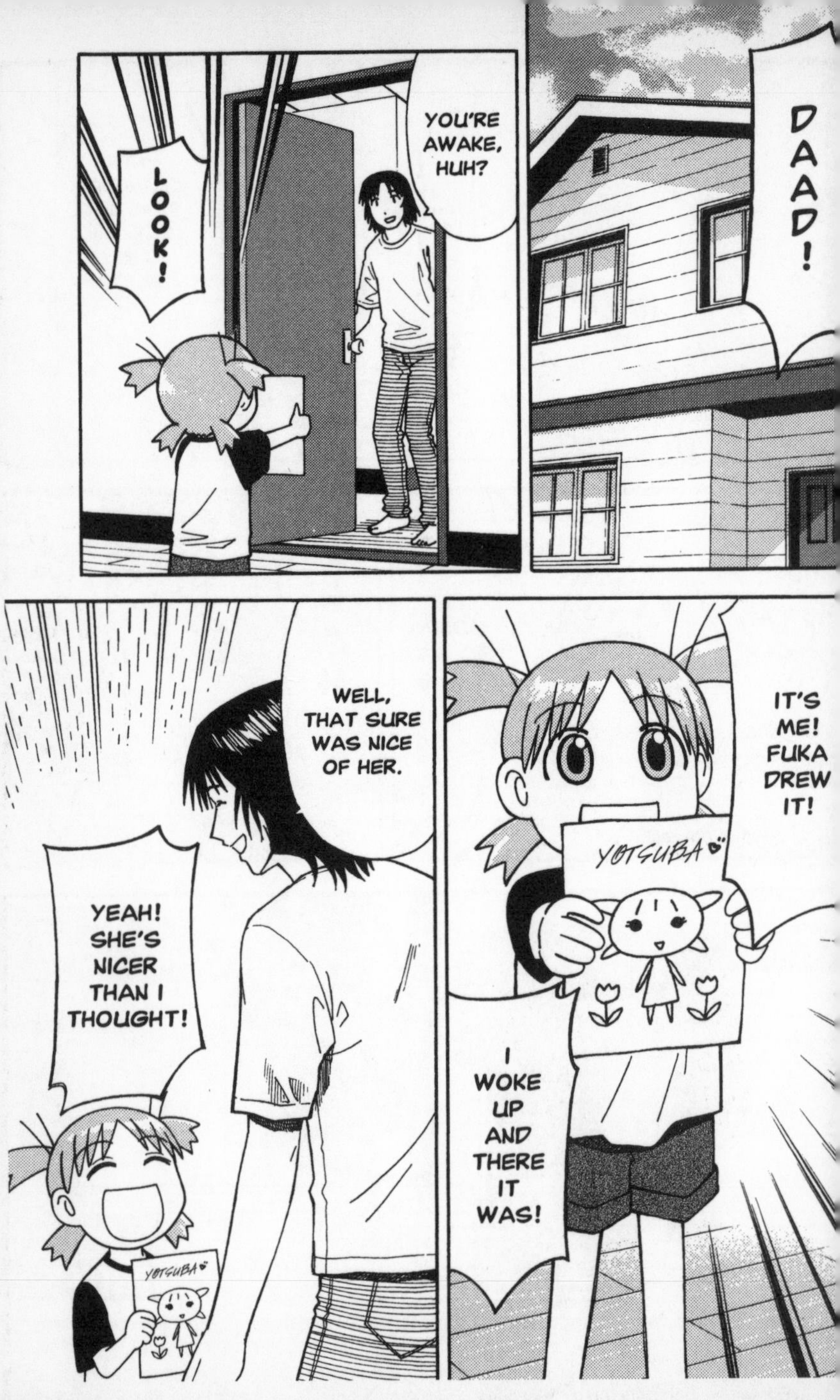
DAAAD!
YOU'RE AWAKE, HUH?
LOOK!
IT'S ME! FUKA DREW IT!
YOTSUBA
I WOKE UP AND THERE IT WAS!
WELL, THAT SURE WAS NICE OF HER.
YEAH! SHE'S NICER THAN I THOUGHT!
YOTSUBA

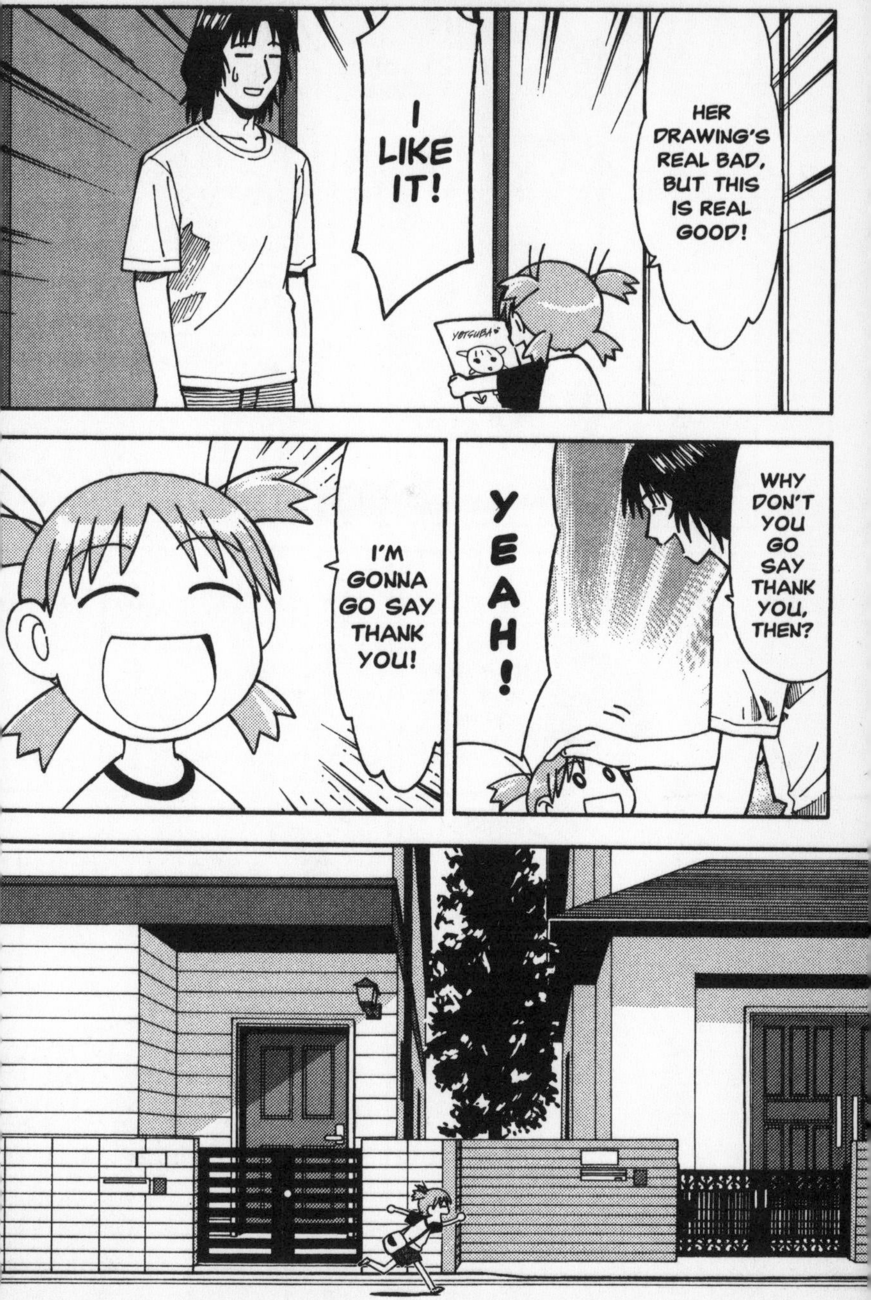
HER DRAWING'S REAL BAD, BUT THIS IS REAL GOOD!
YOTSUBA
I LIKE IT!
WHY DON'T YOU GO SAY THANK YOU, THEN?
YEAH!
I'M GONNA GO SAY THANK YOU!

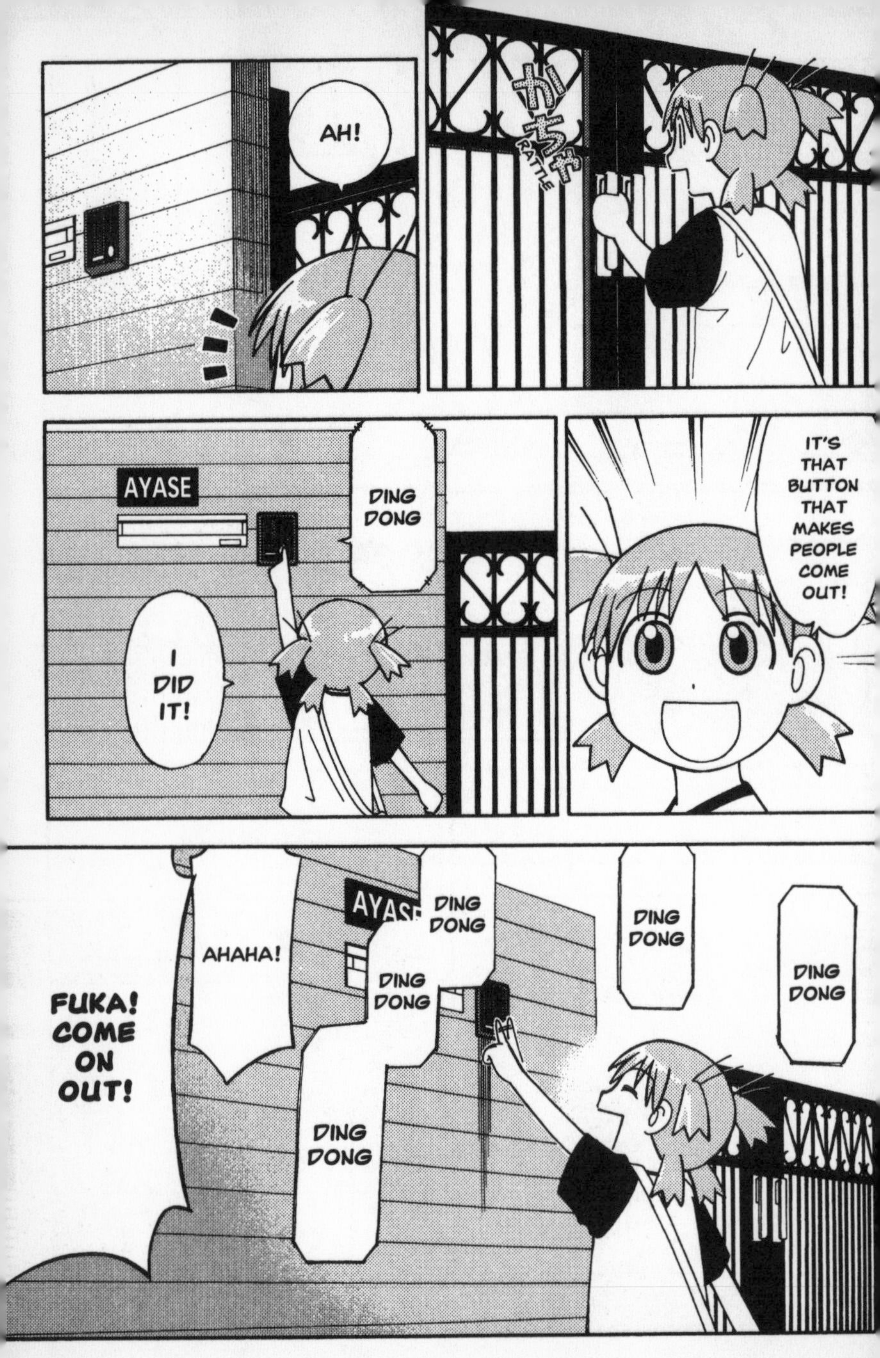
RATTLE
AH!
IT'S THAT BUTTON THAT MAKES PEOPLE COME OUT!
AYASE
DING DONG
I DID IT!
DING DONG
DING DONG
DING DONG
DING DONG
AYASE
DING DONG
AHAHA!
FUKA! COME ON OUT!

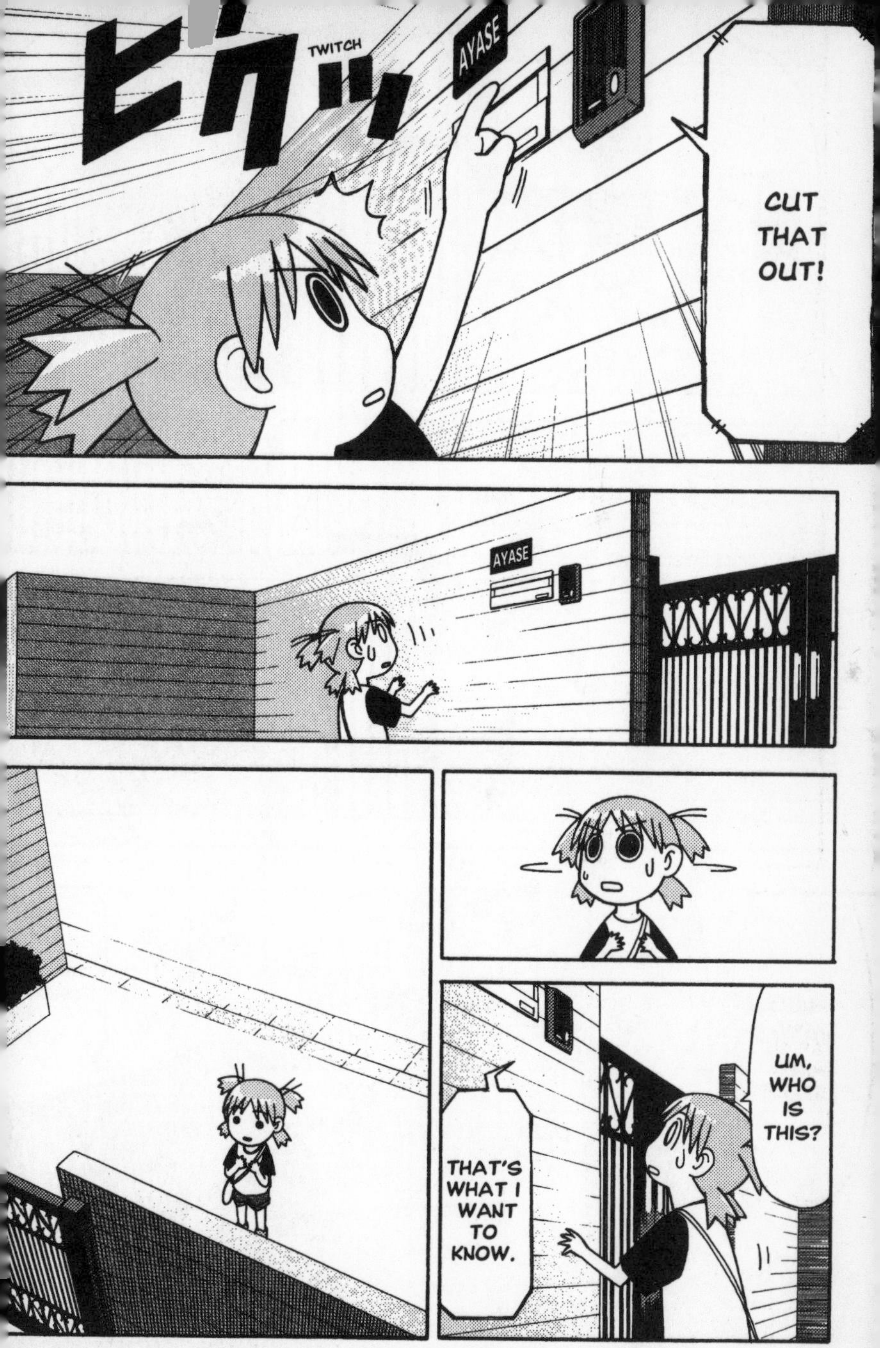
CUT THAT OUT!
AYASE
ビクッ
TWITCH
AYASE
UM, WHO IS THIS?
THAT'S WHAT I WANT TO KNOW.

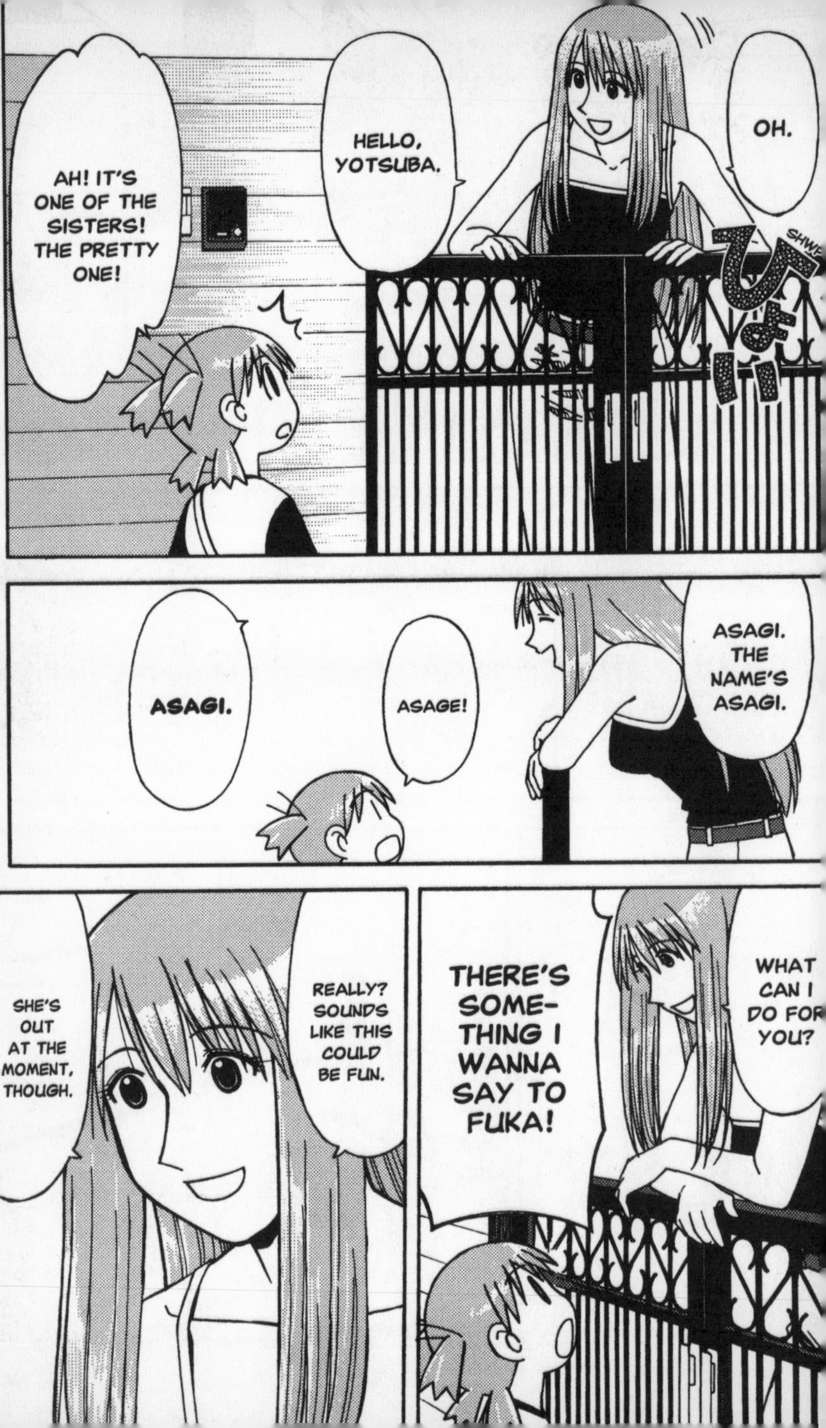
OH.
SHWP
HELLO, YOTSUBA.
AH! IT'S ONE OF THE SISTERS! THE PRETTY ONE!
ASAGI. THE NAME'S ASAGI.
ASAGE!
ASAGI.
WHAT CAN I DO FOR YOU?
THERE'S SOME-THING I WANNA SAY TO FUKA!
REALLY? SOUNDS LIKE THIS COULD BE FUN.
SHE'S OUT AT THE MOMENT, THOUGH.

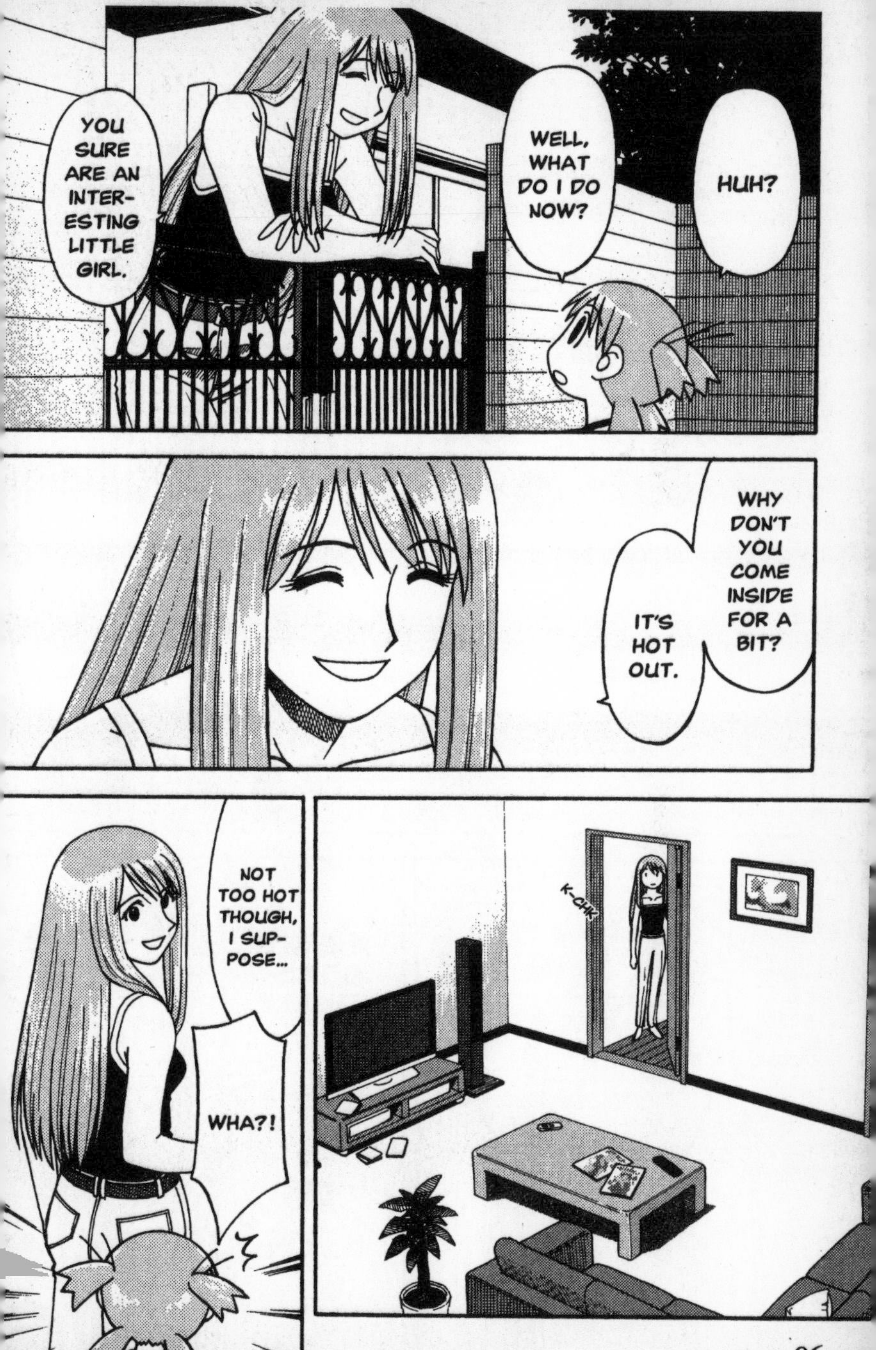
HUH?
WELL, WHAT DO I DO NOW?
YOU SURE ARE AN INTER-ESTING LITTLE GIRL.
WHY DON'T YOU COME INSIDE FOR A BIT?
IT'S HOT OUT.
K-CHK
NOT TOO HOT THOUGH, I SUP-POSE...
WHA?!

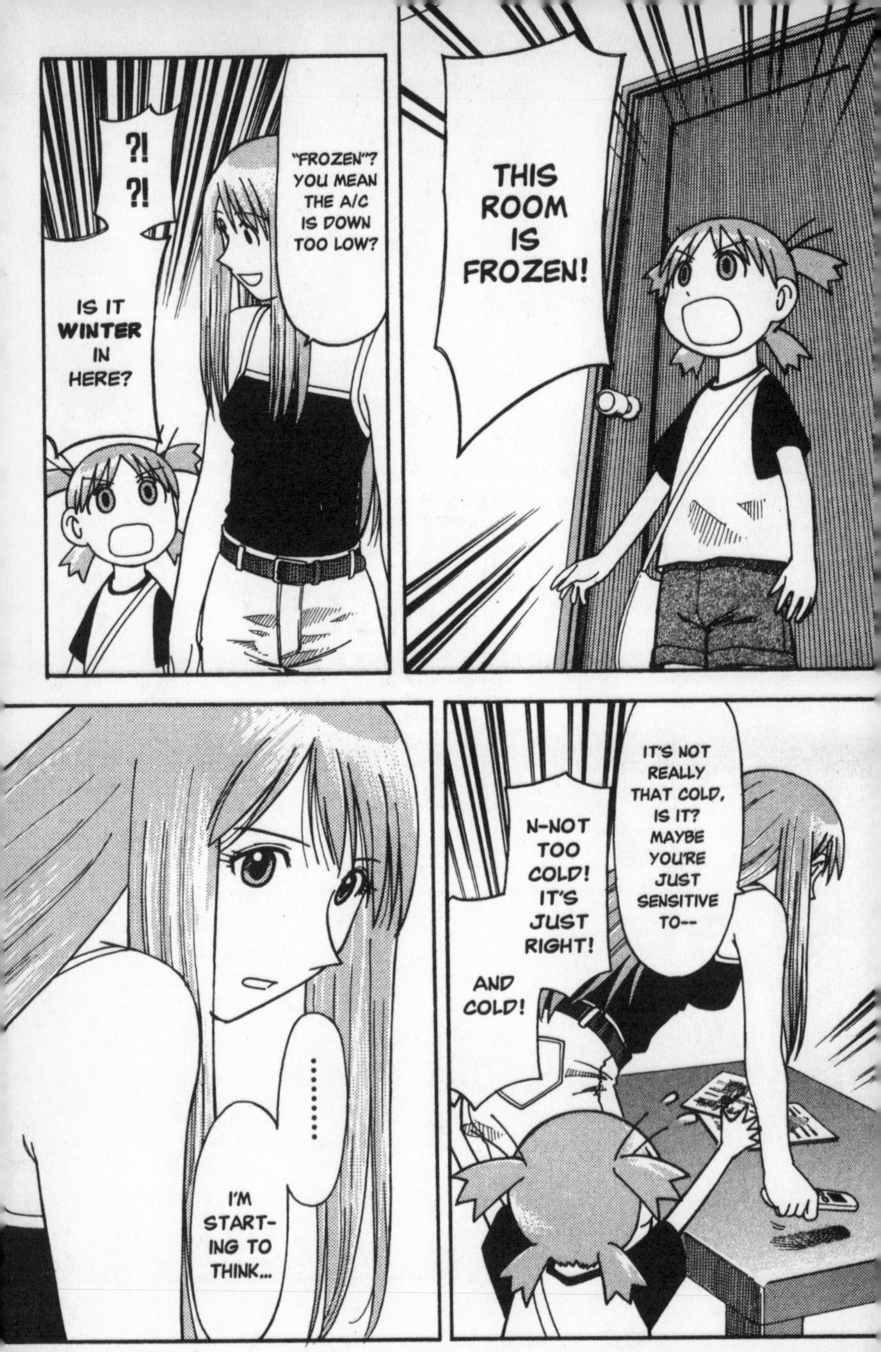
THIS ROOM IS FROZEN!
"FROZEN"? YOU MEAN THE A/C IS DOWN TOO LOW?
?! ?!
IS IT WINTER IN HERE?
IT'S NOT REALLY THAT COLD, IS IT? MAYBE YOU'RE JUST SENSITIVE TO--
N-NOT TOO COLD! IT'S JUST RIGHT!
AND COLD!
....
I'M START-ING TO THINK...

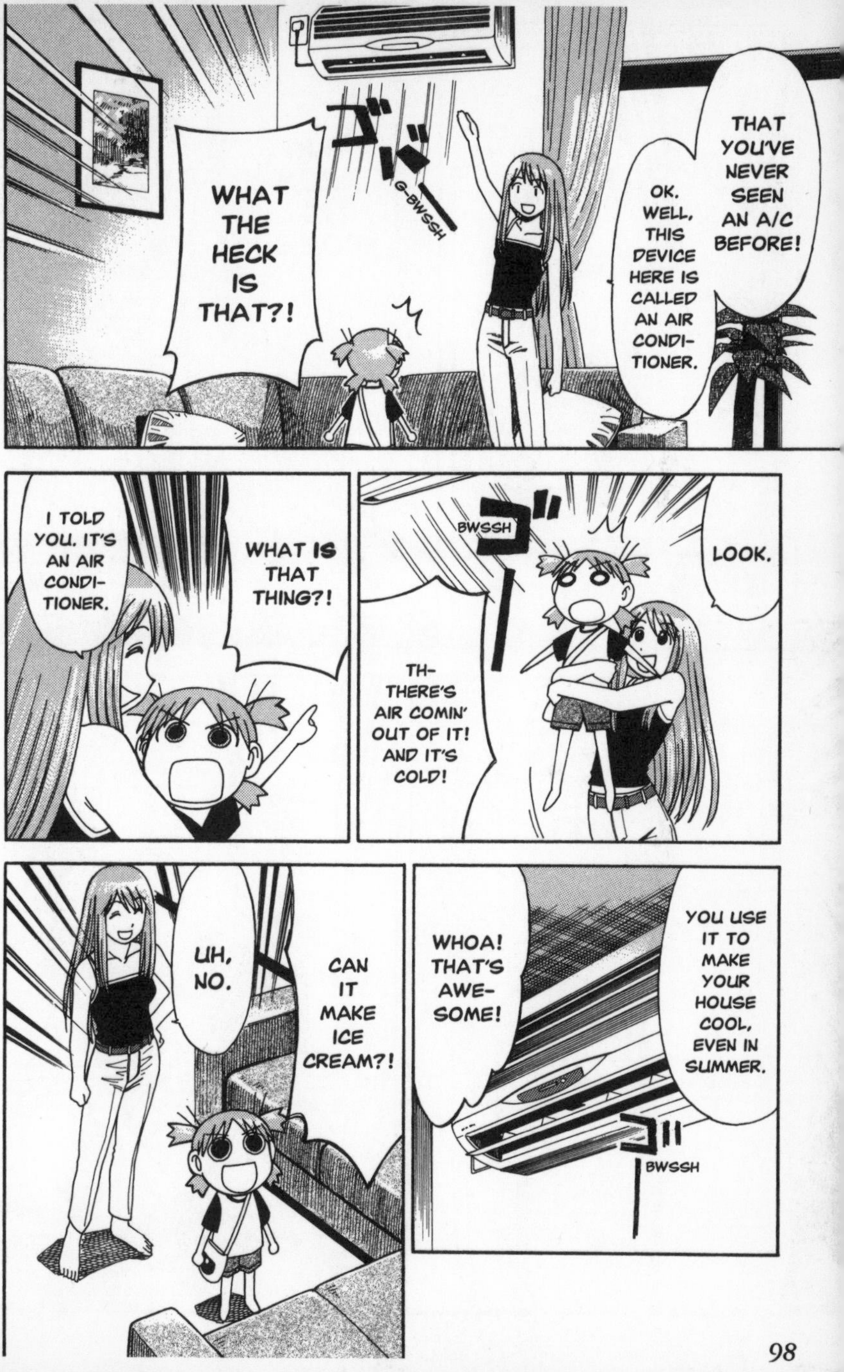
THAT YOU'VE NEVER SEEN AN A/C BEFORE!
OK. WELL, THIS DEVICE HERE IS CALLED AN AIR CONDITIONER.
G-BWSSH
WHAT THE HECK IS THAT?!
LOOK.
BWSSH
TH- THERE'S AIR COMIN' OUT OF IT! AND IT'S COLD!
WHAT IS THAT THING?!
I TOLD YOU. IT'S AN AIR CONDITIONER.
YOU USE IT TO MAKE YOUR HOUSE COOL, EVEN IN SUMMER.
WHOA! THAT'S AWESOME!
BWSSH
CAN IT MAKE ICE CREAM?!
UH, NO.

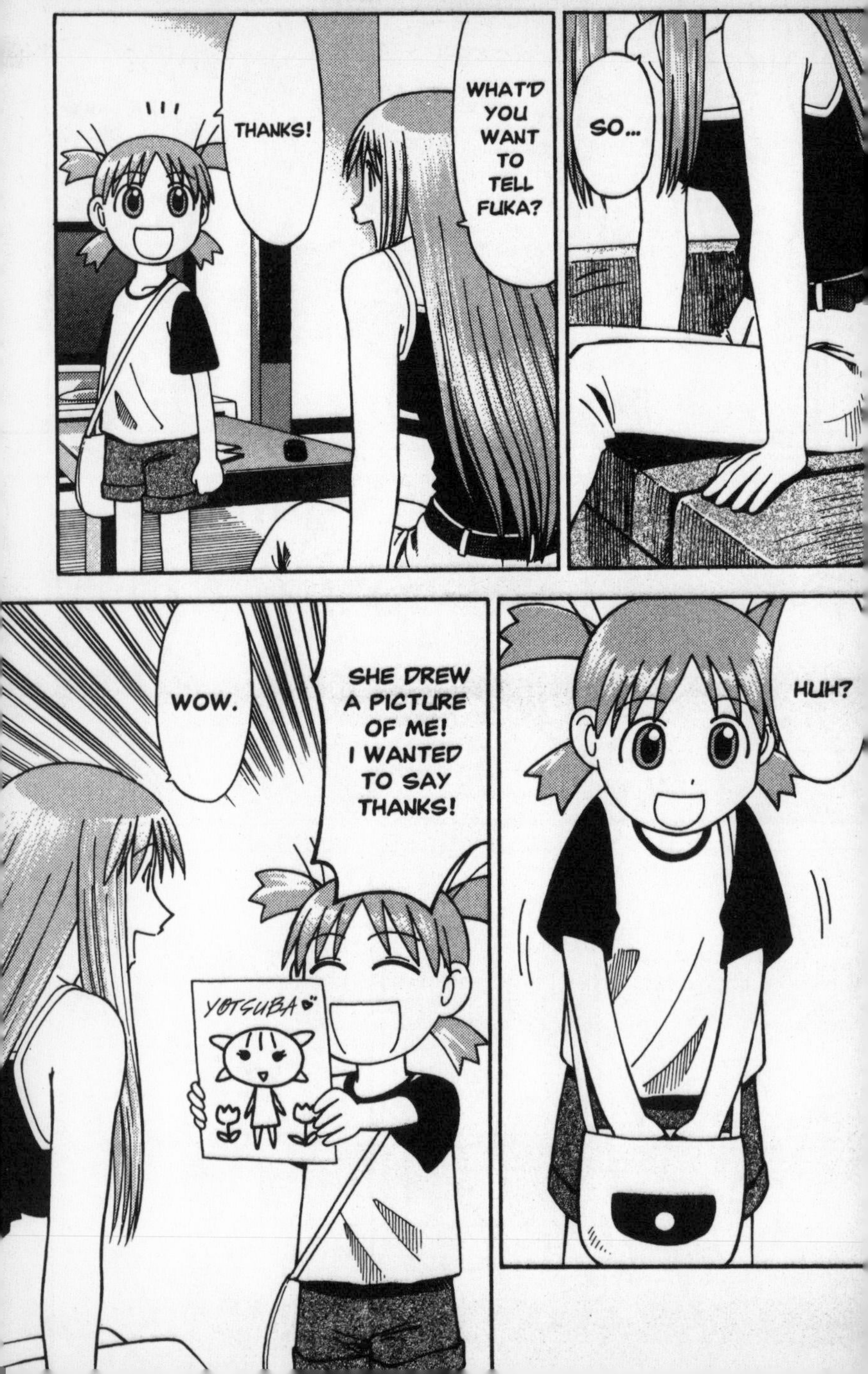
SO...
WHAT'D YOU WANT TO TELL FUKA?
THANKS!
HUH?
SHE DREW A PICTURE OF ME! I WANTED TO SAY THANKS!
WOW.
YOTSUBA

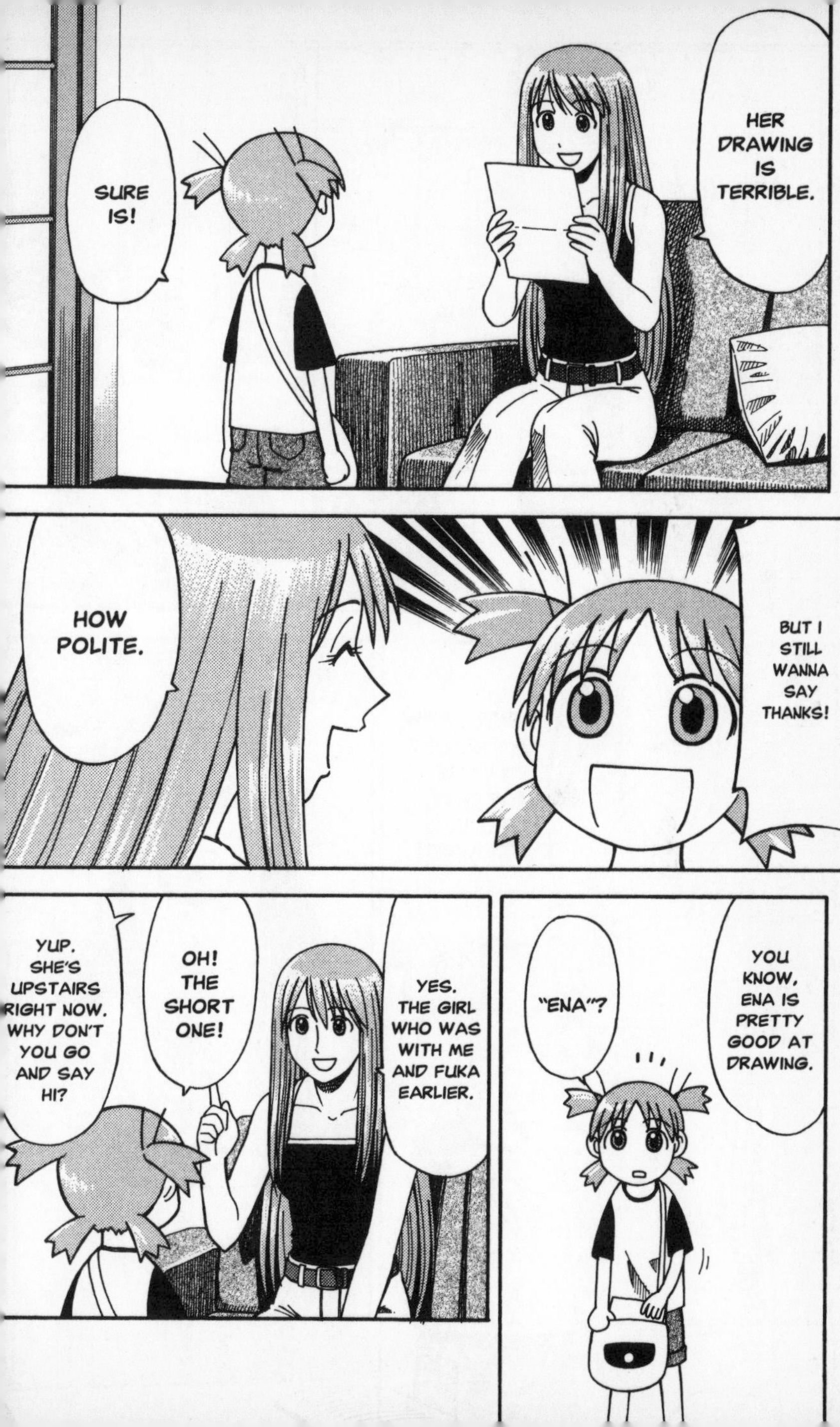
HER DRAWING IS TERRIBLE.
SURE IS!
BUT I STILL WANNA SAY THANKS!
HOW POLITE.
YOU KNOW, ENA IS PRETTY GOOD AT DRAWING.
"ENA"?
YES. THE GIRL WHO WAS WITH ME AND FUKA EARLIER.
OH! THE SHORT ONE!
YUP. SHE'S UPSTAIRS RIGHT NOW. WHY DON'T YOU GO AND SAY HI?

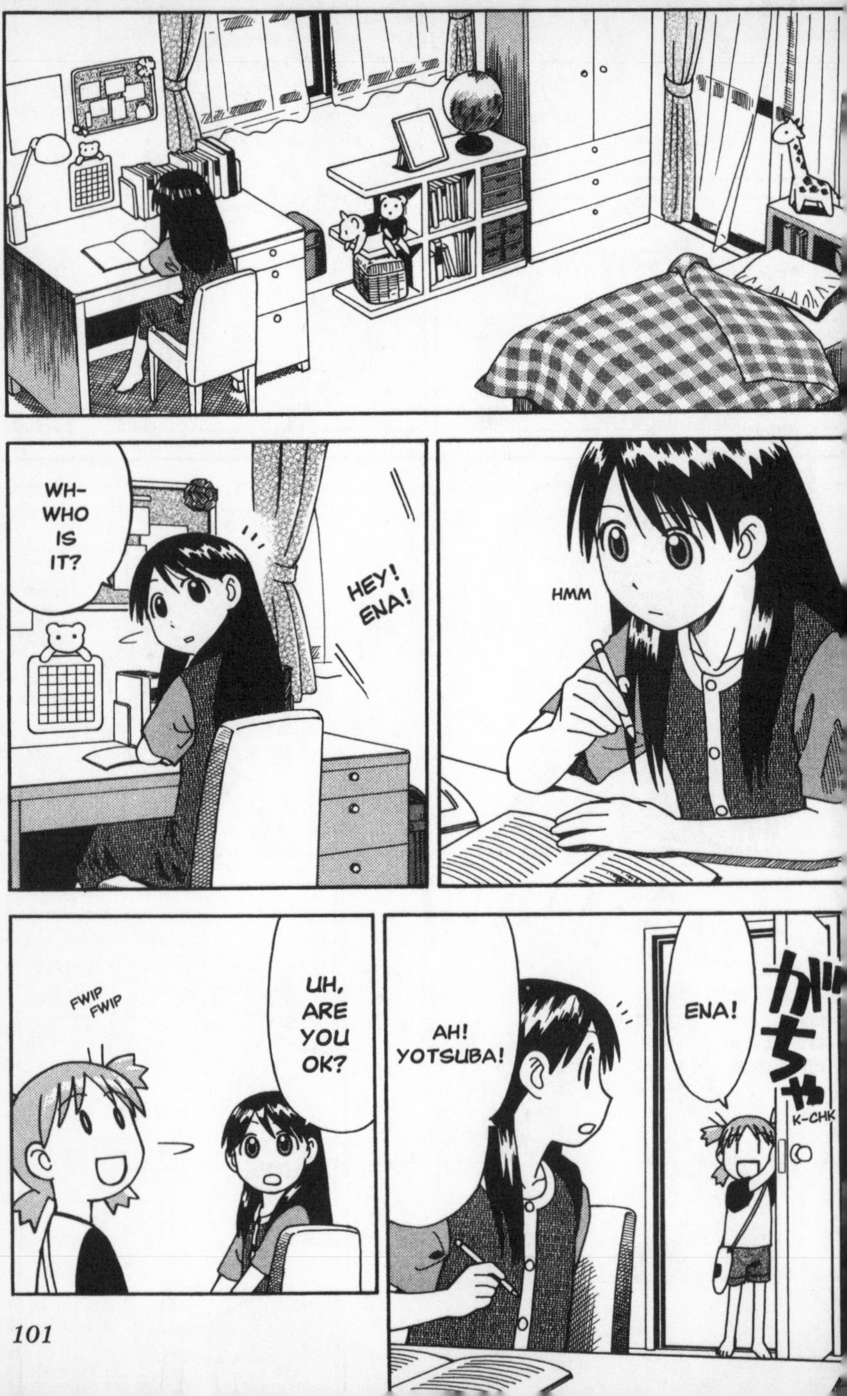
HMM
HEY! ENA!
WH- WHO IS IT?
がちゃ
K-CHK
ENA!
AH! YOTSUBA!
UH, ARE YOU OK?
FWIP FWIP

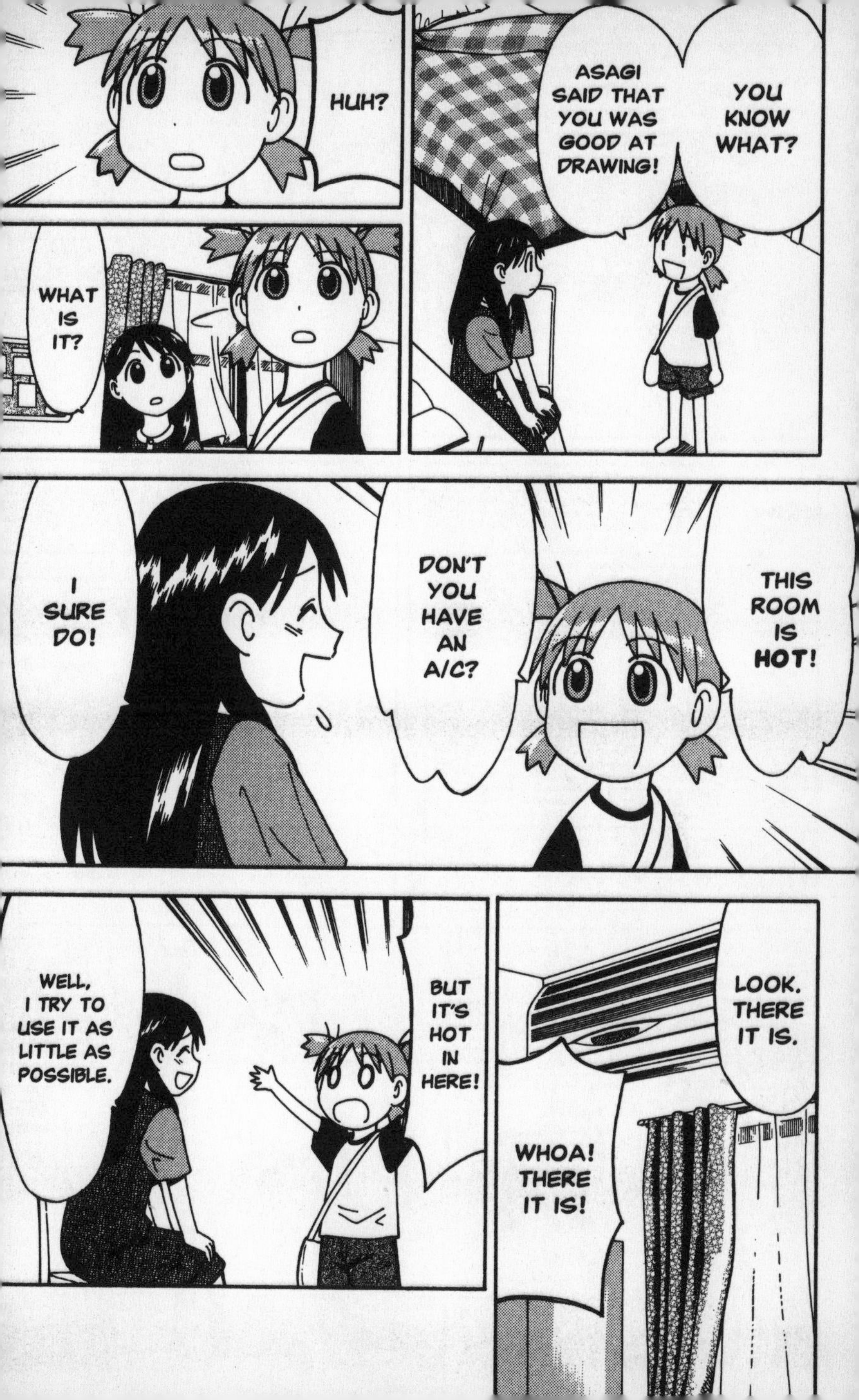
YOU KNOW WHAT?
ASAGI SAID THAT YOU WAS GOOD AT DRAWING!
HUH?
WHAT IS IT?
THIS ROOM IS HOT!
DON'T YOU HAVE AN A/C?
I SURE DO!
LOOK. THERE IT IS.
WHOA! THERE IT IS!
BUT IT'S HOT IN HERE!
WELL, I TRY TO USE IT AS LITTLE AS POSSIBLE.

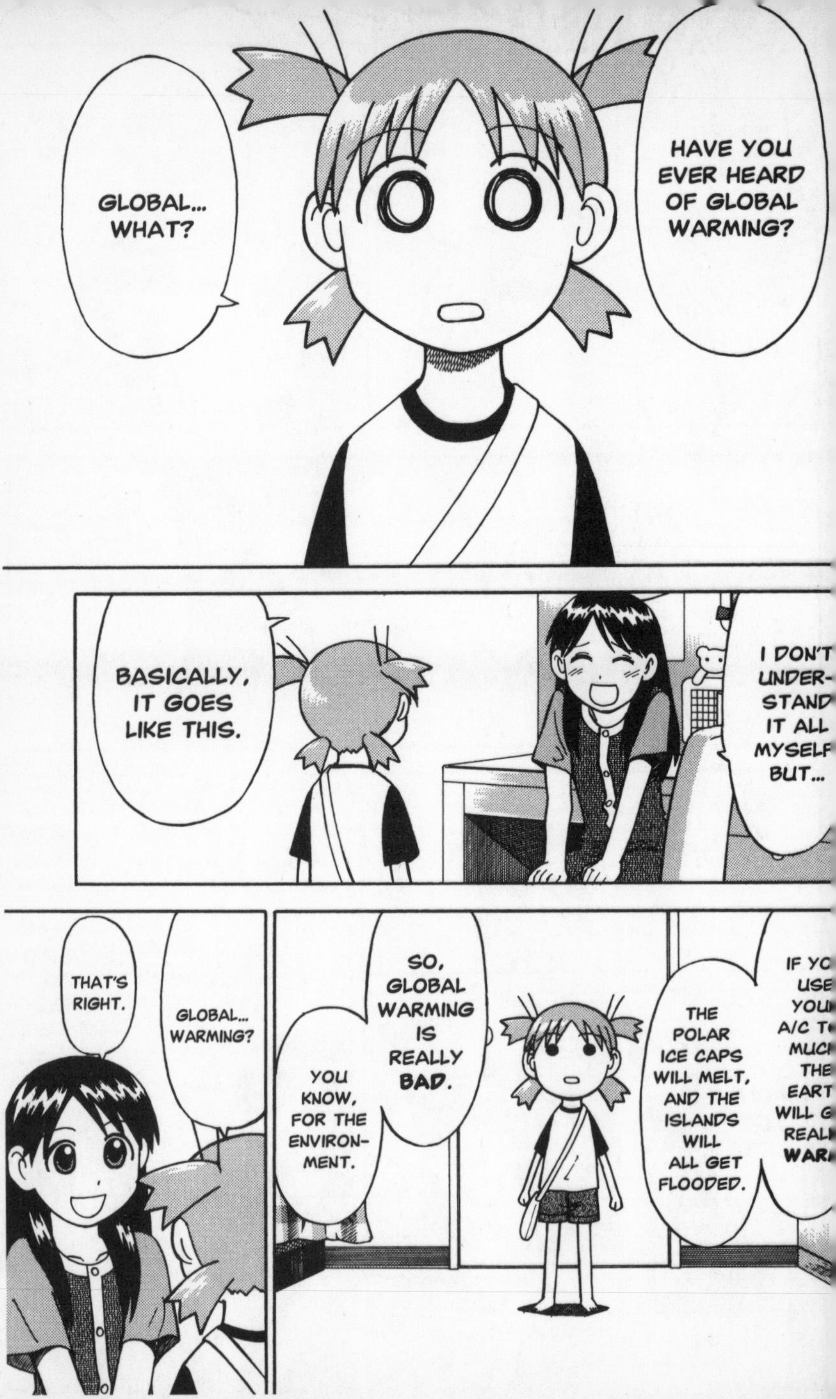
HAVE YOU EVER HEARD OF GLOBAL WARMING?
GLOBAL... WHAT?
I DON'T UNDER-STAND IT ALL MYSELF BUT...
BASICALLY, IT GOES LIKE THIS.
IF YO USE YOU A/C T MUC THE EART WILL G REAL WAR
THE POLAR ICE CAPS WILL MELT, AND THE ISLANDS WILL ALL GET FLOODED.
SO, GLOBAL WARMING IS REALLY **BAD**.
YOU KNOW, FOR THE ENVIRON-MENT.
GLOBAL... WARMING?
THAT'S RIGHT.

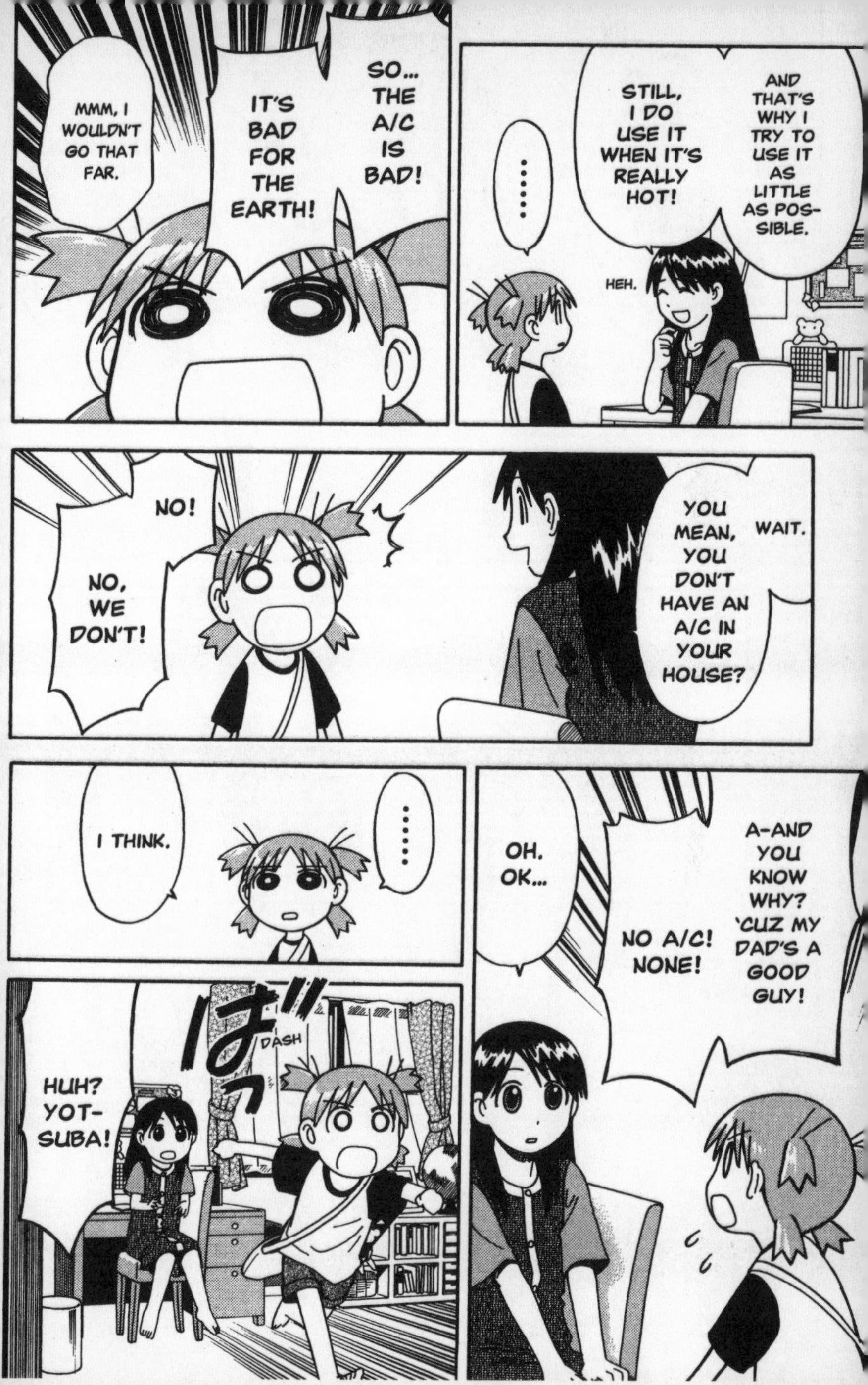
AND THAT'S WHY I TRY TO USE IT AS LITTLE AS POSSIBLE.
STILL, I DO USE IT WHEN IT'S REALLY HOT!
HEH.
......
SO... THE A/C IS BAD!
IT'S BAD FOR THE EARTH!
MMM, I WOULDN'T GO THAT FAR.
WAIT.
YOU MEAN, YOU DON'T HAVE AN A/C IN YOUR HOUSE?
NO!
NO, WE DON'T!
A-AND YOU KNOW WHY? 'CUZ MY DAD'S A GOOD GUY!
NO A/C! NONE!
OH. OK...
......
I THINK.
DASH
HUH? YOTSUBA!

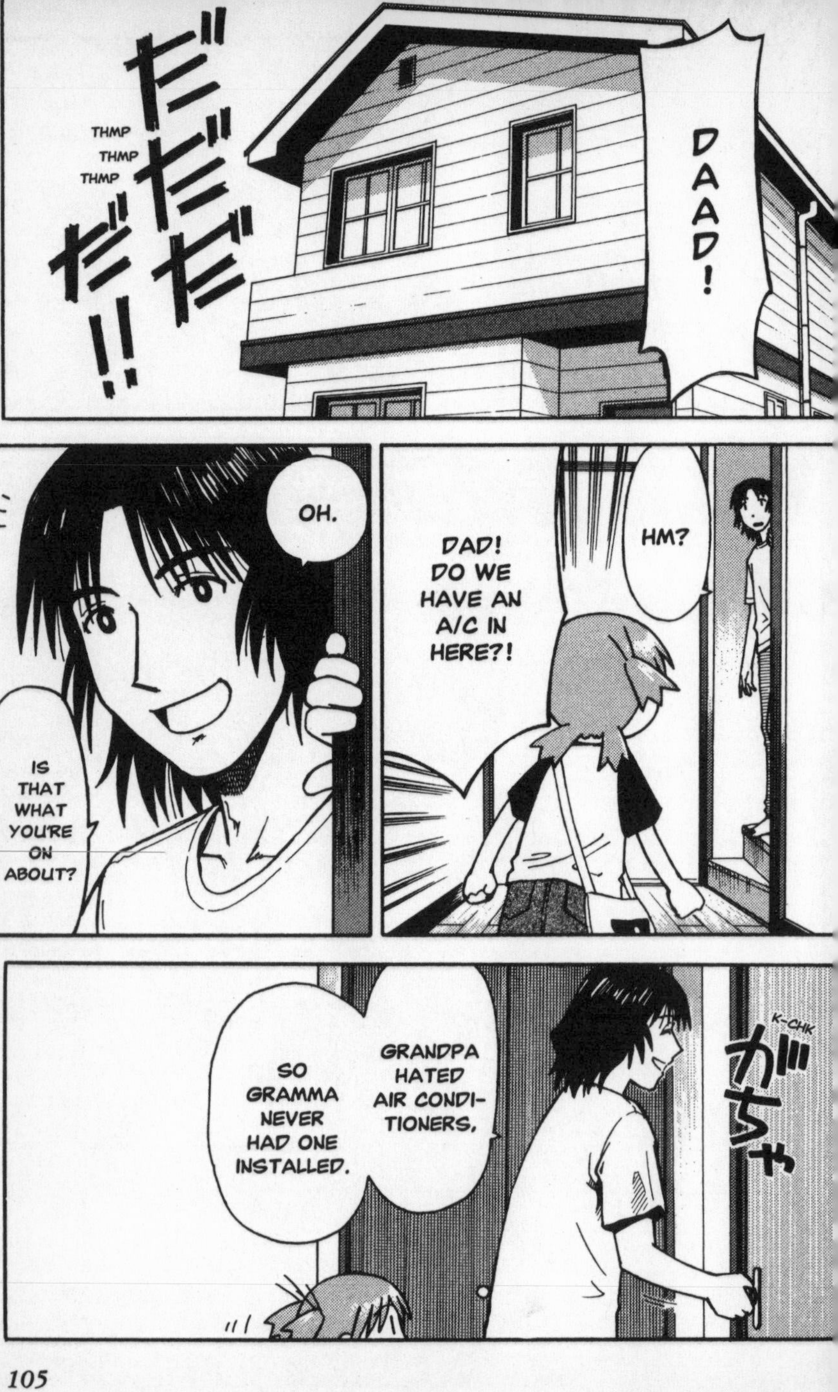
DAAD!
だだだだ!!
THMP THMP THMP
DAD! DO WE HAVE AN A/C IN HERE?!
HM?
OH.
IS THAT WHAT YOU'RE ON ABOUT?
K-CHK
がちゃ
GRANDPA HATED AIR CONDITIONERS,
SO GRAMMA NEVER HAD ONE INSTALLED.

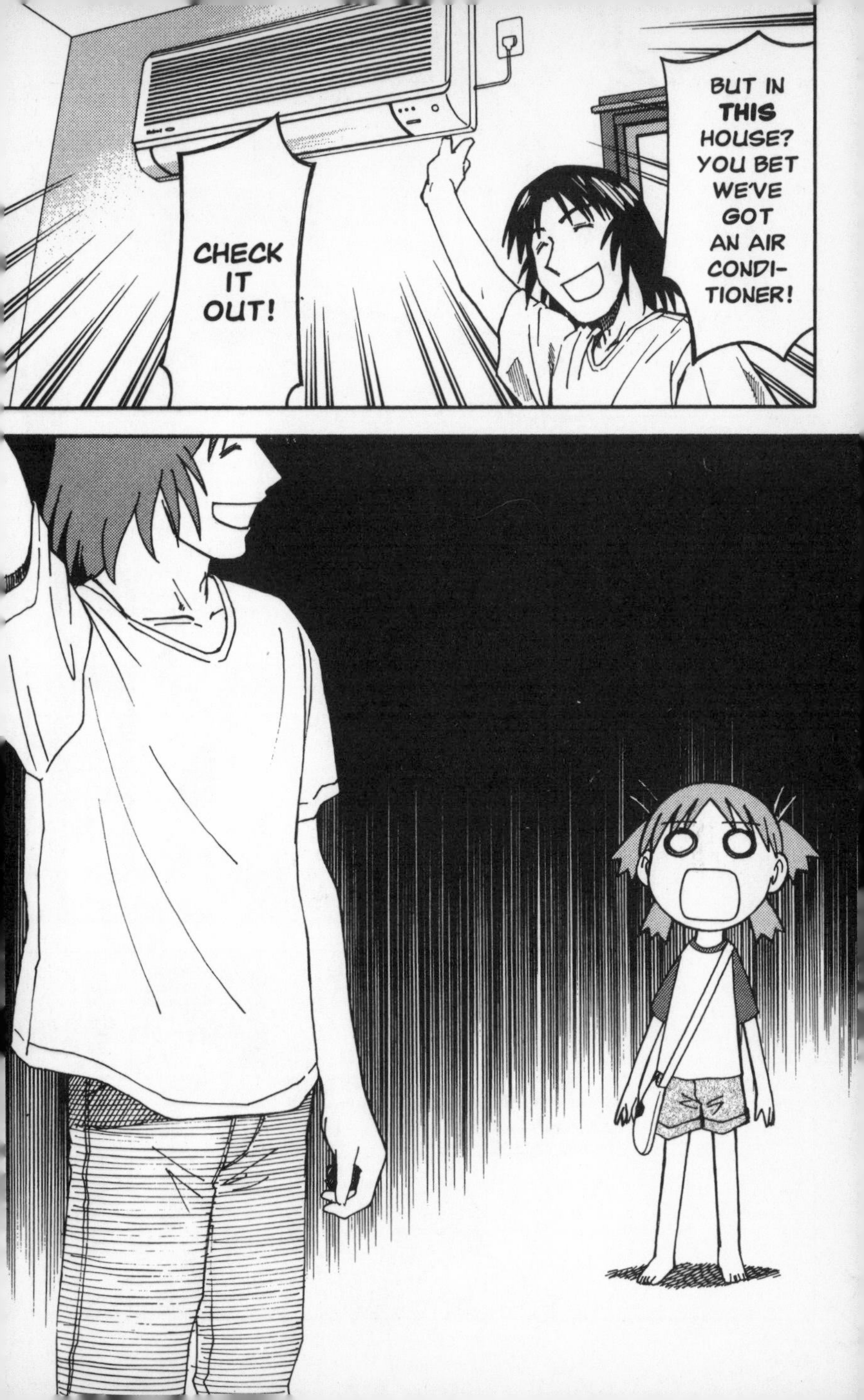
BUT IN **THIS** HOUSE? YOU BET WE'VE GOT AN AIR CONDI-TIONER!
CHECK IT OUT!

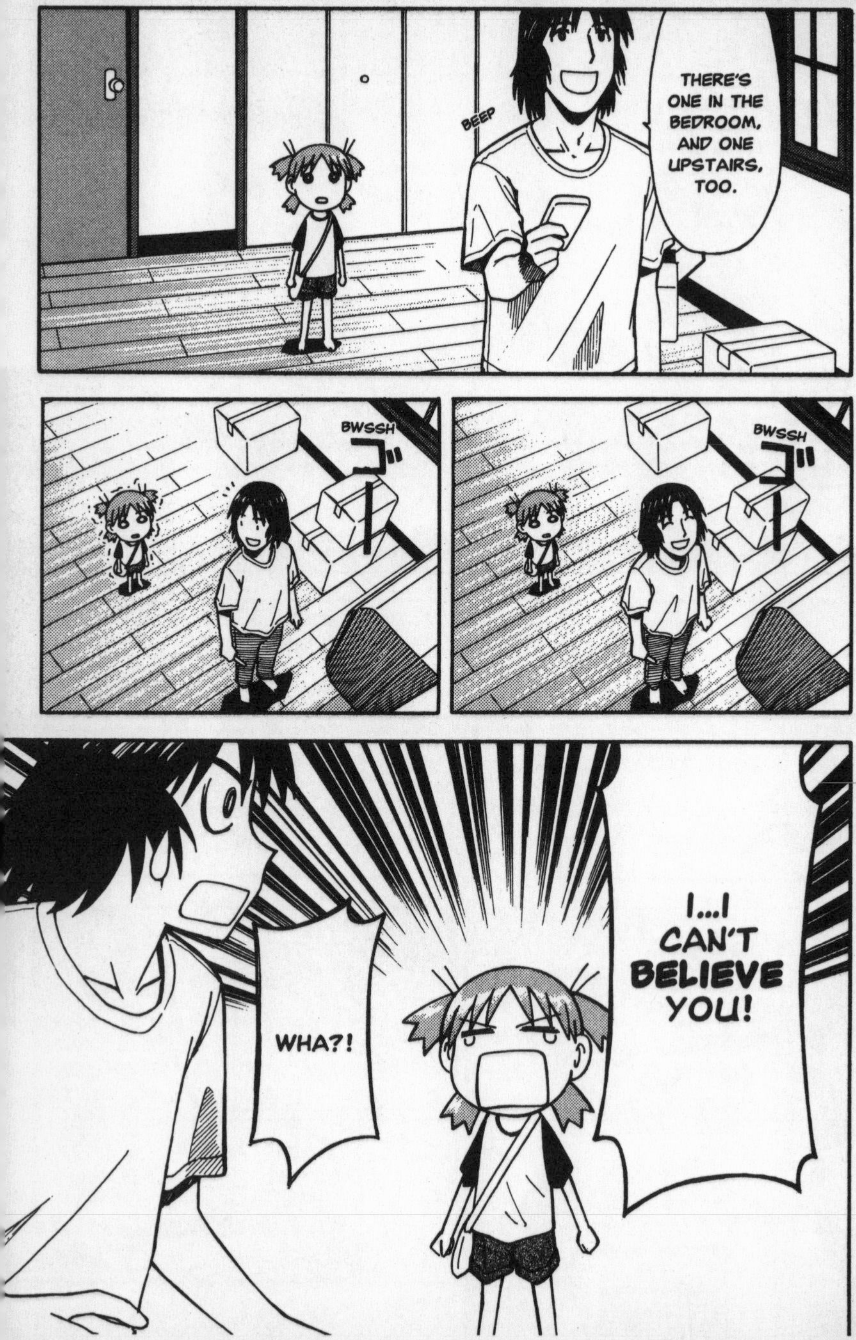
THERE'S ONE IN THE BEDROOM, AND ONE UPSTAIRS, TOO.
BEEP
BWSSH
ゴ
BWSSH
ゴ
I...I CAN'T BELIEVE YOU!
WHA?!

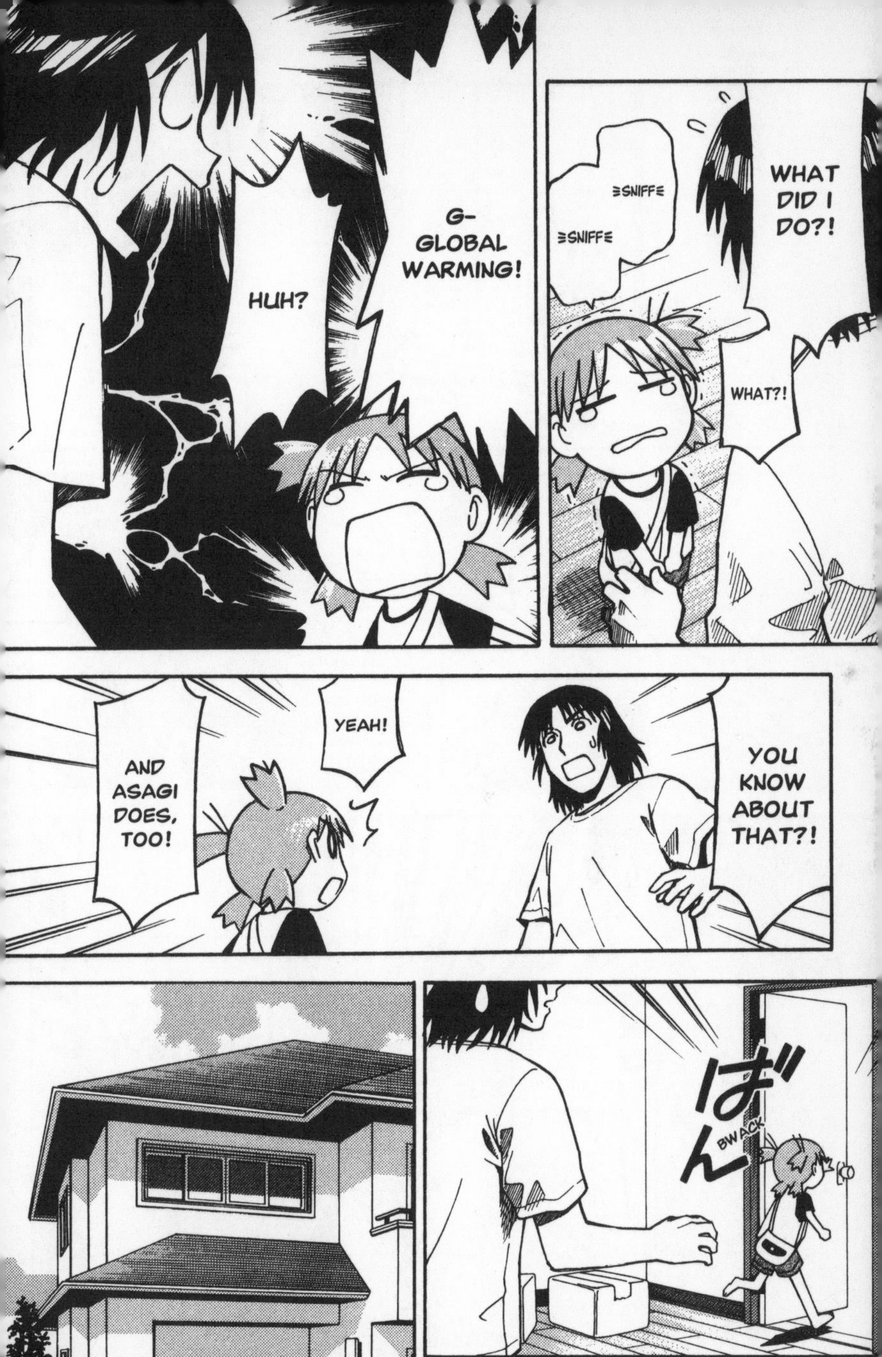
WHAT DID I DO?!
≡SNIFF≡
≡SNIFF≡
WHAT?!
G- GLOBAL WARMING!
HUH?
YOU KNOW ABOUT THAT?!
YEAH!
AND ASAGI DOES, TOO!
ばん
BWACK

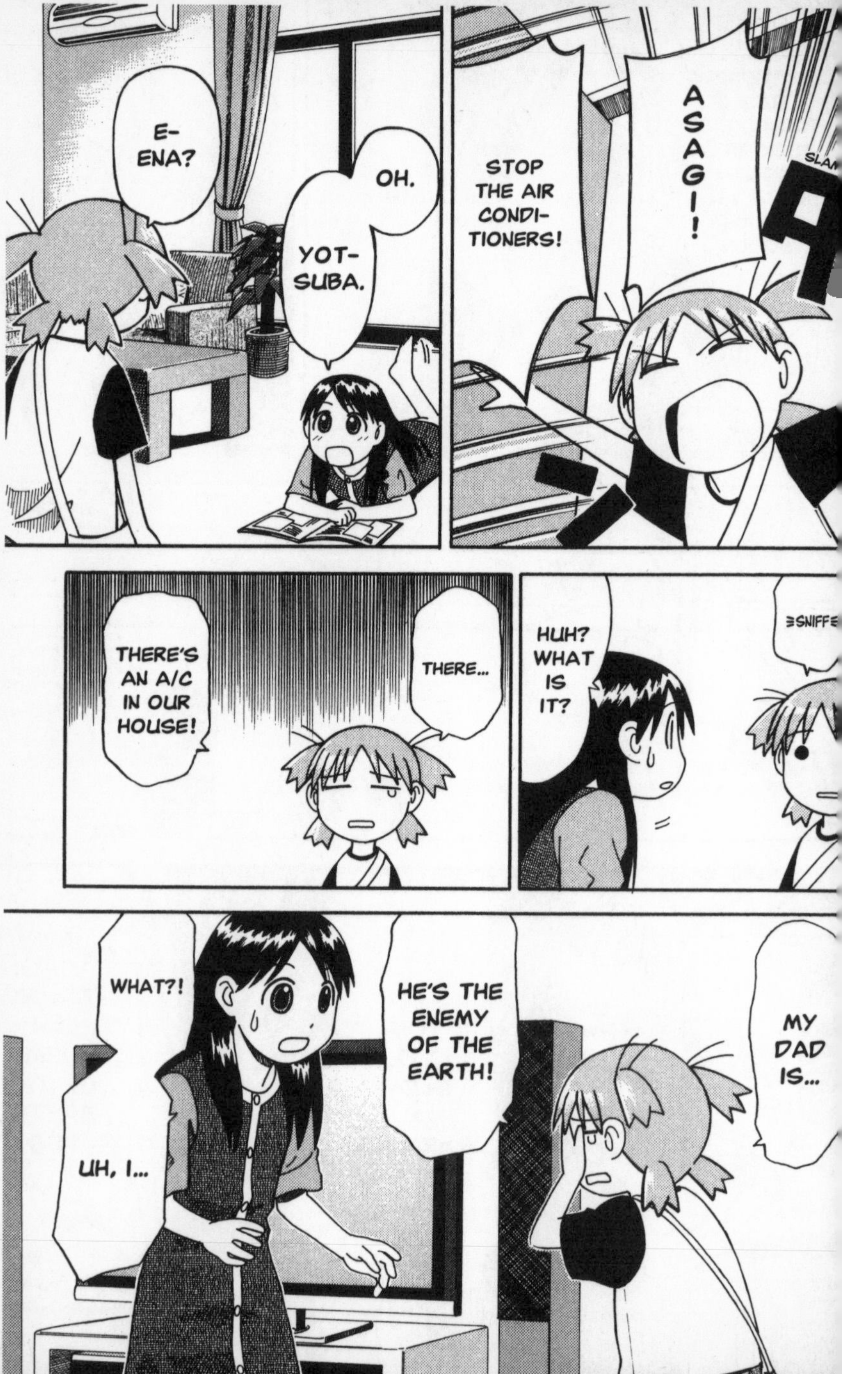
ASAGI!
STOP THE AIR CONDITIONERS!
SLA
OH.
YOT-SUBA.
E-ENA?
≡SNIFF≡
HUH? WHAT IS IT?
THERE...
THERE'S AN A/C IN OUR HOUSE!
MY DAD IS...
HE'S THE ENEMY OF THE EARTH!
WHAT?!
UH, I...

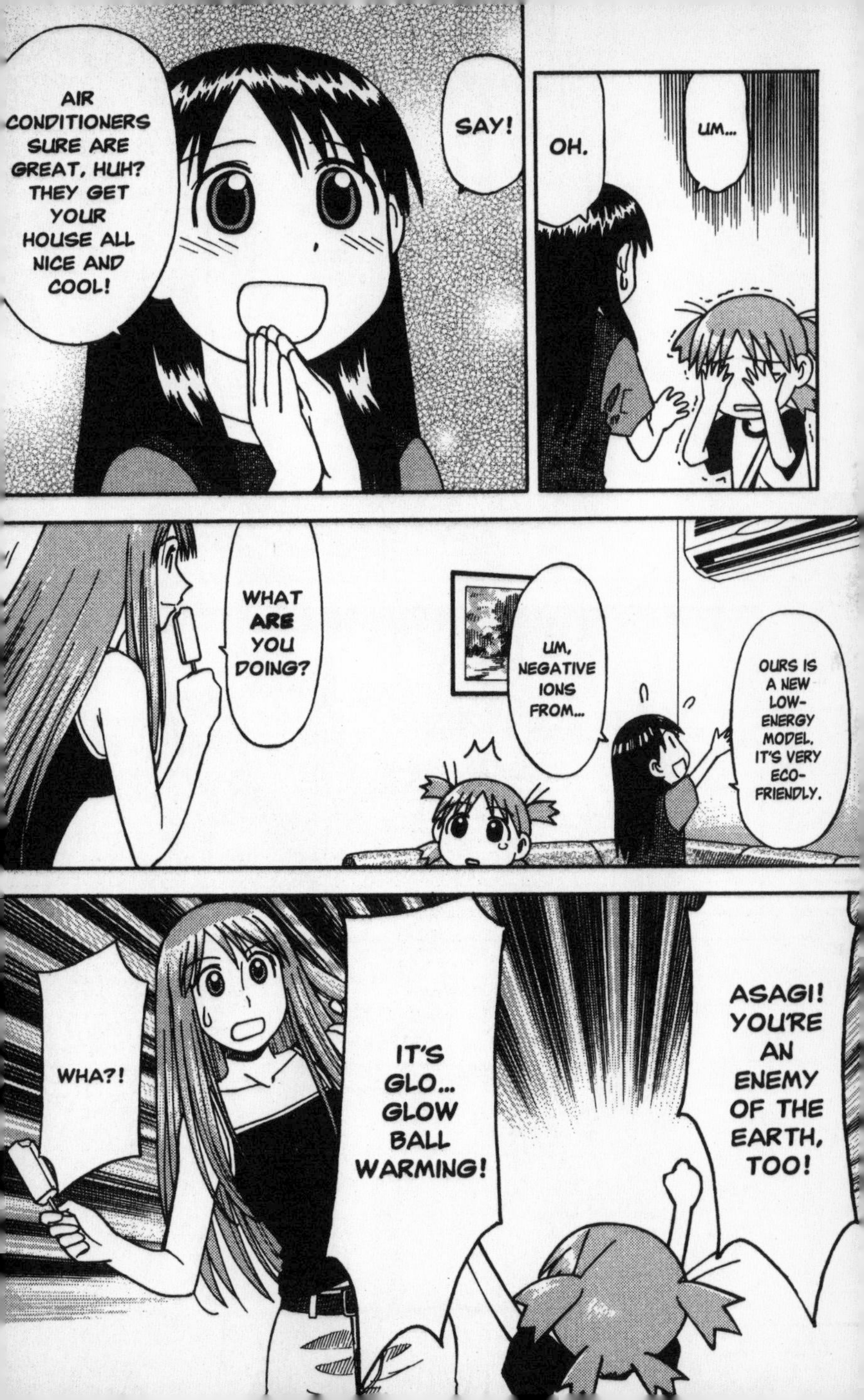
UM...
OH.
SAY!
AIR CONDITIONERS SURE ARE GREAT, HUH? THEY GET YOUR HOUSE ALL NICE AND COOL!
OURS IS A NEW LOW-ENERGY MODEL. IT'S VERY ECO-FRIENDLY.
UM, NEGATIVE IONS FROM...
WHAT ARE YOU DOING?
ASAGI! YOU'RE AN ENEMY OF THE EARTH, TOO!
IT'S GLO... GLOW BALL WARMING!
WHA?!

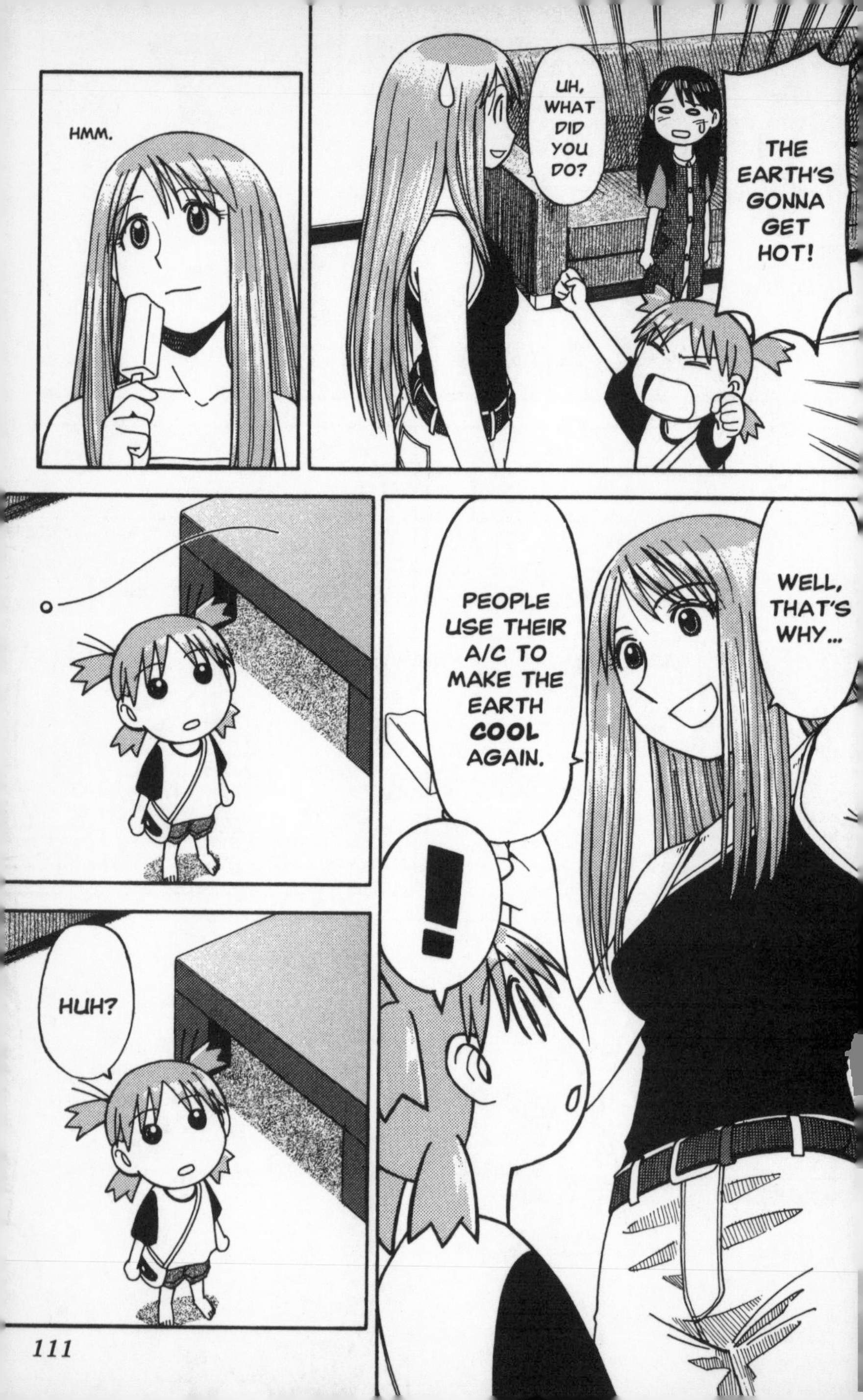
THE EARTH'S GONNA GET HOT!
UH, WHAT DID YOU DO?
HMM.
WELL, THAT'S WHY...
PEOPLE USE THEIR A/C TO MAKE THE EARTH COOL AGAIN.
!
HUH?

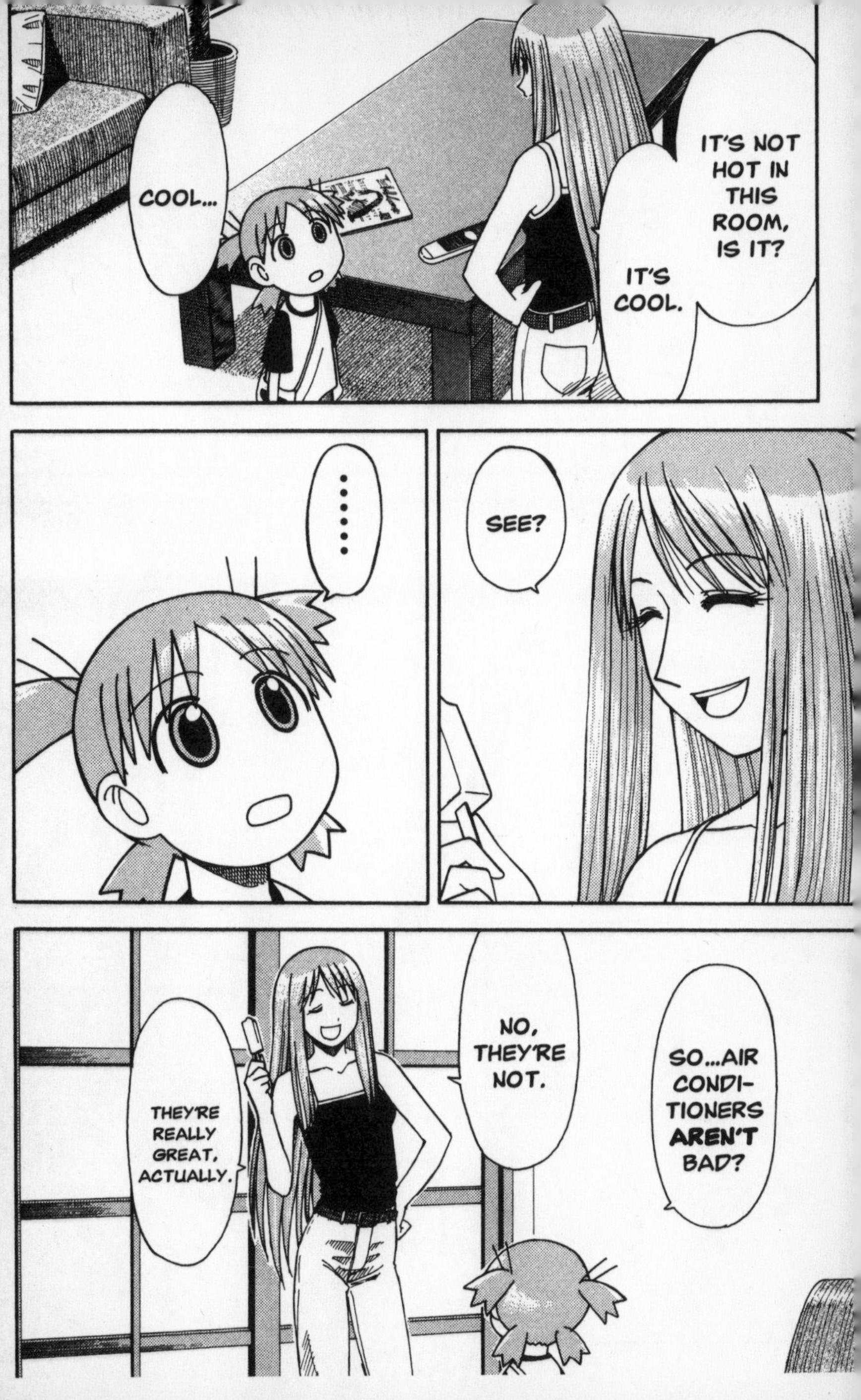
IT'S NOT HOT IN THIS ROOM, IS IT?
IT'S COOL.
COOL...
SEE?
......
SO...AIR CONDITIONERS **AREN'T** BAD?
NO, THEY'RE NOT.
THEY'RE REALLY GREAT, ACTUALLY.

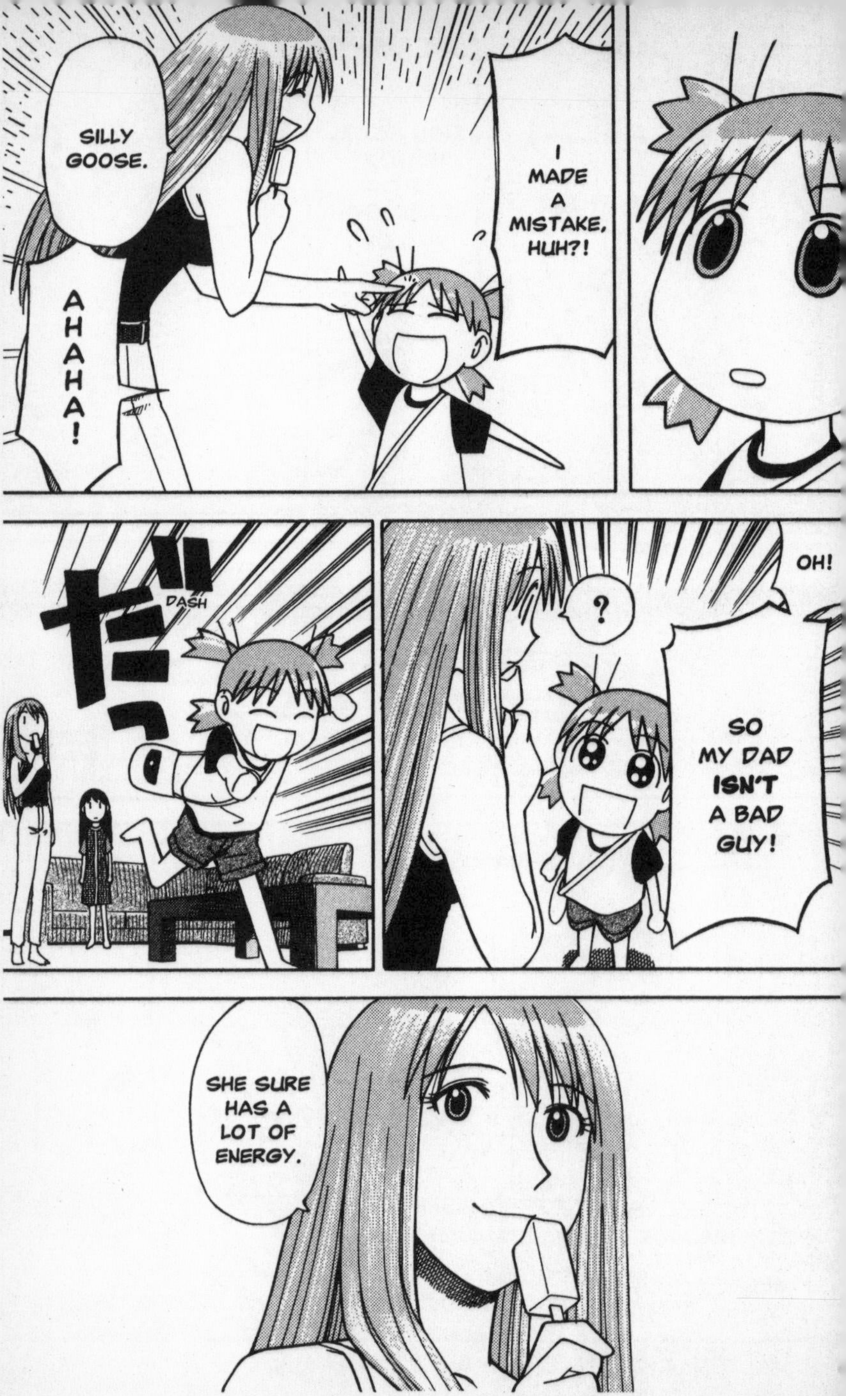
I MADE A MISTAKE, HUH?!
SILLY GOOSE.
AHAHA!
OH!
SO MY DAD ISN'T A BAD GUY!
?
DASH
SHE SURE HAS A LOT OF ENERGY.

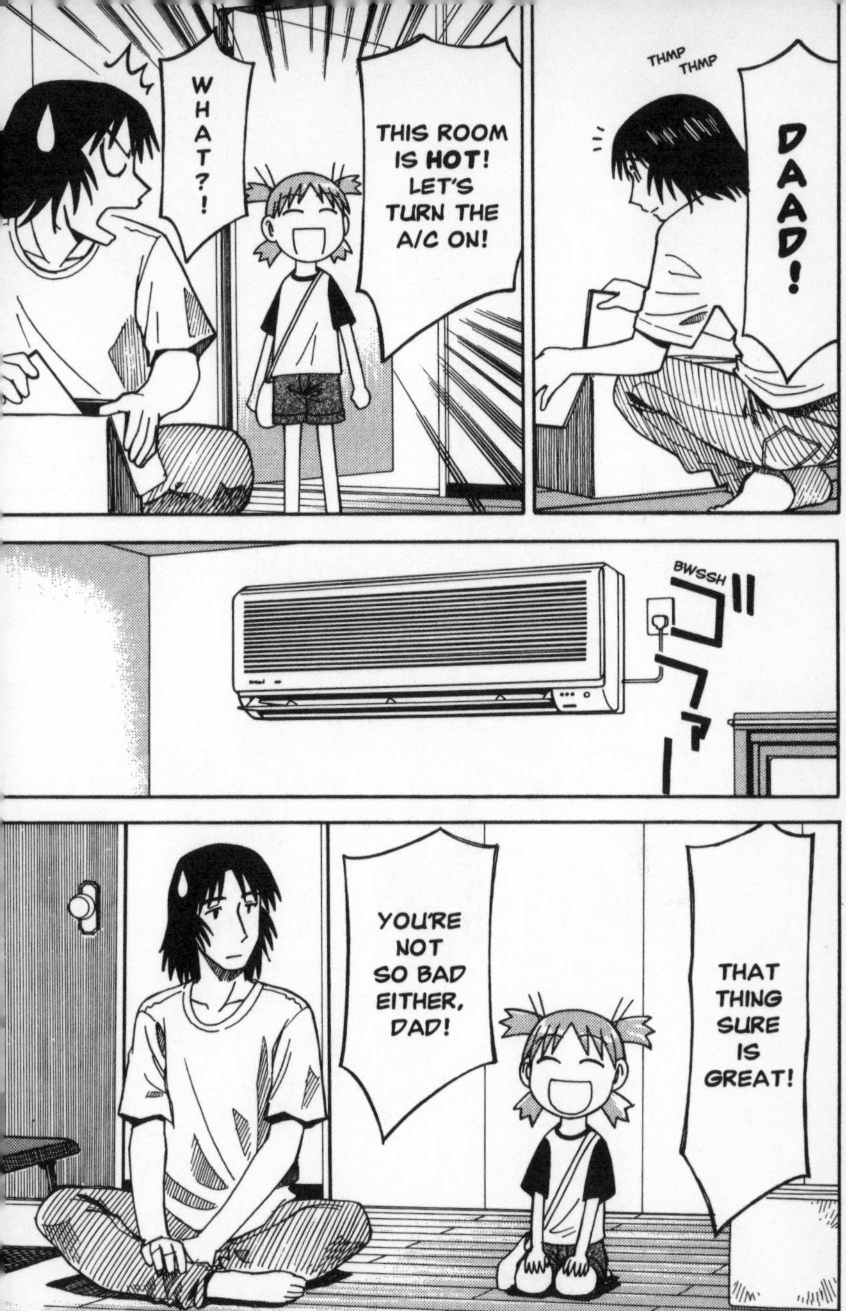
THMP THMP
DAAD!
THIS ROOM IS HOT! LET'S TURN THE A/C ON!
WHAT?!
BWSSH
THAT THING SURE IS GREAT!
YOU'RE NOT SO BAD EITHER, DAD!

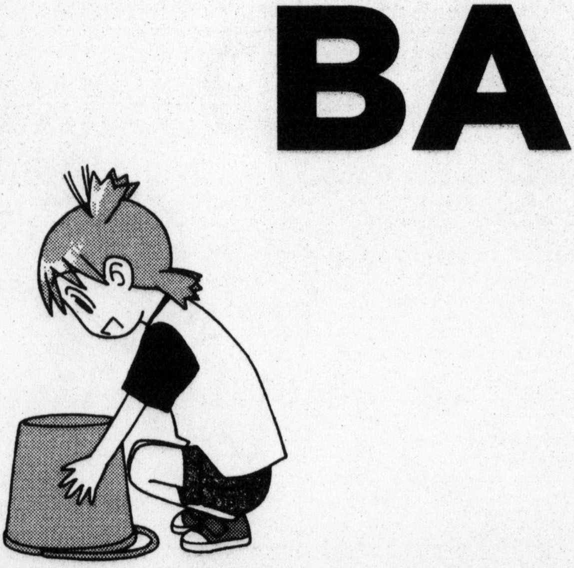
BA

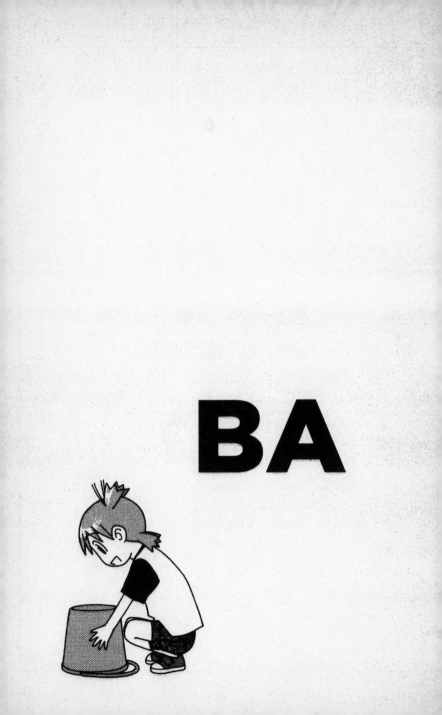

TO

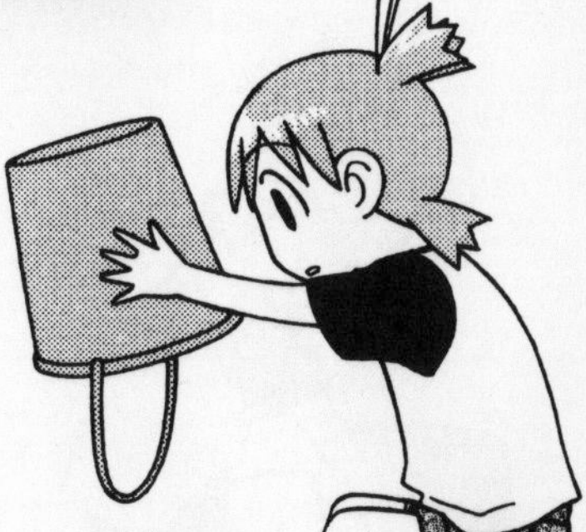

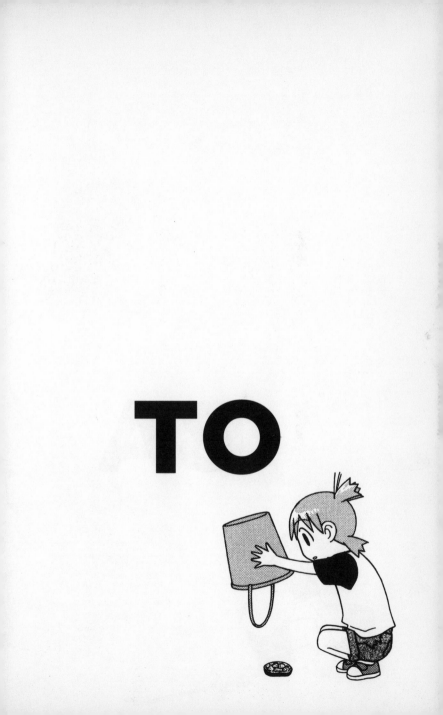

YOTSUBA&!

CHAPTER 4
TV

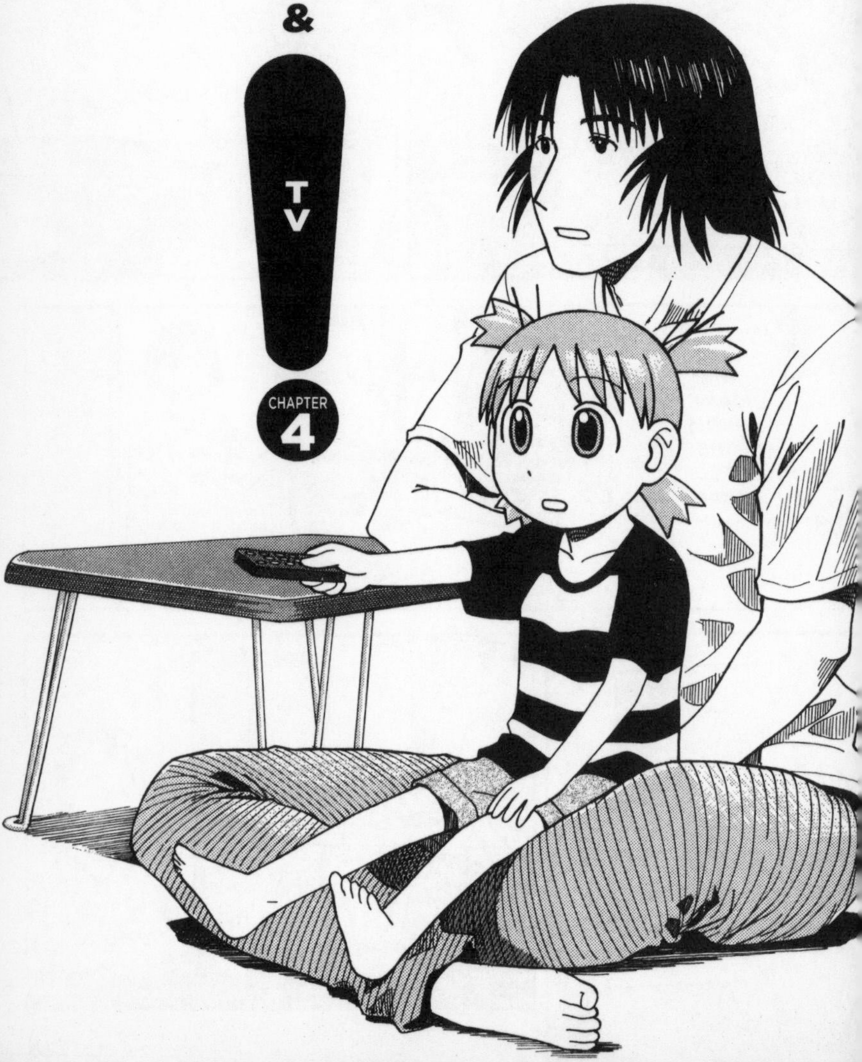

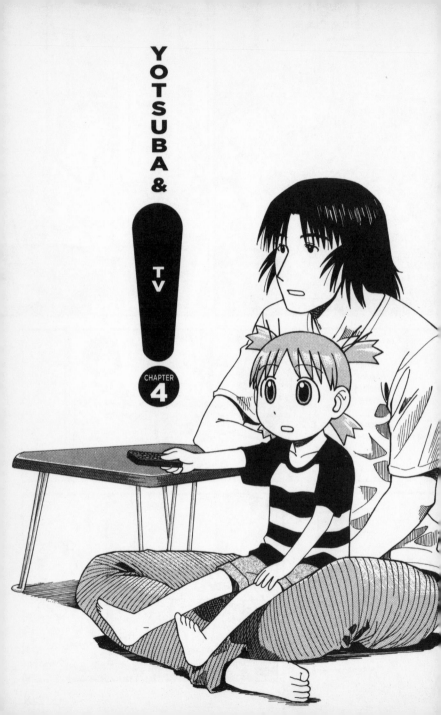

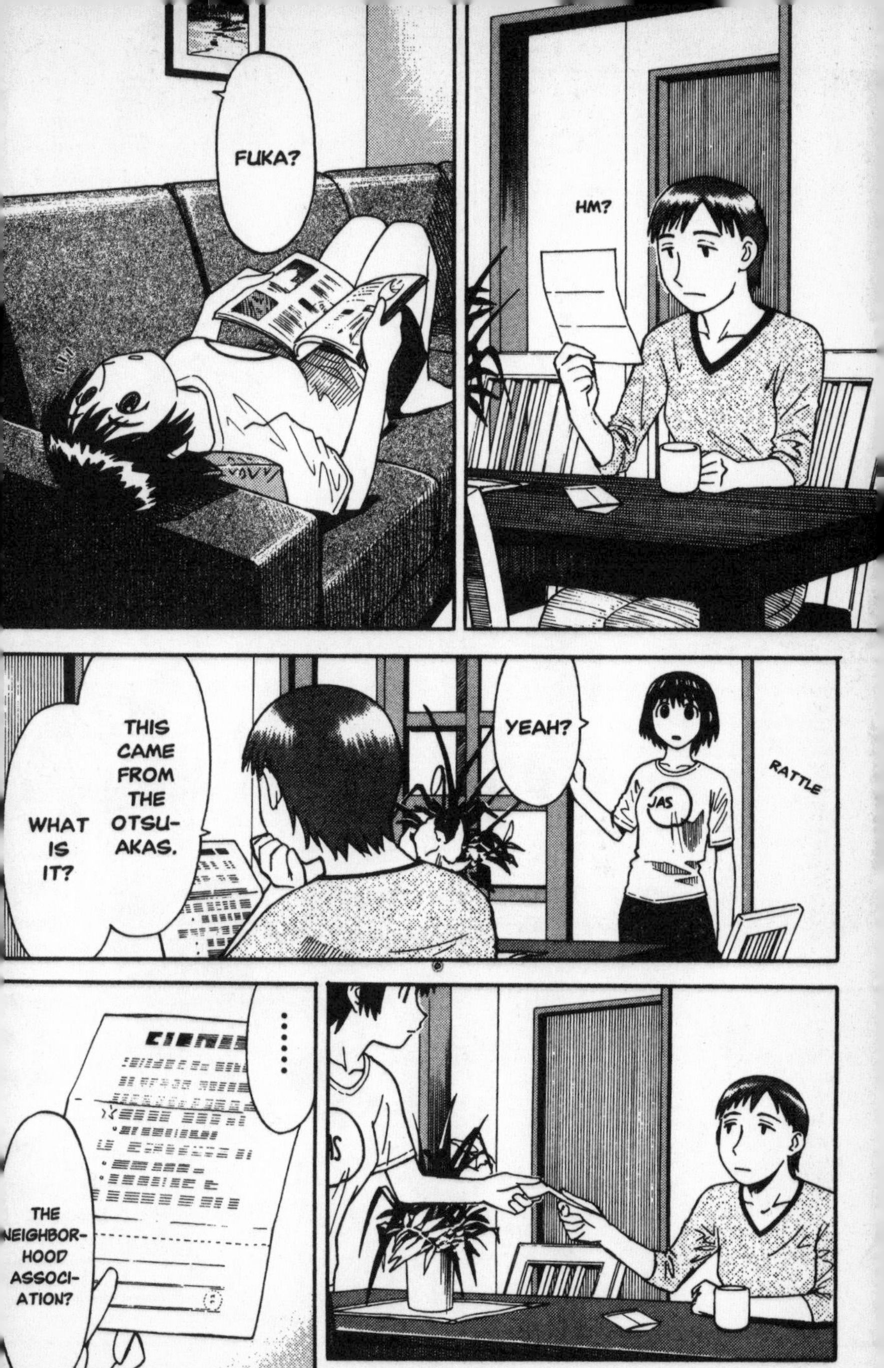
HM?
FUKA?
RATTLE
YEAH?
THIS CAME FROM THE OTSU-AKAS.
WHAT IS IT?
......
THE NEIGHBOR-HOOD ASSOCI-ATION?

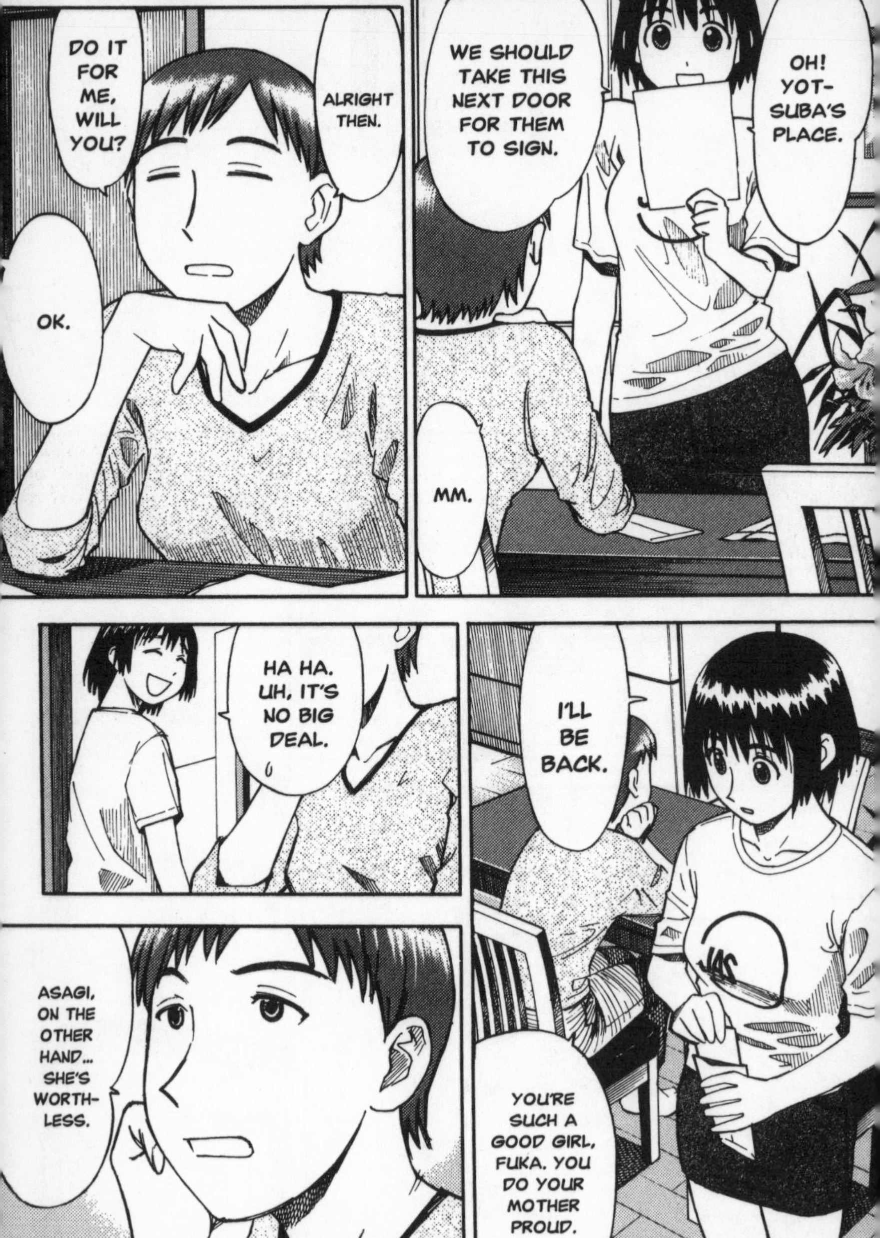
OH! YOT-SUBA'S PLACE.
WE SHOULD TAKE THIS NEXT DOOR FOR THEM TO SIGN.
MM.
ALRIGHT THEN.
DO IT FOR ME, WILL YOU?
OK.
I'LL BE BACK.
YOU'RE SUCH A GOOD GIRL, FUKA. YOU DO YOUR MOTHER PROUD.
HA HA. UH, IT'S NO BIG DEAL.
ASAGI, ON THE OTHER HAND... SHE'S WORTH-LESS.

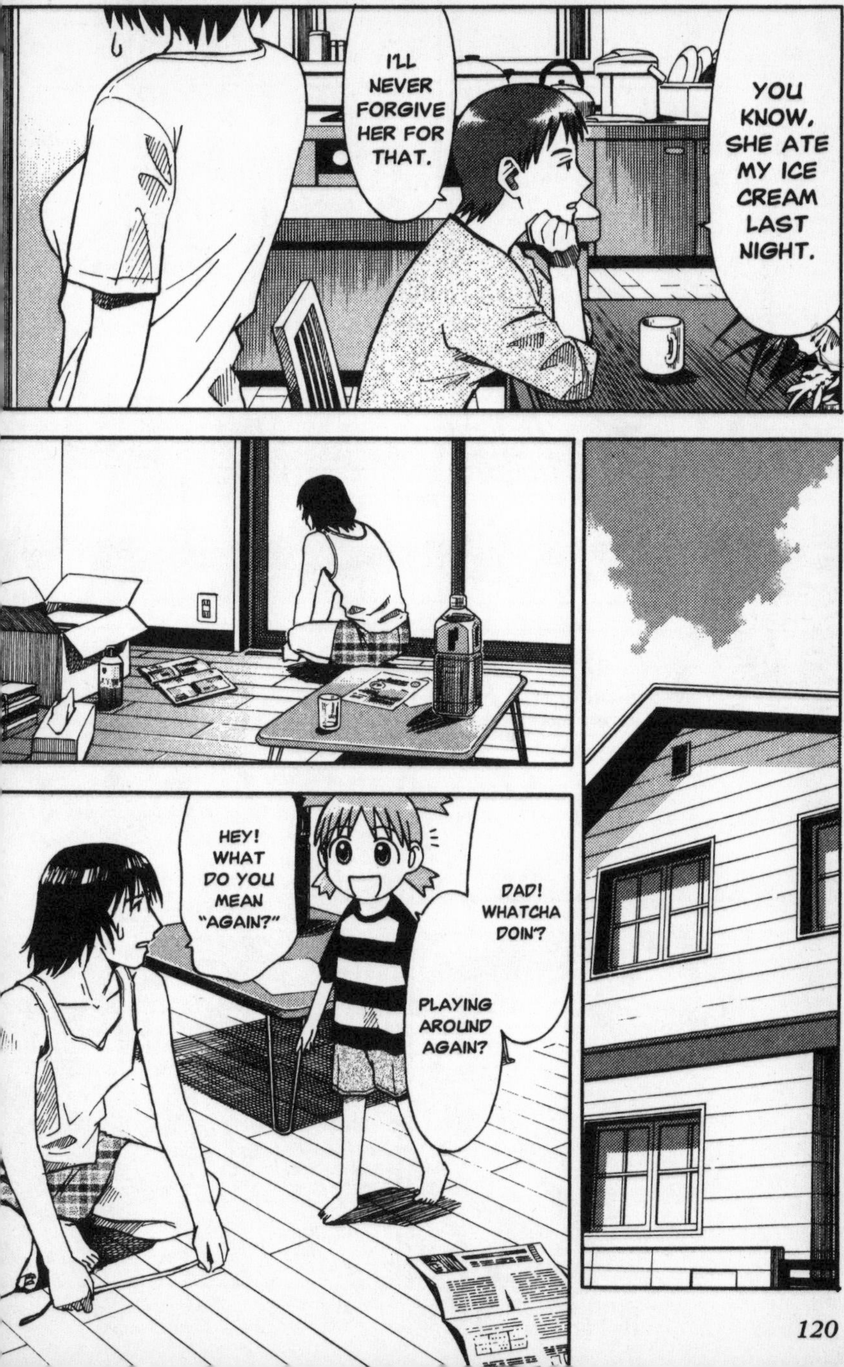
YOU KNOW, SHE ATE MY ICE CREAM LAST NIGHT.
I'LL NEVER FORGIVE HER FOR THAT.
DAD! WHATCHA DOIN'?
PLAYING AROUND AGAIN?
HEY! WHAT DO YOU MEAN "AGAIN?"

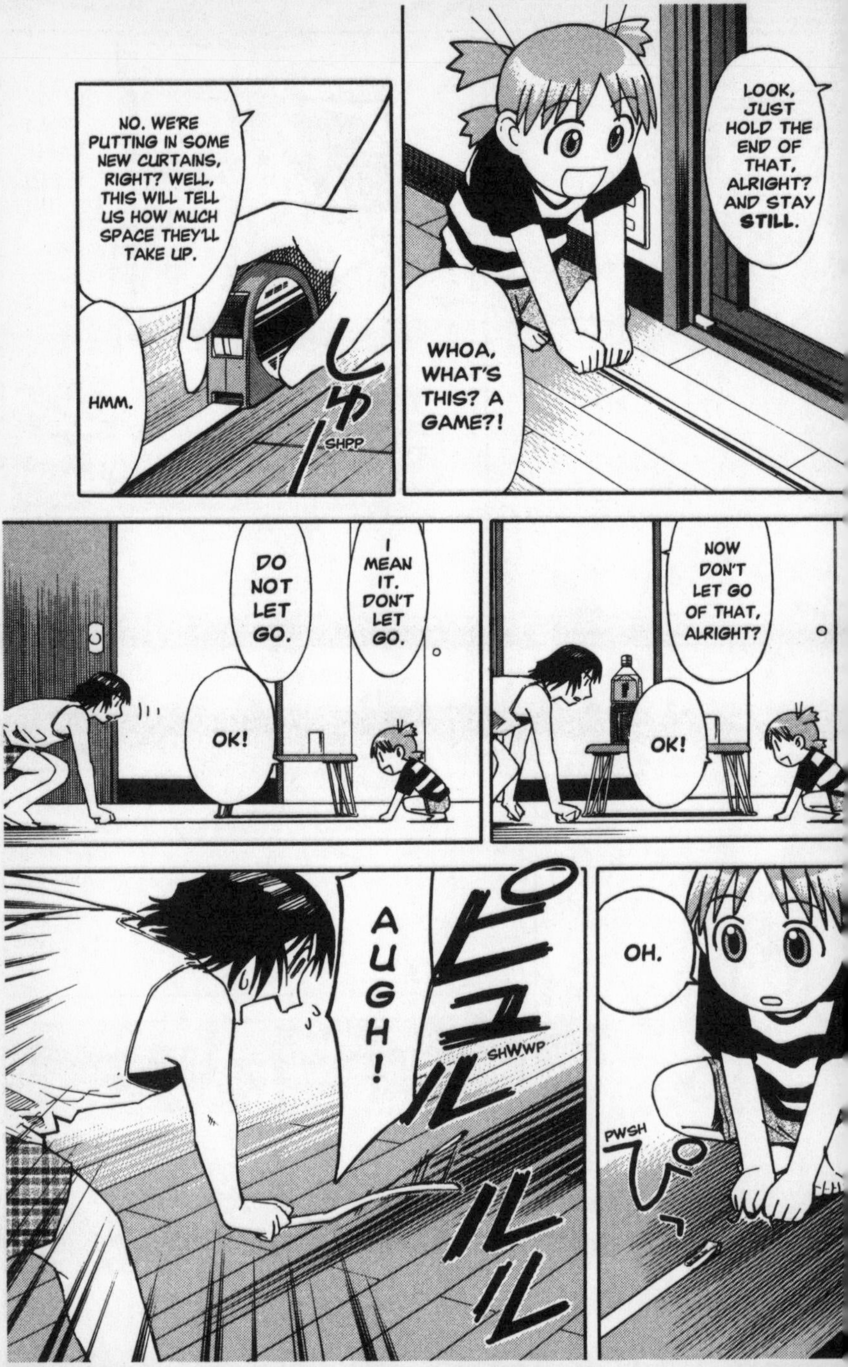
LOOK, JUST HOLD THE END OF THAT, ALRIGHT? AND STAY **STILL**.
WHOA, WHAT'S THIS? A GAME?!
NO. WE'RE PUTTING IN SOME NEW CURTAINS, RIGHT? WELL, THIS WILL TELL US HOW MUCH SPACE THEY'LL TAKE UP.
HMM.
SHPP
NOW DON'T LET GO OF THAT, ALRIGHT?
OK!
I MEAN IT. DON'T LET GO.
DO NOT LET GO.
OK!
OH.
PWSH
AUGH!
SHWWP

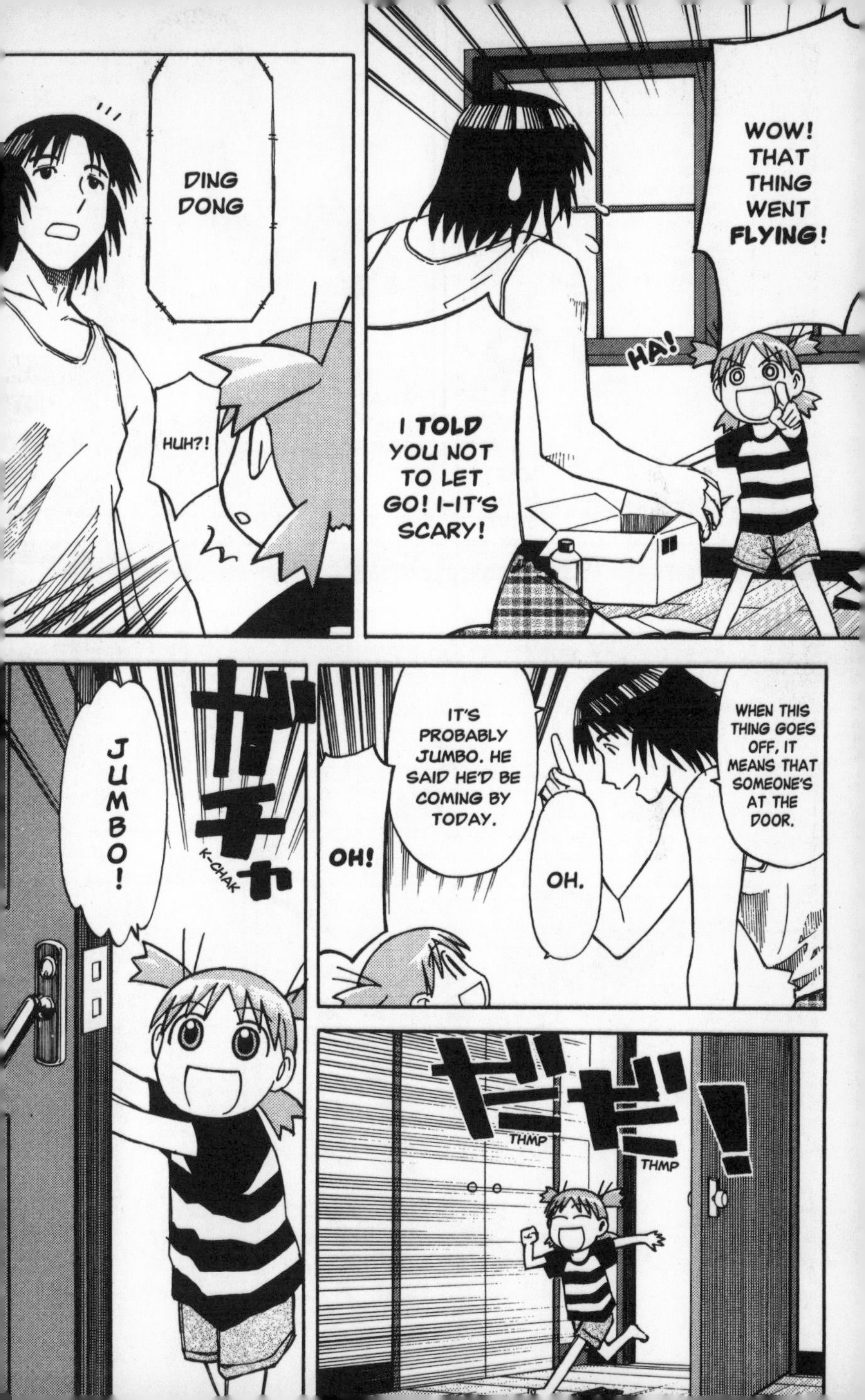
WOW! THAT THING WENT FLYING!
HA!
I TOLD YOU NOT TO LET GO! I-IT'S SCARY!
DING DONG
HUH?!
WHEN THIS THING GOES OFF, IT MEANS THAT SOMEONE'S AT THE DOOR.
OH.
IT'S PROBABLY JUMBO. HE SAID HE'D BE COMING BY TODAY.
OH!
THMP
THMP
K-CHAK
JUMBO!

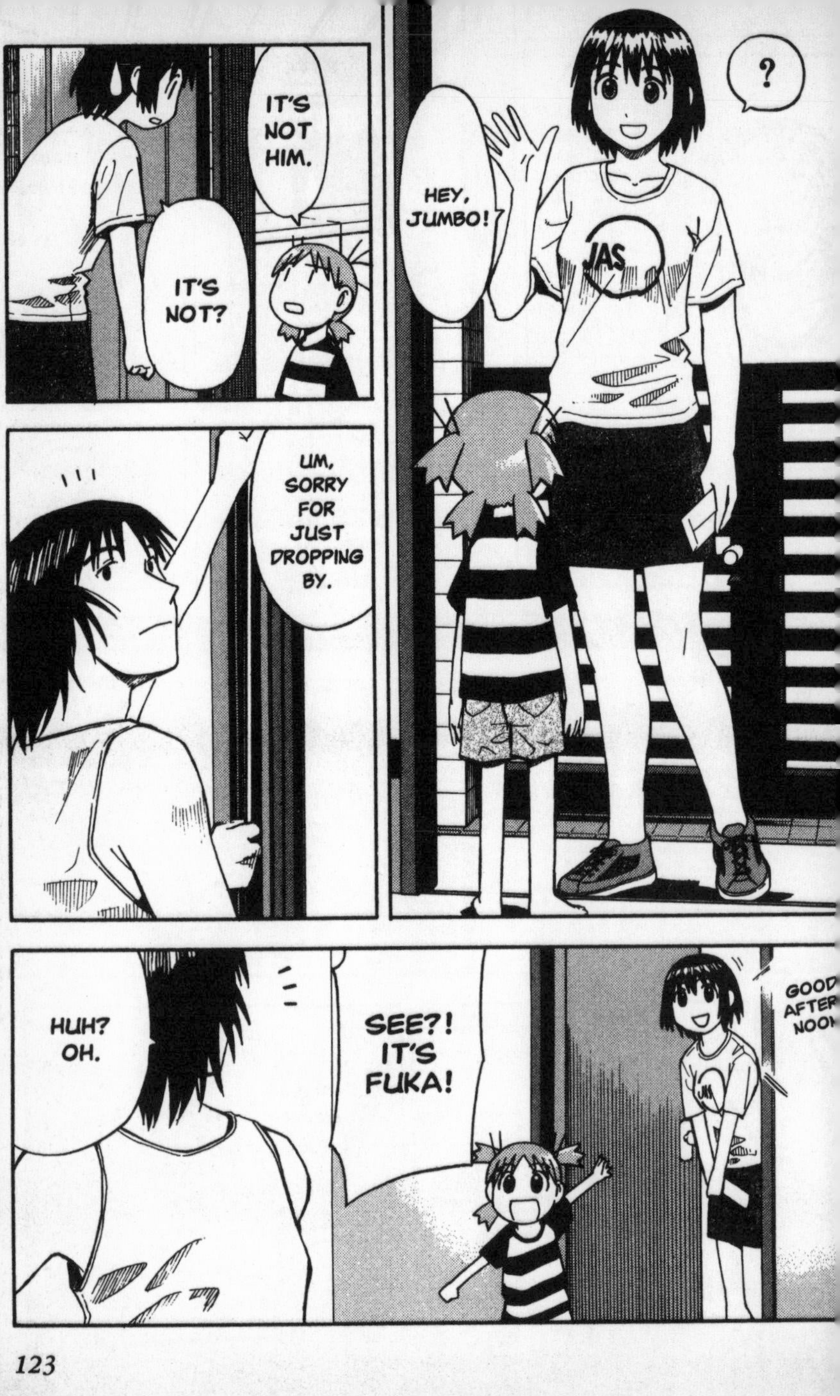
?
HEY, JUMBO!
IT'S NOT HIM.
IT'S NOT?
UM, SORRY FOR JUST DROPPING BY.
GOOD AFTER NOO
SEE?! IT'S FUKA!
HUH? OH.

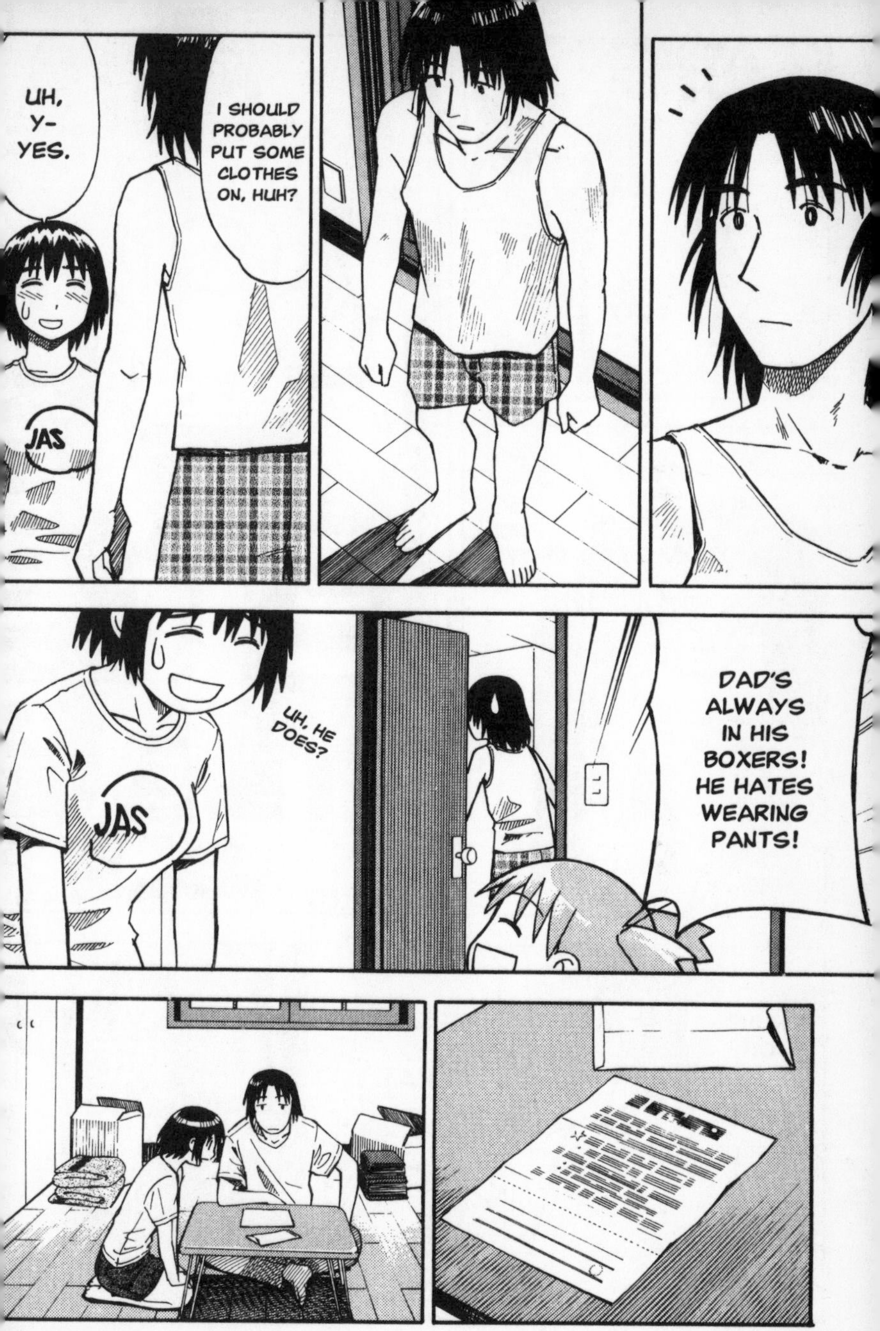
I SHOULD PROBABLY PUT SOME CLOTHES ON, HUH?
UH, Y-YES.
DAD'S ALWAYS IN HIS BOXERS! HE HATES WEARING PANTS!
UH, HE DOES?

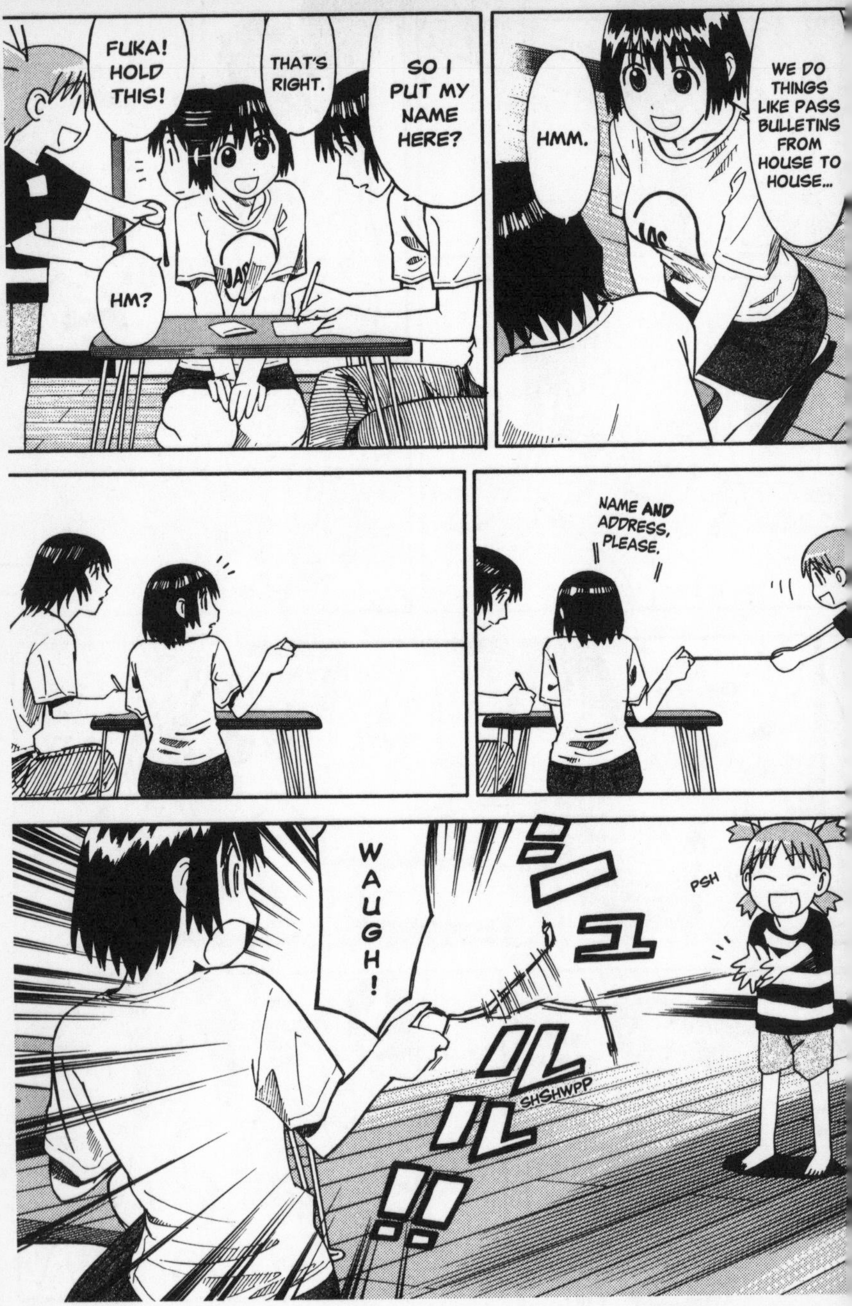
WE DO THINGS LIKE PASS BULLETINS FROM HOUSE TO HOUSE...
HMM.
SO I PUT MY NAME HERE?
THAT'S RIGHT.
FUKA! HOLD THIS!
HM?
NAME AND ADDRESS, PLEASE.
PSH
WAUGH!
SHSHWPP

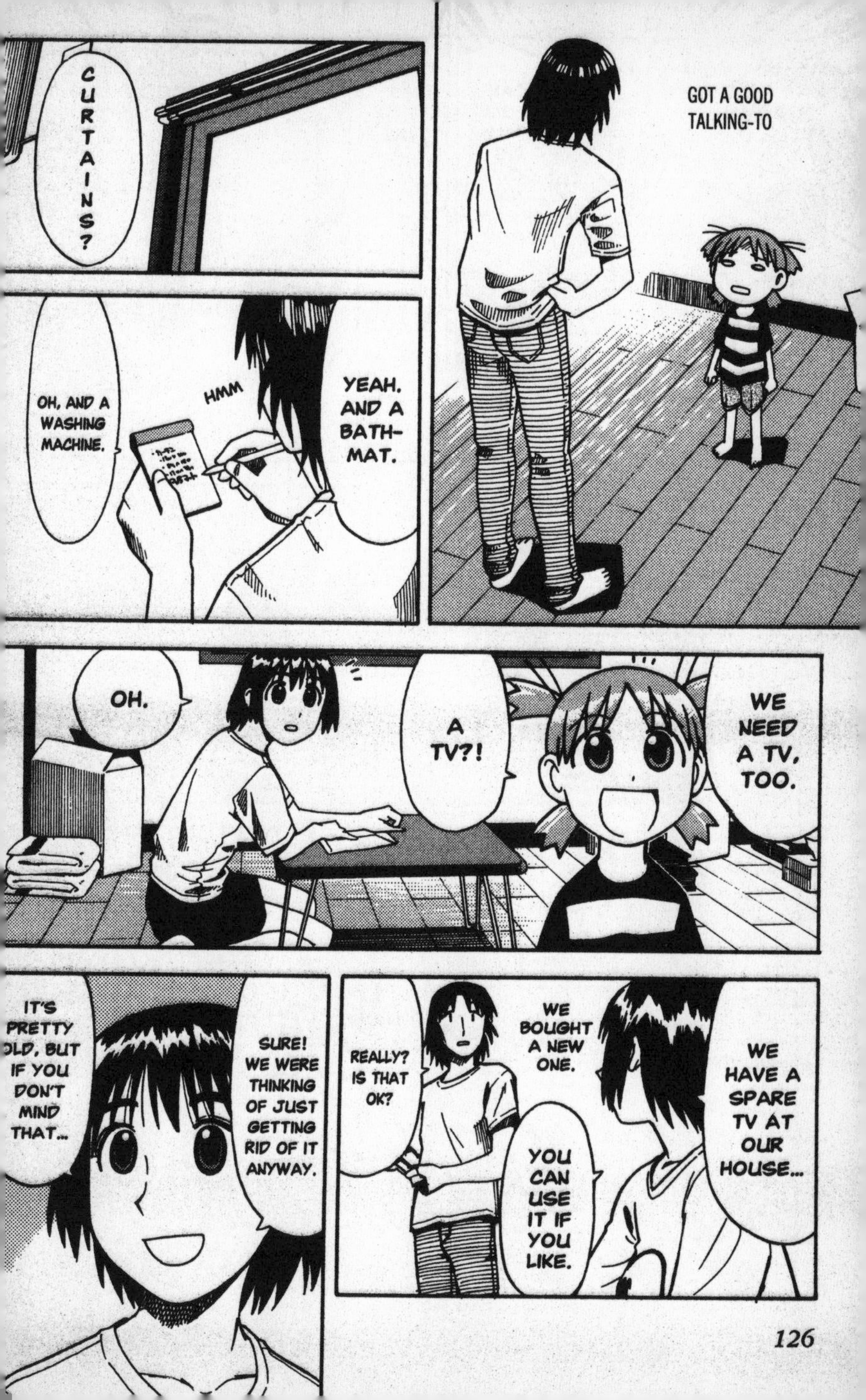
GOT A GOOD TALKING-TO
CURTAINS?
YEAH. AND A BATH-MAT.
HMM
OH, AND A WASHING MACHINE.
WE NEED A TV, TOO.
A TV?!
OH.
WE HAVE A SPARE TV AT OUR HOUSE...
WE BOUGHT A NEW ONE.
YOU CAN USE IT IF YOU LIKE.
REALLY? IS THAT OK?
SURE! WE WERE THINKING OF JUST GETTING RID OF IT ANYWAY.
IT'S PRETTY OLD, BUT IF YOU DON'T MIND THAT...

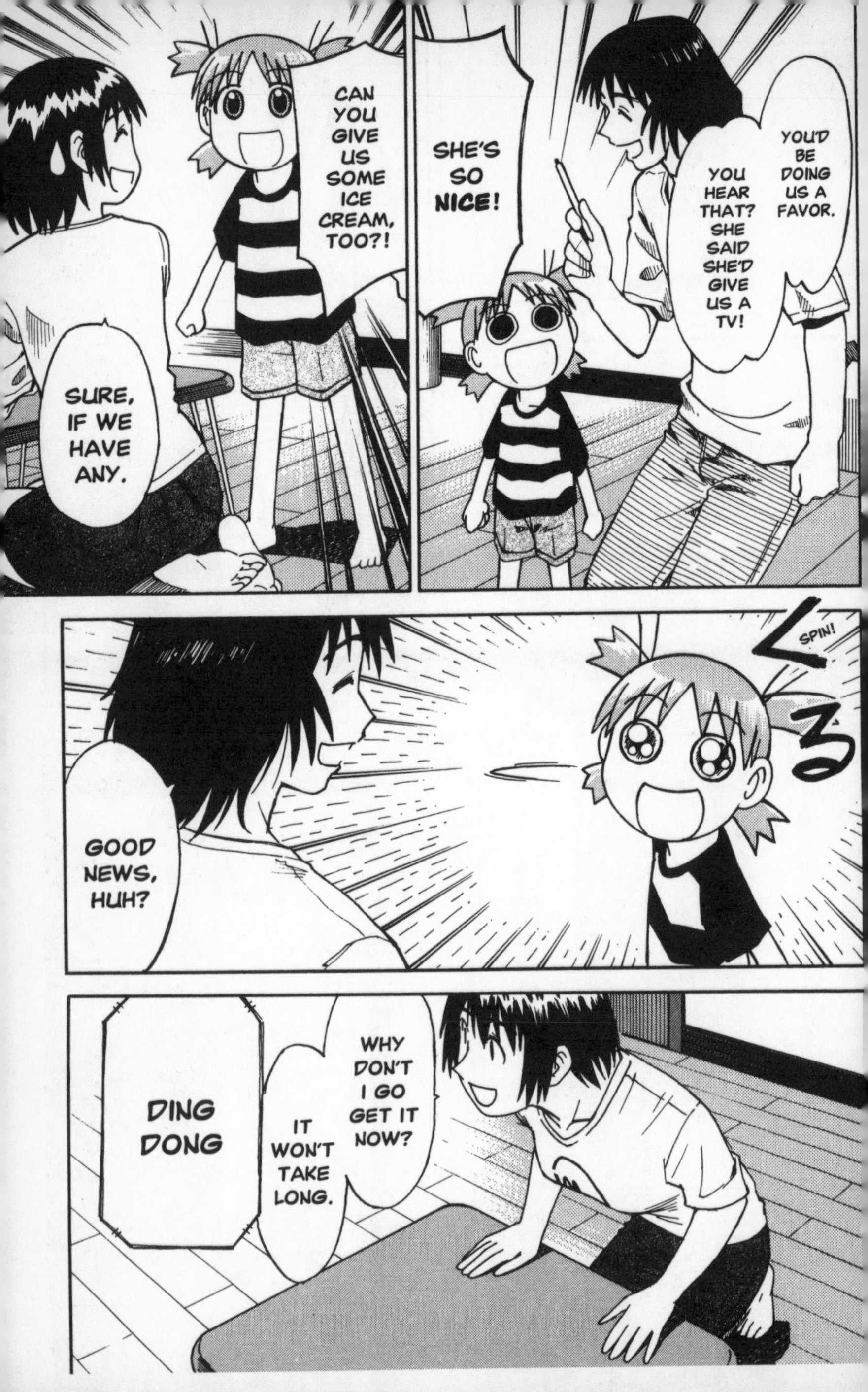
YOU'D BE DOING US A FAVOR.
YOU HEAR THAT? SHE SAID SHE'D GIVE US A TV!
SHE'S SO NICE!
CAN YOU GIVE US SOME ICE CREAM, TOO?!
SURE, IF WE HAVE ANY.
SPIN!
GOOD NEWS, HUH?
WHY DON'T I GO GET IT NOW?
IT WON'T TAKE LONG.
DING DONG

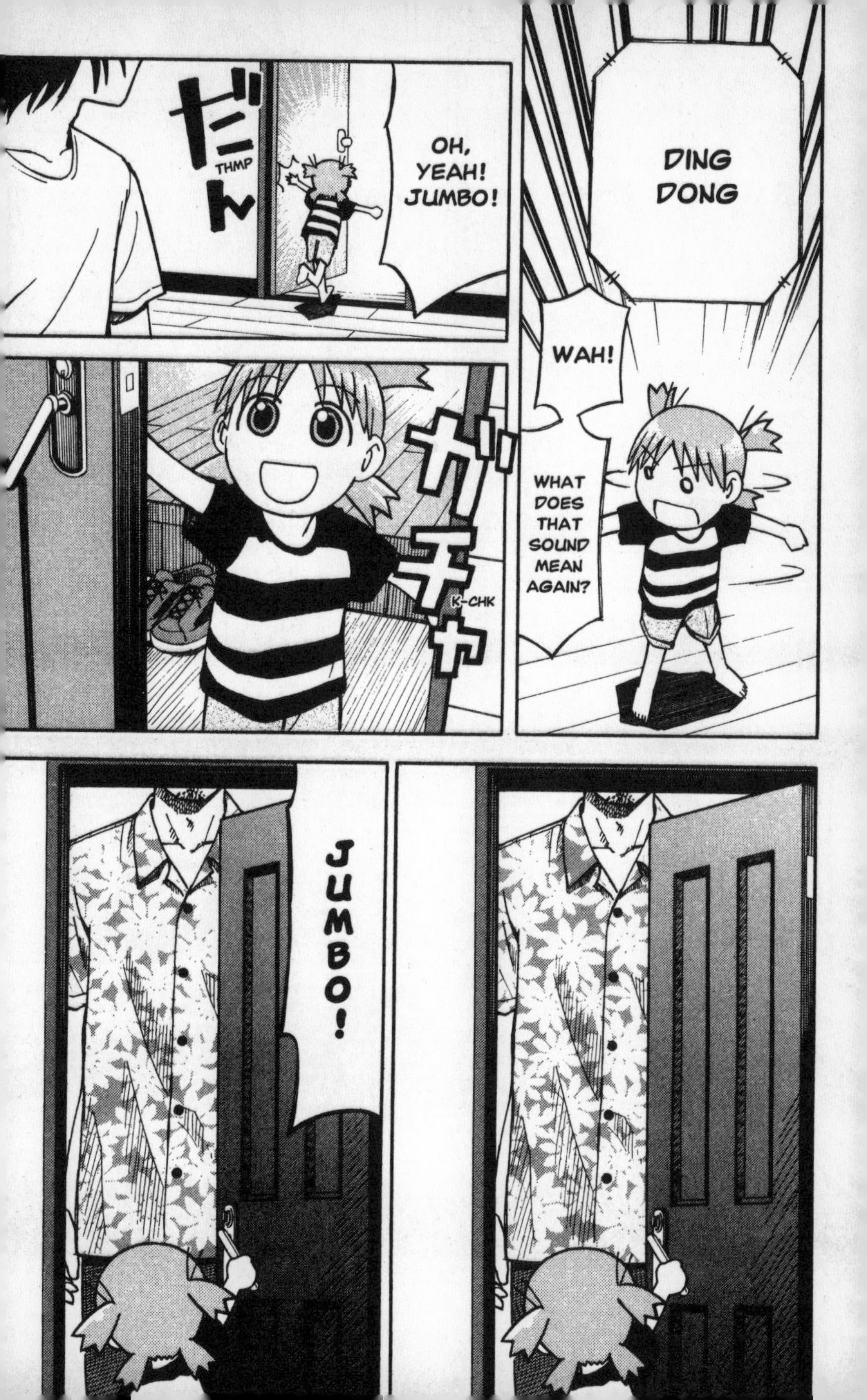
DING DONG
WAH!
WHAT DOES THAT SOUND MEAN AGAIN?
OH, YEAH! JUMBO!
THMP
K-CHK
JUMBO!

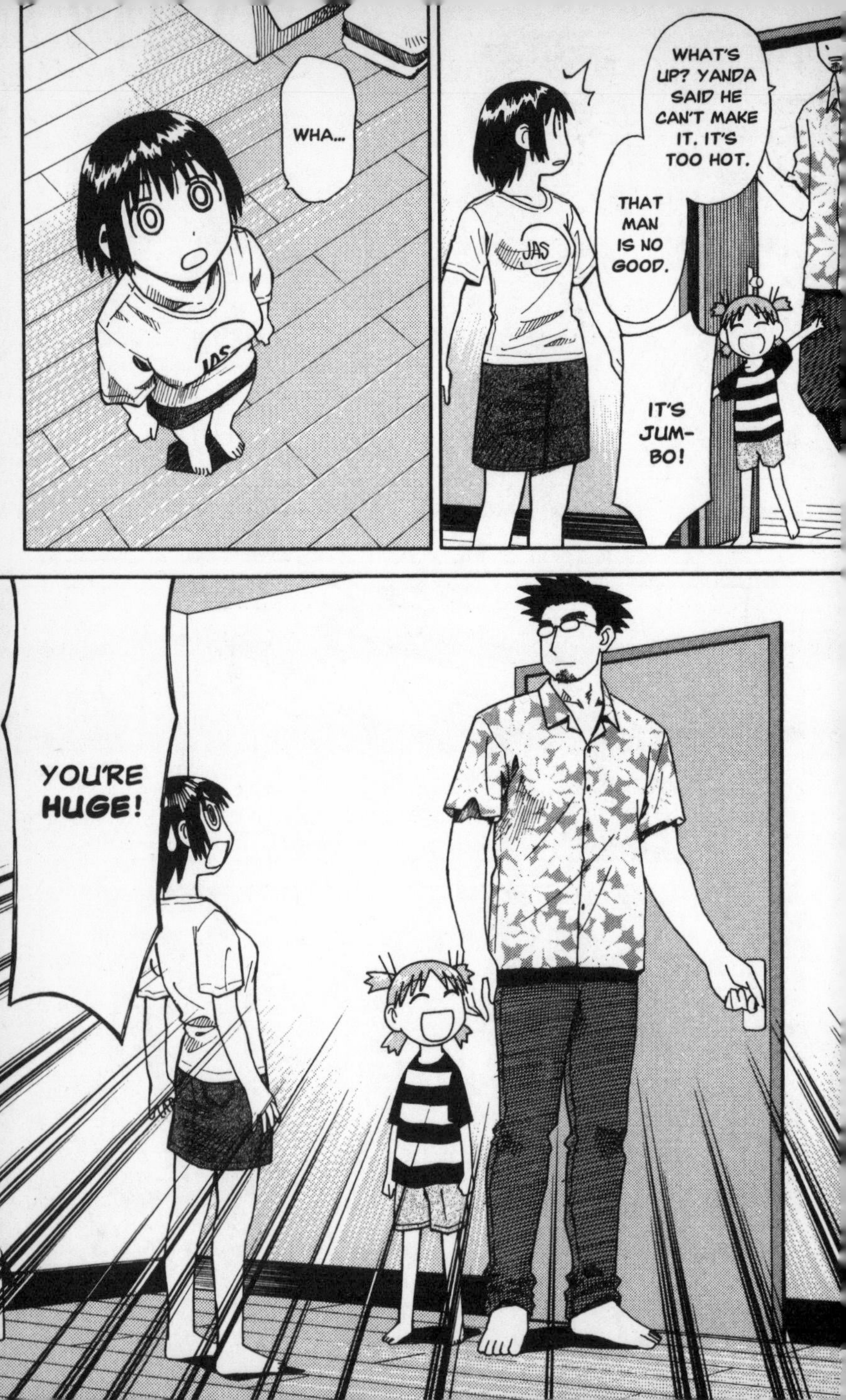
WHAT'S UP? YANDA SAID HE CAN'T MAKE IT. IT'S TOO HOT.
THAT MAN IS NO GOOD.
IT'S JUM-BO!
WHA...
YOU'RE HUGE!

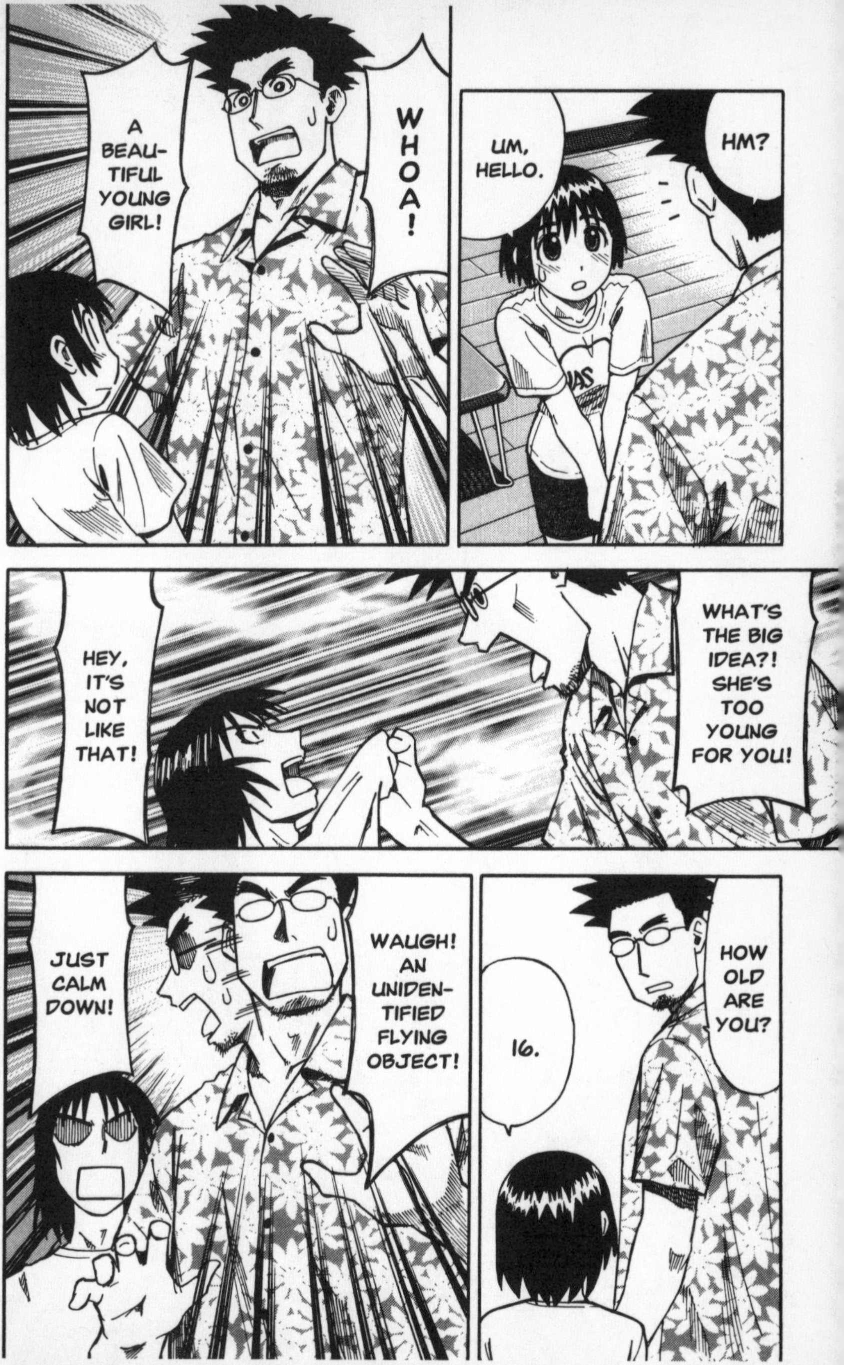
HM?
UM, HELLO.
WHOA!
A BEAUTIFUL YOUNG GIRL!
WHAT'S THE BIG IDEA?! SHE'S TOO YOUNG FOR YOU!
HEY, IT'S NOT LIKE THAT!
HOW OLD ARE YOU?
16.
WAUGH! AN UNIDENTIFIED FLYING OBJECT!
JUST CALM DOWN!

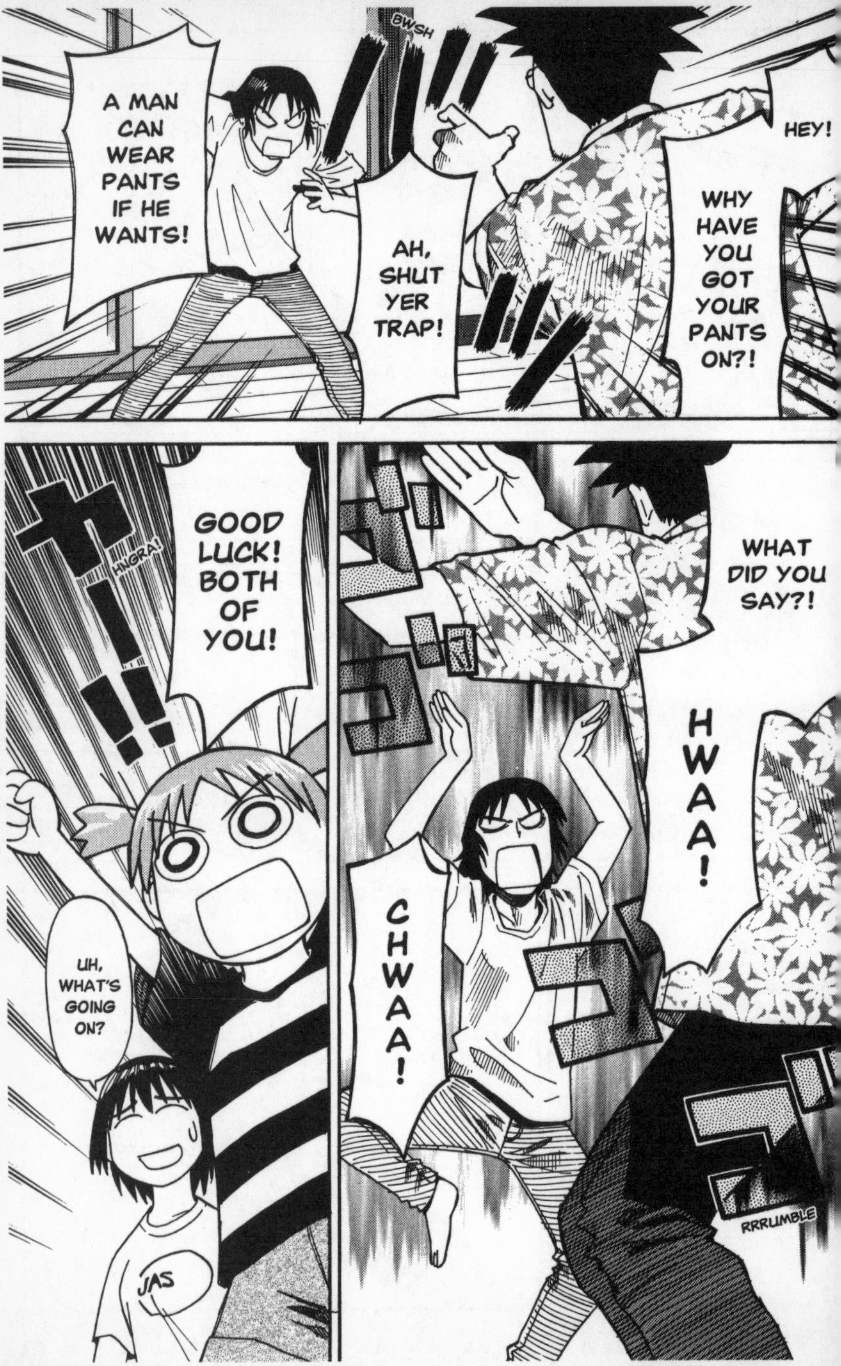
HEY!
WHY HAVE YOU GOT YOUR PANTS ON?!
BWSH
AH, SHUT YER TRAP!
A MAN CAN WEAR PANTS IF HE WANTS!
WHAT DID YOU SAY?!
HWAA!
CHWAA!
RRRUMBLE
GOOD LUCK! BOTH OF YOU!
HNGRA!
UH, WHAT'S GOING ON?
JAS

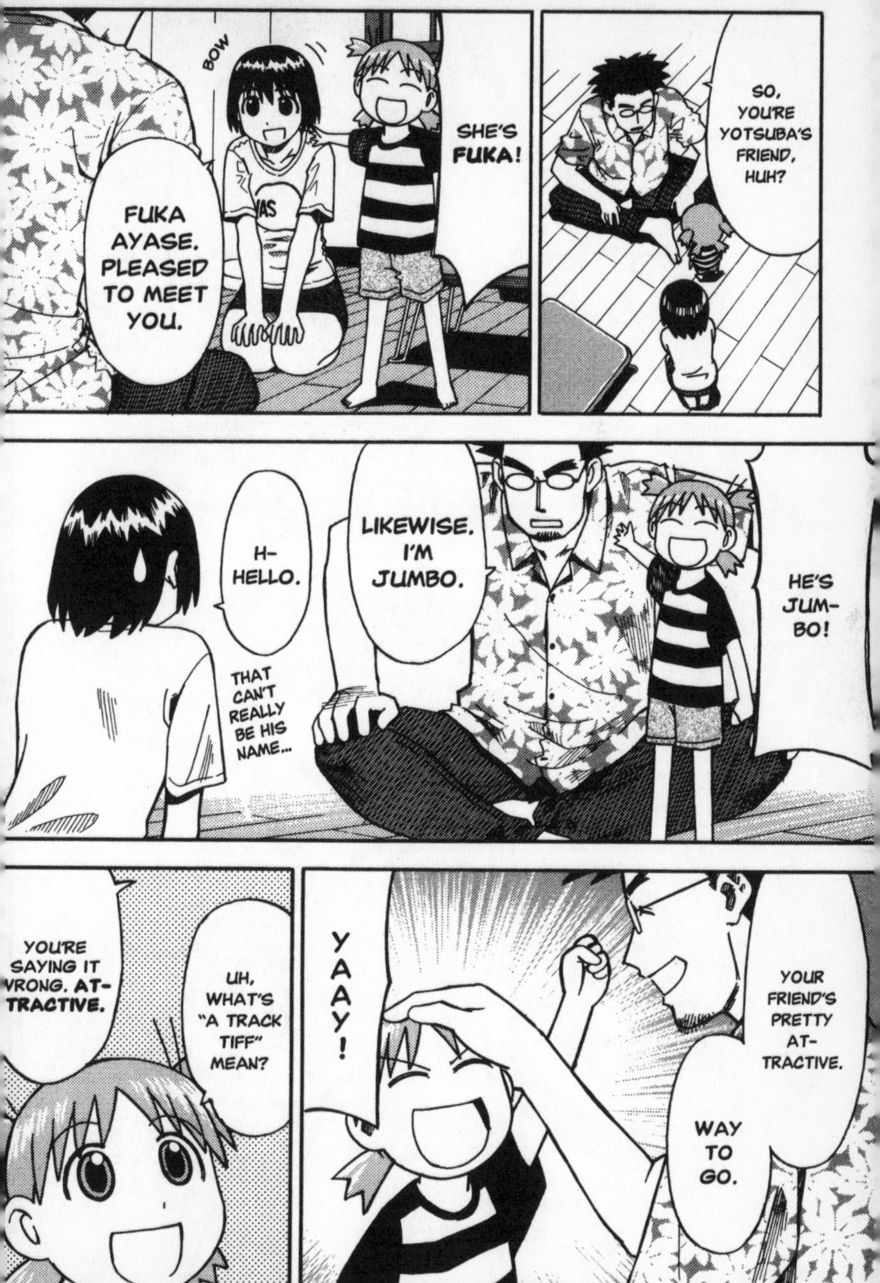
SO, YOU'RE YOTSUBA'S FRIEND, HUH?
SHE'S **FUKA!**
BOW
FUKA AYASE. PLEASED TO MEET YOU.
HE'S JUMBO!
LIKEWISE. I'M JUMBO.
H- HELLO.
THAT CAN'T REALLY BE HIS NAME...
YOUR FRIEND'S PRETTY AT-TRACTIVE.
WAY TO GO.
YAAAY!
UH, WHAT'S "A TRACK TIFF" MEAN?
YOU'RE SAYING IT WRONG. AT-TRACTIVE.

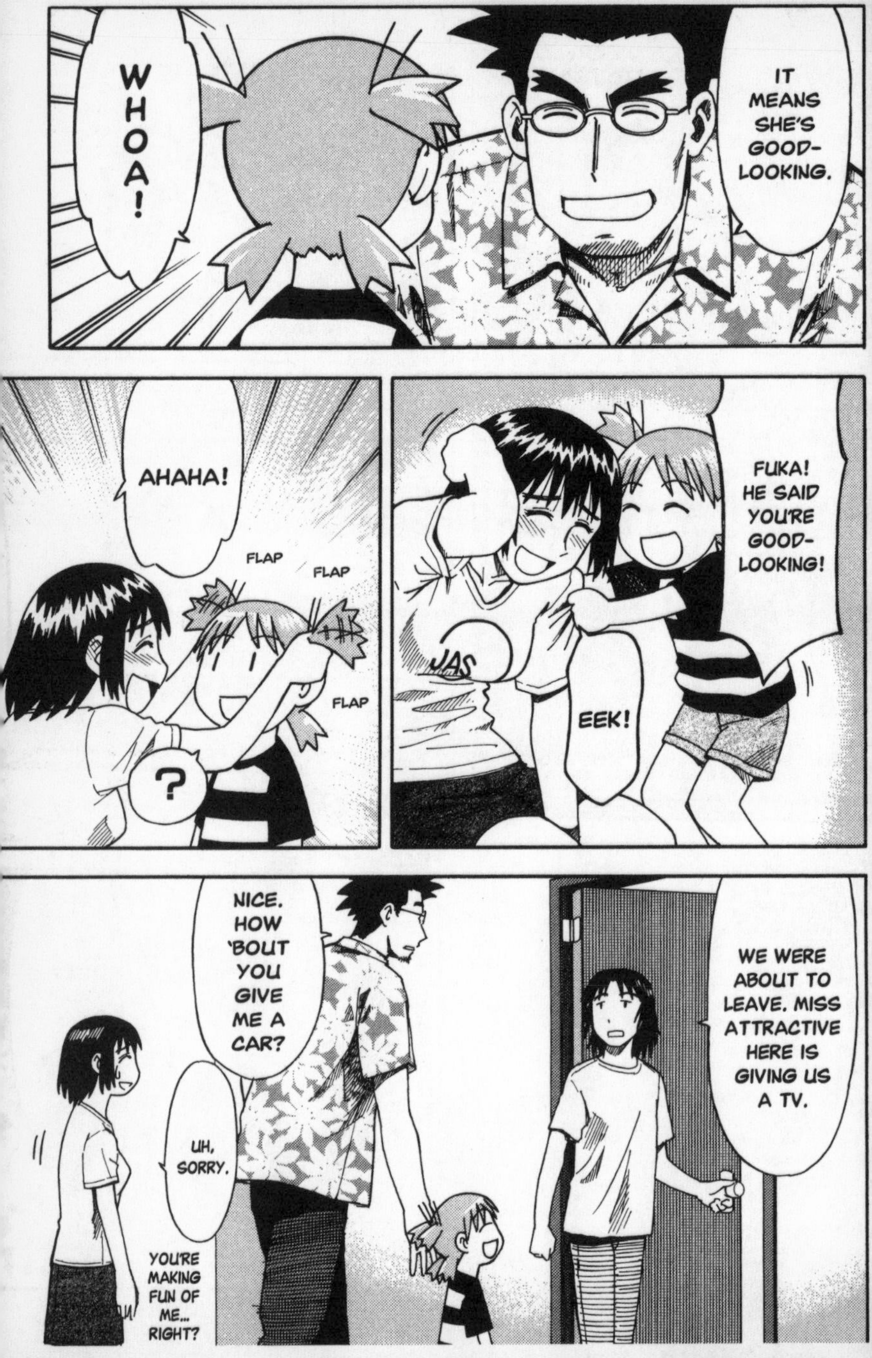
IT MEANS SHE'S GOOD-LOOKING.
WHOA!
FUKA! HE SAID YOU'RE GOOD-LOOKING!
JAS
EEK!
AHAHA!
FLAP
FLAP
FLAP
?
WE WERE ABOUT TO LEAVE. MISS ATTRACTIVE HERE IS GIVING US A TV.
NICE. HOW 'BOUT YOU GIVE ME A CAR?
UH, SORRY.
YOU'RE MAKING FUN OF ME... RIGHT?

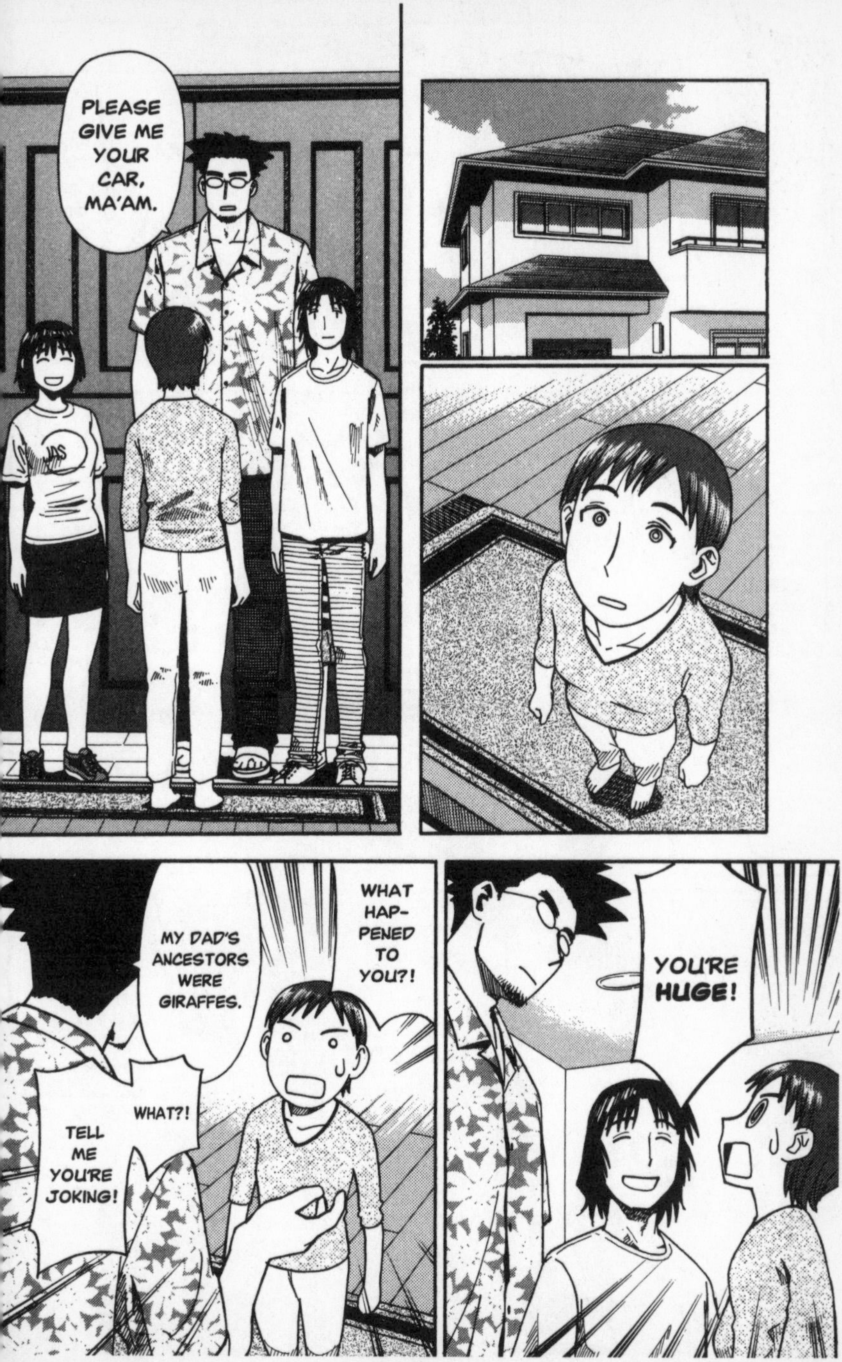
PLEASE GIVE ME YOUR CAR, MA'AM.
YOU'RE HUGE!
WHAT HAP-PENED TO YOU?!
MY DAD'S ANCESTORS WERE GIRAFFES.
WHAT?!
TELL ME YOU'RE JOKING!

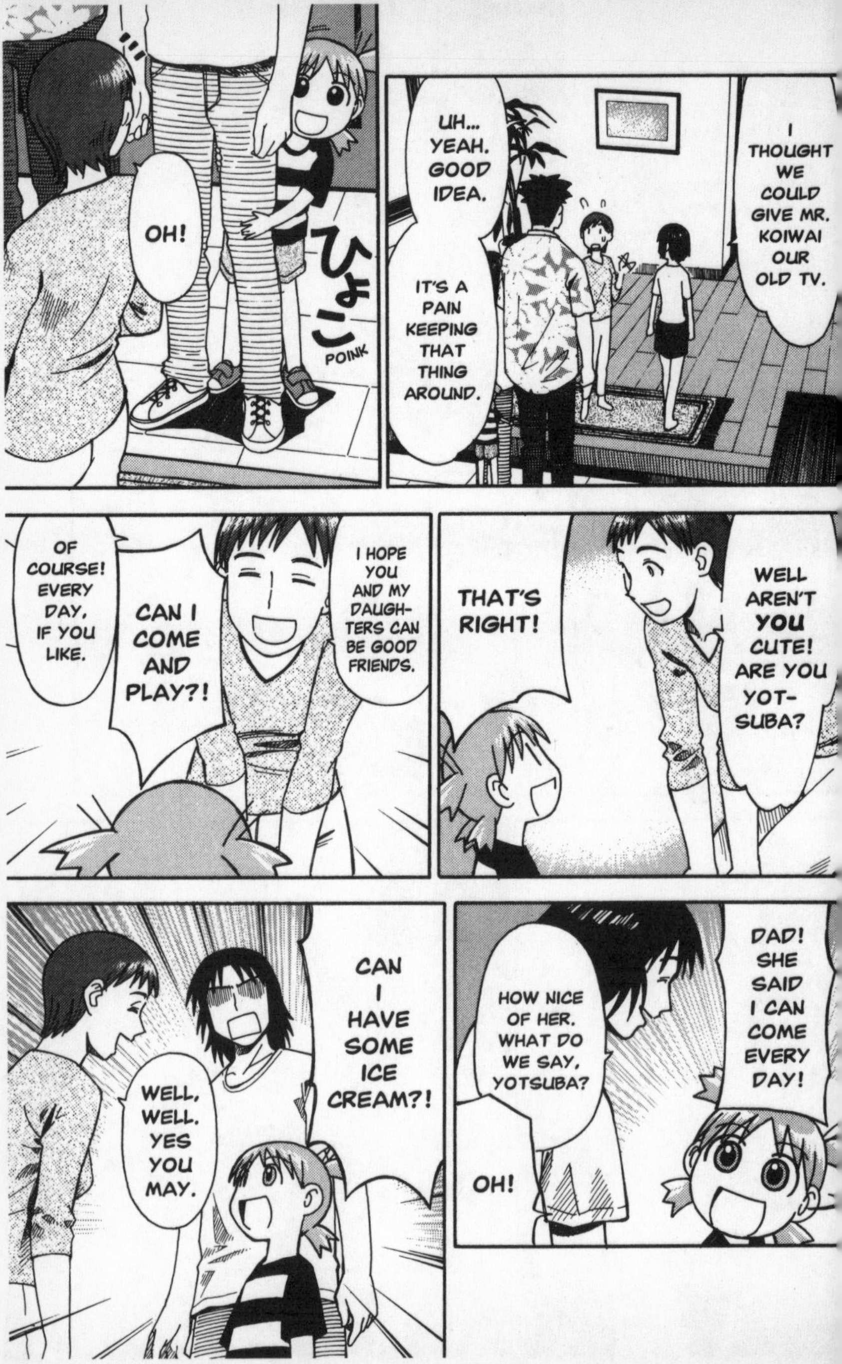
I THOUGHT WE COULD GIVE MR. KOIWAI OUR OLD TV.
UH... YEAH. GOOD IDEA.
IT'S A PAIN KEEPING THAT THING AROUND.
ひょこ
POINK
OH!
WELL AREN'T YOU CUTE! ARE YOU YOT-SUBA?
THAT'S RIGHT!
I HOPE YOU AND MY DAUGH-TERS CAN BE GOOD FRIENDS.
CAN I COME AND PLAY?!
OF COURSE! EVERY DAY, IF YOU LIKE.
DAD! SHE SAID I CAN COME EVERY DAY!
HOW NICE OF HER. WHAT DO WE SAY, YOTSUBA?
OH!
CAN I HAVE SOME ICE CREAM?!
WELL, WELL. YES YOU MAY.

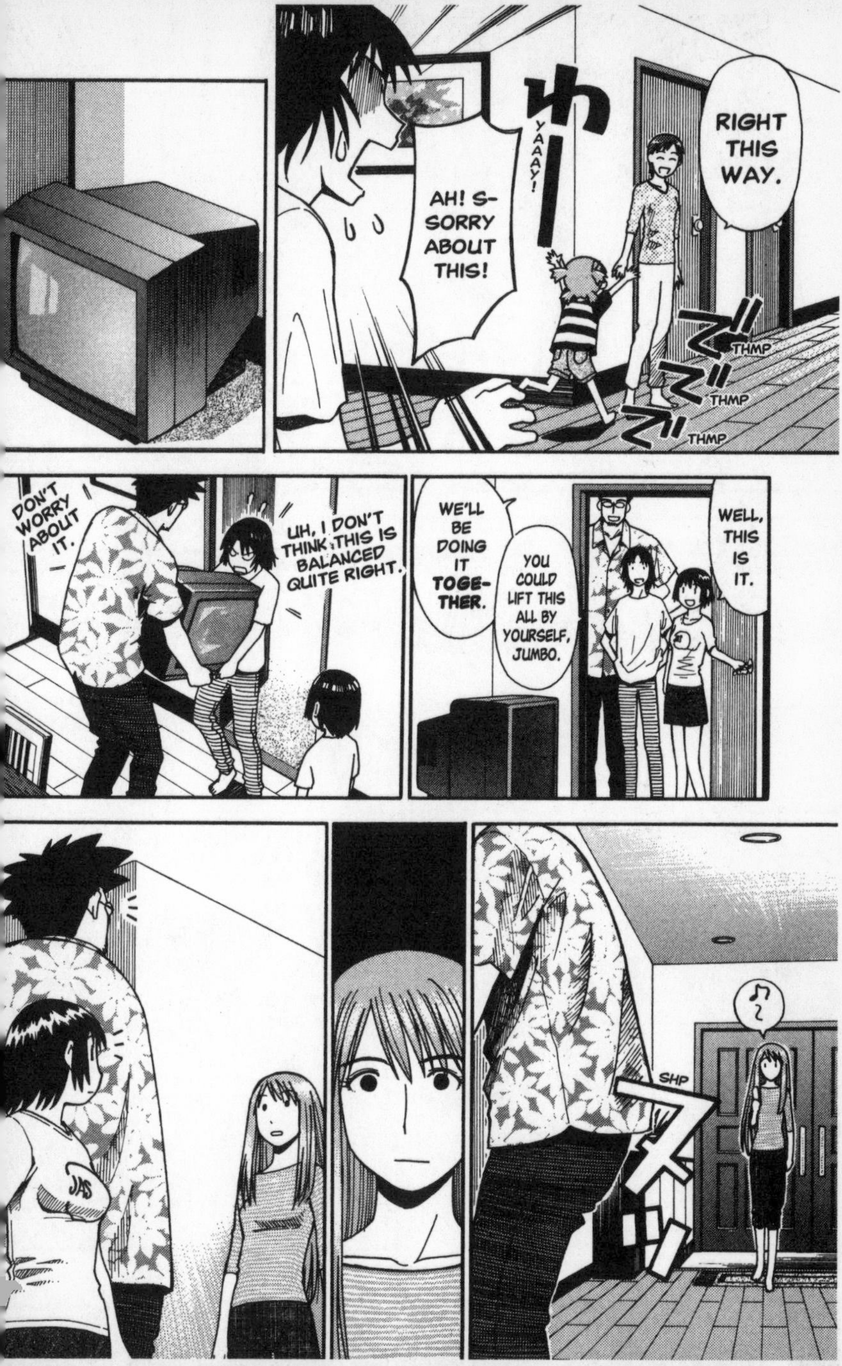
RIGHT THIS WAY.
YAAAAY!
AH! S-SORRY ABOUT THIS!
THMP
THMP
THMP
WELL, THIS IS IT.
YOU COULD LIFT THIS ALL BY YOURSELF, JUMBO.
WE'LL BE DOING IT TOGETHER.
UH, I DON'T THINK THIS IS BALANCED QUITE RIGHT.
DON'T WORRY ABOUT IT.
♪
SHP

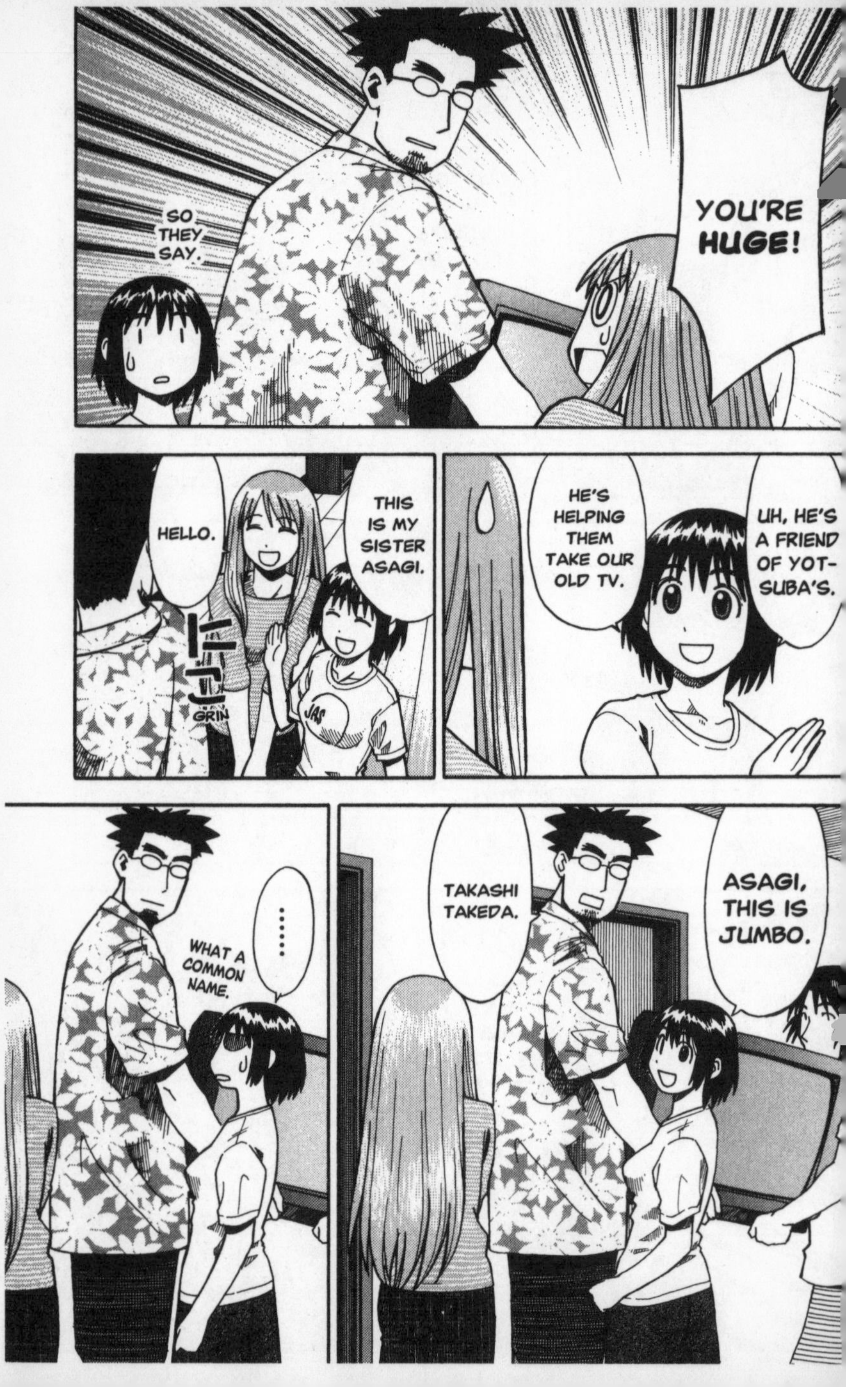
YOU'RE **HUGE!**
SO THEY SAY.
UH, HE'S A FRIEND OF YOT-SUBA'S.
HE'S HELPING THEM TAKE OUR OLD TV.
THIS IS MY SISTER ASAGI.
HELLO.
GRIN
ASAGI, THIS IS JUMBO.
TAKASHI TAKEDA.
......
WHAT A COMMON NAME.

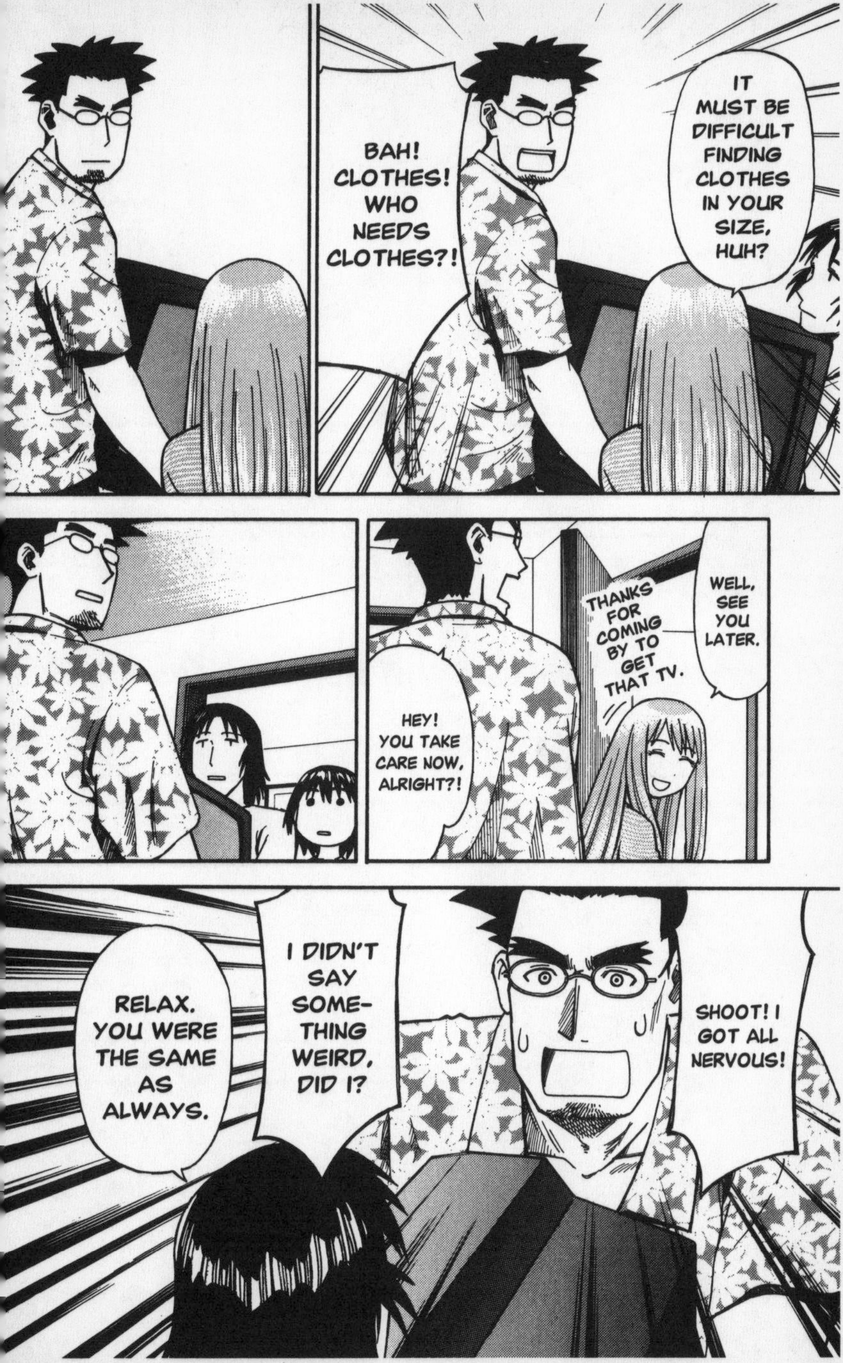
IT MUST BE DIFFICULT FINDING CLOTHES IN YOUR SIZE, HUH?
BAH! CLOTHES! WHO NEEDS CLOTHES?!
WELL, SEE YOU LATER.
THANKS FOR COMING BY TO GET THAT TV.
HEY! YOU TAKE CARE NOW, ALRIGHT?!
SHOOT!! I GOT ALL NERVOUS!
I DIDN'T SAY SOMETHING WEIRD, DID I?
RELAX. YOU WERE THE SAME AS ALWAYS.

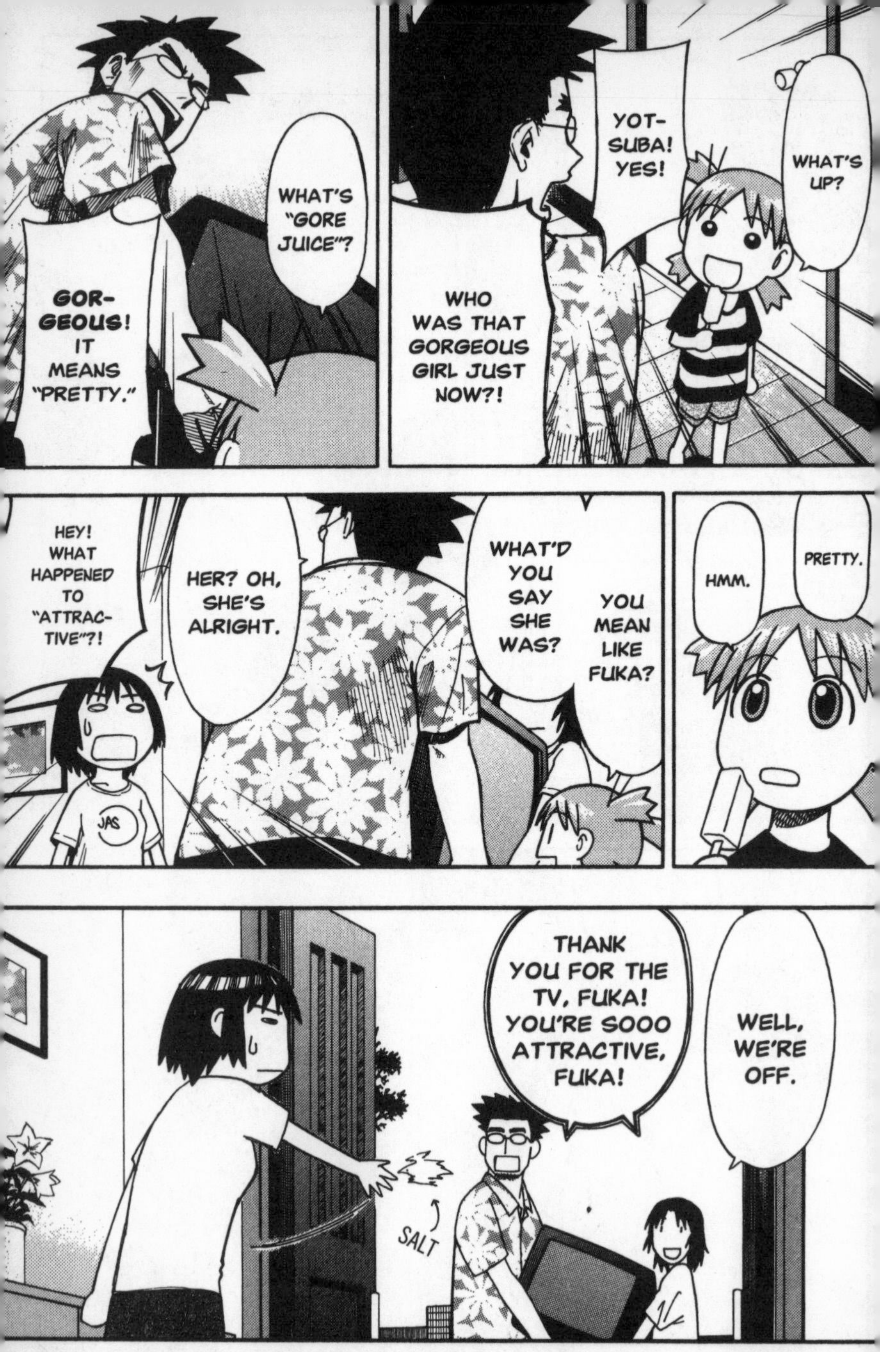
WHAT'S UP?
YOT-SUBA! YES!
WHO WAS THAT GORGEOUS GIRL JUST NOW?!
WHAT'S "GORE JUICE"?
GORGEOUS! IT MEANS "PRETTY."
PRETTY.
HMM.
YOU MEAN LIKE FUKA?
WHAT'D YOU SAY SHE WAS?
HER? OH, SHE'S ALRIGHT.
HEY! WHAT HAPPENED TO "ATTRACTIVE"?!
WELL, WE'RE OFF.
THANK YOU FOR THE TV, FUKA! YOU'RE SOOO ATTRACTIVE, FUKA!
SALT

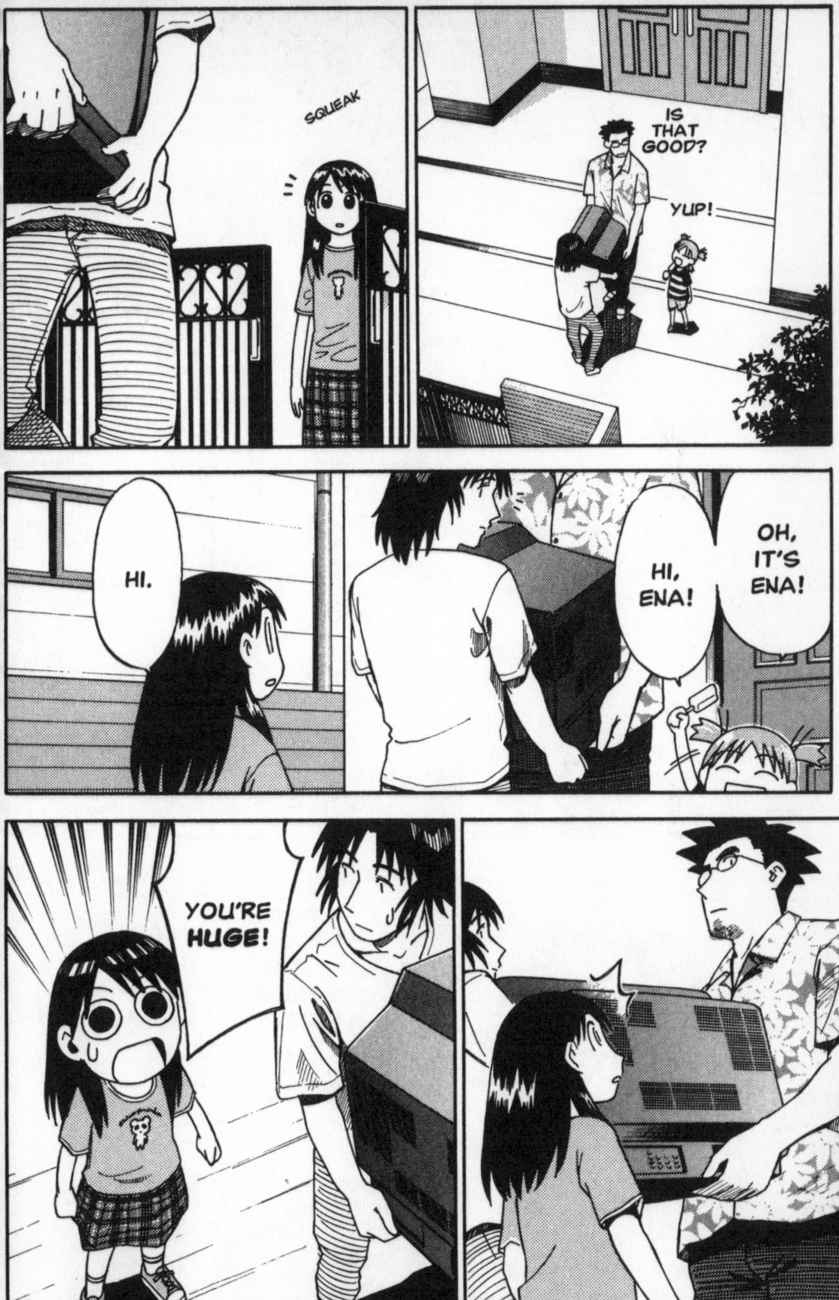
IS THAT GOOD?
YUP!
SQUEAK
OH, IT'S ENA!
HI, ENA!
HI.
YOU'RE HUGE!

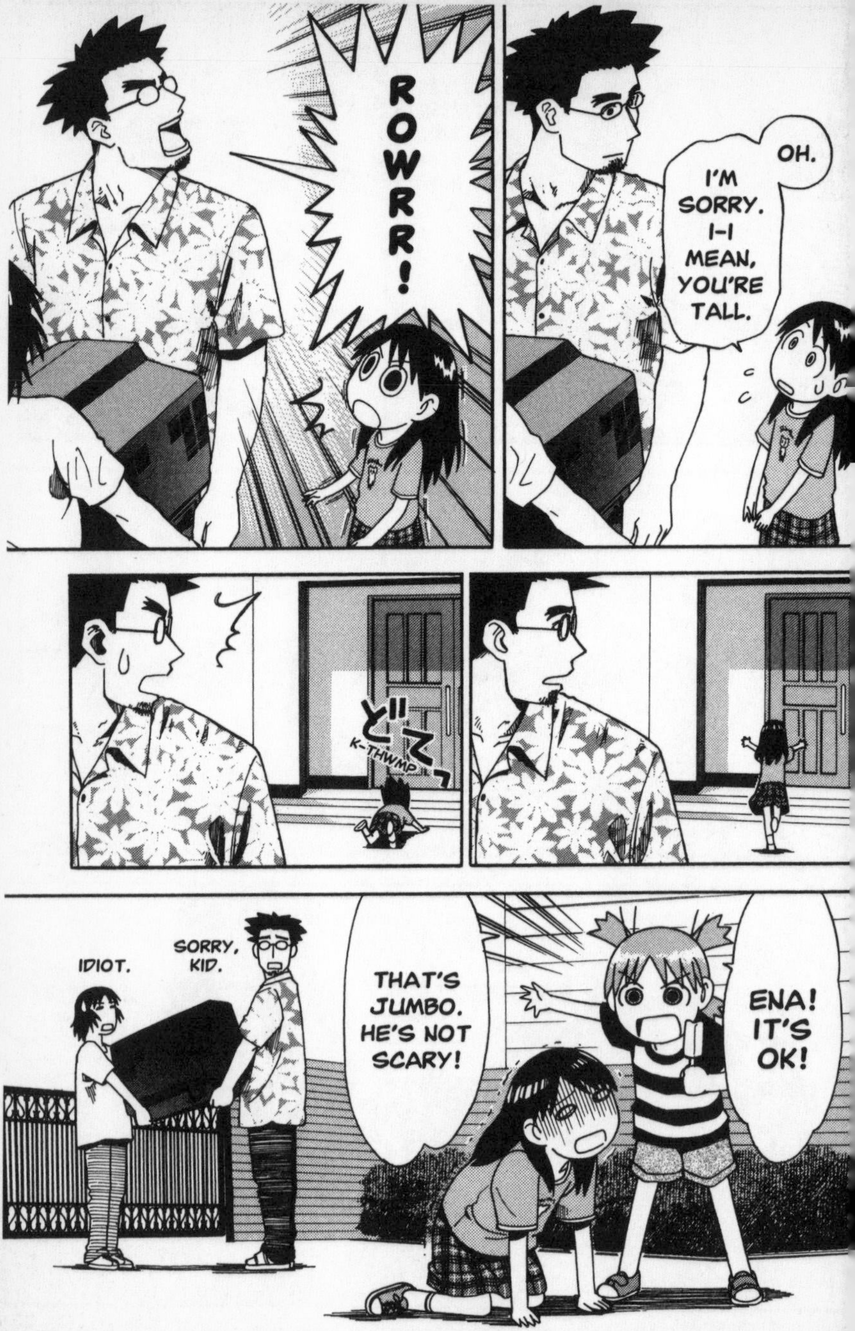
OH.
I'M SORRY. I-I MEAN, YOU'RE TALL.
ROWRR!
K-THWMP
ENA! IT'S OK!
THAT'S JUMBO. HE'S NOT SCARY!
SORRY, KID.
IDIOT.

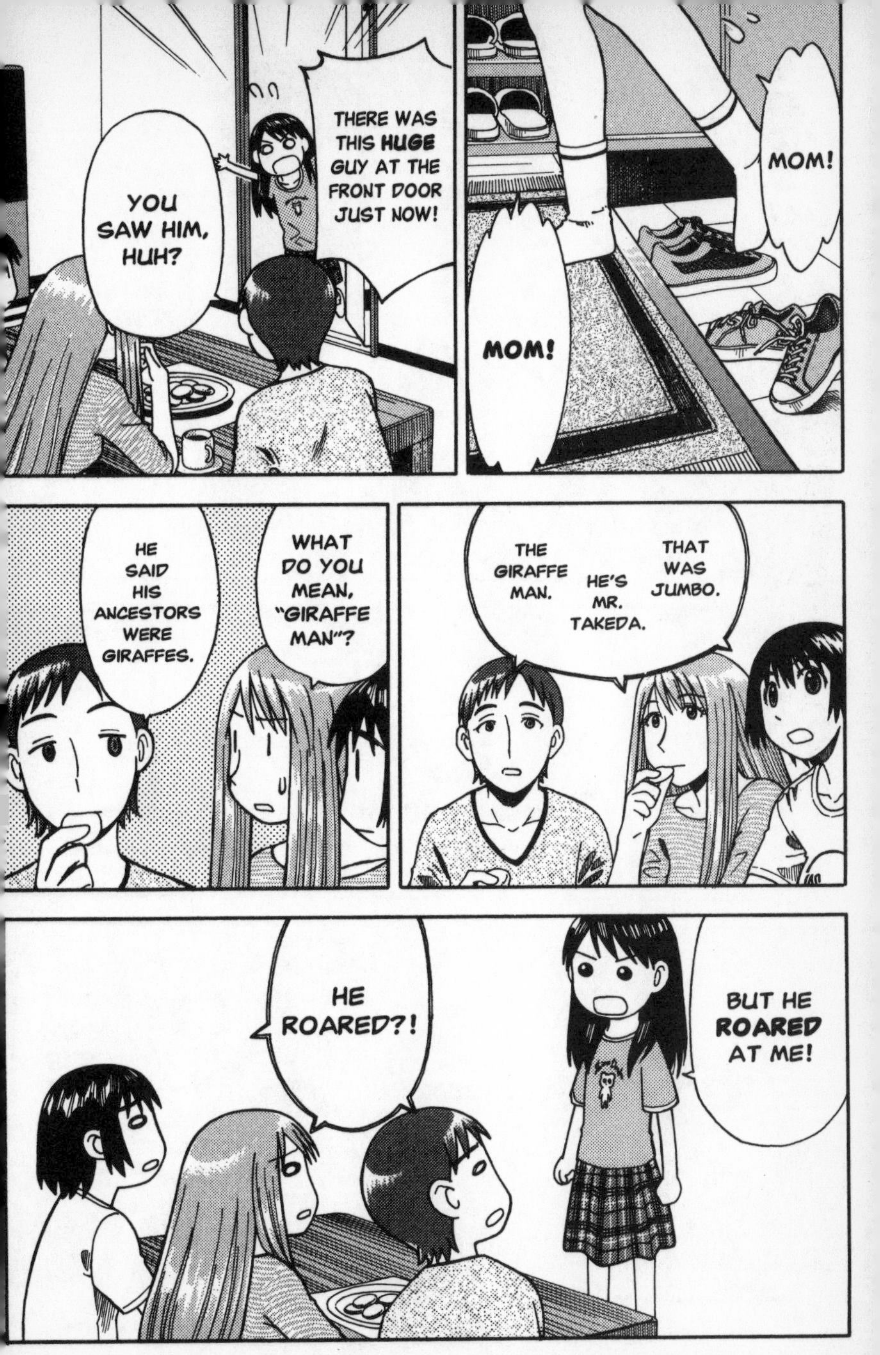
MOM!
MOM!
THERE WAS THIS HUGE GUY AT THE FRONT DOOR JUST NOW!
YOU SAW HIM, HUH?
THAT WAS JUMBO.
HE'S MR. TAKEDA.
THE GIRAFFE MAN.
WHAT DO YOU MEAN, "GIRAFFE MAN"?
HE SAID HIS ANCESTORS WERE GIRAFFES.
BUT HE ROARED AT ME!
HE ROARED?!

YOTSUBA & SHOPPING

CHAPTER 5

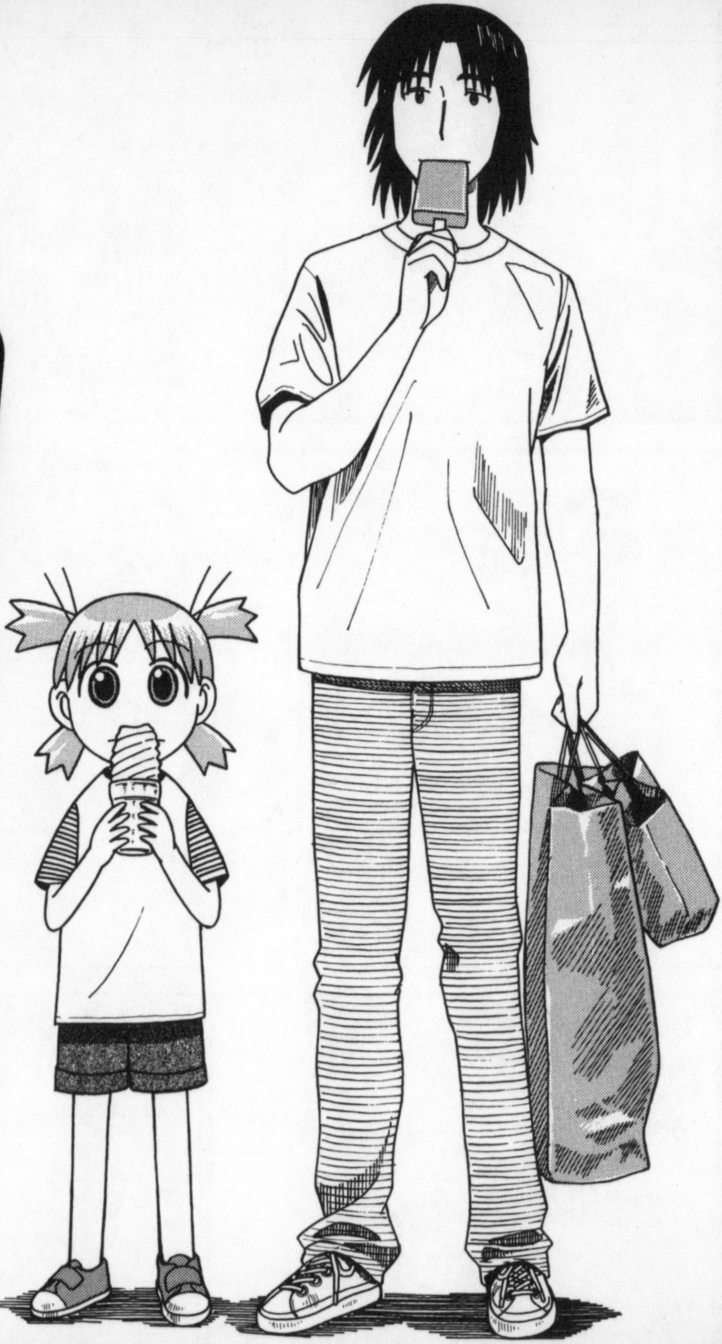

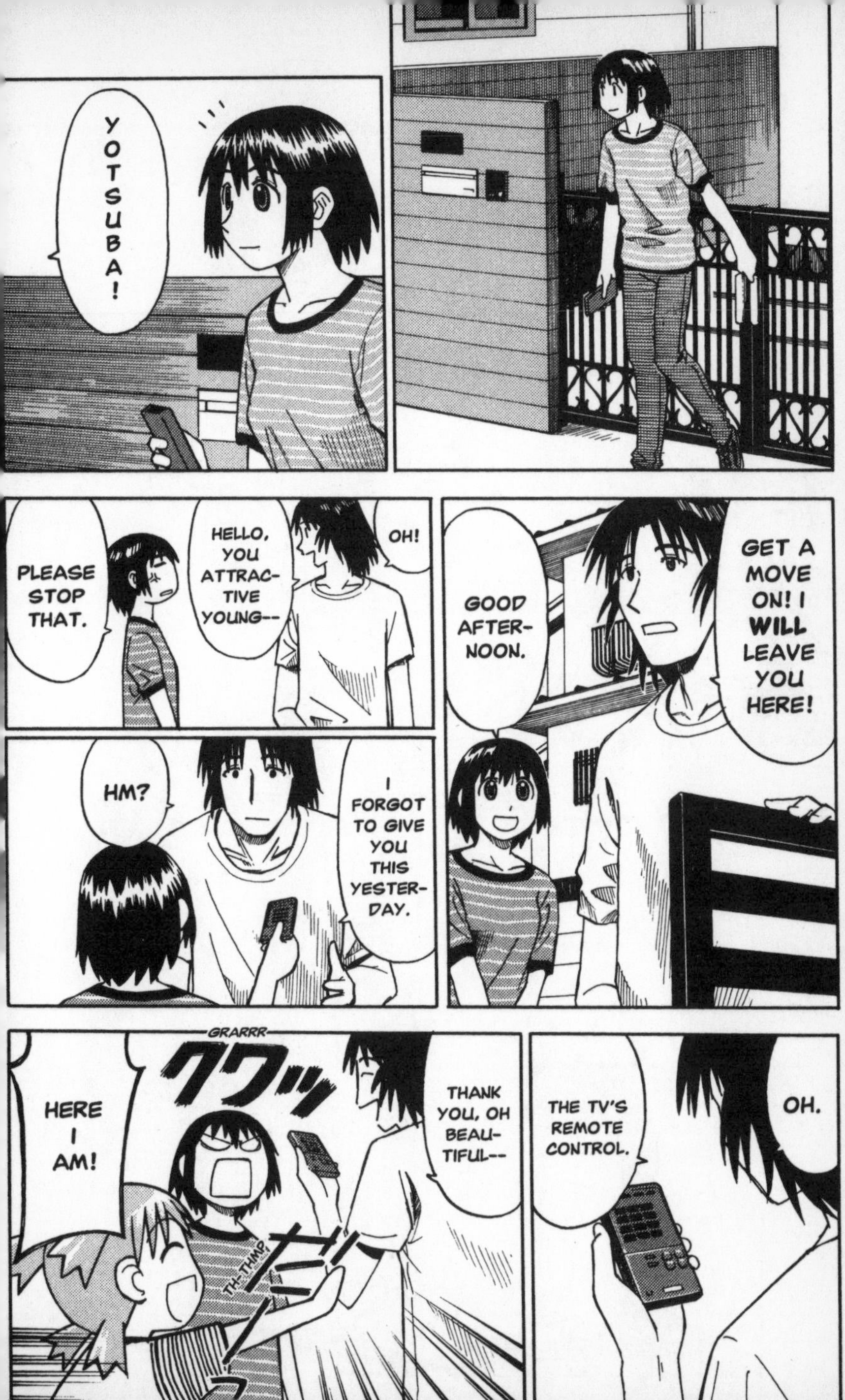
YOTSUBA!
GET A MOVE ON! I WILL LEAVE YOU HERE!
GOOD AFTERNOON.
OH!
HELLO, YOU ATTRACTIVE YOUNG--
PLEASE STOP THAT.
I FORGOT TO GIVE YOU THIS YESTERDAY.
HM?
OH.
THE TV'S REMOTE CONTROL.
THANK YOU, OH BEAUTIFUL--
GRARRR
HERE I AM!
TH-THMP

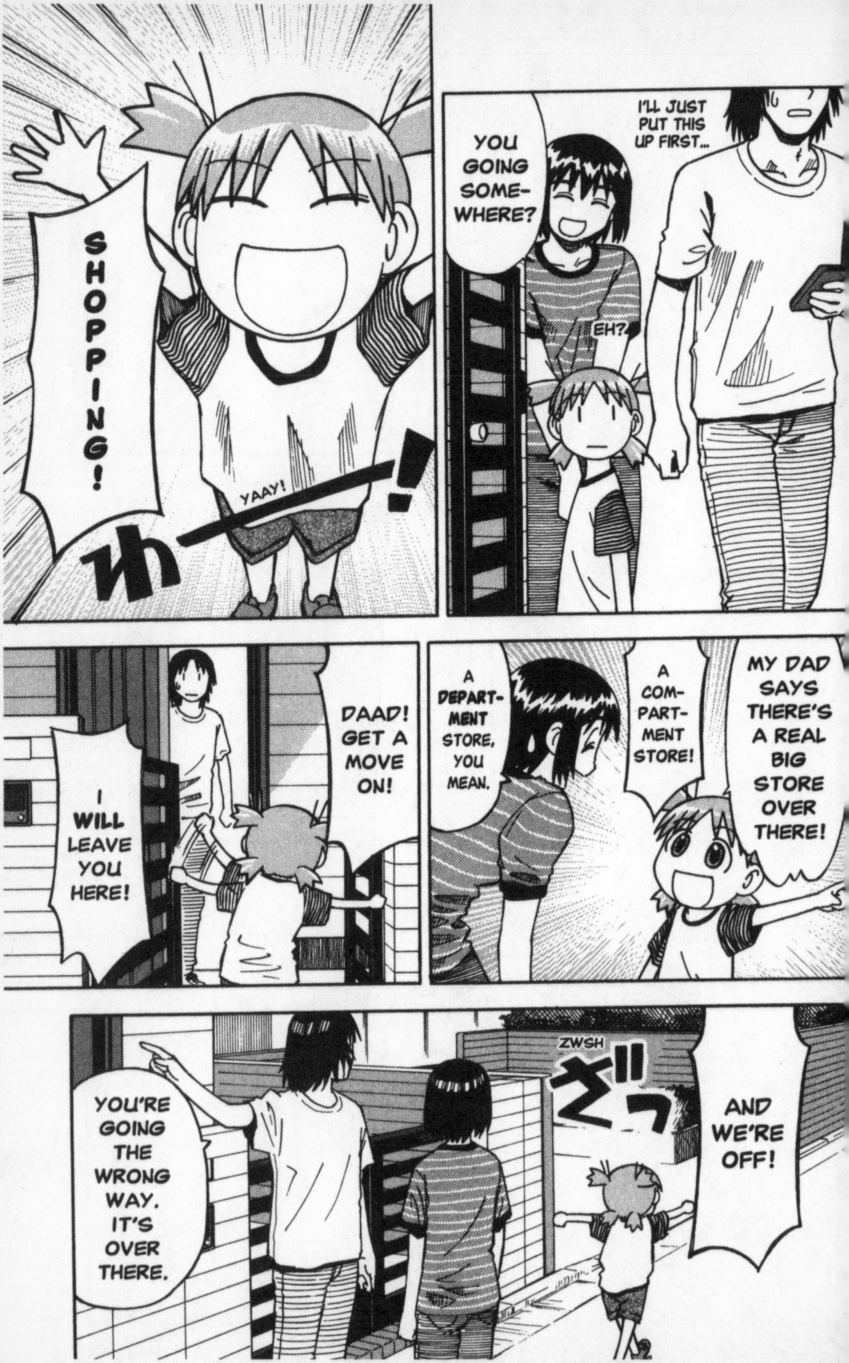
I'LL JUST PUT THIS UP FIRST...
YOU GOING SOMEWHERE?
EH?
SHOPPING!
YAAY!
わー!
MY DAD SAYS THERE'S A REAL BIG STORE OVER THERE!
A COMPARTMENT STORE!
A DEPARTMENT STORE, YOU MEAN.
DAAD! GET A MOVE ON!
I WILL LEAVE YOU HERE!
AND WE'RE OFF!
ZWSH
ざっ
YOU'RE GOING THE WRONG WAY. IT'S OVER THERE.

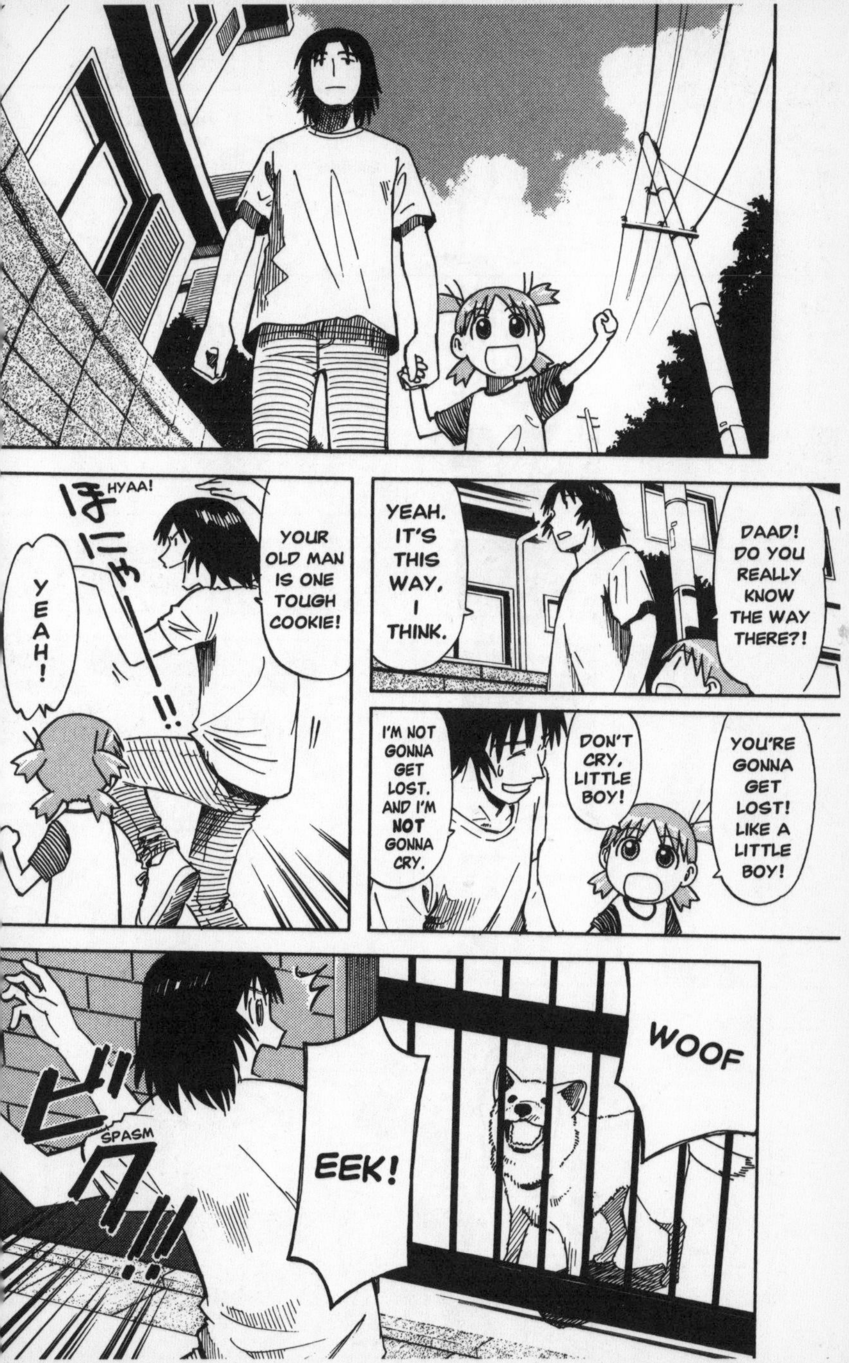
DAAD! DO YOU REALLY KNOW THE WAY THERE?!
YEAH. IT'S THIS WAY, I THINK.
YOU'RE GONNA GET LOST! LIKE A LITTLE BOY!
DON'T CRY, LITTLE BOY!
I'M NOT GONNA GET LOST. AND I'M NOT GONNA CRY.
YOUR OLD MAN IS ONE TOUGH COOKIE!
ほにゃーー!!
HYAA!
YEAH!
WOOF
EEK!
ビクッ!!
SPASM

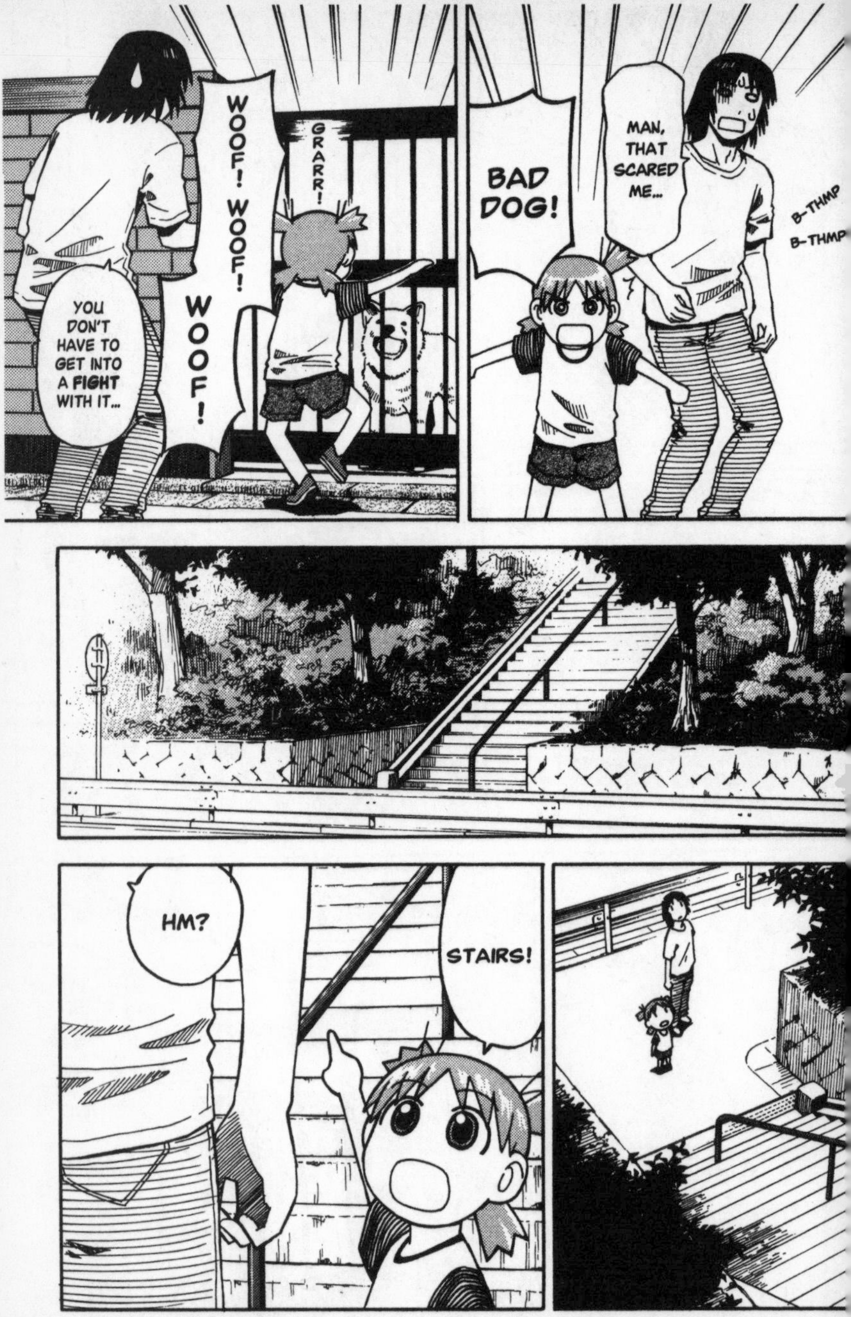
MAN, THAT SCARED ME...
B-THMP
B-THMP
BAD DOG!
GRARR!
WOOF! WOOF!
WOOF!
YOU DON'T HAVE TO GET INTO A **FIGHT** WITH IT...
STAIRS!
HM?

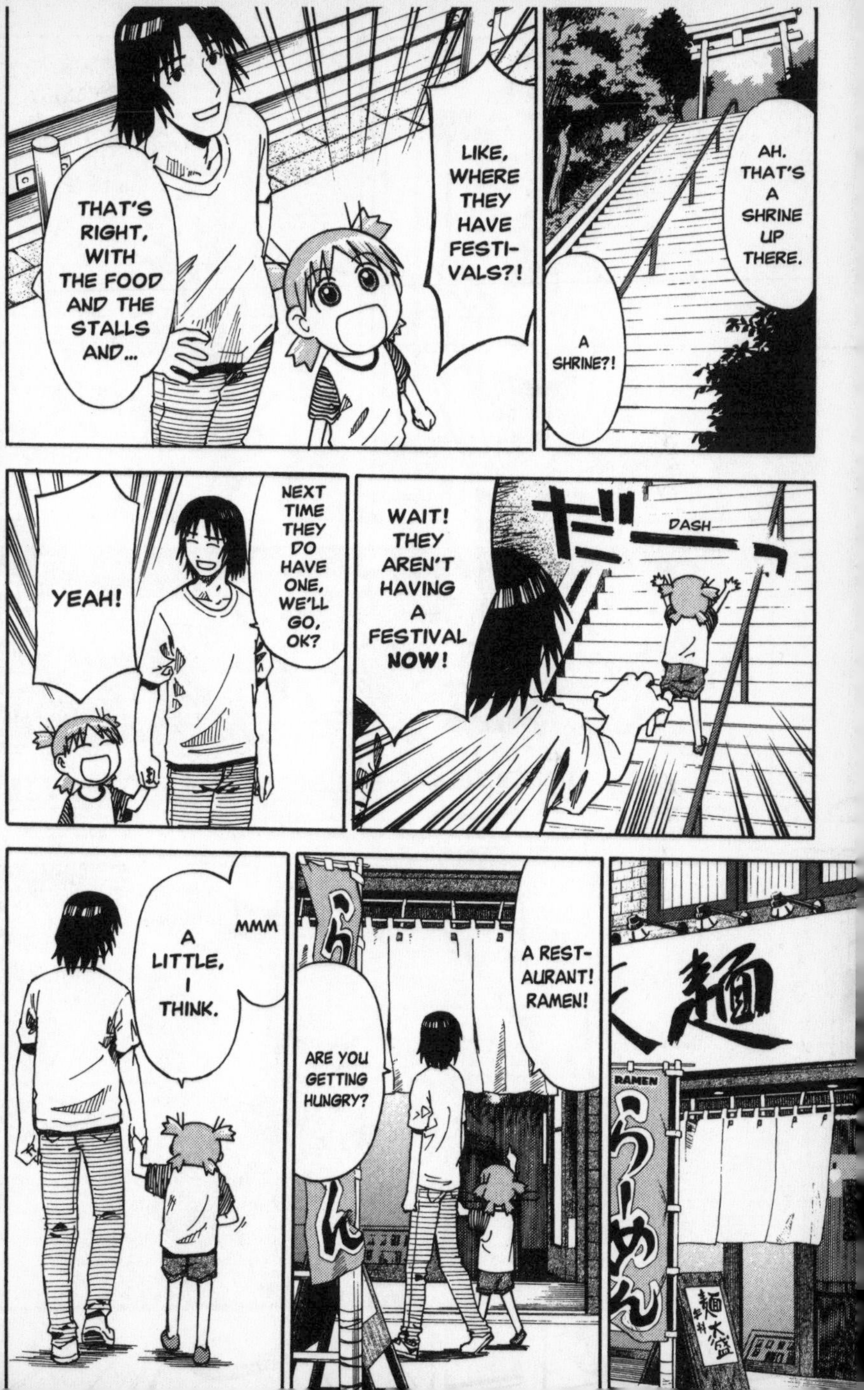
AH. THAT'S A SHRINE UP THERE.
A SHRINE?!
LIKE, WHERE THEY HAVE FESTIVALS?!
THAT'S RIGHT, WITH THE FOOD AND THE STALLS AND...
DASH
WAIT! THEY AREN'T HAVING A FESTIVAL NOW!
NEXT TIME THEY DO HAVE ONE, WE'LL GO, OK?
YEAH!
RAMEN
A RESTAURANT! RAMEN!
ARE YOU GETTING HUNGRY?
MMM
A LITTLE, I THINK.

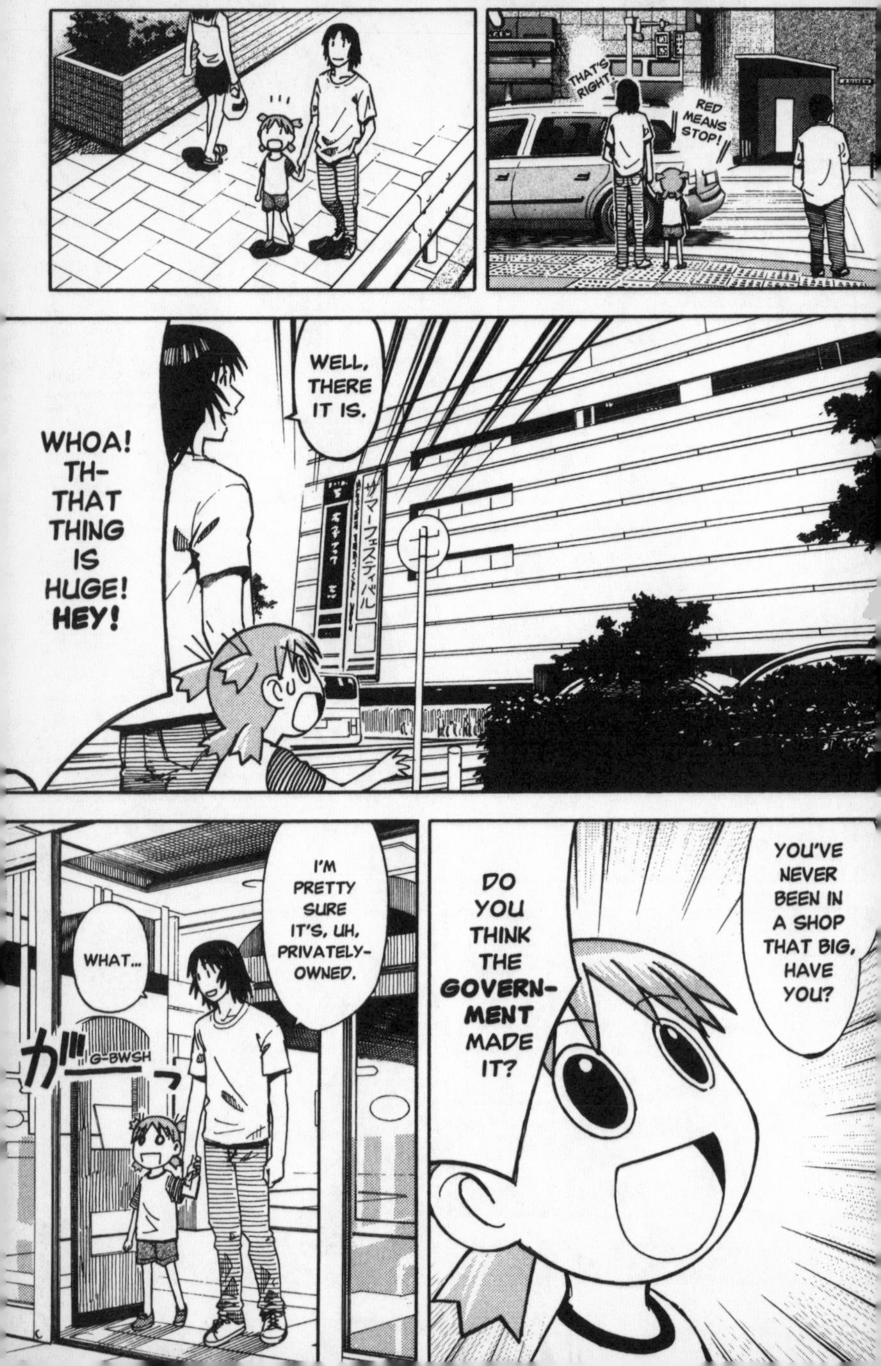
RED MEANS STOP!
THAT'S RIGHT.
WELL, THERE IT IS.
WHOA! TH-THAT THING IS HUGE! HEY!
サマーフェスティバル
YOU'VE NEVER BEEN IN A SHOP THAT BIG, HAVE YOU?
DO YOU THINK THE GOVERNMENT MADE IT?
I'M PRETTY SURE IT'S, UH, PRIVATELY-OWNED.
WHAT...
ガー G-BWSH

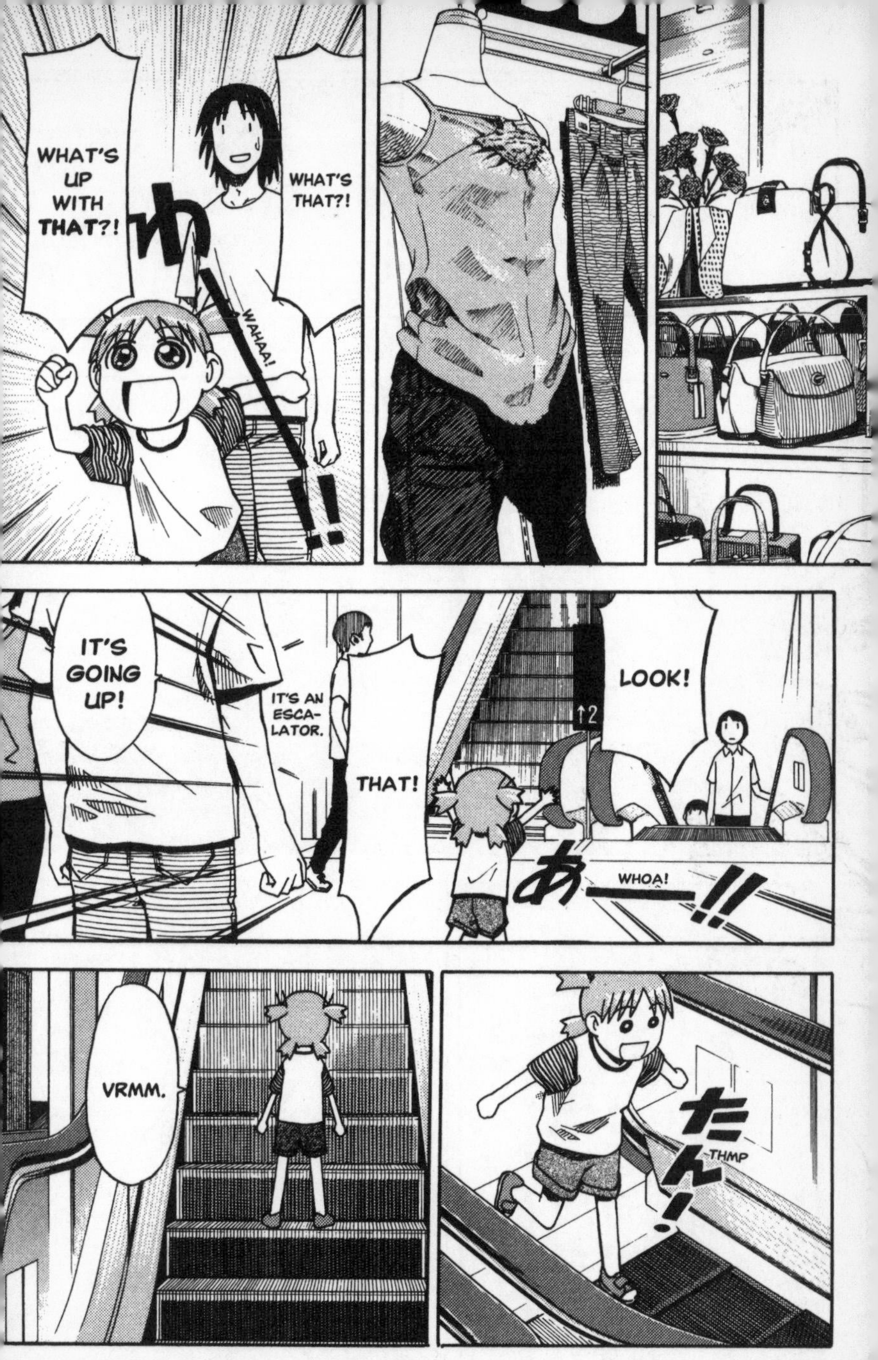
WHAT'S THAT?!
WHAT'S UP WITH THAT?!
わ
WAHAA!
!!
LOOK!
THAT!
IT'S AN ESCALATOR.
IT'S GOING UP!
あー!!
WHOA!
たん!
THMP
VRMM.

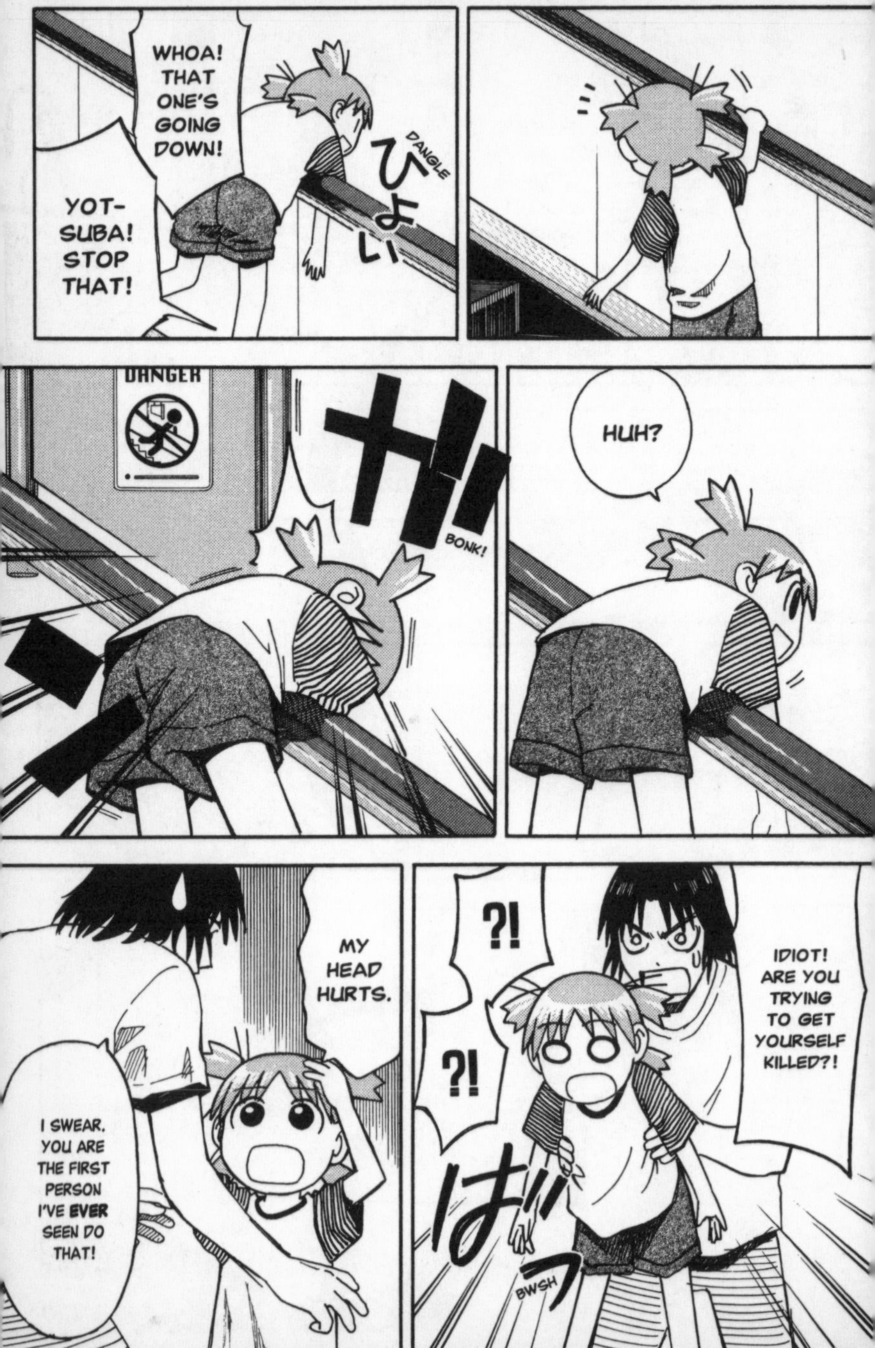
WHOA! THAT ONE'S GOING DOWN!
ひょい
DANGLE
YOT-SUBA! STOP THAT!
HUH?
DANGER
ガッ
BONK!
?!
?!
IDIOT! ARE YOU TRYING TO GET YOURSELF KILLED?!
ばっ
BWSH
MY HEAD HURTS.
I SWEAR. YOU ARE THE FIRST PERSON I'VE EVER SEEN DO THAT!

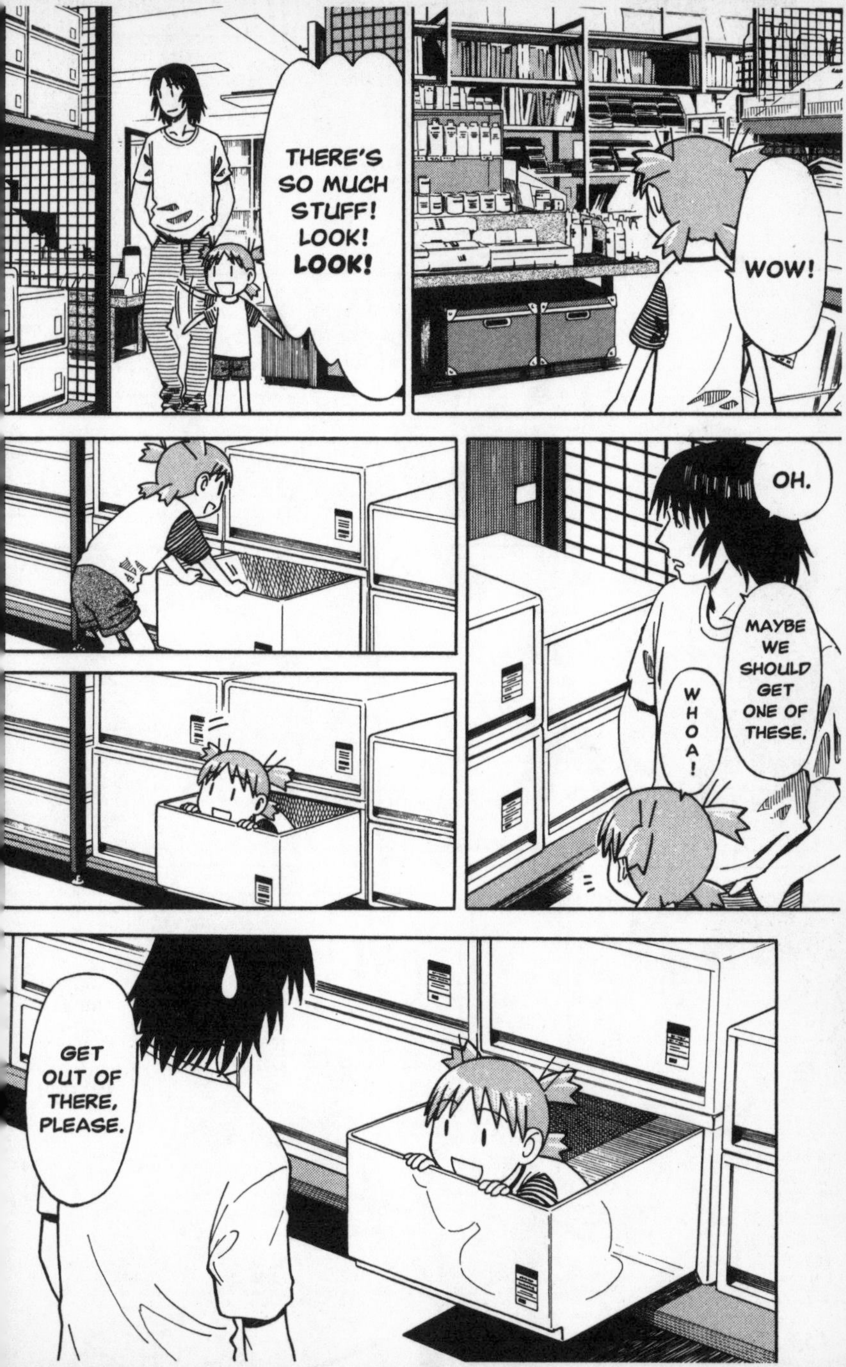
WOW!
THERE'S SO MUCH STUFF! LOOK! LOOK!
OH.
MAYBE WE SHOULD GET ONE OF THESE.
WHOA!
GET OUT OF THERE, PLEASE.

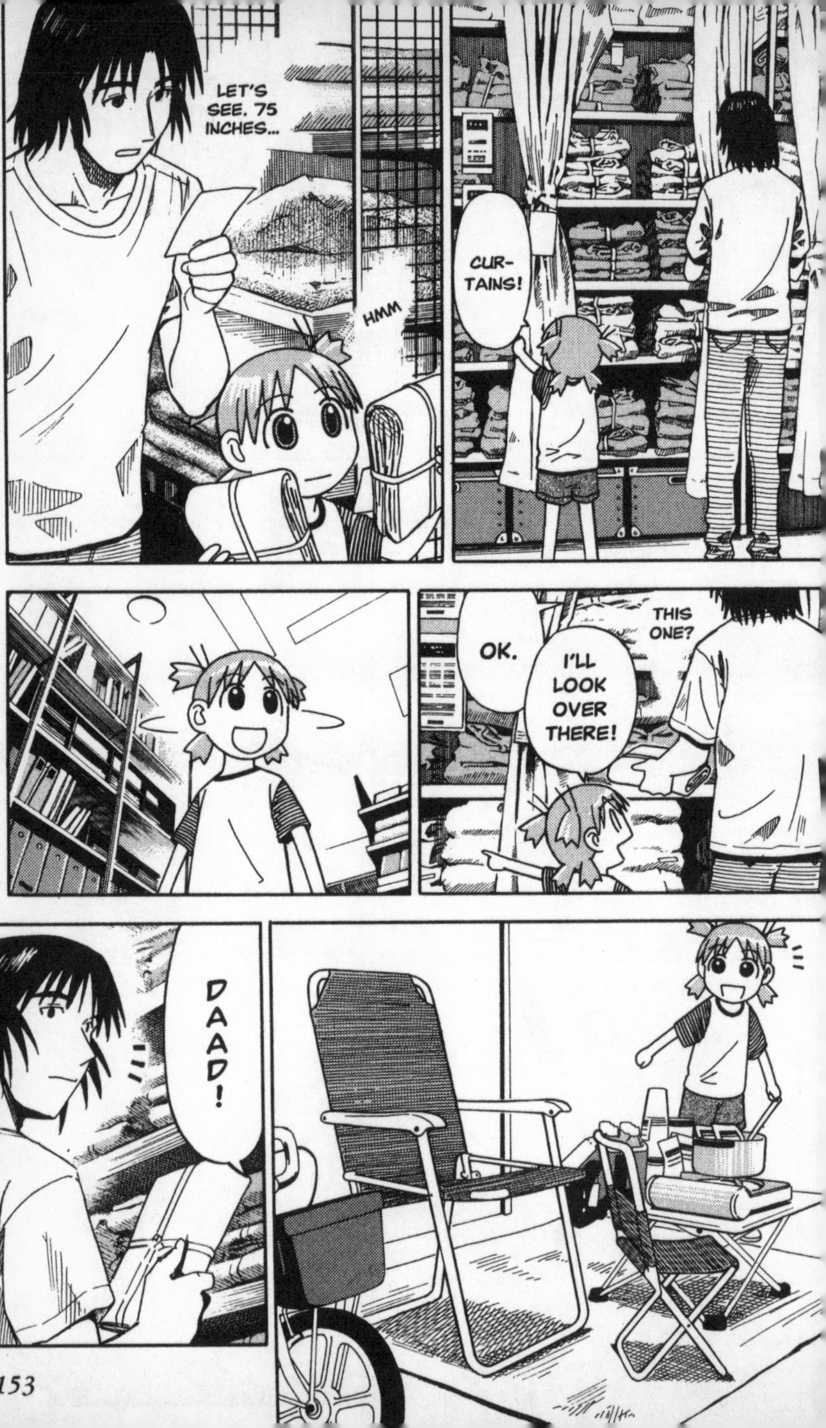
CUR-TAINS!
LET'S SEE. 75 INCHES...
HMM
THIS ONE?
OK.
I'LL LOOK OVER THERE!
DAAD!

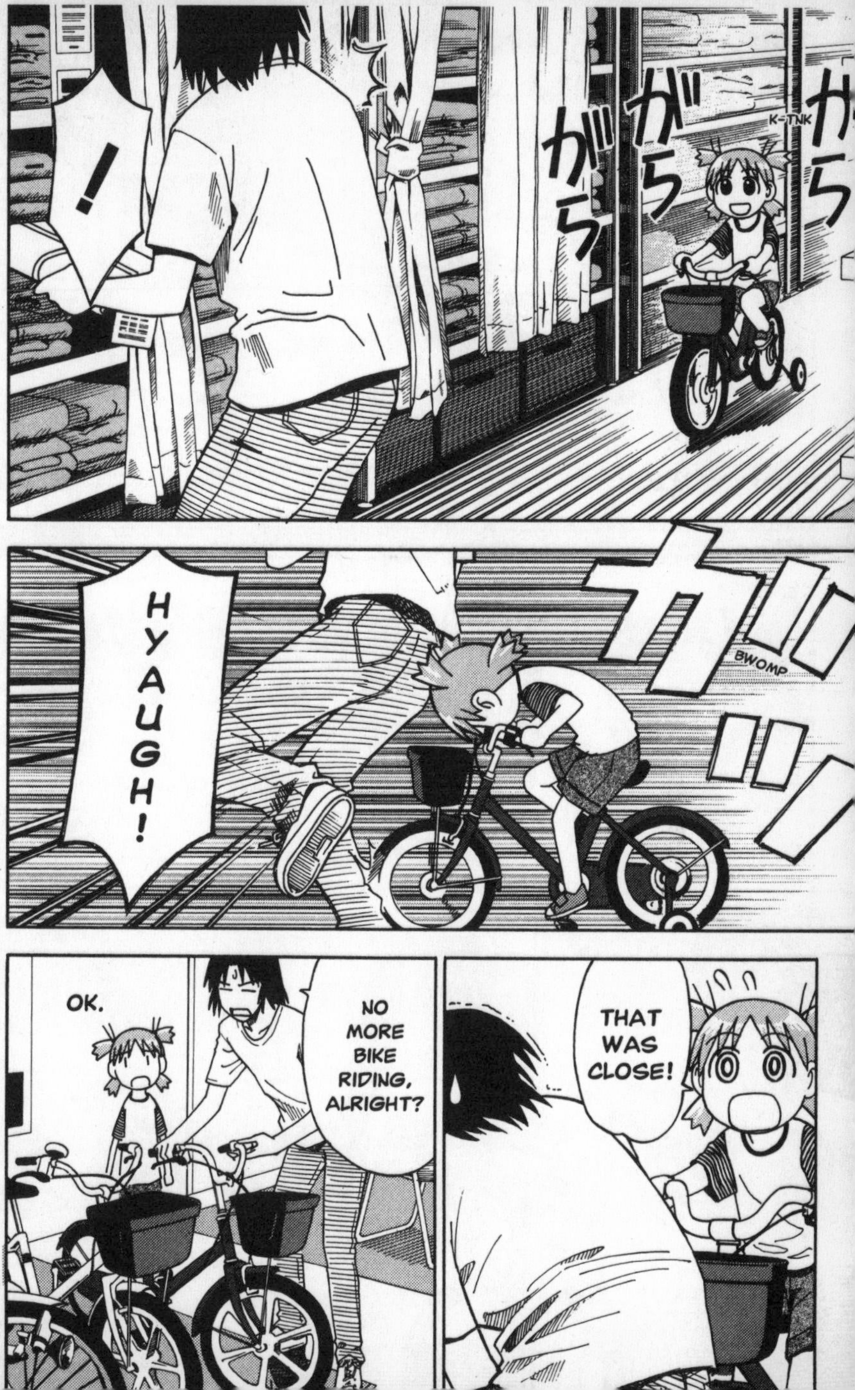
から
K-TNK
がら
がら
!
ガッ
BWOMP
HYAUGH!
THAT WAS CLOSE!
...
NO MORE BIKE RIDING, ALRIGHT?
OK.

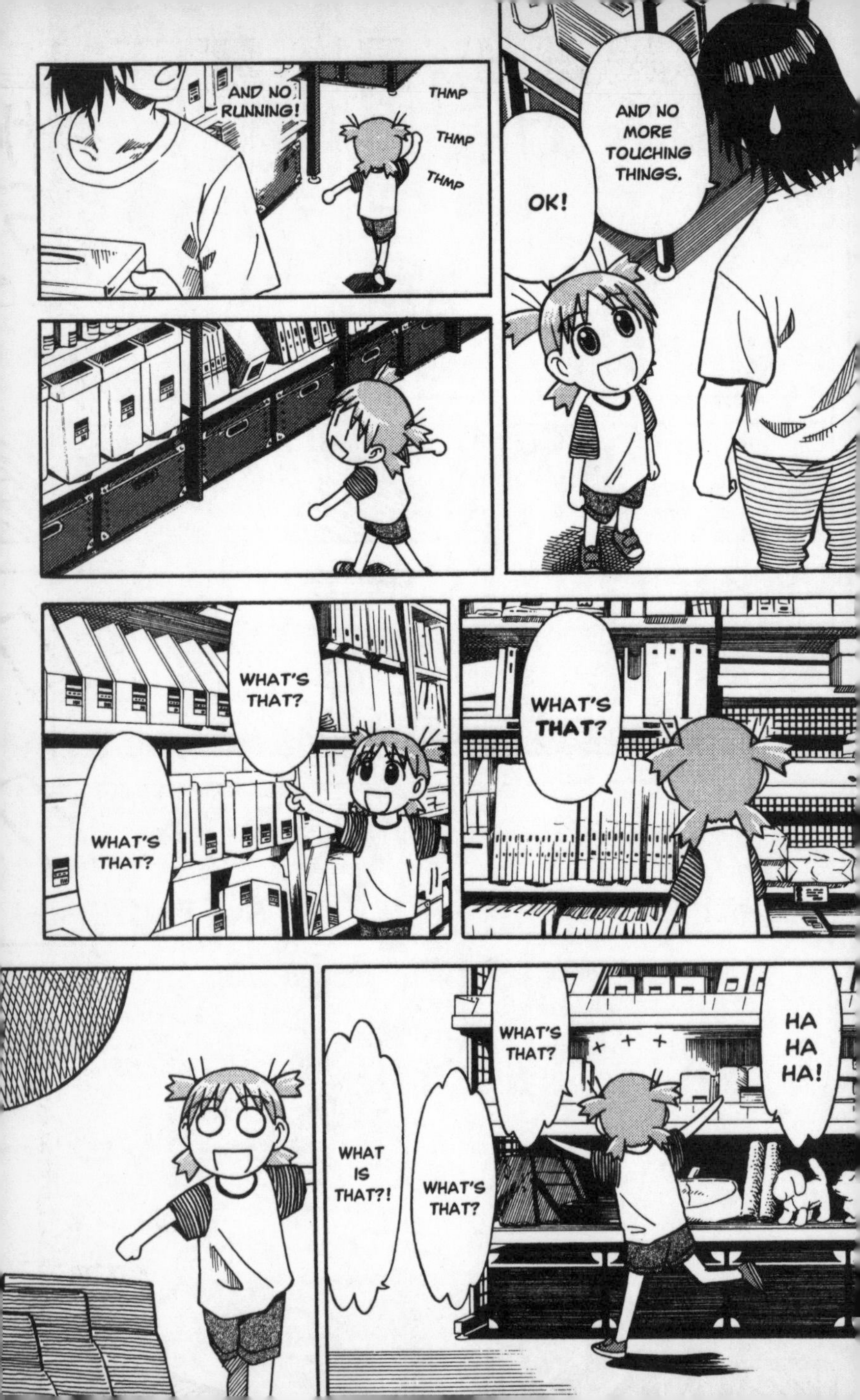
AND NO MORE TOUCHING THINGS.
OK!
AND NO RUNNING!
THMP
THMP
THMP
WHAT'S THAT?
WHAT'S THAT?
WHAT'S THAT?
HA HA HA!
WHAT'S THAT?
WHAT'S THAT?
WHAT IS THAT?!

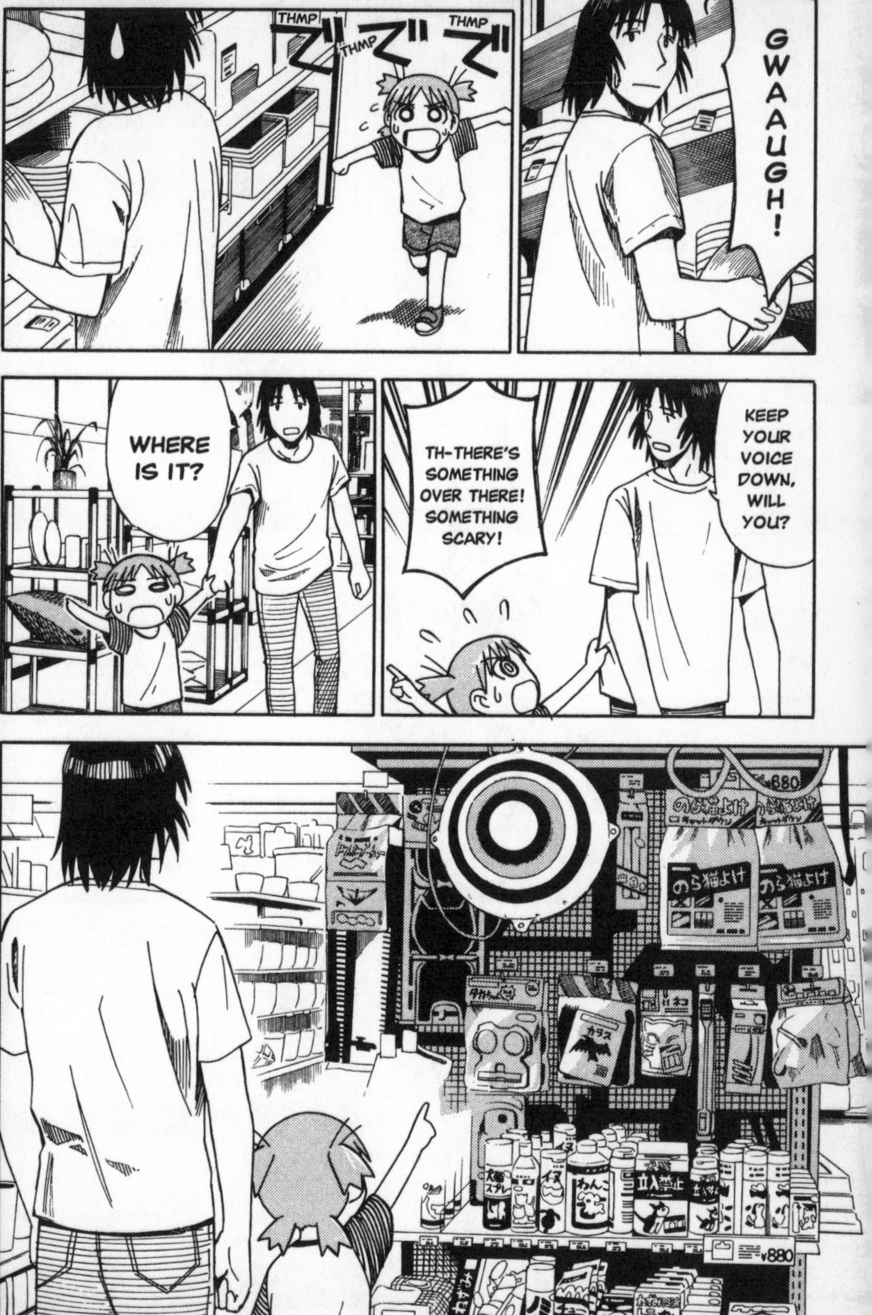
GWAAUGH!
THMP
THMP
THMP
KEEP YOUR VOICE DOWN, WILL YOU?
TH-THERE'S SOMETHING OVER THERE! SOMETHING SCARY!
WHERE IS IT?
¥880
のら猫よけ
のら猫よけ
のら猫よけ
のら猫よけ
カラス
わんこ
立入禁止
¥880

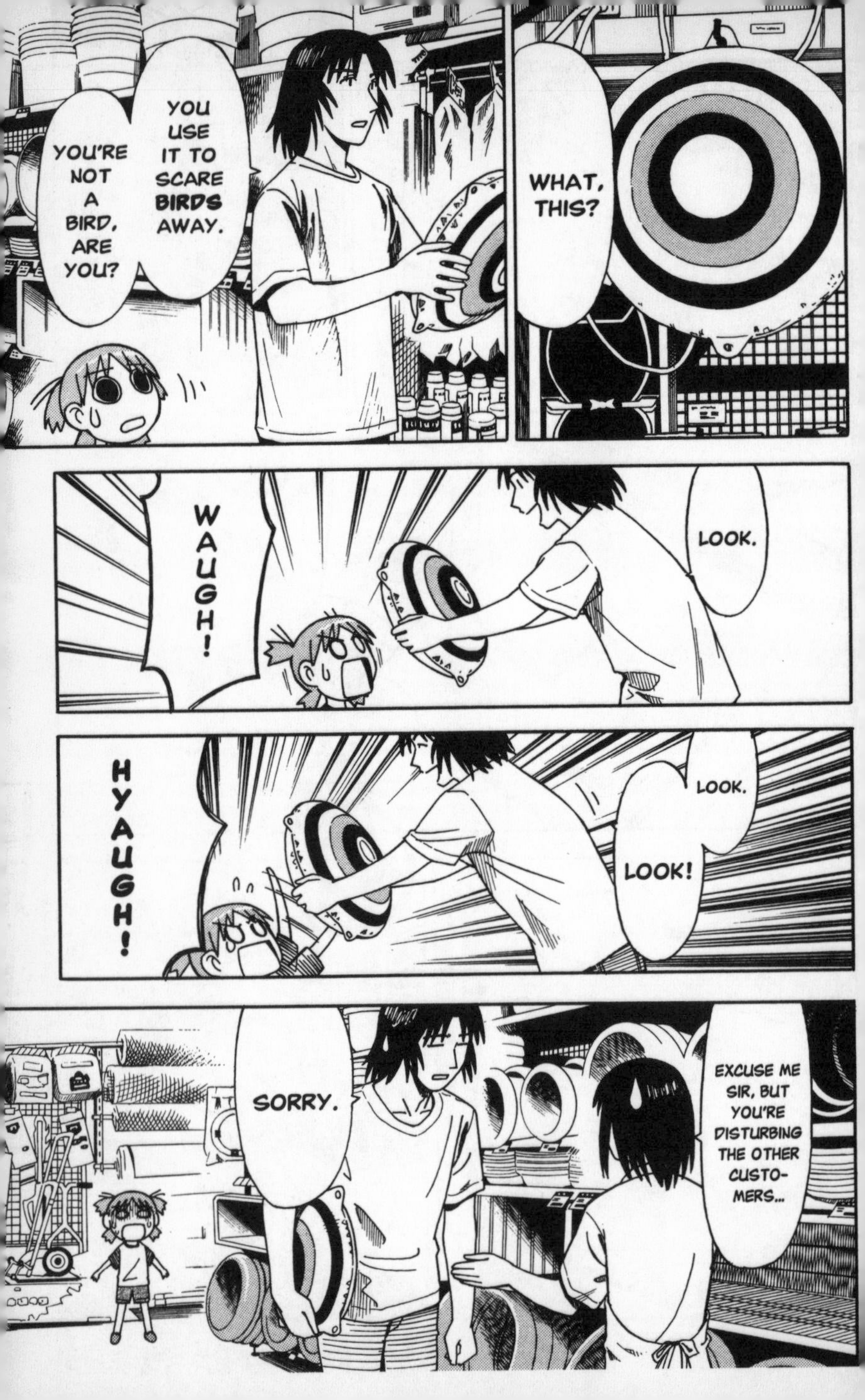
WHAT, THIS?
YOU USE IT TO SCARE **BIRDS** AWAY.
YOU'RE NOT A BIRD, ARE YOU?
LOOK.
WAUGH!
LOOK.
LOOK!
HYAUGH!
EXCUSE ME SIR, BUT YOU'RE DISTURBING THE OTHER CUSTOMERS...
SORRY.

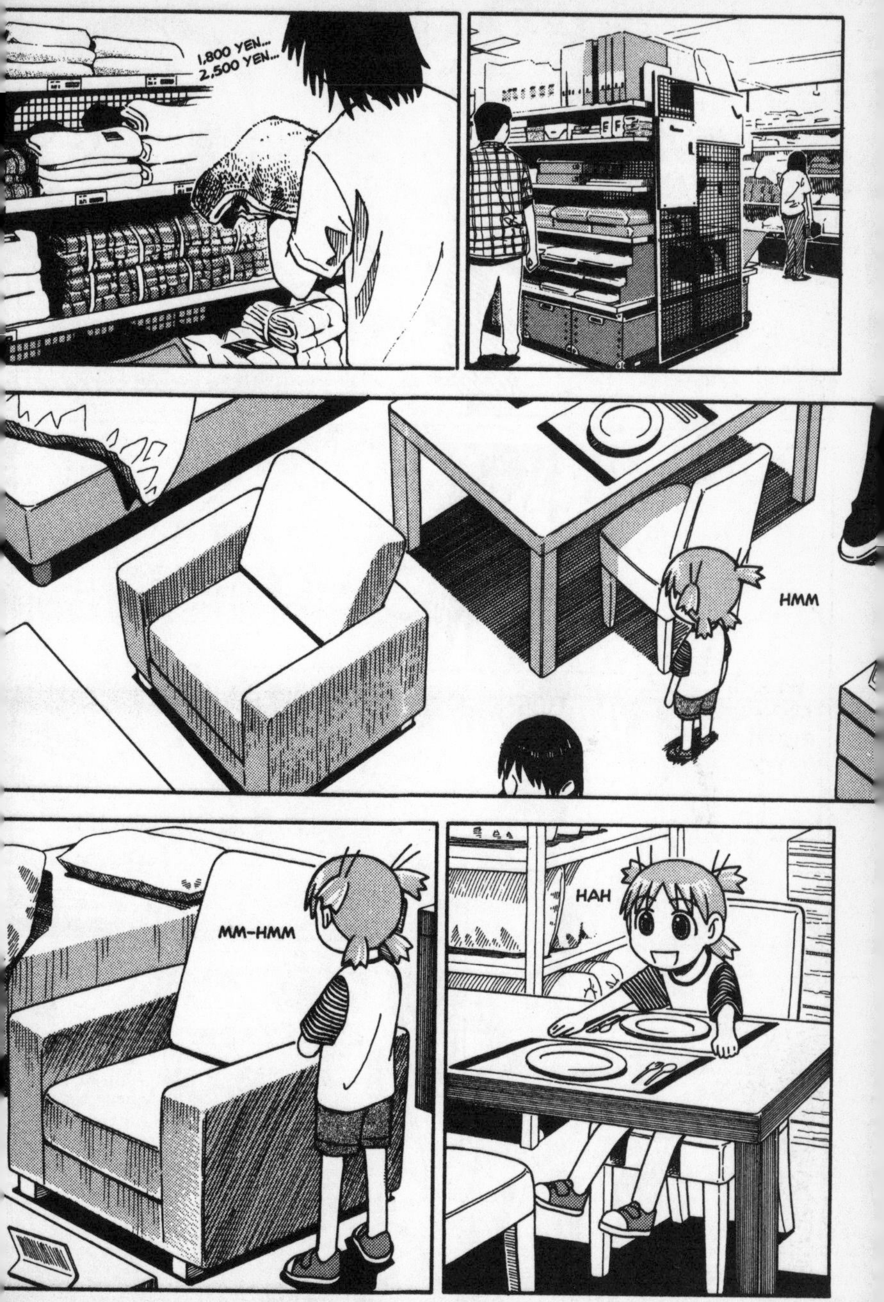
1,800 YEN...
2,500 YEN...
HMM
HAH
MM-HMM

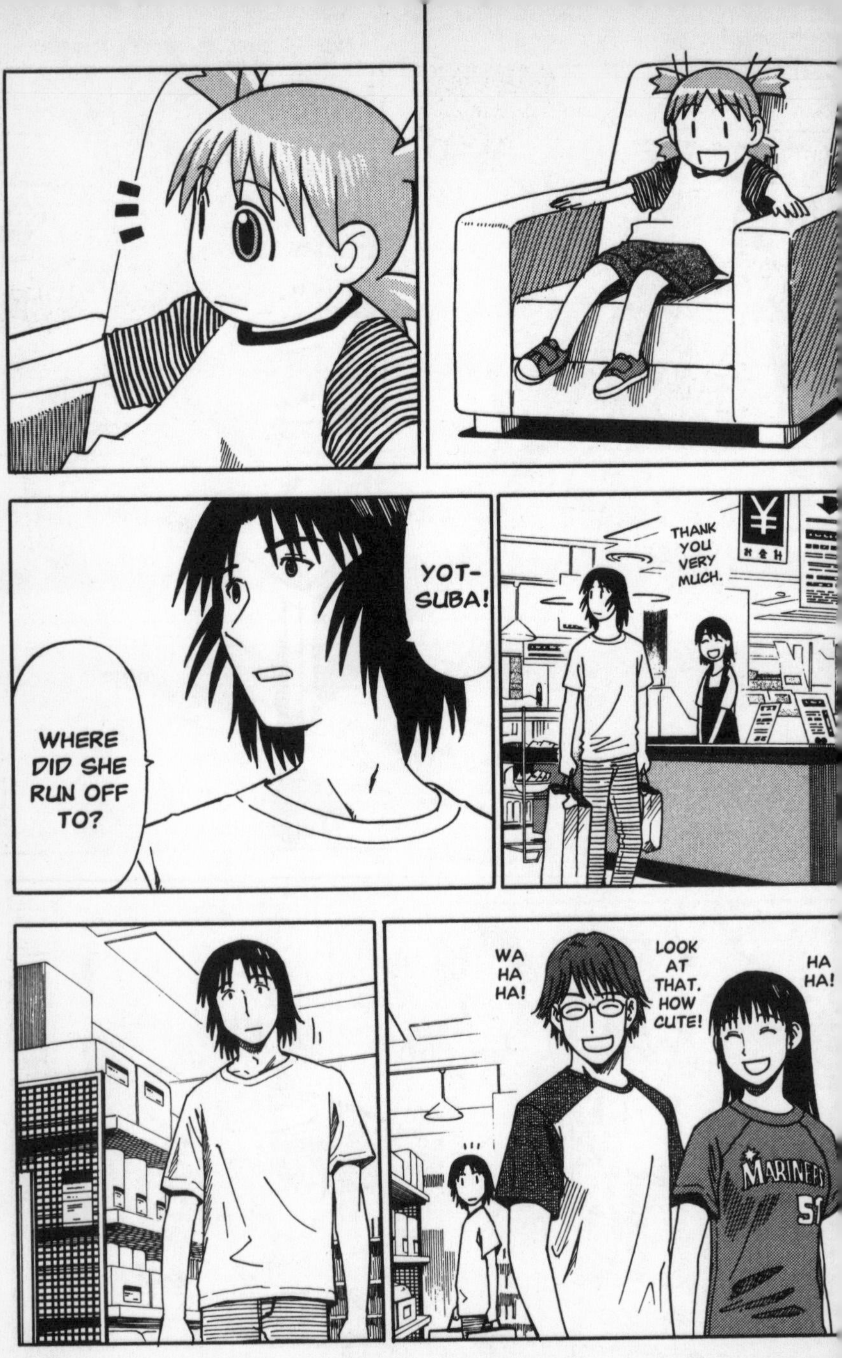
THANK YOU VERY MUCH.
YOT-SUBA!
WHERE DID SHE RUN OFF TO?
HA HA!
LOOK AT THAT. HOW CUTE!
WA HA HA!
MARINERS

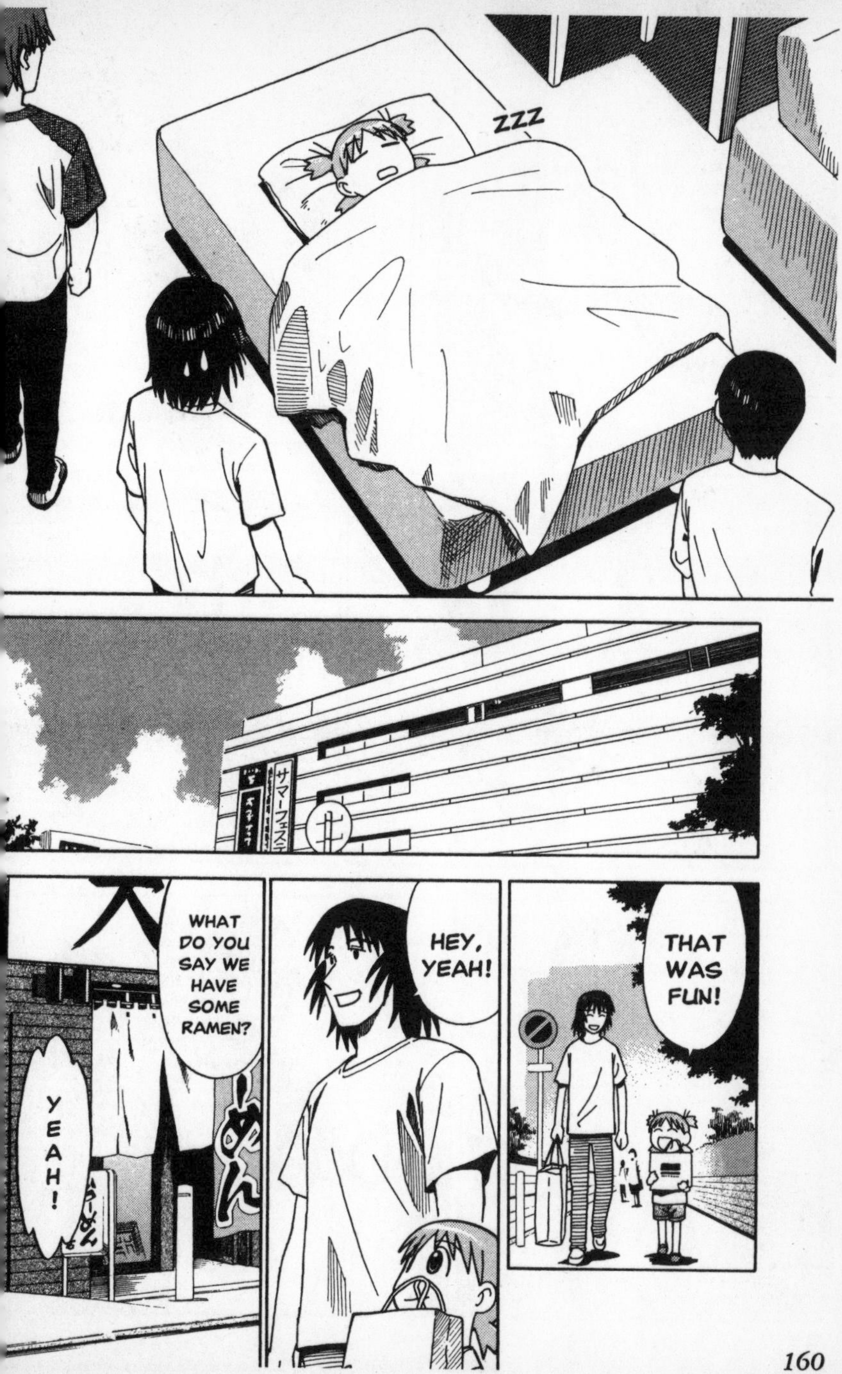
ZZZ
THAT WAS FUN!
HEY, YEAH!
WHAT DO YOU SAY WE HAVE SOME RAMEN?
YEAH!

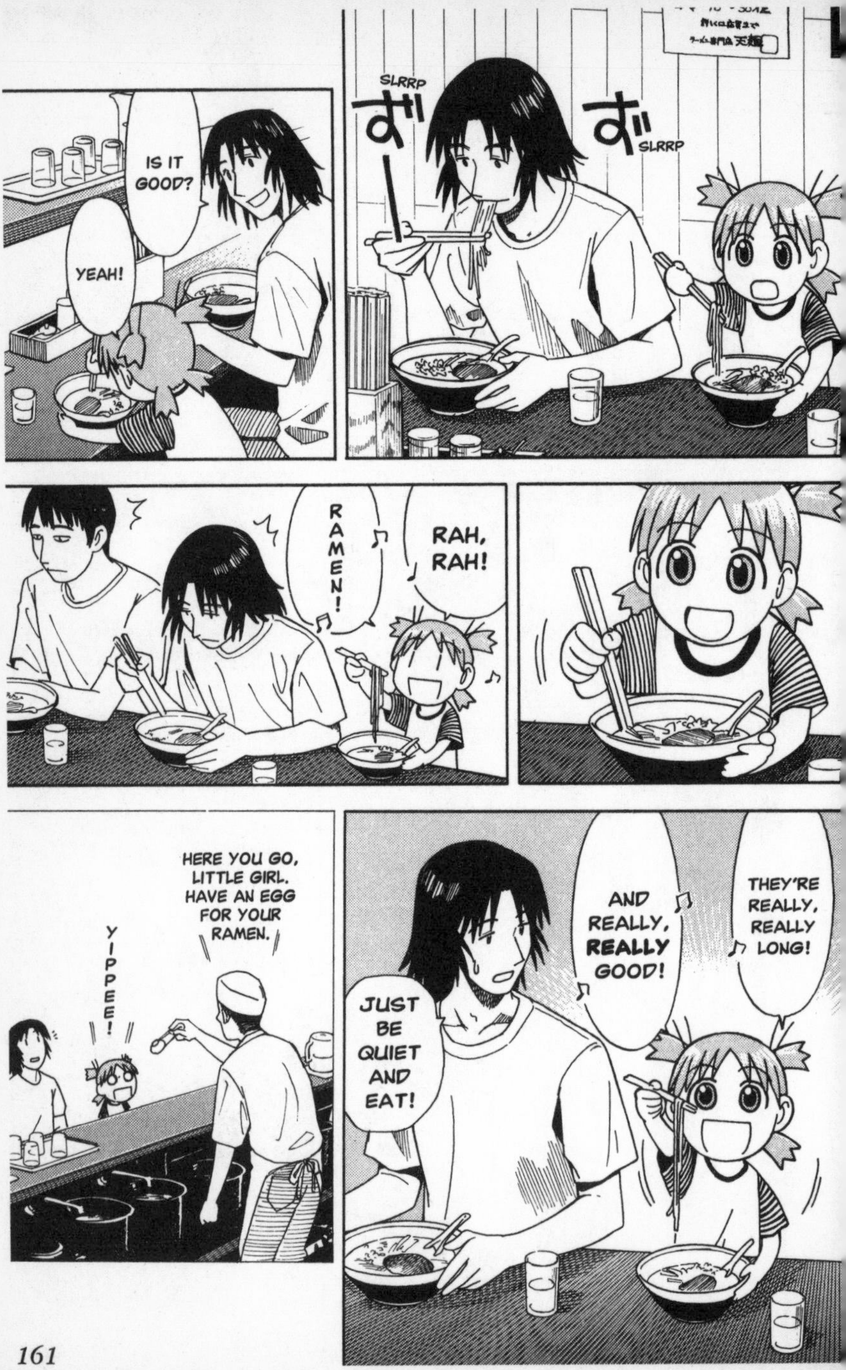
ず
SLRRP
ず
SLRRP
IS IT GOOD?
YEAH!
RAH, RAH!
RAMEN!
THEY'RE REALLY, REALLY LONG!
AND REALLY, **REALLY** GOOD!
JUST BE QUIET AND EAT!
HERE YOU GO, LITTLE GIRL. HAVE AN EGG FOR YOUR RAMEN.
YIPPEE!

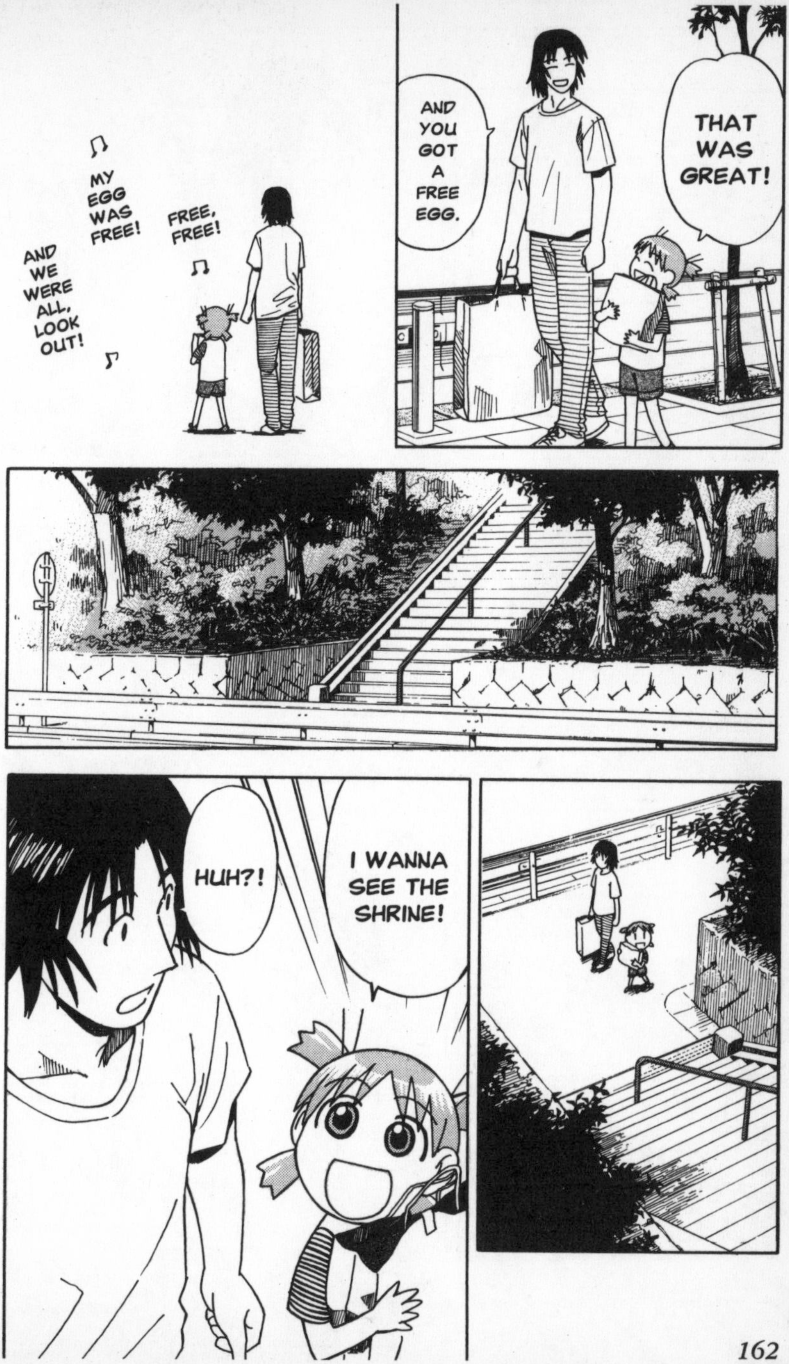
THAT WAS GREAT!
AND YOU GOT A FREE EGG.
MY EGG WAS FREE!
FREE, FREE!
AND WE WERE ALL, LOOK OUT!
I WANNA SEE THE SHRINE!
HUH?!

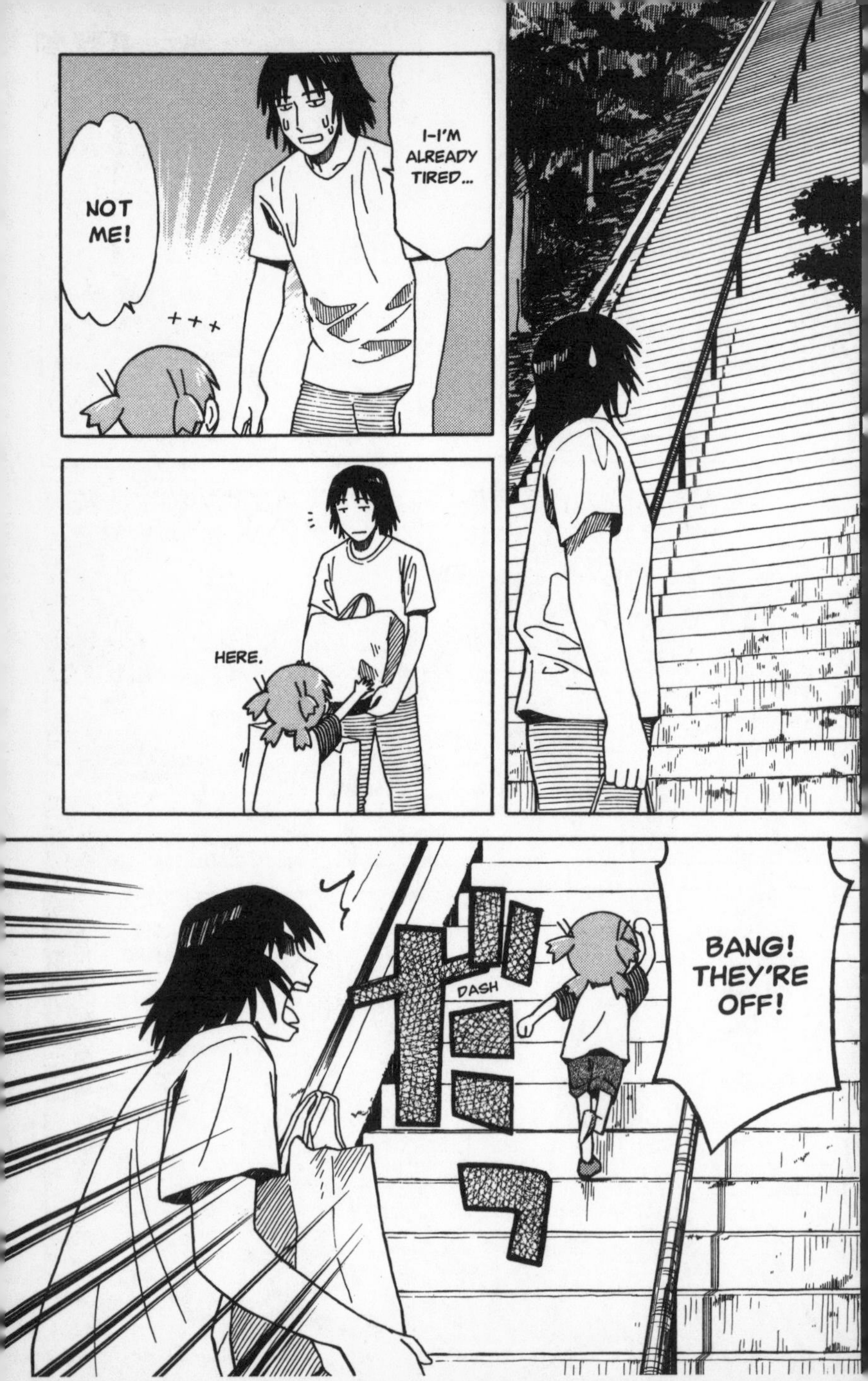
I-I'M ALREADY TIRED...
NOT ME!
HERE.
BANG! THEY'RE OFF!
DASH

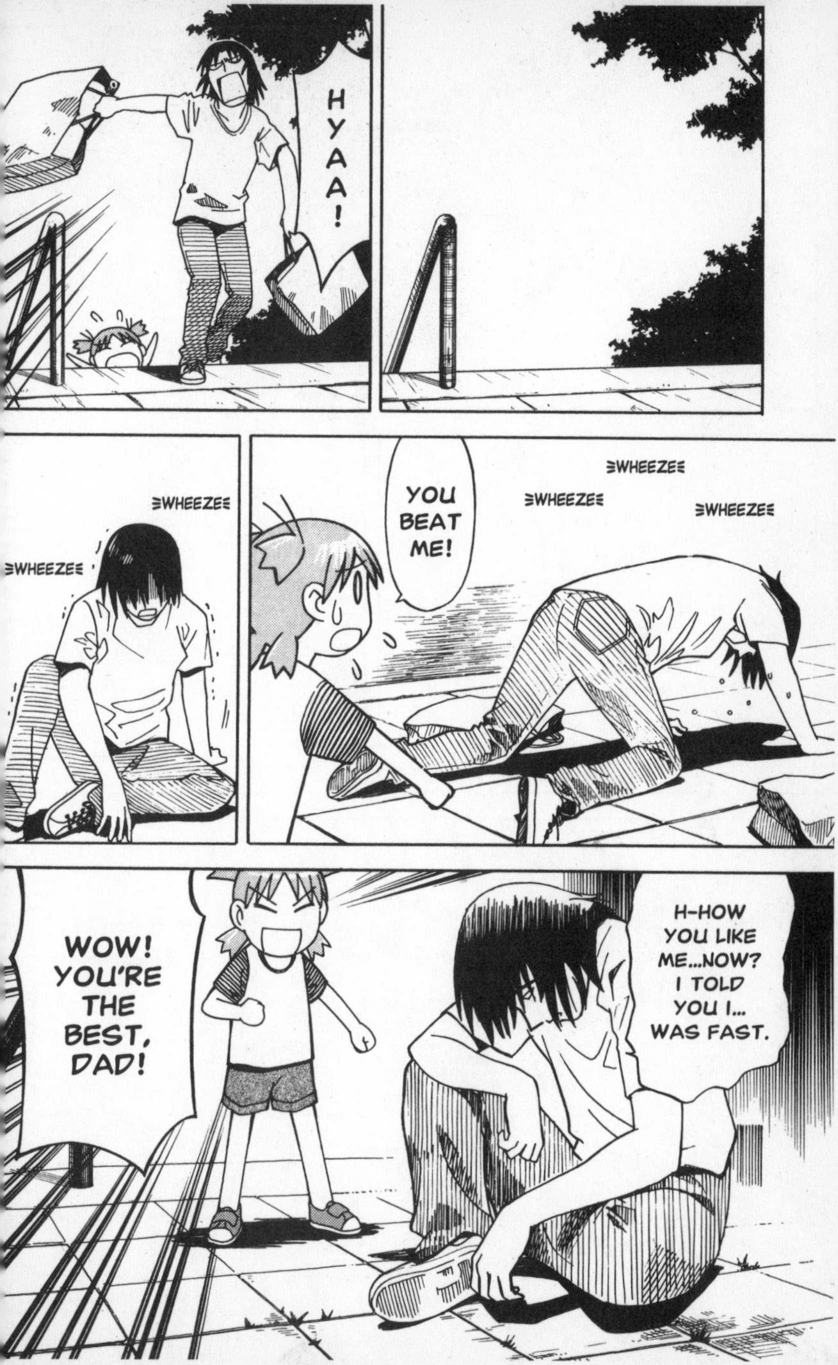
HYAA!
≡WHEEZE≡
≡WHEEZE≡
≡WHEEZE≡
YOU BEAT ME!
≡WHEEZE≡
≡WHEEZE≡
H-HOW YOU LIKE ME...NOW? I TOLD YOU I... WAS FAST.
WOW! YOU'RE THE BEST, DAD!

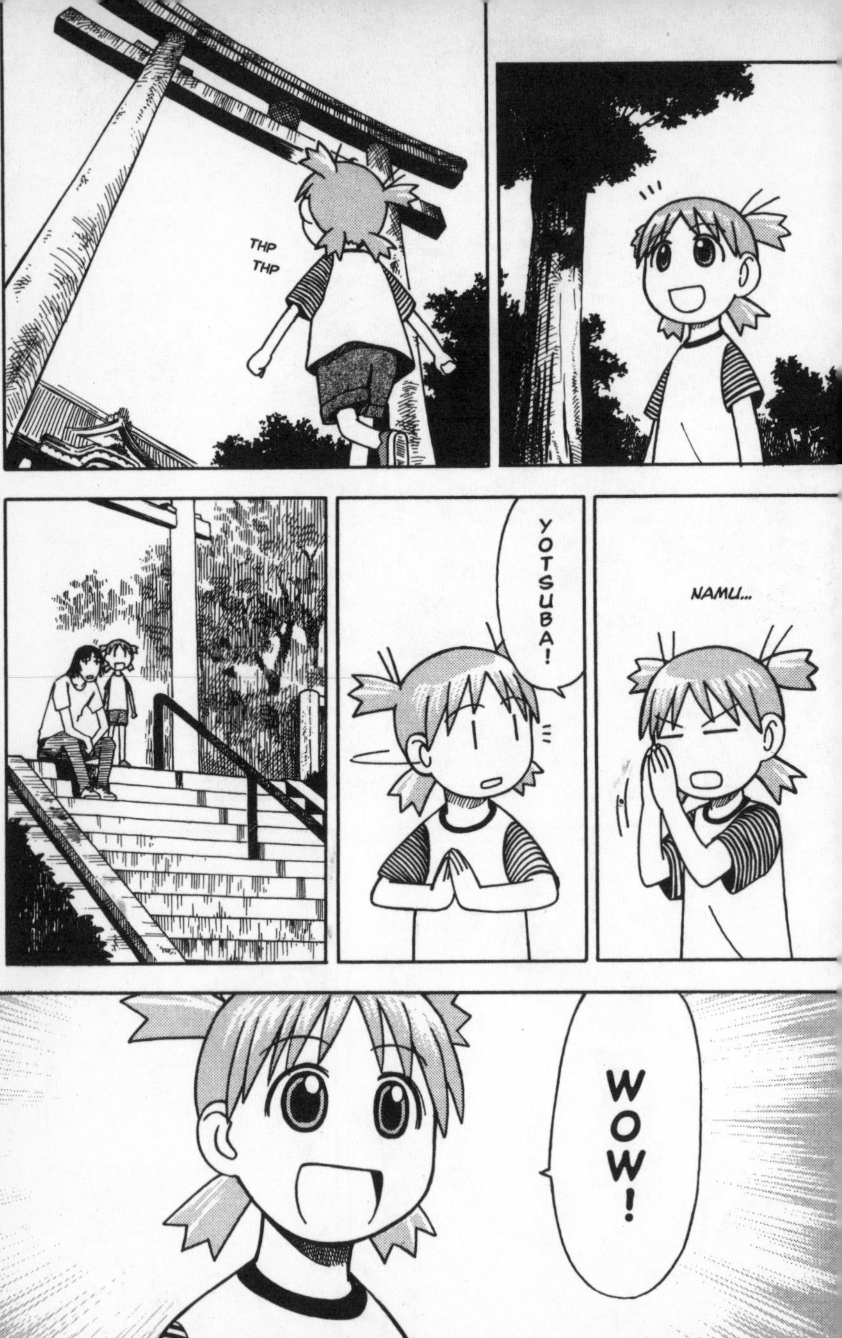
THP
THP
NAMU...
YOTSUBA!
WOW!

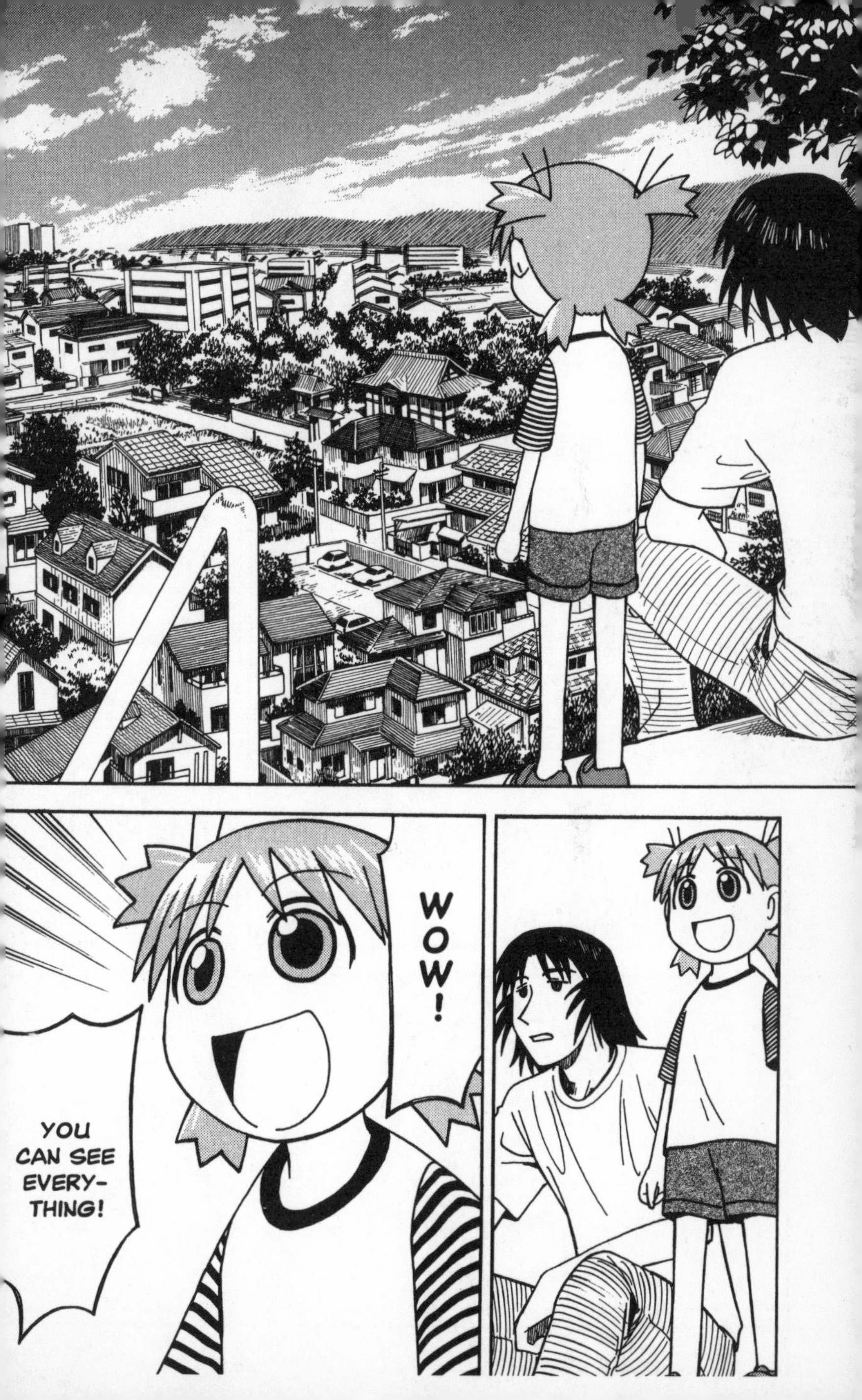
WOW!
YOU CAN SEE EVERYTHING!

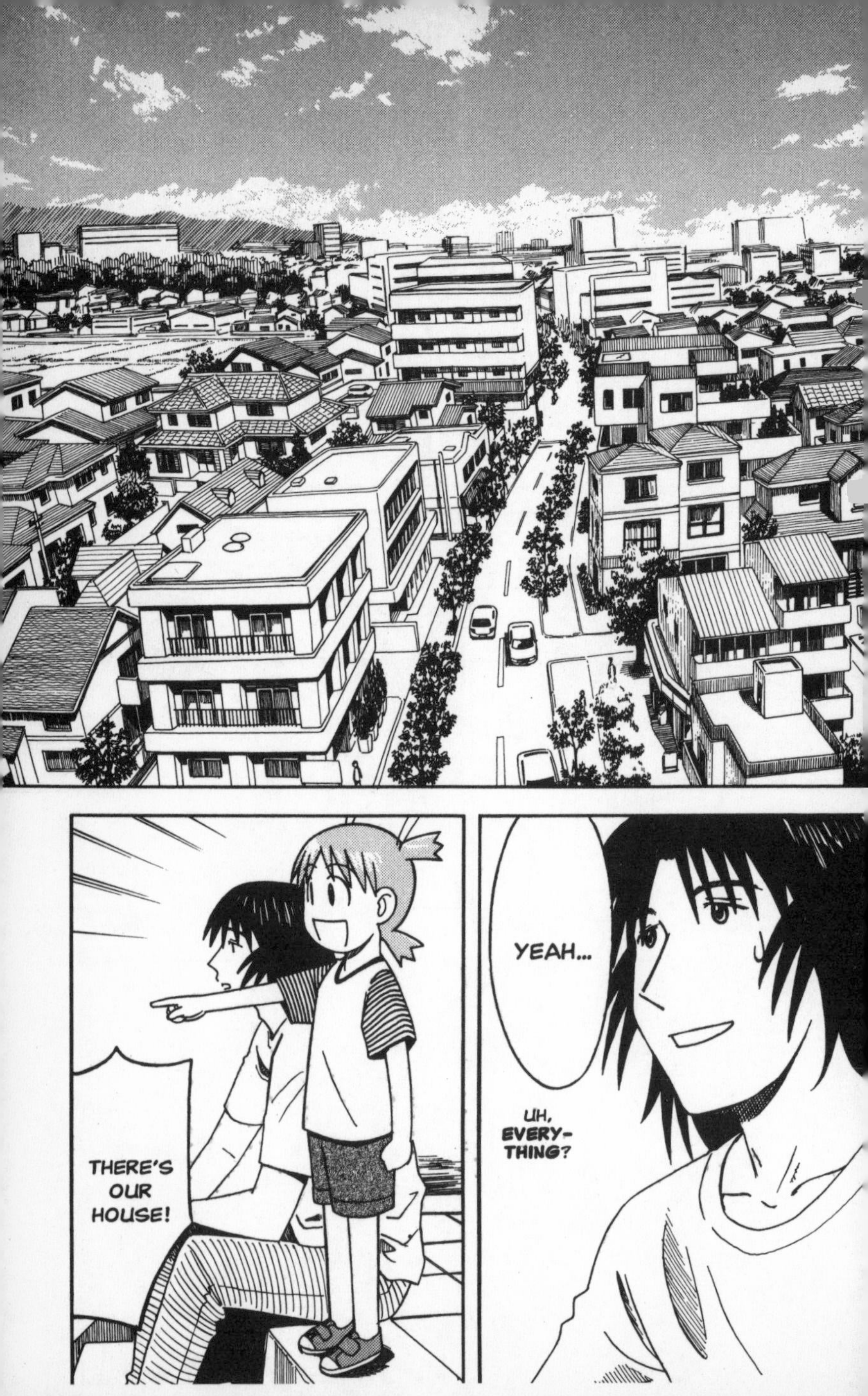
YEAH...
UH, EVERY-THING?
THERE'S OUR HOUSE!

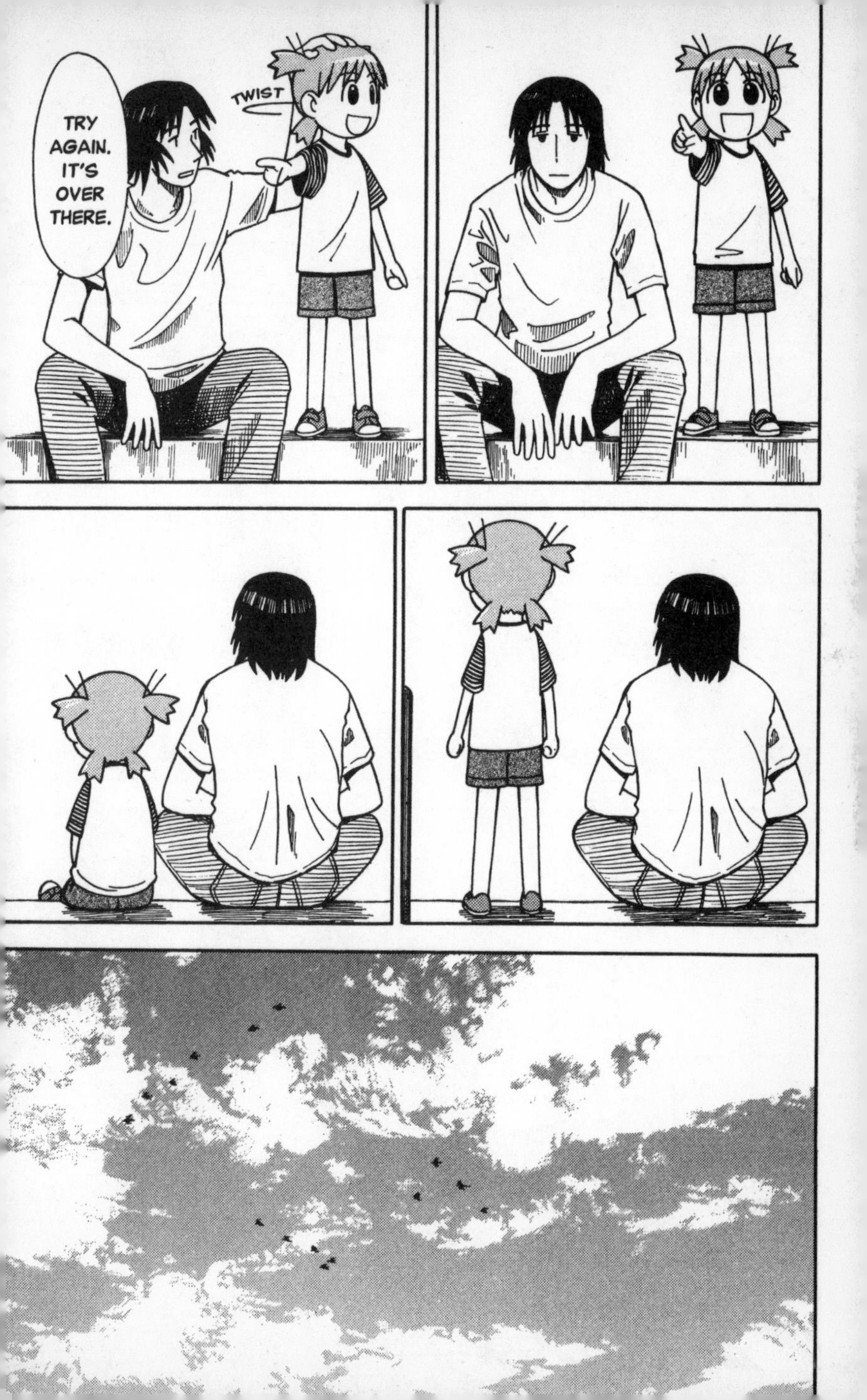
TRY AGAIN. IT'S OVER THERE.
TWIST

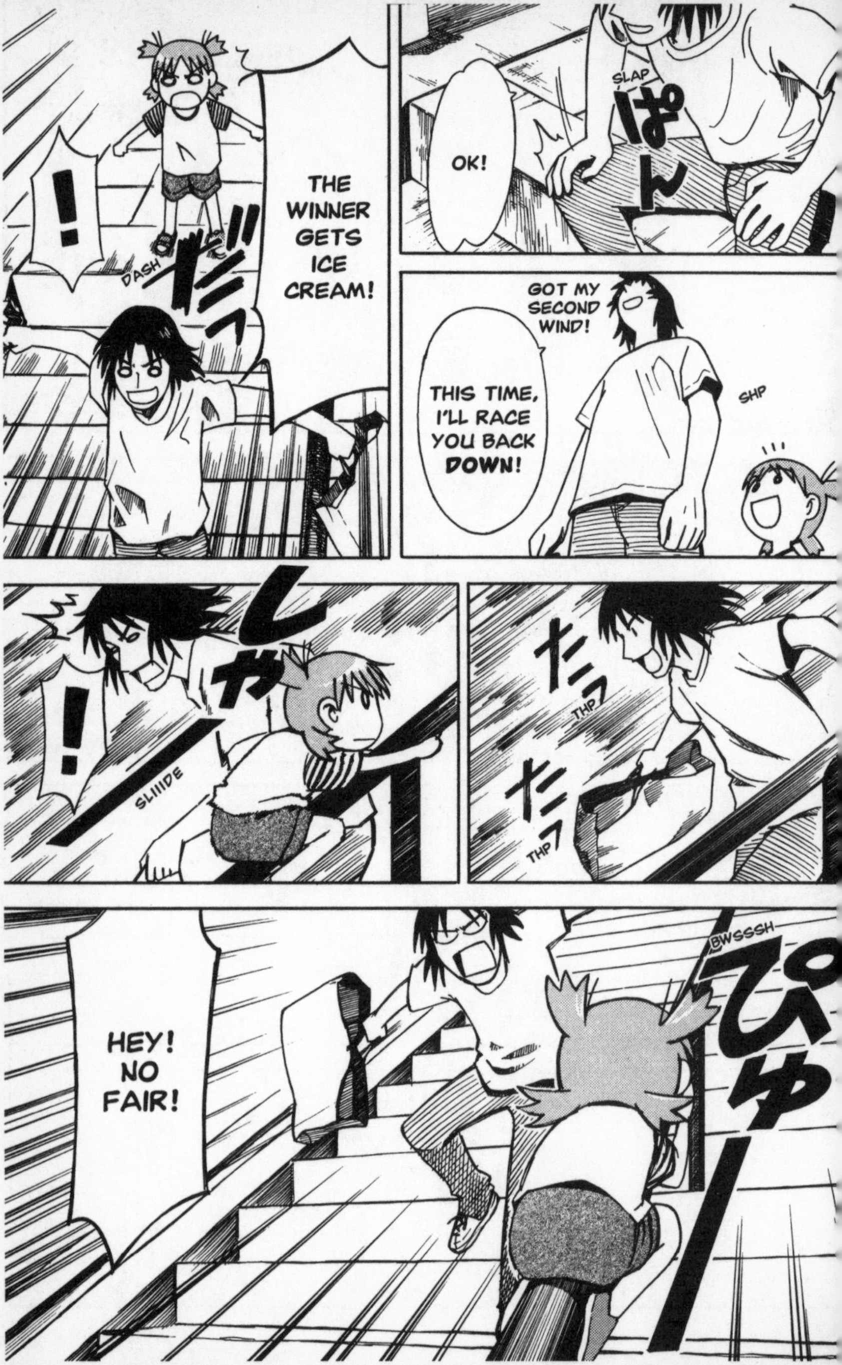
SLAP
ぱん
OK!
GOT MY SECOND WIND!
THIS TIME, I'LL RACE YOU BACK DOWN!
SHP
THE WINNER GETS ICE CREAM!
DASH
ダッ
!
たっ
THP
たっ
THP
しゃ
!
SLIIDE
BWSSSH
ぴゅー
HEY! NO FAIR!

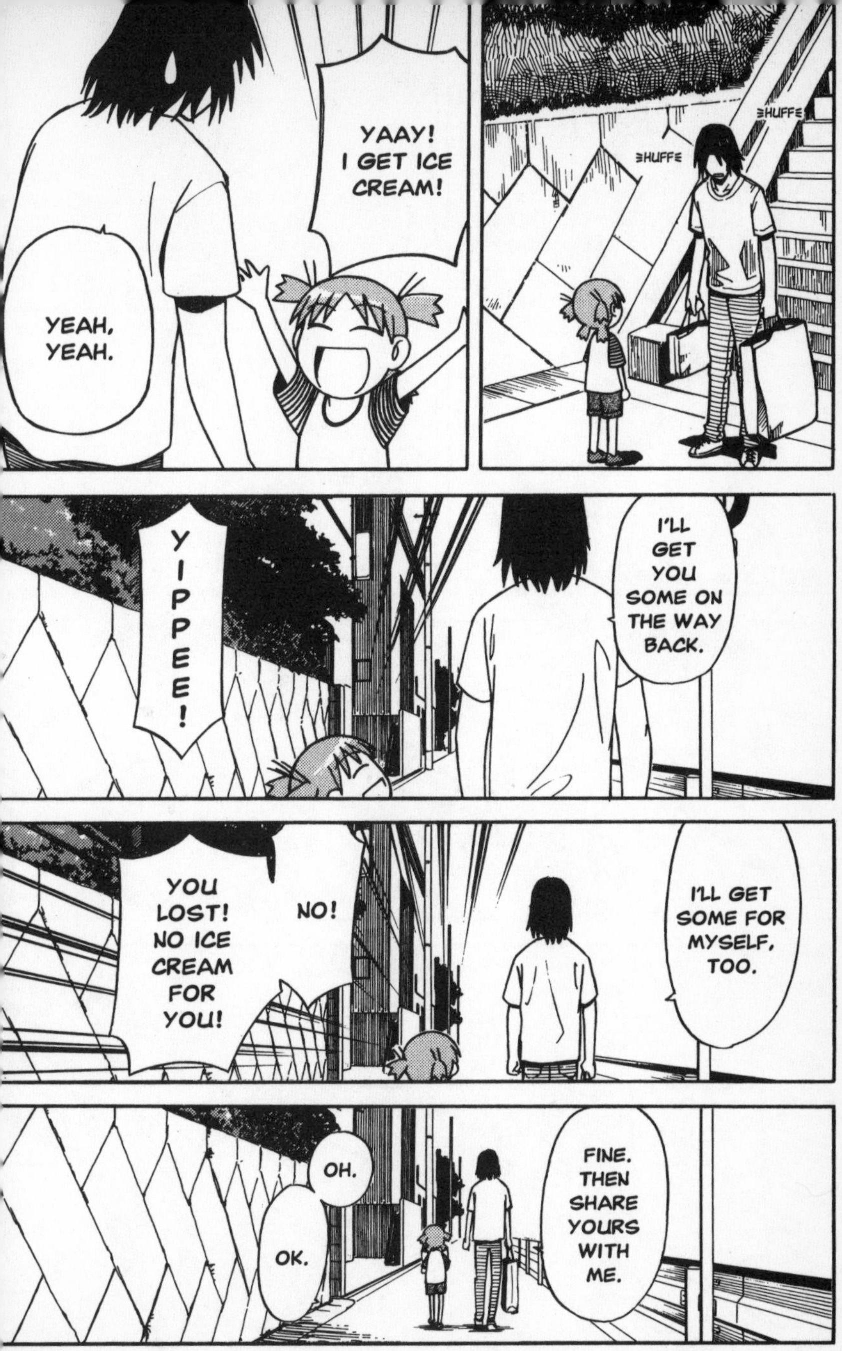
HUFF
HUFF
YAAY! I GET ICE CREAM!
YEAH, YEAH.
I'LL GET YOU SOME ON THE WAY BACK.
YIPPEE!
I'LL GET SOME FOR MYSELF, TOO.
NO!
YOU LOST! NO ICE CREAM FOR YOU!
FINE. THEN SHARE YOURS WITH ME.
OH.
OK.

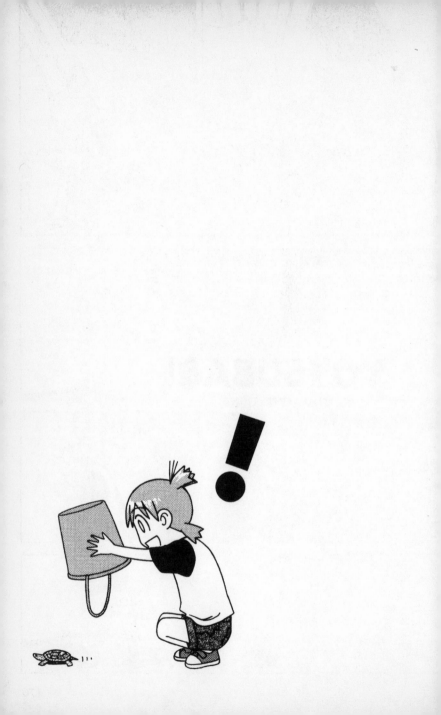

YOTSUBA&!

ENJOY EVERYTHING.

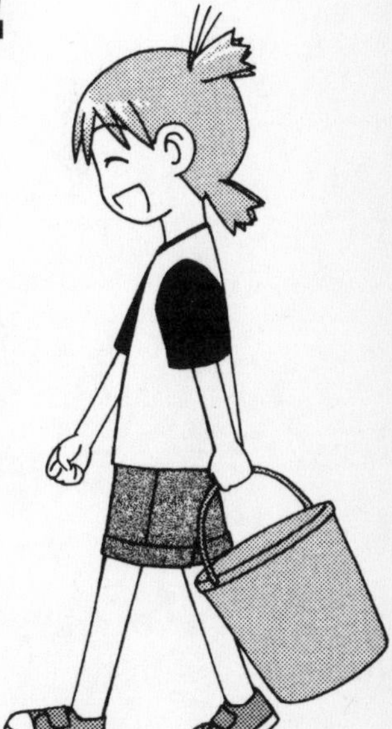

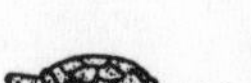

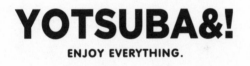

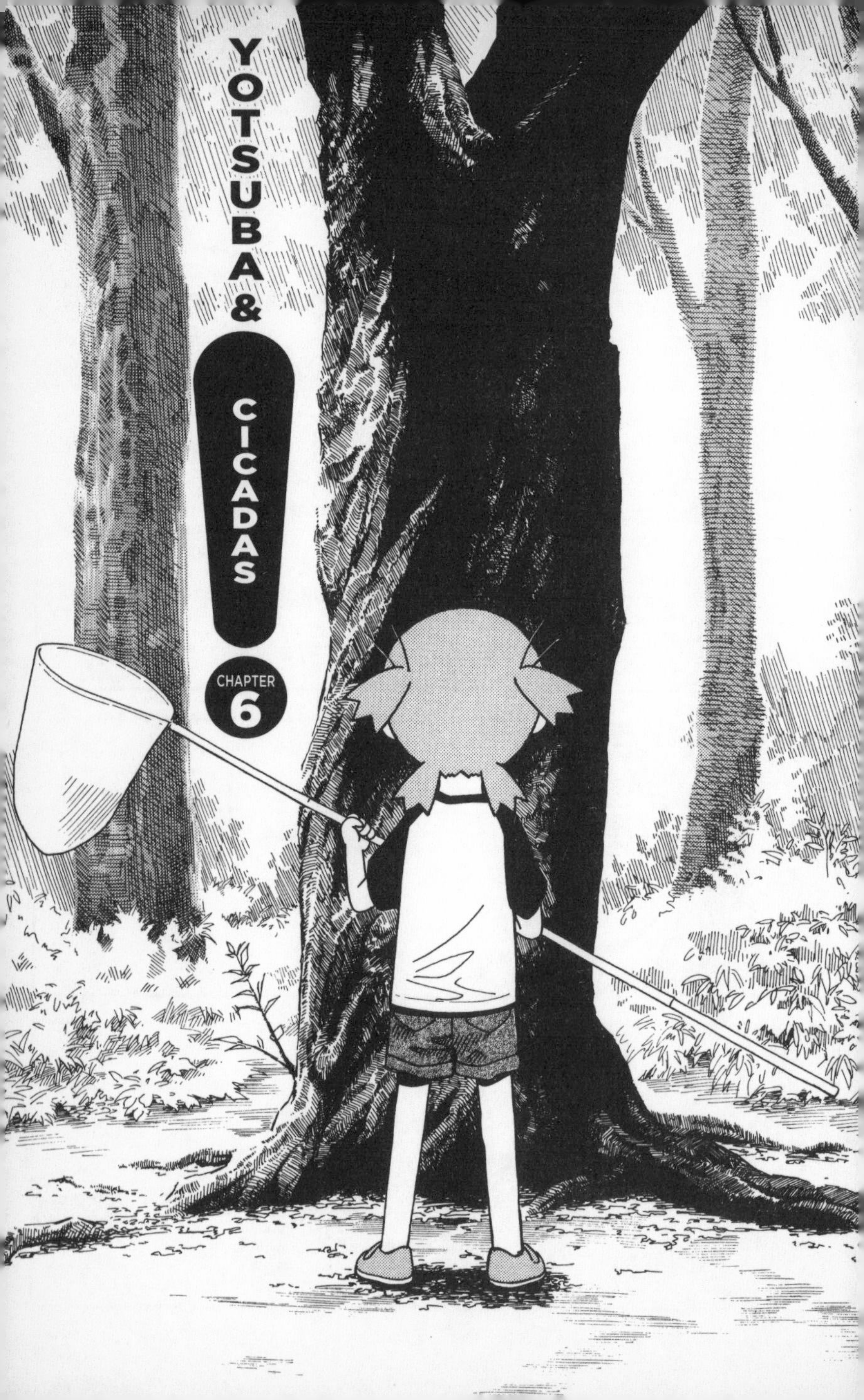
YOTSUBA&
CICADAS
CHAPTER 6

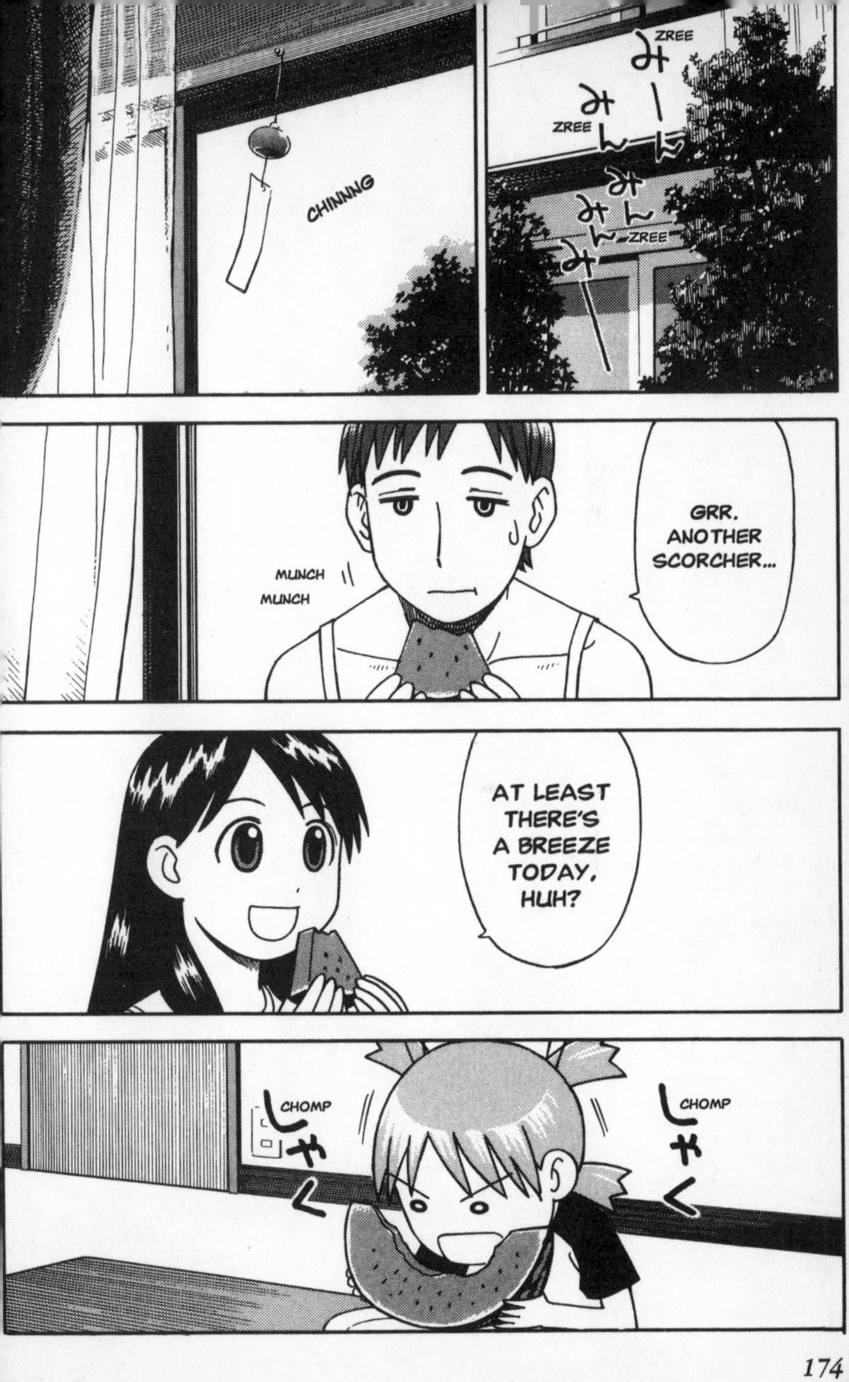
みーん
ZREE
ZREE
みんみんみー
ZREE
CHINNNG
GRR. ANOTHER SCORCHER...
MUNCH MUNCH
AT LEAST THERE'S A BREEZE TODAY, HUH?
しゃく
CHOMP
しゃく
CHOMP

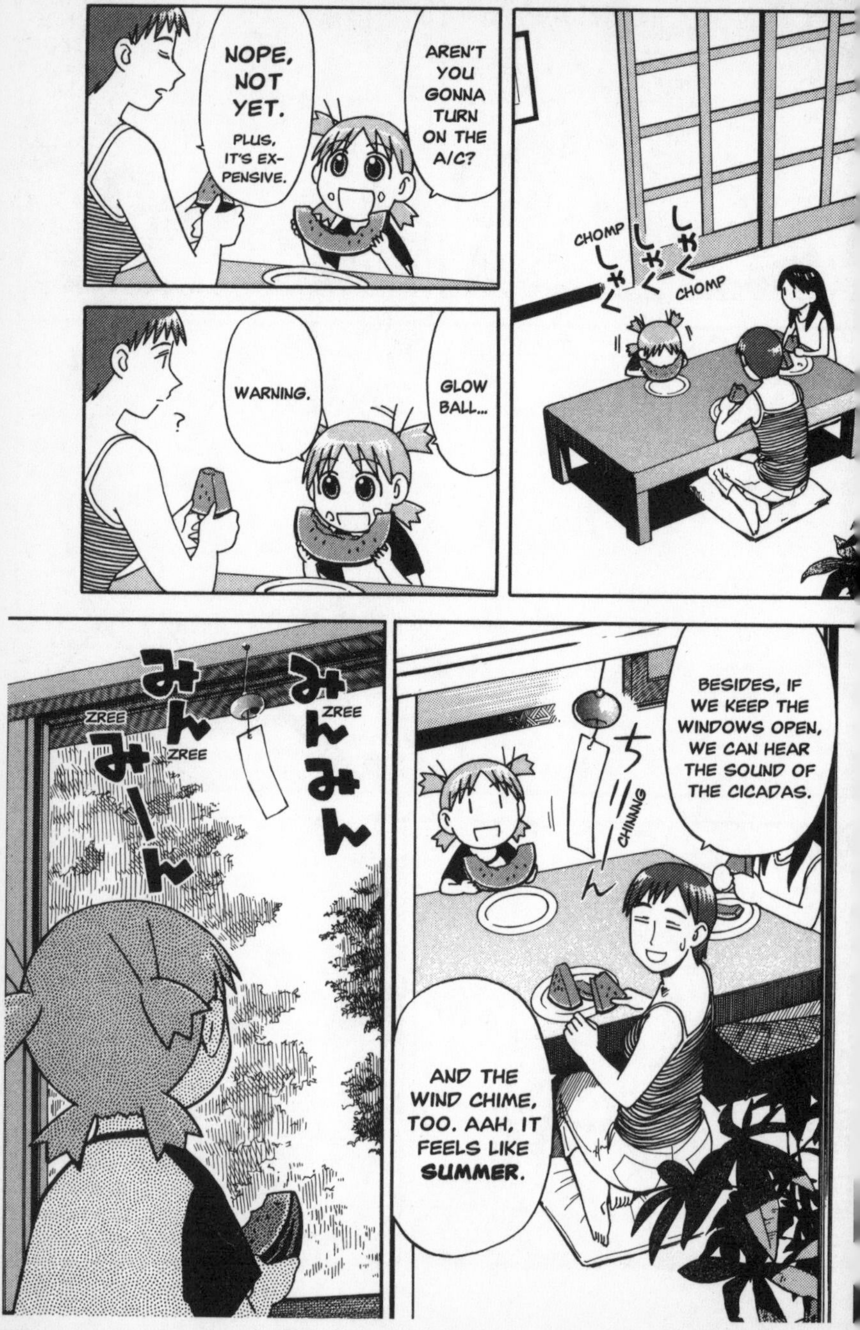
しゃく
しゃく
しゃく
CHOMP
CHOMP
AREN'T YOU GONNA TURN ON THE A/C?
NOPE, NOT YET.
PLUS, IT'S EX-PENSIVE.
GLOW BALL...
WARNING.
?
BESIDES, IF WE KEEP THE WINDOWS OPEN, WE CAN HEAR THE SOUND OF THE CICADAS.
ちりーん
CHINNNG
AND THE WIND CHIME, TOO. AAH, IT FEELS LIKE **SUMMER**.
みんみんみーん
ZREE
ZREE

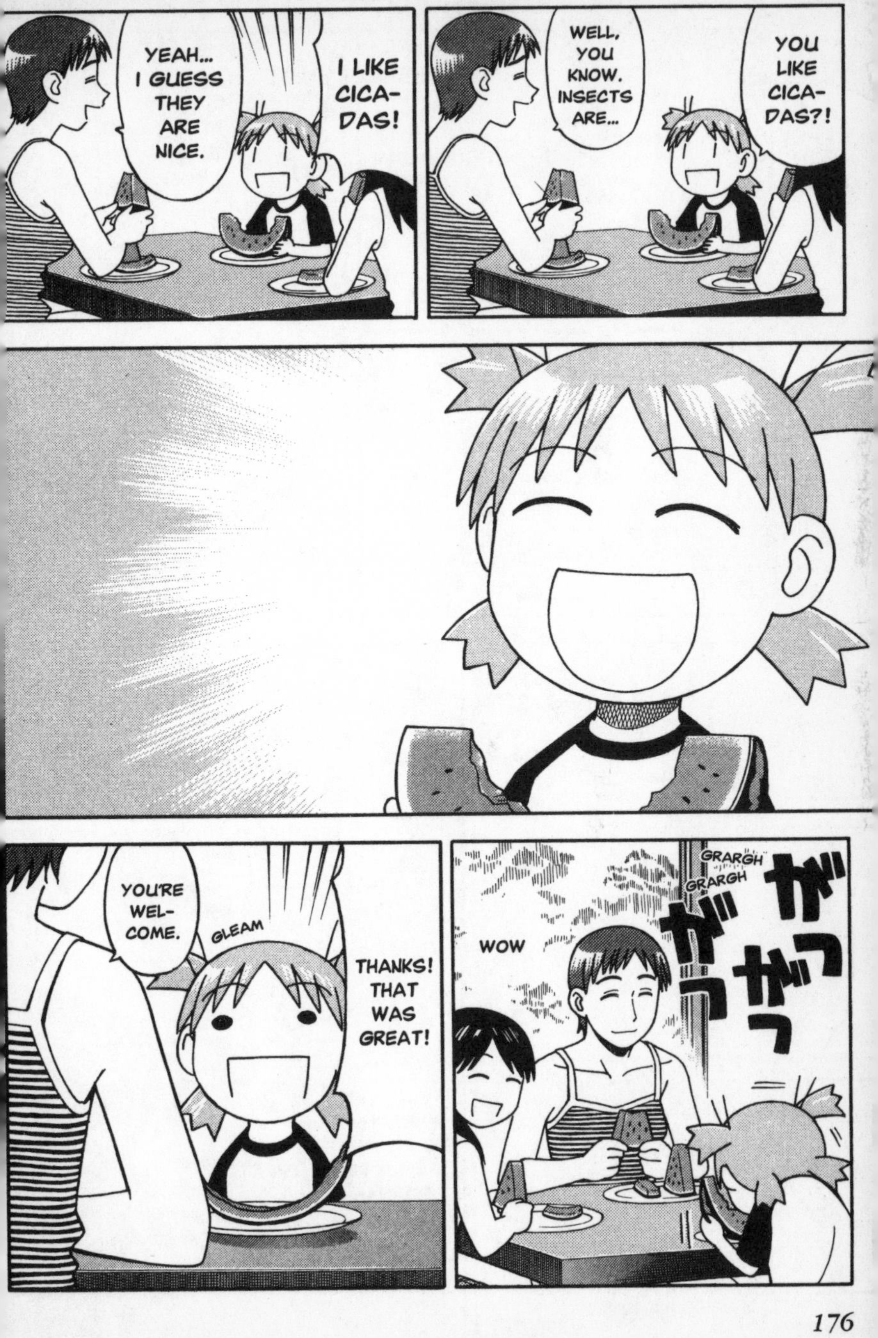

YOU LIKE CICA-DAS?!
WELL, YOU KNOW. INSECTS ARE...
I LIKE CICA-DAS!
YEAH... I GUESS THEY ARE NICE.
GRARGH GRARGH
がっがっ
がっ
WOW
THANKS! THAT WAS GREAT!
GLEAM
YOU'RE WEL-COME.

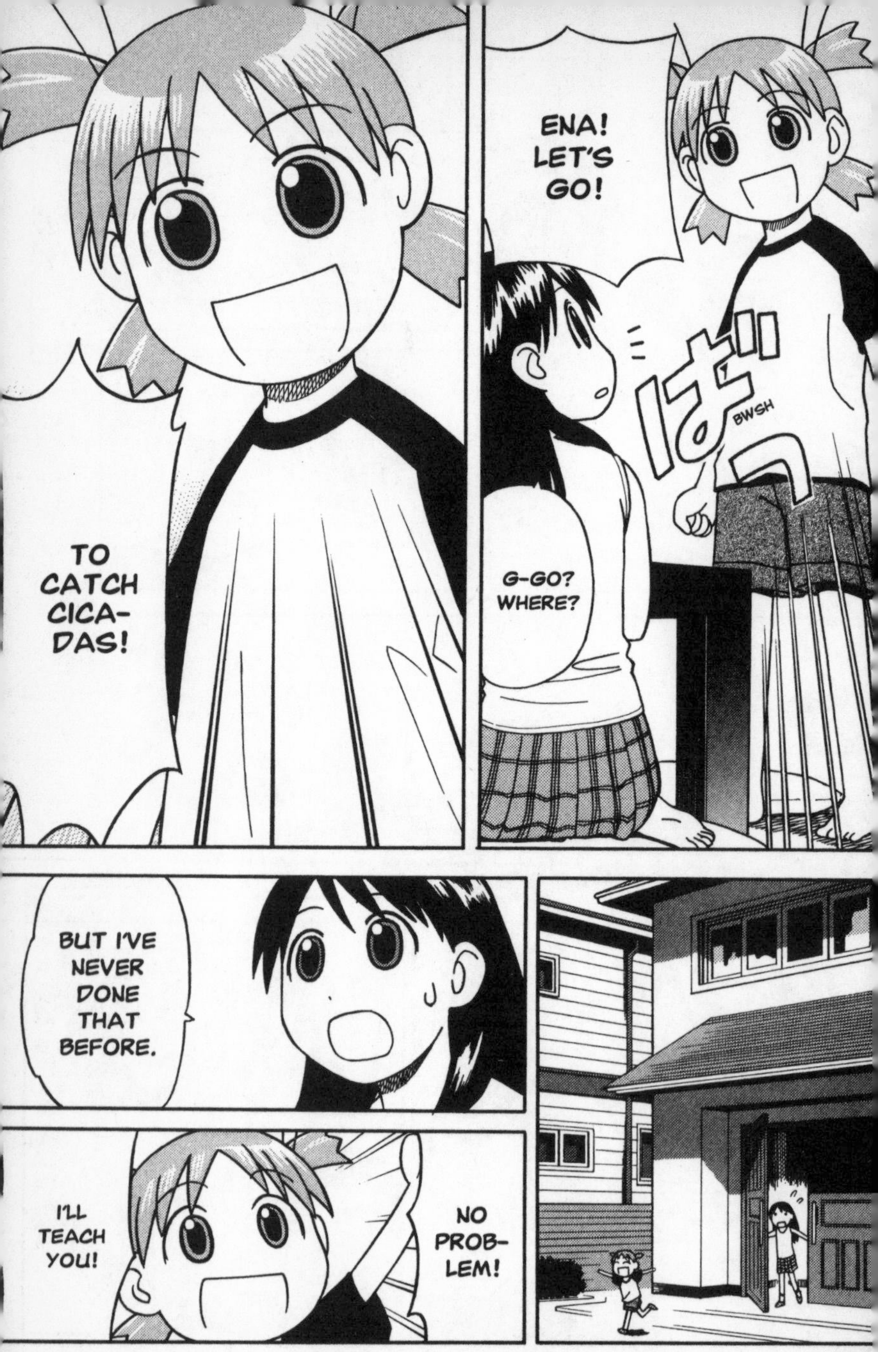
ENA! LET'S GO!
ばっ
BWSH
G-GO? WHERE?
TO CATCH CICA-DAS!
BUT I'VE NEVER DONE THAT BEFORE.
NO PROB-LEM!
I'LL TEACH YOU!

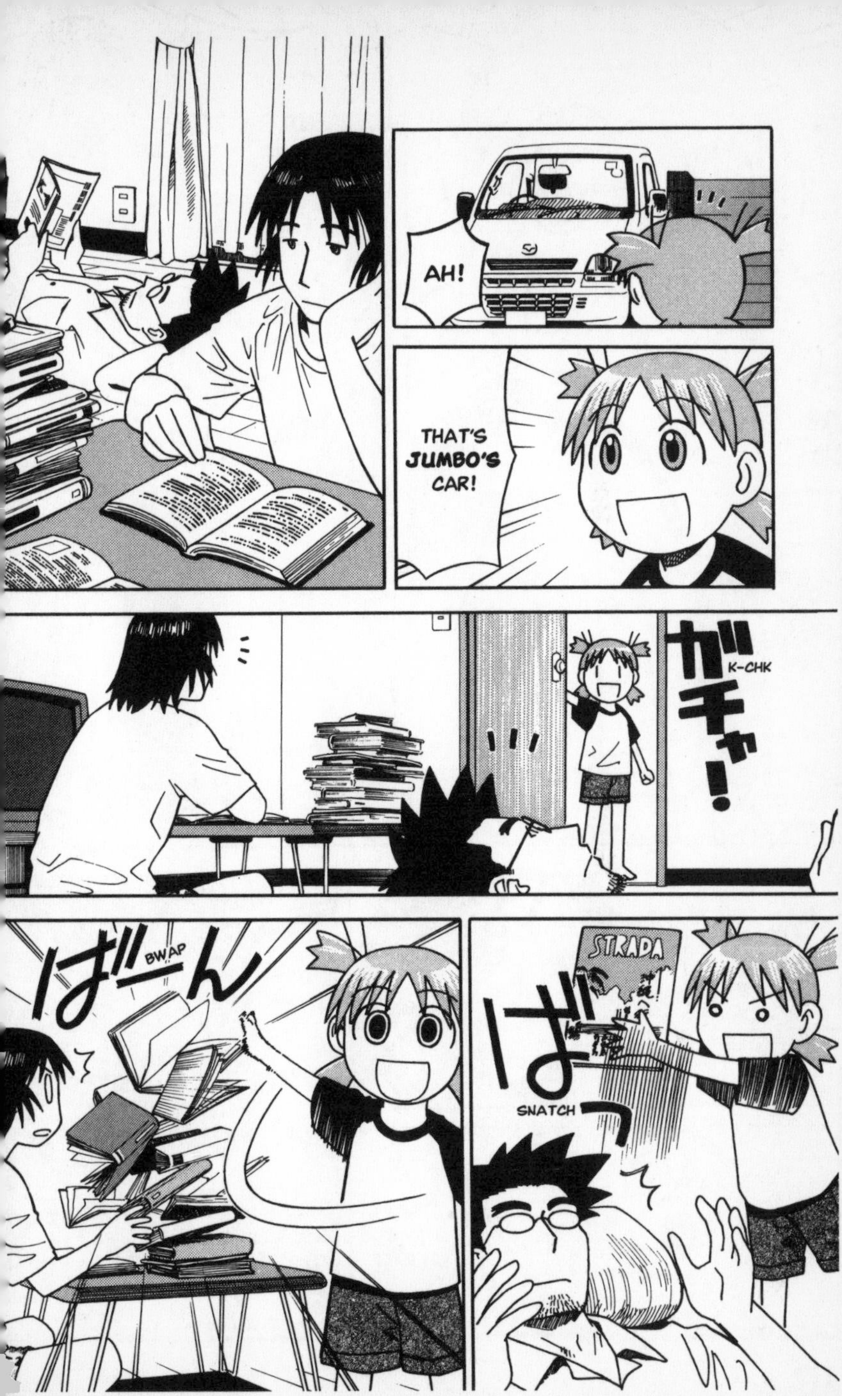
AH!
THAT'S JUMBO'S CAR!
ガチャ!
K-CHK
STRADA
ばっ
SNATCH
ばーん
BWAP

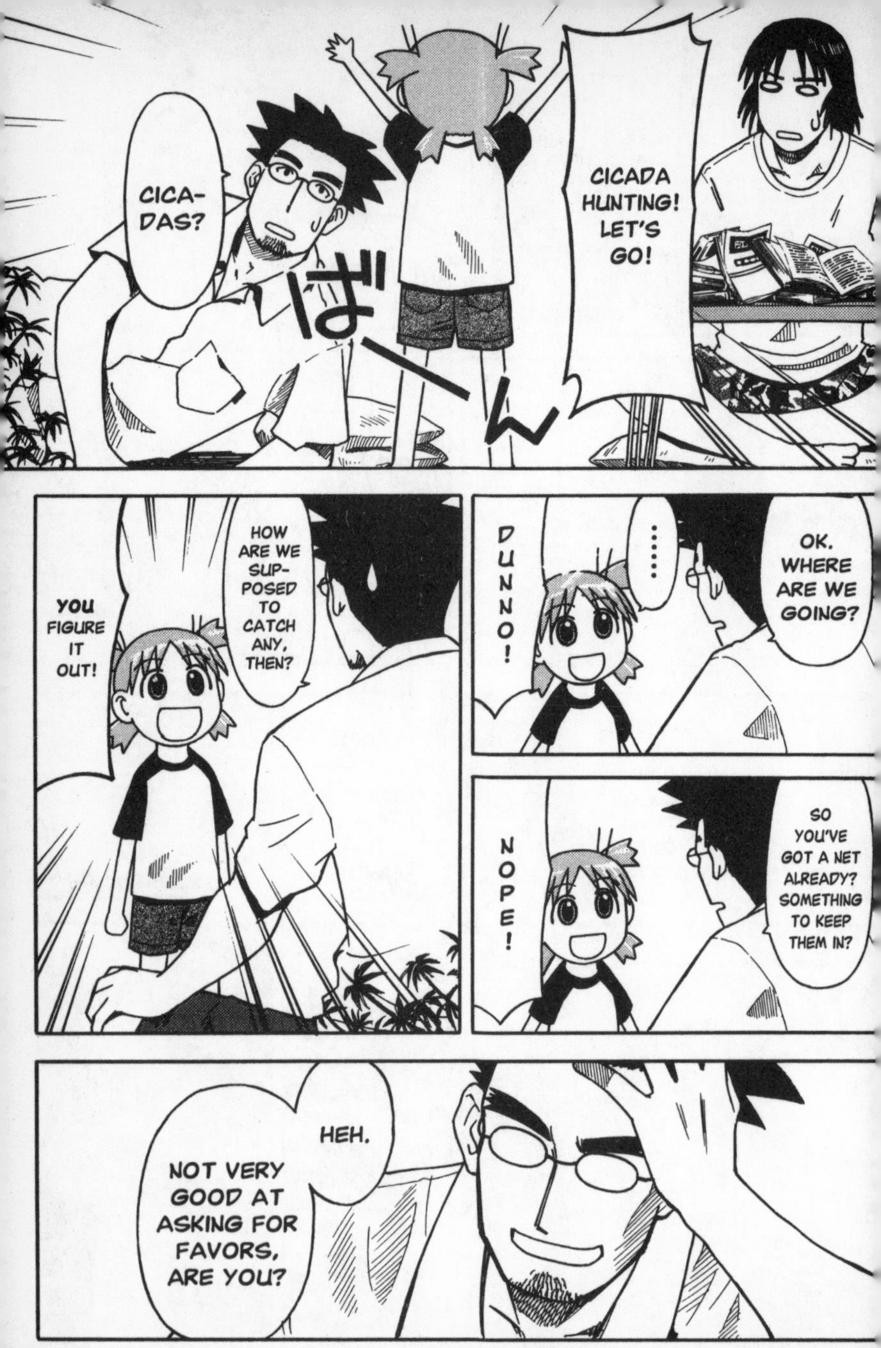
CICADA HUNTING! LET'S GO!
ばーん
CICA-DAS?
OK. WHERE ARE WE GOING?
......
DUNNO!
SO YOU'VE GOT A NET ALREADY? SOMETHING TO KEEP THEM IN?
NOPE!
HOW ARE WE SUP-POSED TO CATCH ANY, THEN?
YOU FIGURE IT OUT!
HEH.
NOT VERY GOOD AT ASKING FOR FAVORS, ARE YOU?

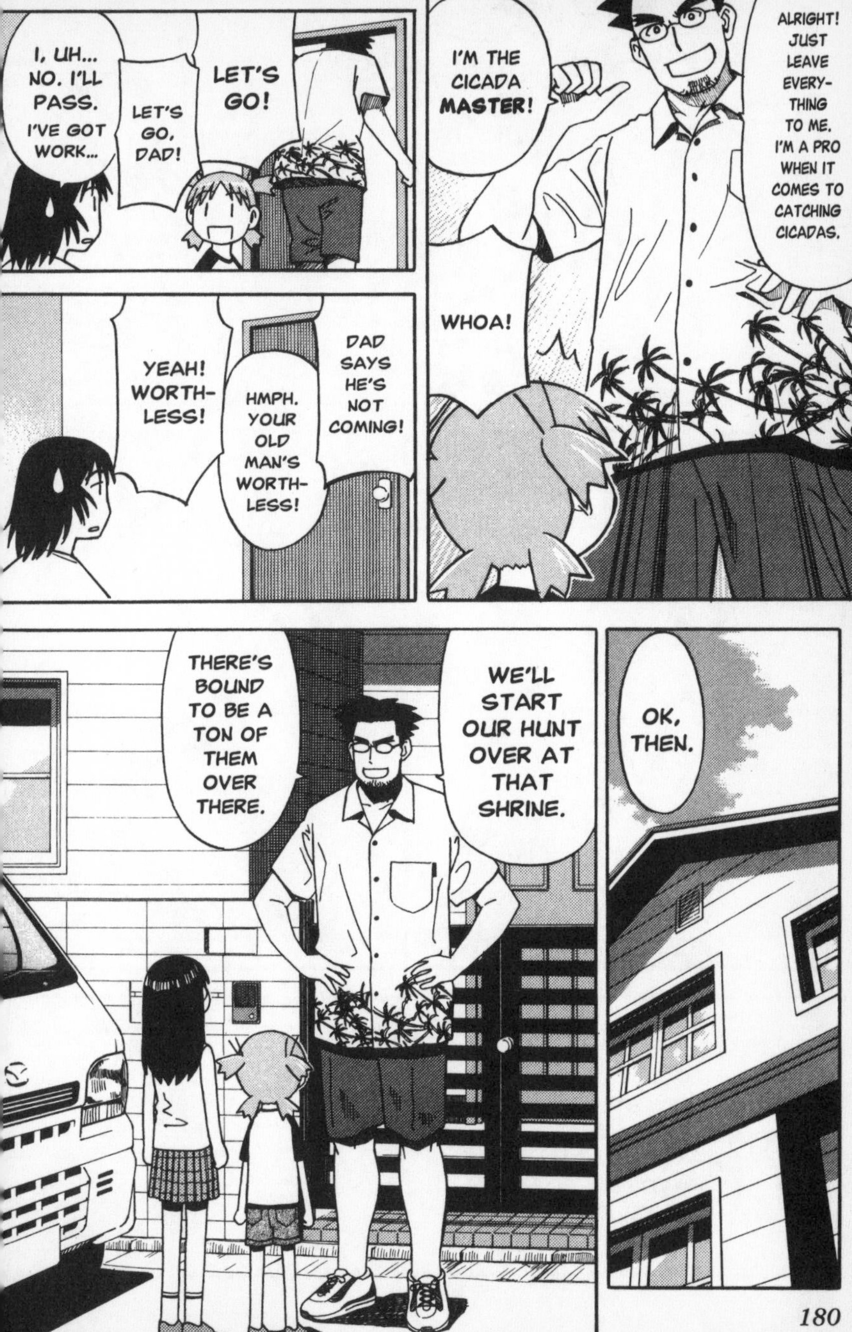
ALRIGHT! JUST LEAVE EVERYTHING TO ME. I'M A PRO WHEN IT COMES TO CATCHING CICADAS.
I'M THE CICADA MASTER!
WHOA!
LET'S GO!
LET'S GO, DAD!
I, UH... NO. I'LL PASS. I'VE GOT WORK...
DAD SAYS HE'S NOT COMING!
HMPH. YOUR OLD MAN'S WORTHLESS!
YEAH! WORTHLESS!
OK, THEN.
WE'LL START OUR HUNT OVER AT THAT SHRINE.
THERE'S BOUND TO BE A TON OF THEM OVER THERE.

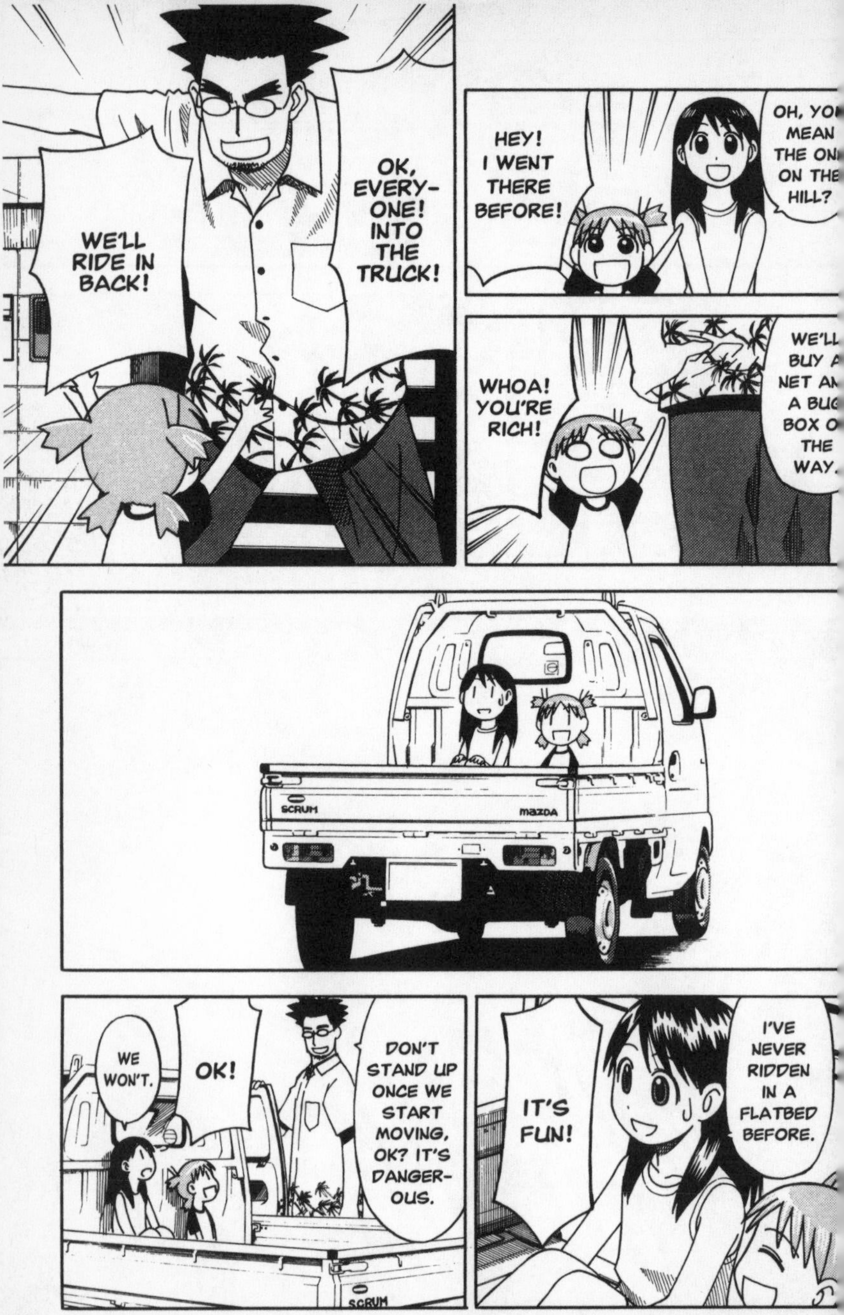
OH, YO MEAN THE ON ON THE HILL?
HEY! I WENT THERE BEFORE!
WE'LL BUY A NET AN A BUG BOX O THE WAY.
WHOA! YOU'RE RICH!
OK, EVERY-ONE! INTO THE TRUCK!
WE'LL RIDE IN BACK!
SCRUM
mazda
I'VE NEVER RIDDEN IN A FLATBED BEFORE.
IT'S FUN!
DON'T STAND UP ONCE WE START MOVING, OK? IT'S DANGER-OUS.
OK!
WE WON'T.
SCRUM

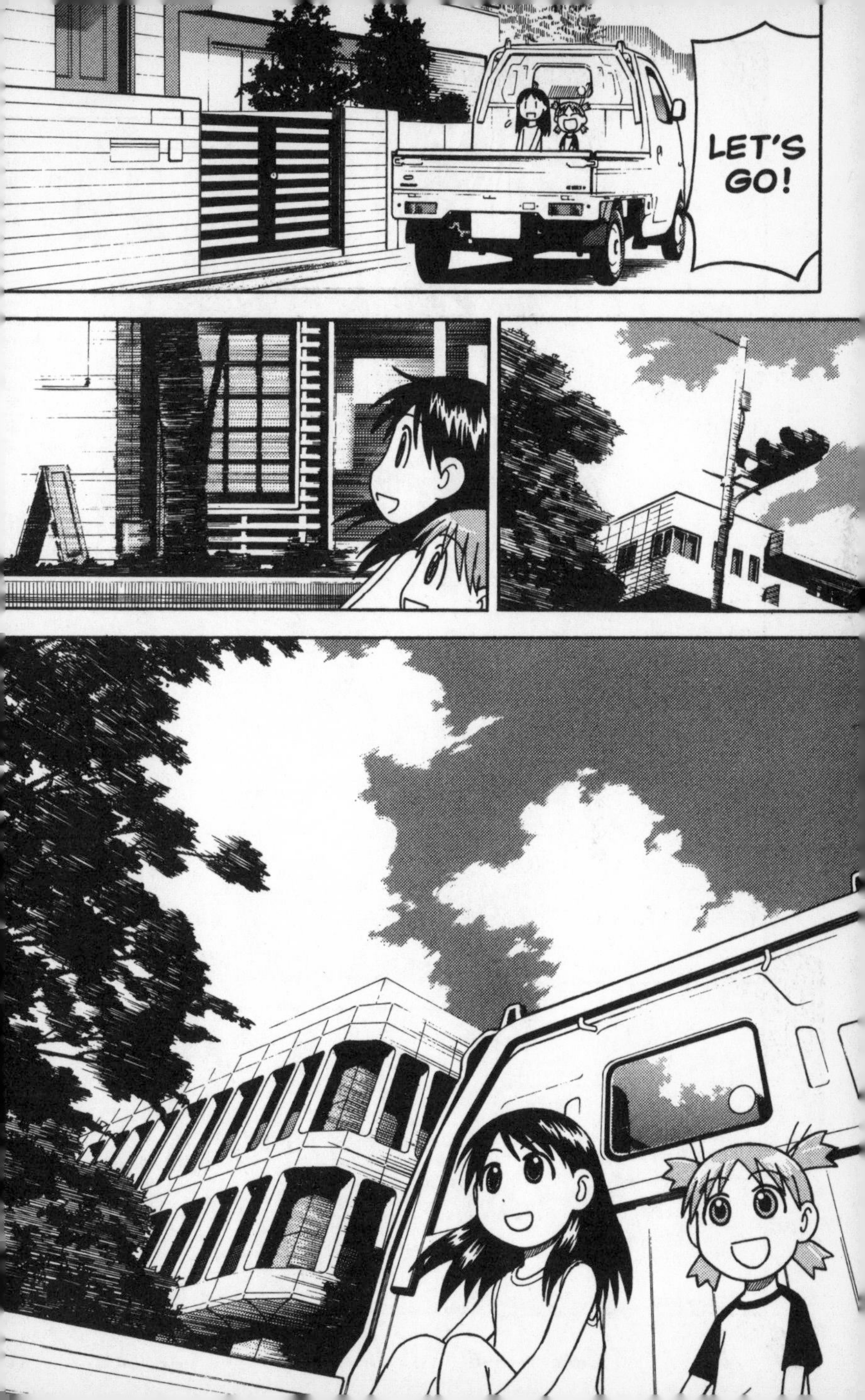
LET'S GO!

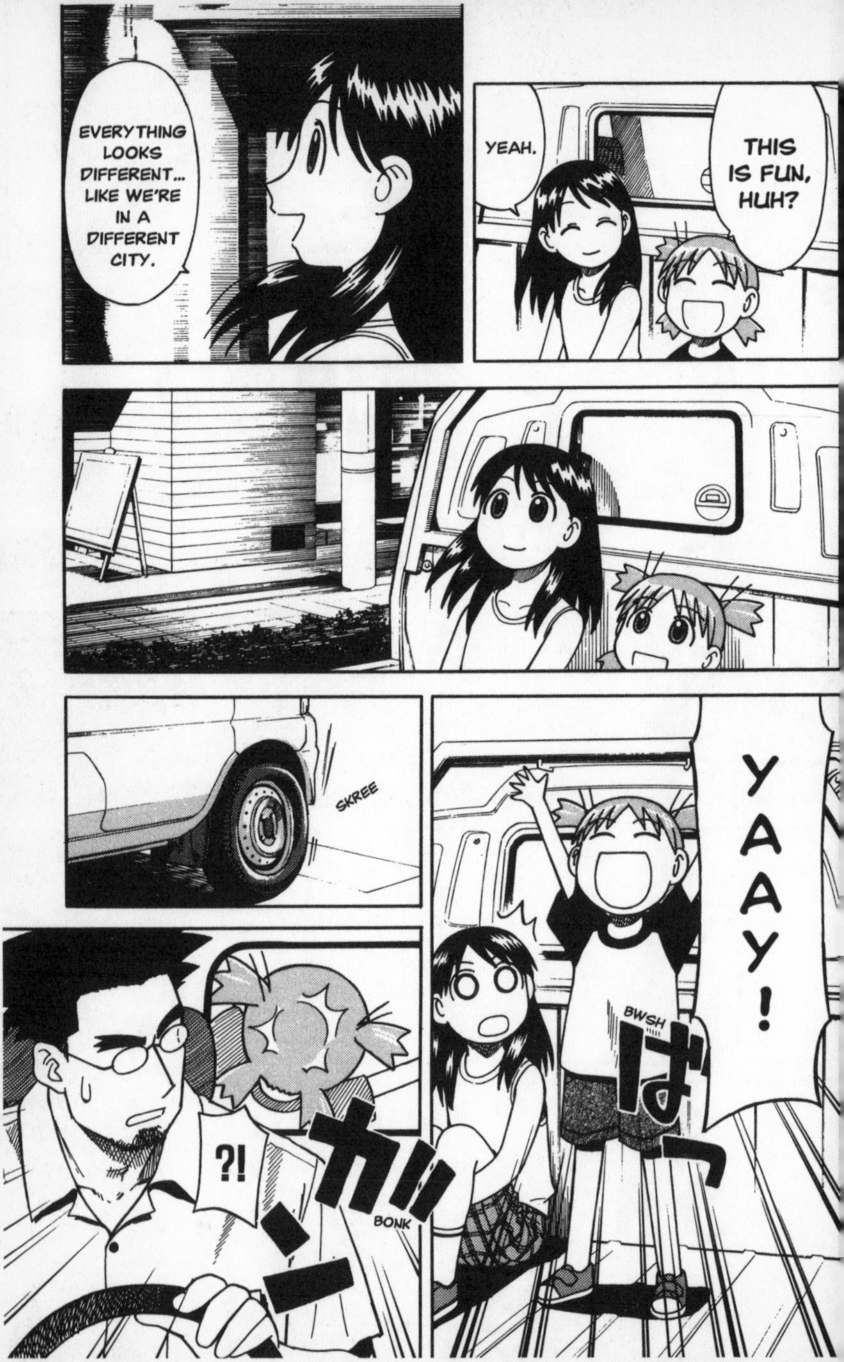

THIS IS FUN, HUH?
YEAH.
EVERYTHING LOOKS DIFFERENT... LIKE WE'RE IN A DIFFERENT CITY.
YAAAY!
BWSH
SKREE
?!
BONK

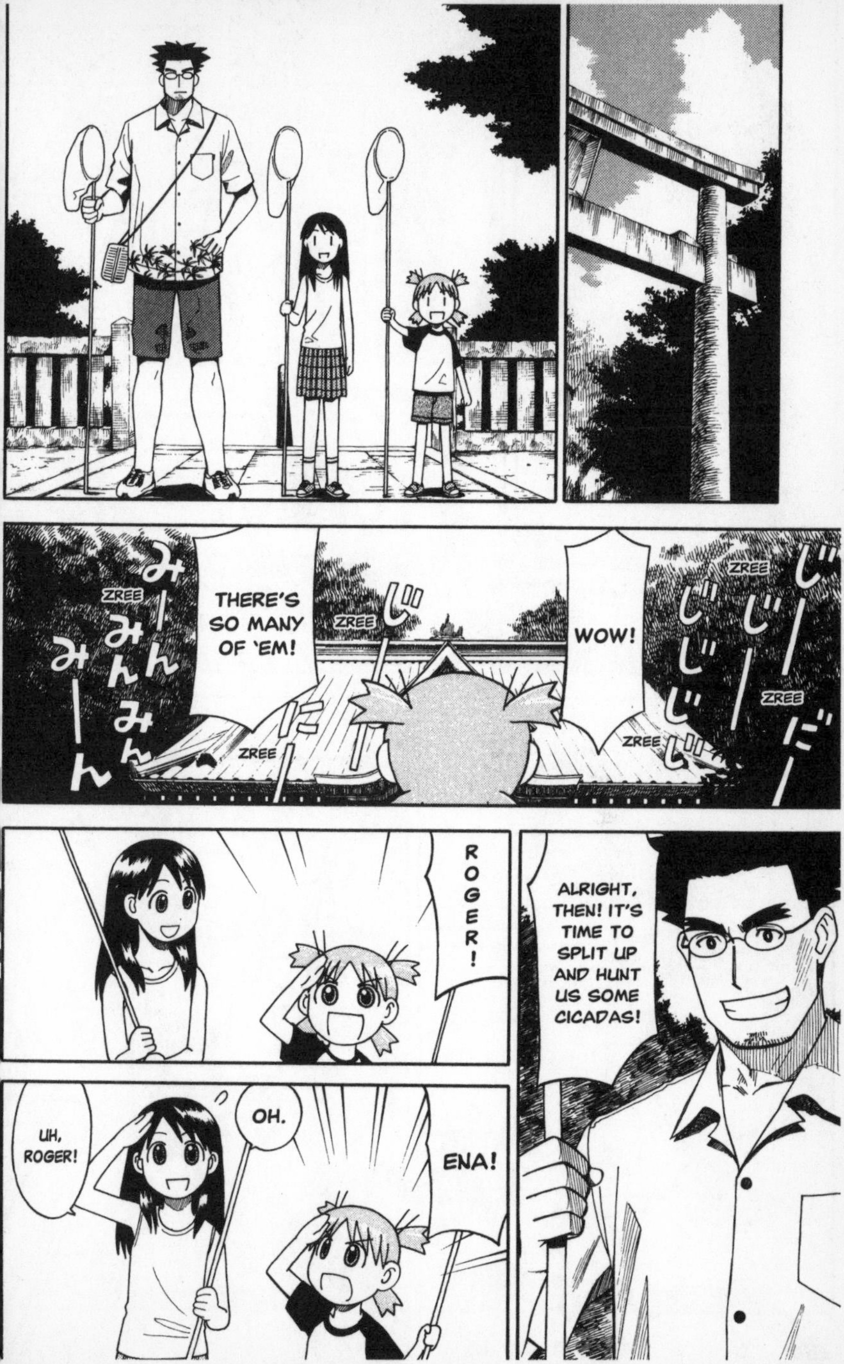
ZREE
じーじーだー
ZREE
じじじじじ
ZREE
WOW!
じ
ZREE
だ
ZREE
THERE'S SO MANY OF 'EM!
ZREE
みーんみんみんみーん
ALRIGHT, THEN! IT'S TIME TO SPLIT UP AND HUNT US SOME CICADAS!
ROGER!
ENA!
OH.
UH, ROGER!

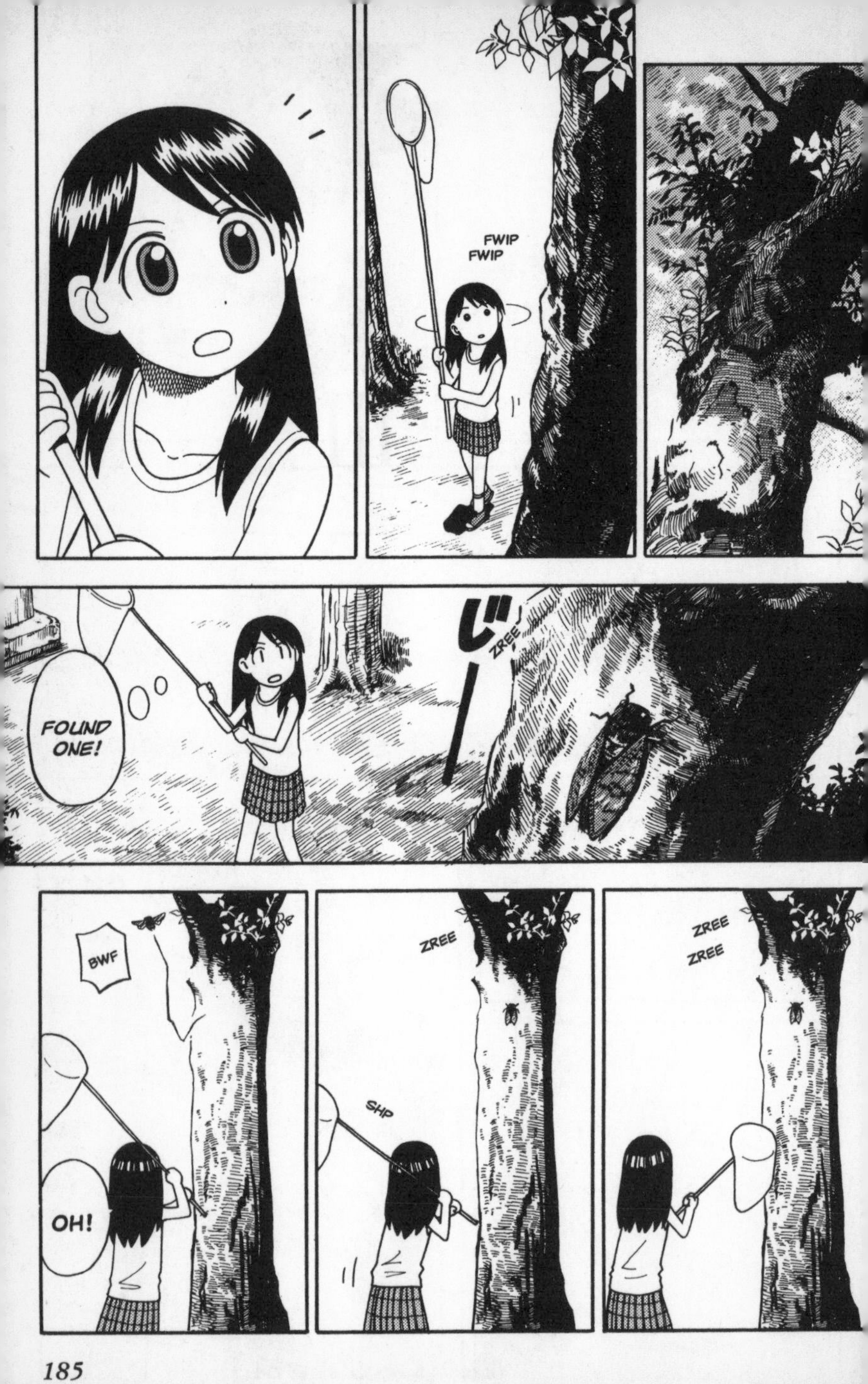
FWIP
FWIP
じ
ZREE
FOUND ONE!
ZREE
ZREE
ZREE
SHP
BWF
OH!

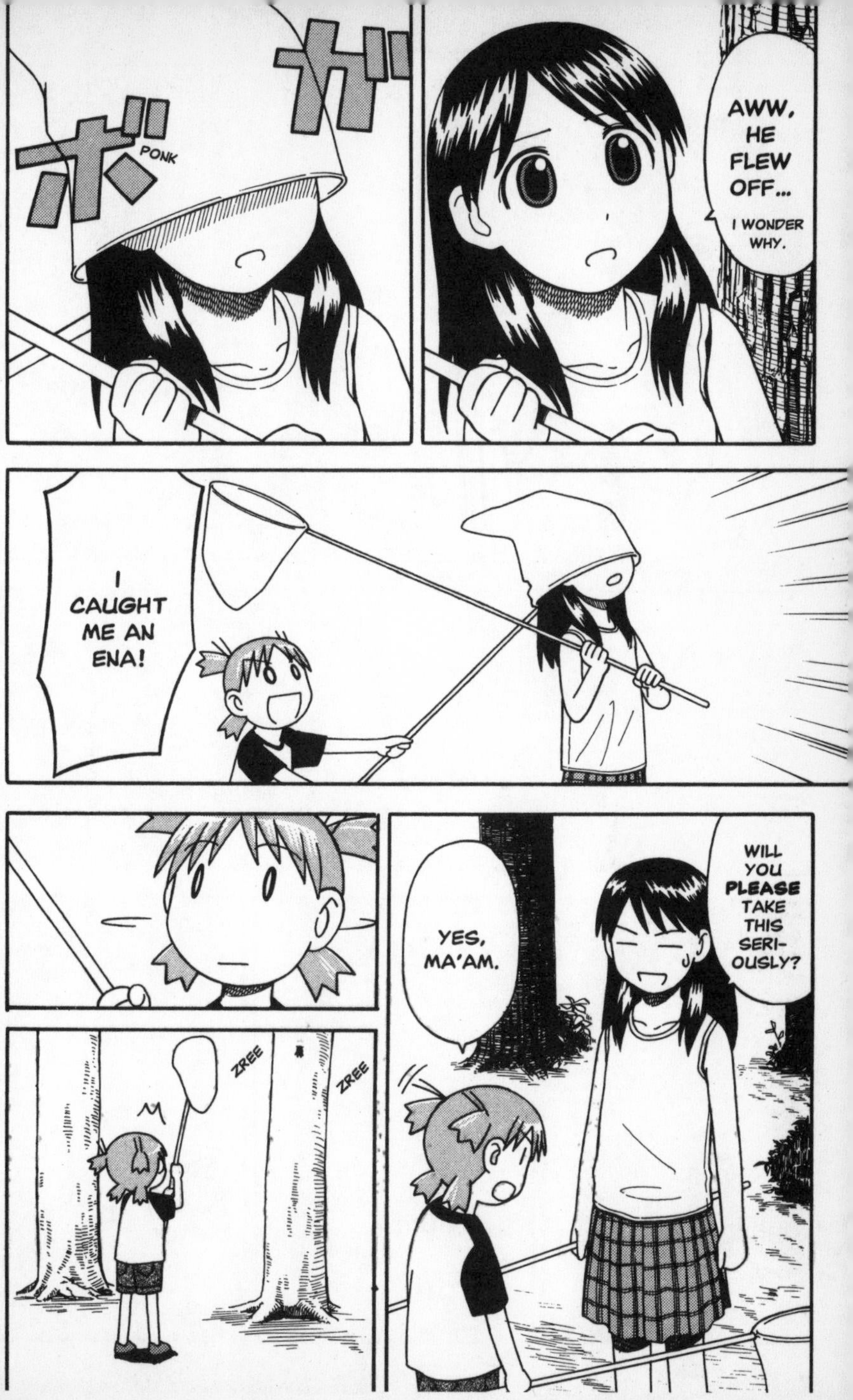
AWW, HE FLEW OFF...
I WONDER WHY.
ガ
ボ
PONK
I CAUGHT ME AN ENA!
WILL YOU **PLEASE** TAKE THIS SERI-OUSLY?
YES, MA'AM.
ZREE
ZREE
M

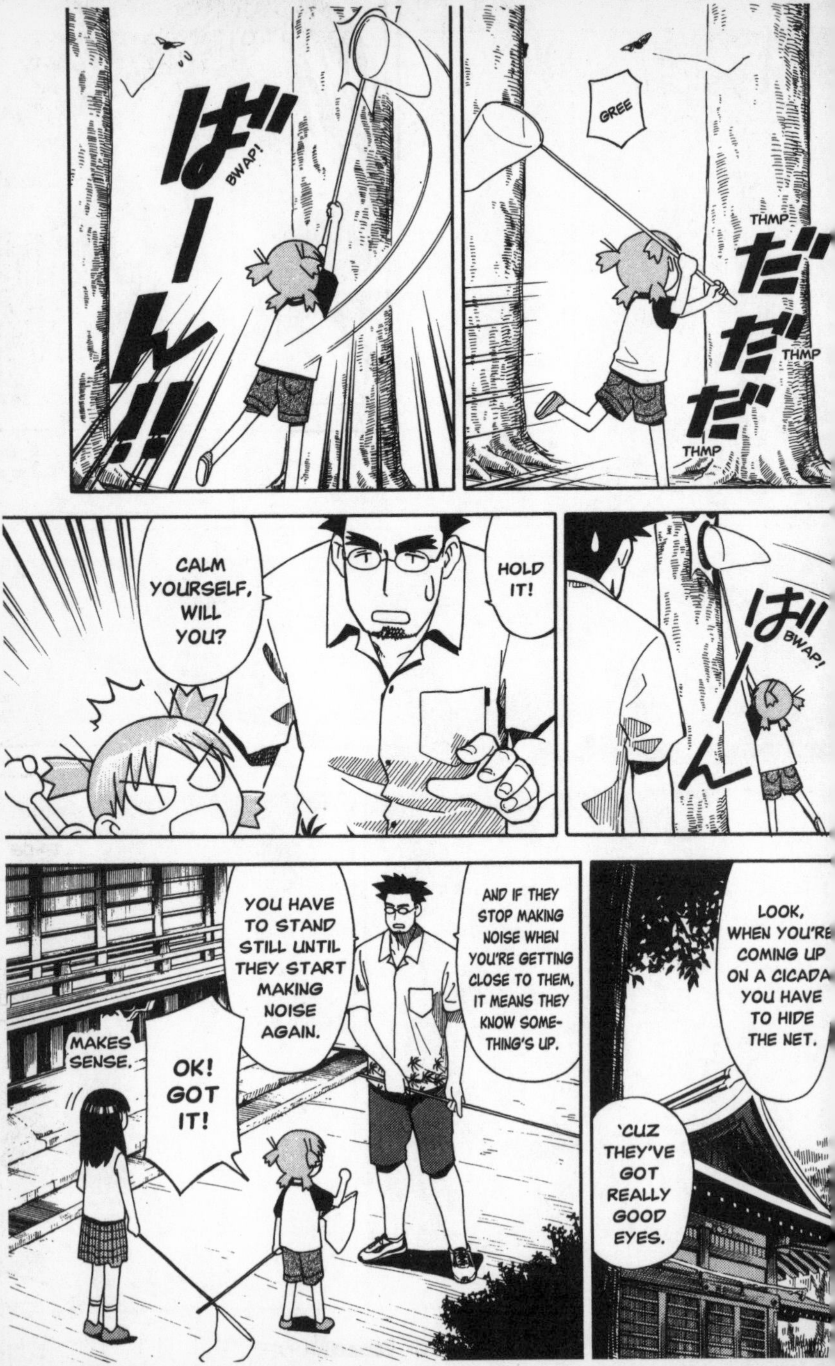
GREE
だだだだ
THMP
THMP
THMP
ばーん!!
BWAP!
ばーん
BWAP!
HOLD IT!
CALM YOURSELF, WILL YOU?
LOOK, WHEN YOU'RE COMING UP ON A CICADA YOU HAVE TO HIDE THE NET.
'CUZ THEY'VE GOT REALLY GOOD EYES.
AND IF THEY STOP MAKING NOISE WHEN YOU'RE GETTING CLOSE TO THEM, IT MEANS THEY KNOW SOME-THING'S UP.
YOU HAVE TO STAND STILL UNTIL THEY START MAKING NOISE AGAIN.
OK! GOT IT!
MAKES SENSE.

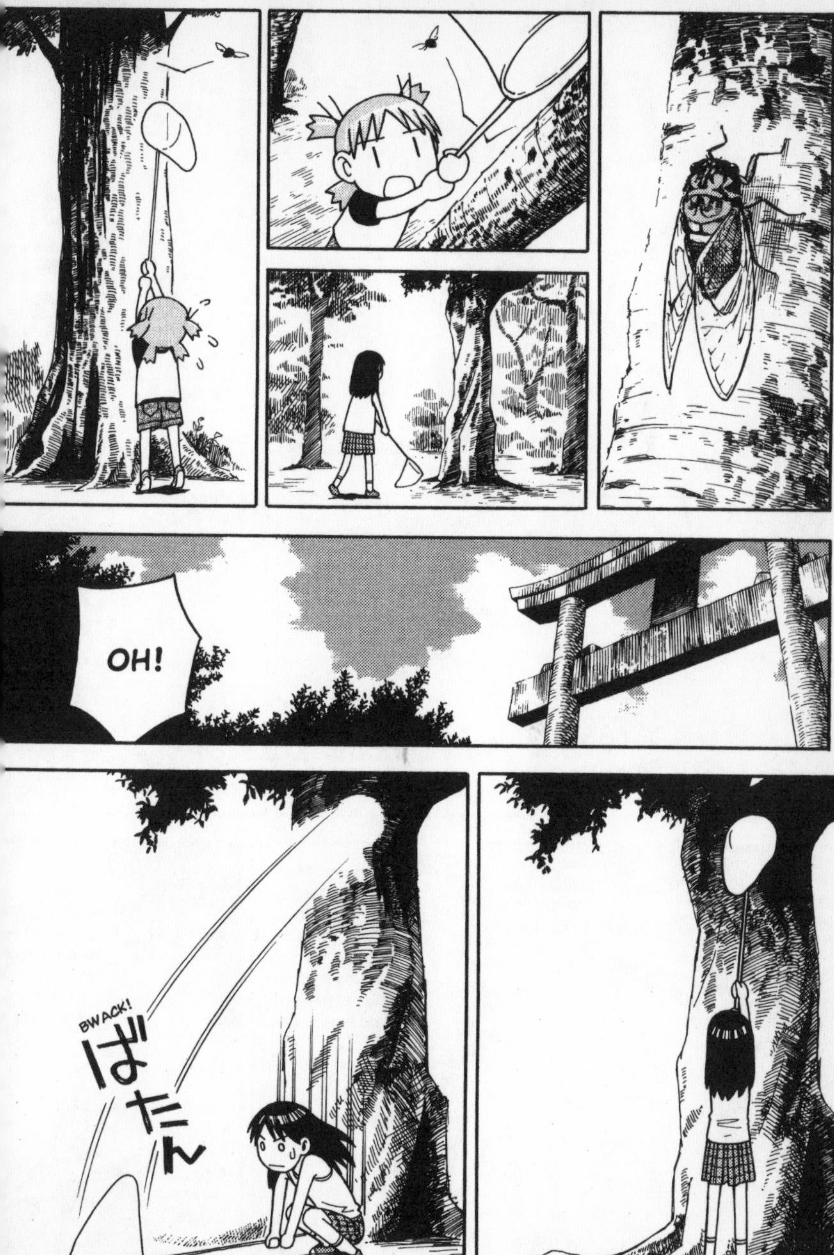
OH!
BWACK!
ばたん

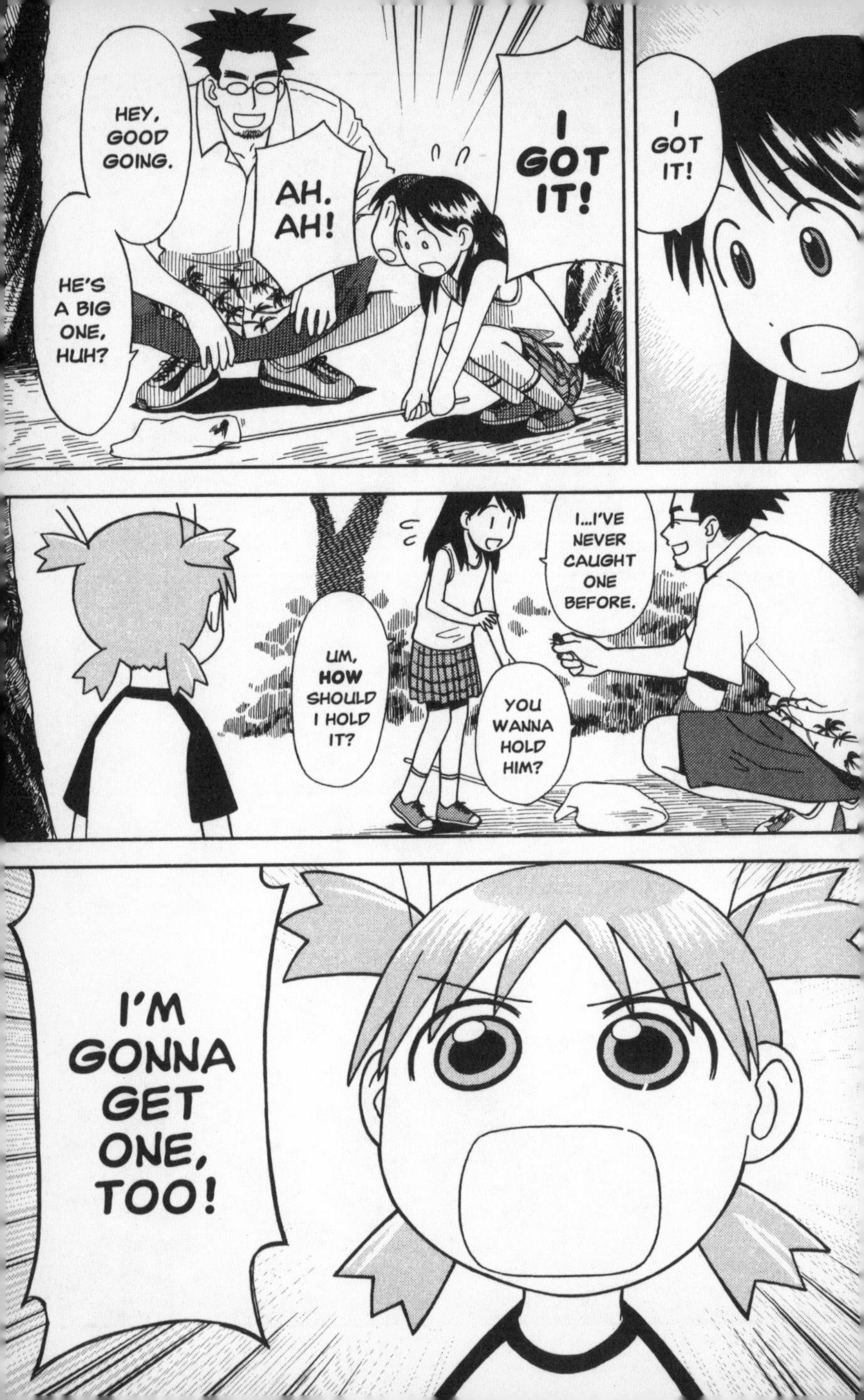
I GOT IT!
I GOT IT!
AH. AH!
HEY, GOOD GOING.
HE'S A BIG ONE, HUH?
I...I'VE NEVER CAUGHT ONE BEFORE.
YOU WANNA HOLD HIM?
UM, **HOW** SHOULD I HOLD IT?
I'M GONNA GET ONE, TOO!

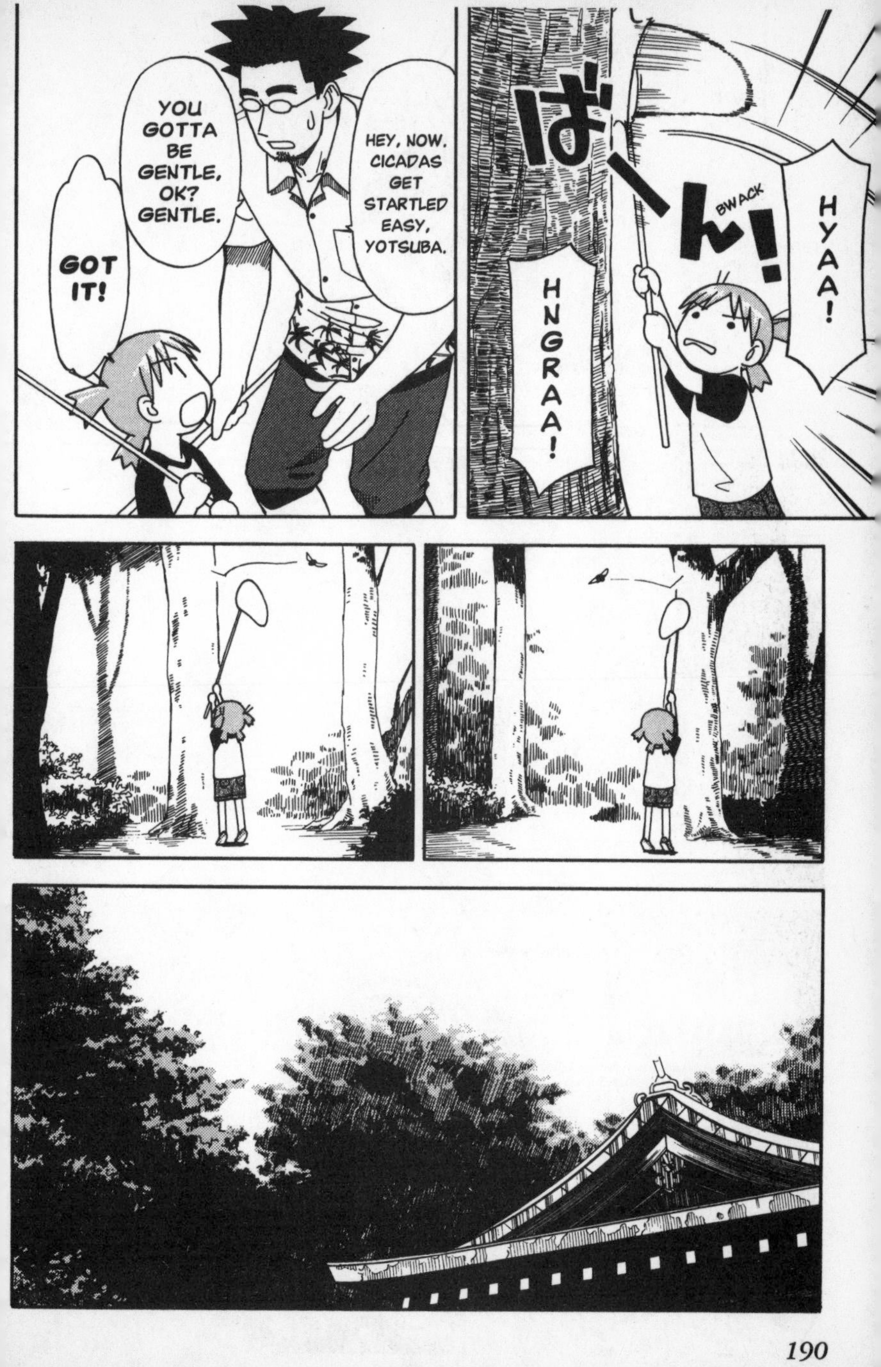
HYAA!
ばーん!
BWACK
HNGRAA!
HEY, NOW. CICADAS GET STARTLED EASY, YOTSUBA.
YOU GOTTA BE GENTLE, OK? GENTLE.
GOT IT!

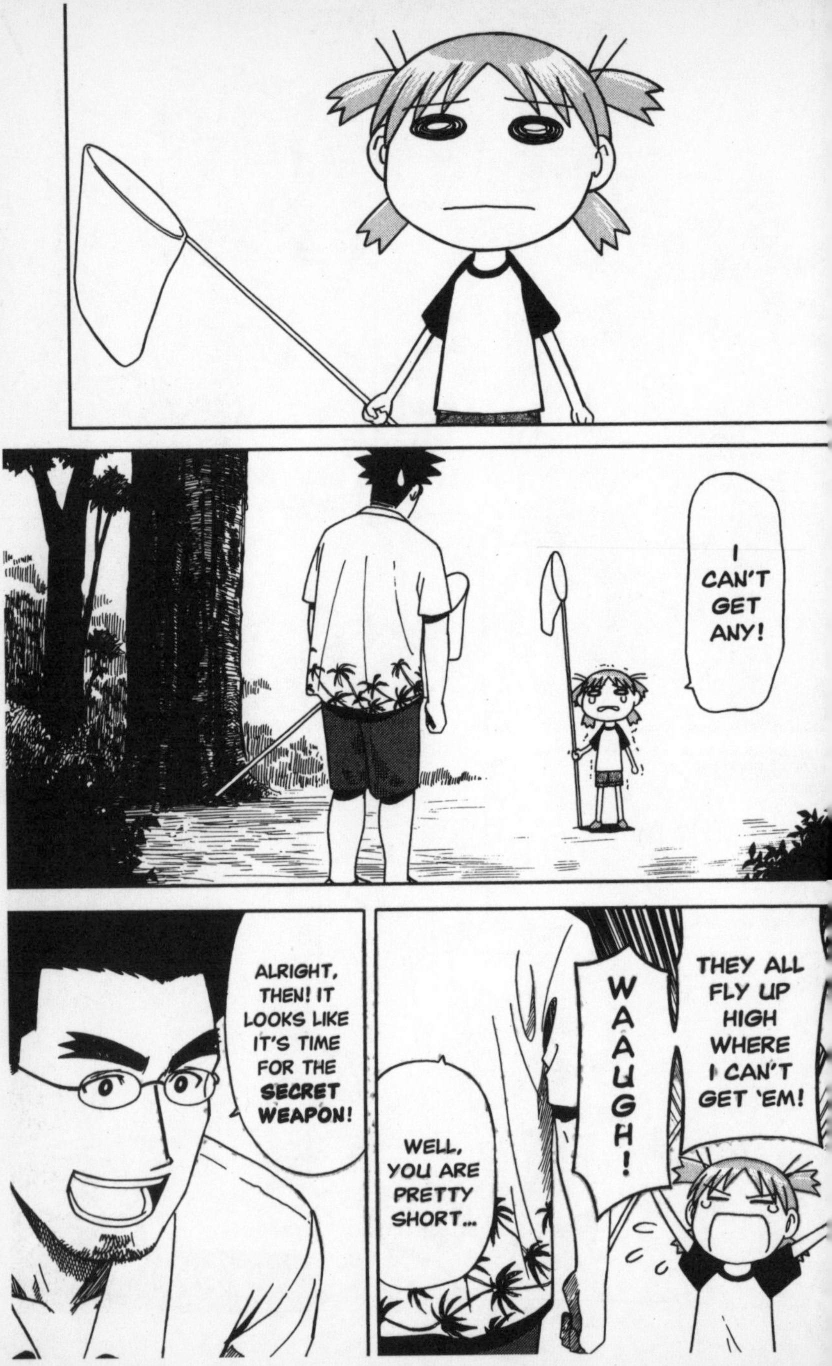
I CAN'T GET ANY!
THEY ALL FLY UP HIGH WHERE I CAN'T GET 'EM!
WAAUGH!
WELL, YOU ARE PRETTY SHORT...
ALRIGHT, THEN! IT LOOKS LIKE IT'S TIME FOR THE SECRET WEAPON!

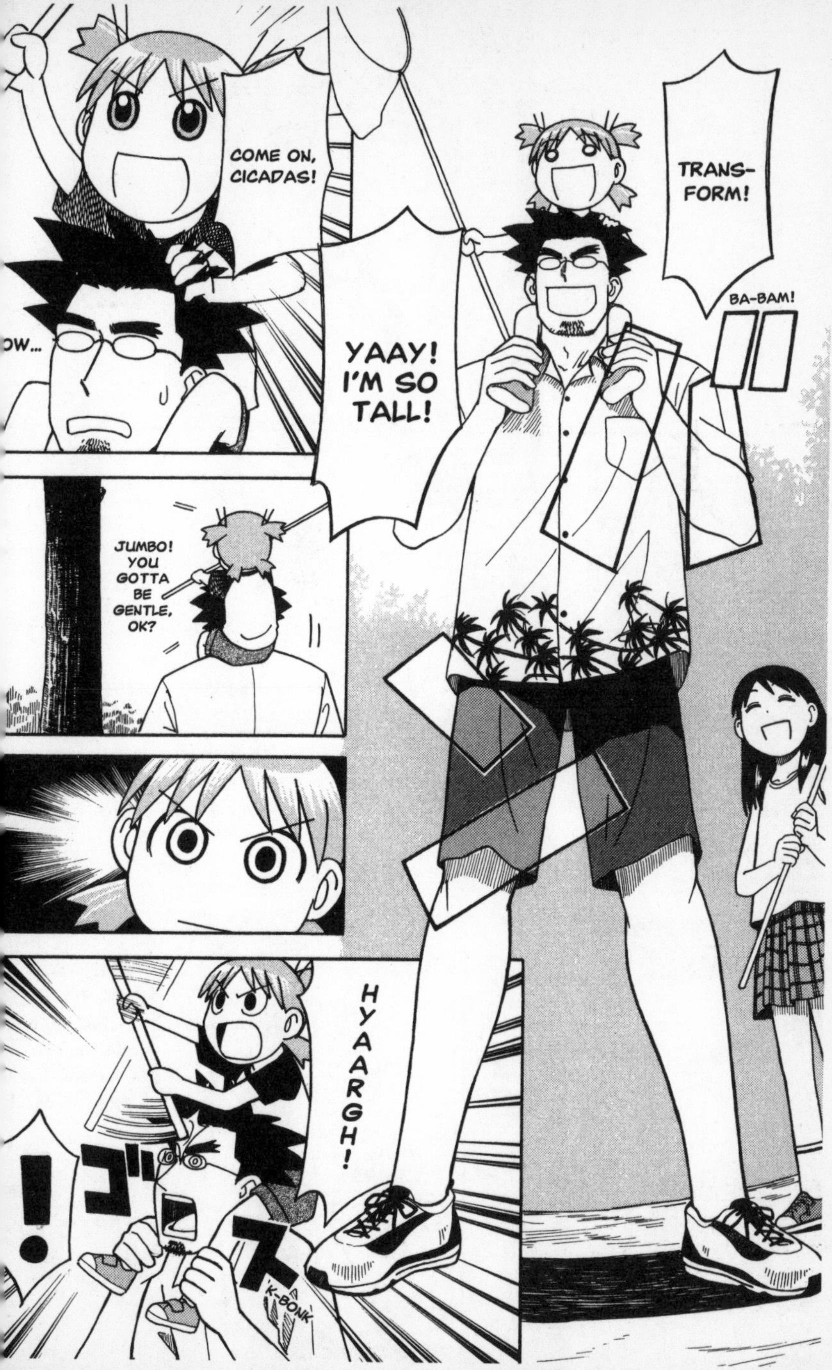

TRANS-FORM!
BA-BAM!
YAAY! I'M SO TALL!
COME ON, CICADAS!
OW...
JUMBO! YOU GOTTA BE GENTLE, OK?
HYAAARGH!
ゴス
K-BONK
!

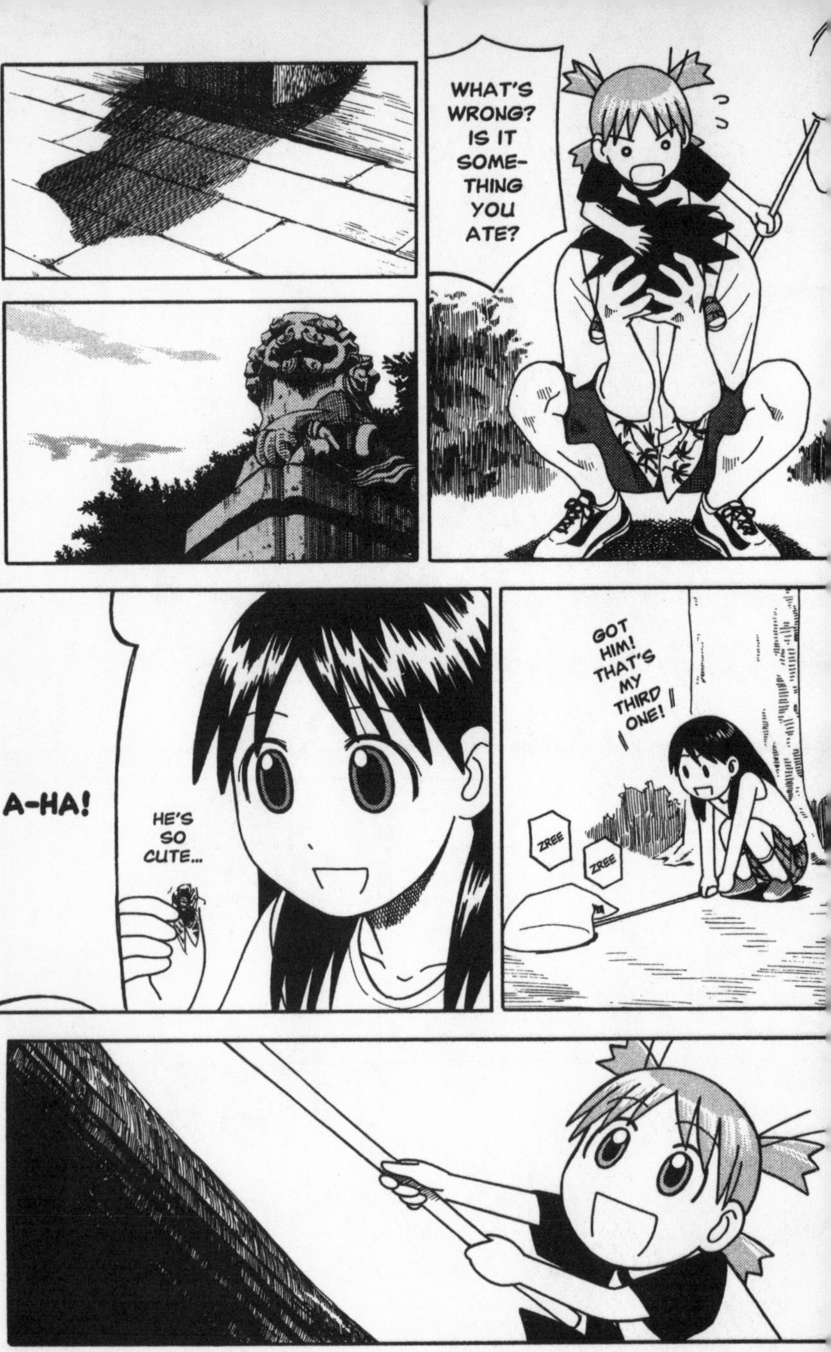
WHAT'S WRONG? IS IT SOME-THING YOU ATE?
GOT HIM! THAT'S MY THIRD ONE!
ZREE
ZREE
HE'S SO CUTE...
A-HA!

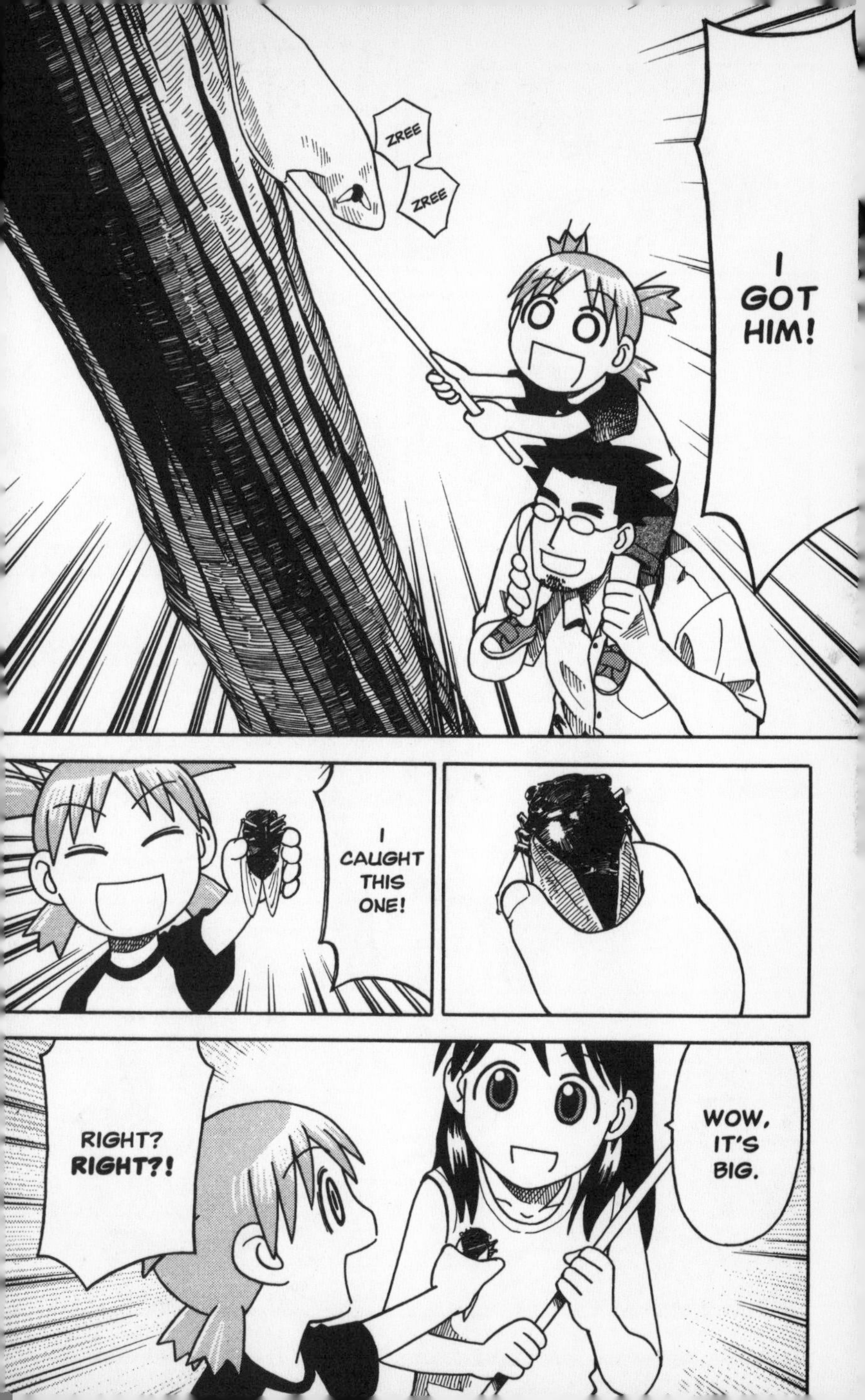
I GOT HIM!
ZREE
ZREE
I CAUGHT THIS ONE!
WOW, IT'S BIG.
RIGHT? RIGHT?!

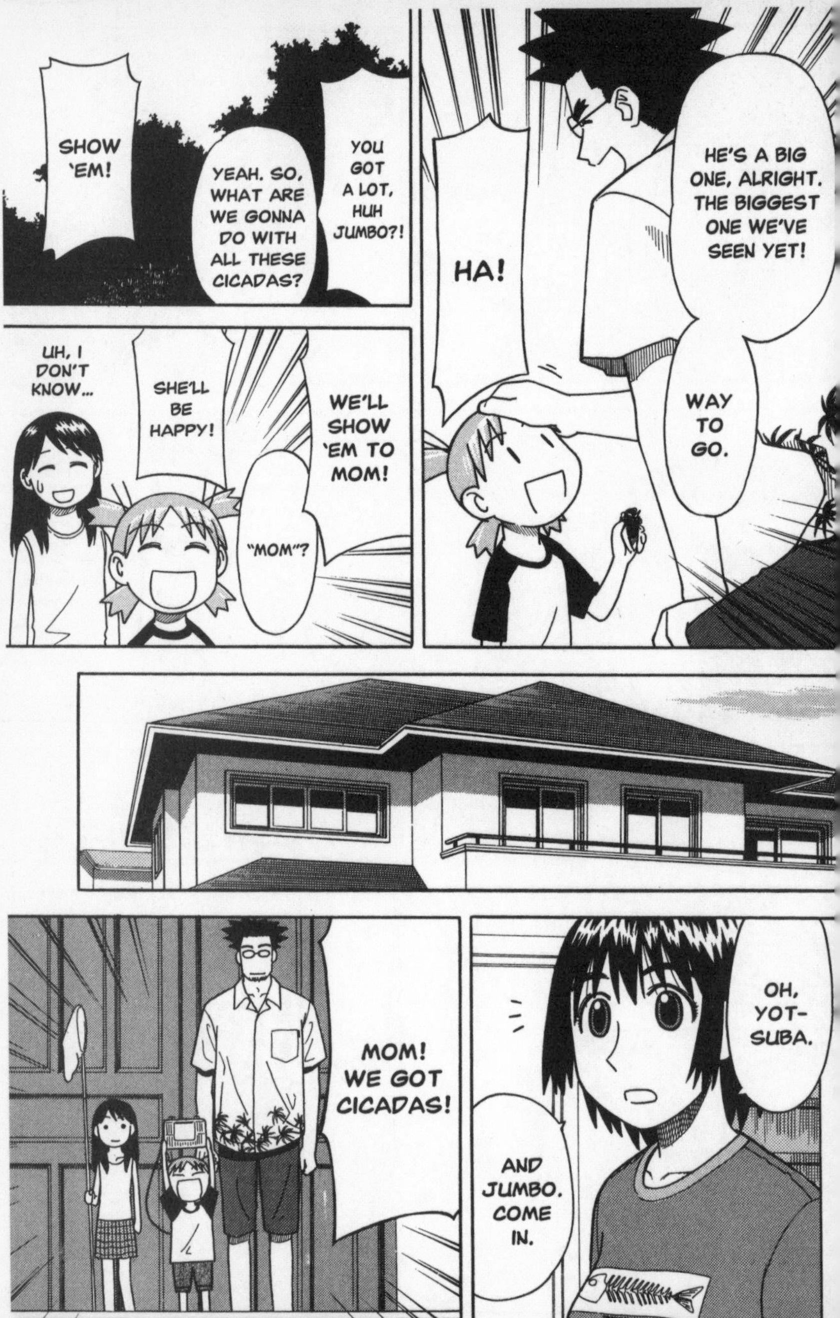
HE'S A BIG ONE, ALRIGHT. THE BIGGEST ONE WE'VE SEEN YET!
HA!
WAY TO GO.
YOU GOT A LOT, HUH JUMBO?!
YEAH. SO, WHAT ARE WE GONNA DO WITH ALL THESE CICADAS?
SHOW 'EM!
WE'LL SHOW 'EM TO MOM!
"MOM"?
SHE'LL BE HAPPY!
UH, I DON'T KNOW...
OH, YOT-SUBA.
AND JUMBO. COME IN.
MOM! WE GOT CICADAS!

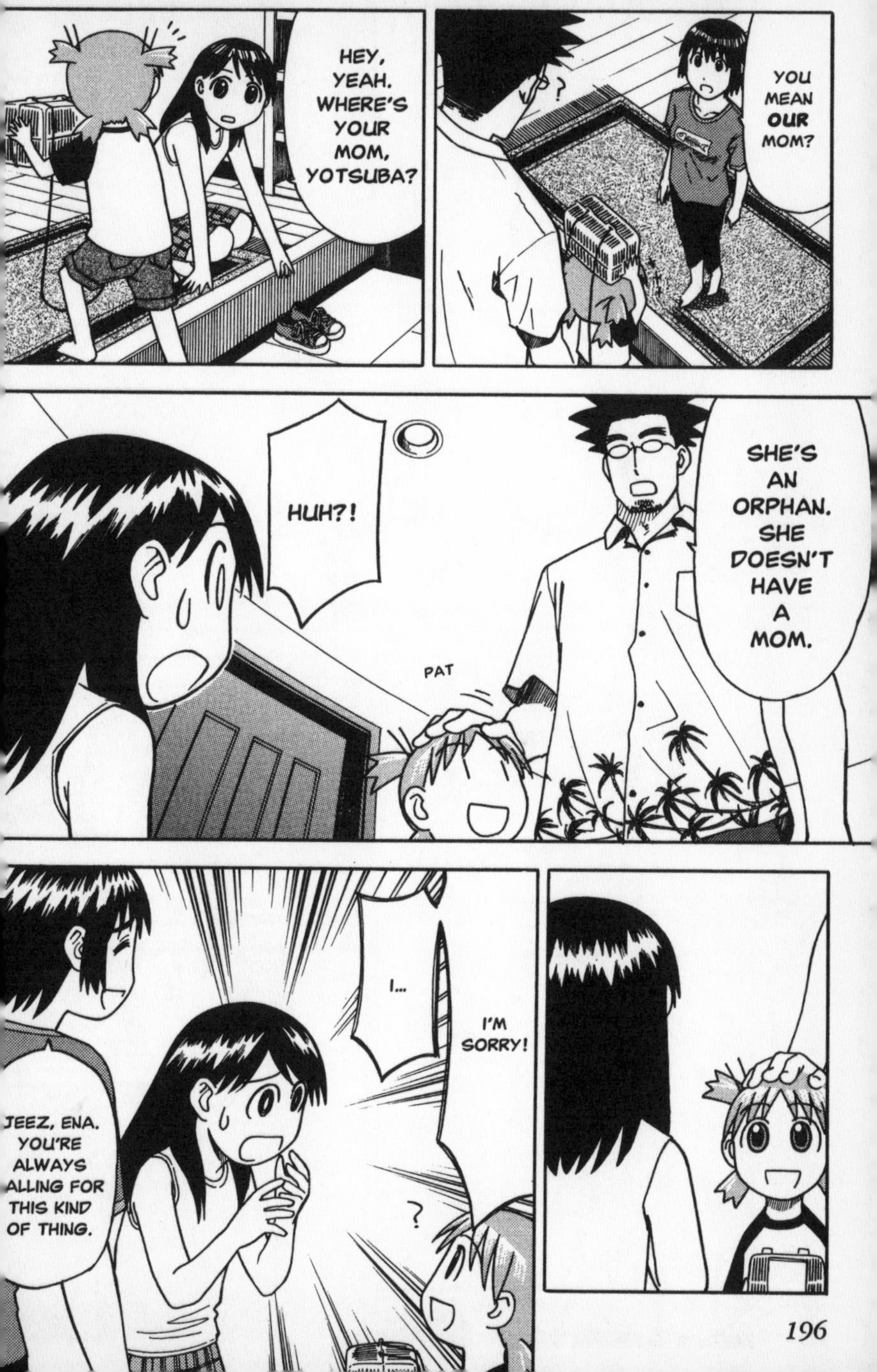
YOU MEAN OUR MOM?
HEY, YEAH. WHERE'S YOUR MOM, YOTSUBA?
SHE'S AN ORPHAN. SHE DOESN'T HAVE A MOM.
PAT
HUH?!
I...
I'M SORRY!
?
JEEZ, ENA. YOU'RE ALWAYS ALLING FOR THIS KIND OF THING.

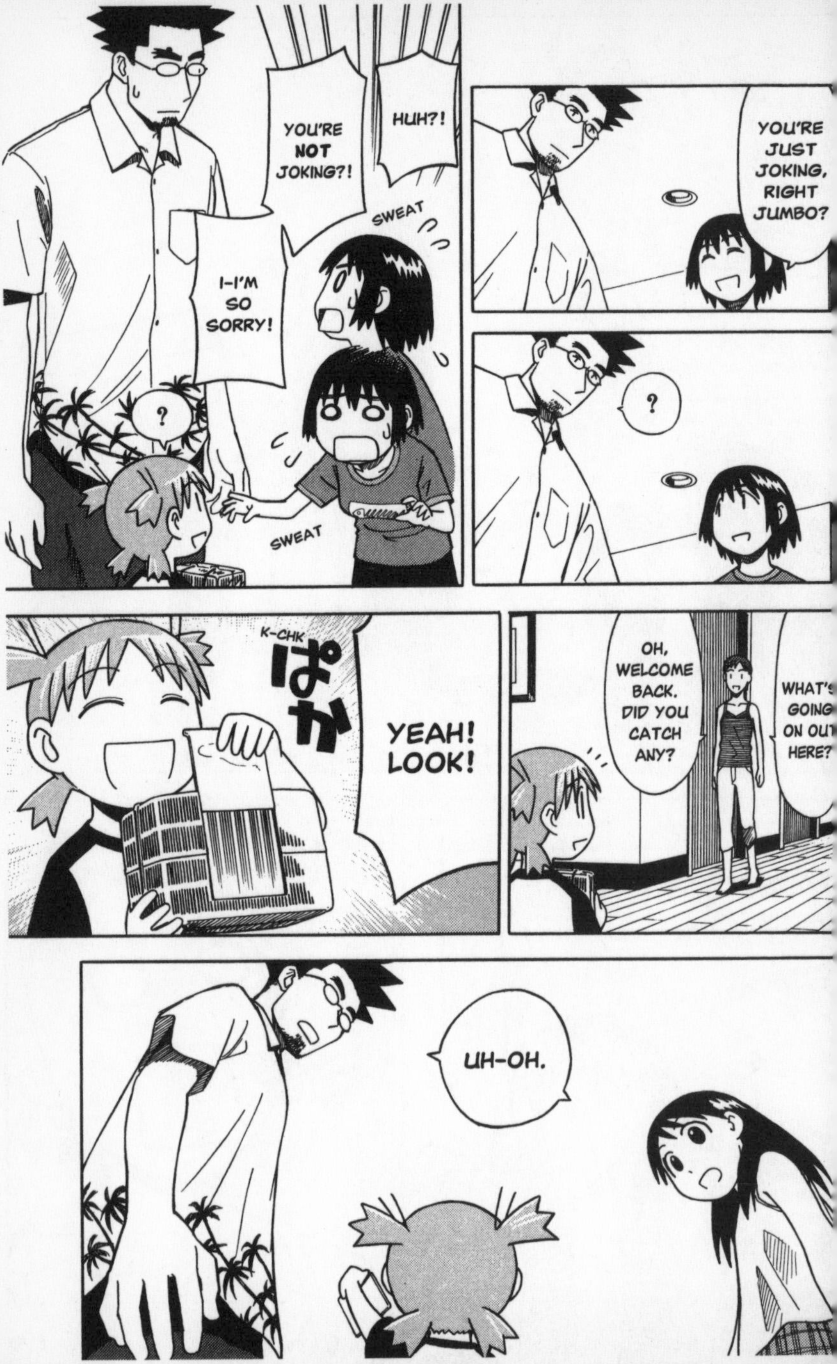
YOU'RE JUST JOKING, RIGHT JUMBO?
?
HUH?!
YOU'RE NOT JOKING?!
SWEAT
I-I'M SO SORRY!
?
SWEAT
WHAT'S GOING ON OUT HERE?
OH, WELCOME BACK. DID YOU CATCH ANY?
YEAH! LOOK!
K-CHK
ぱか
UH-OH.

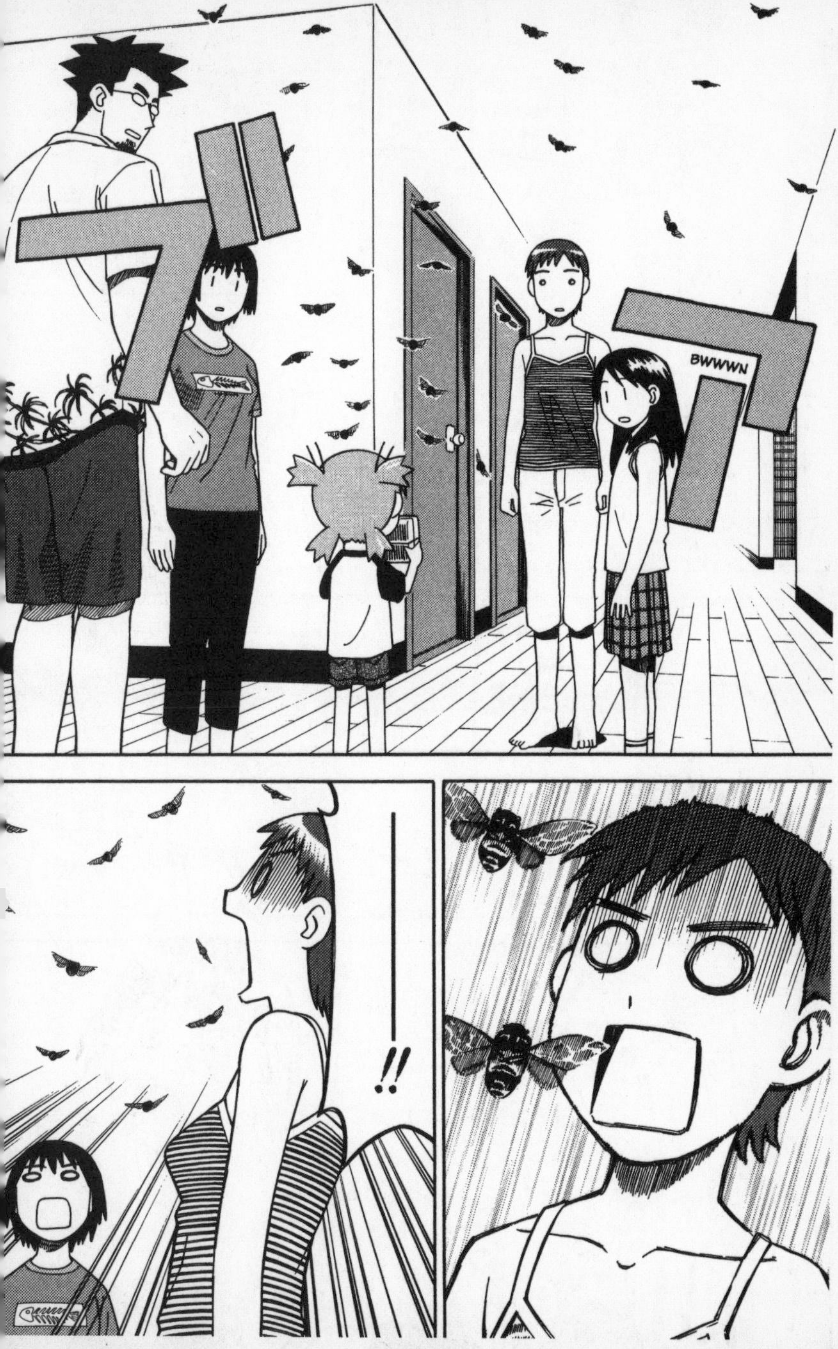
BWWWN
!!

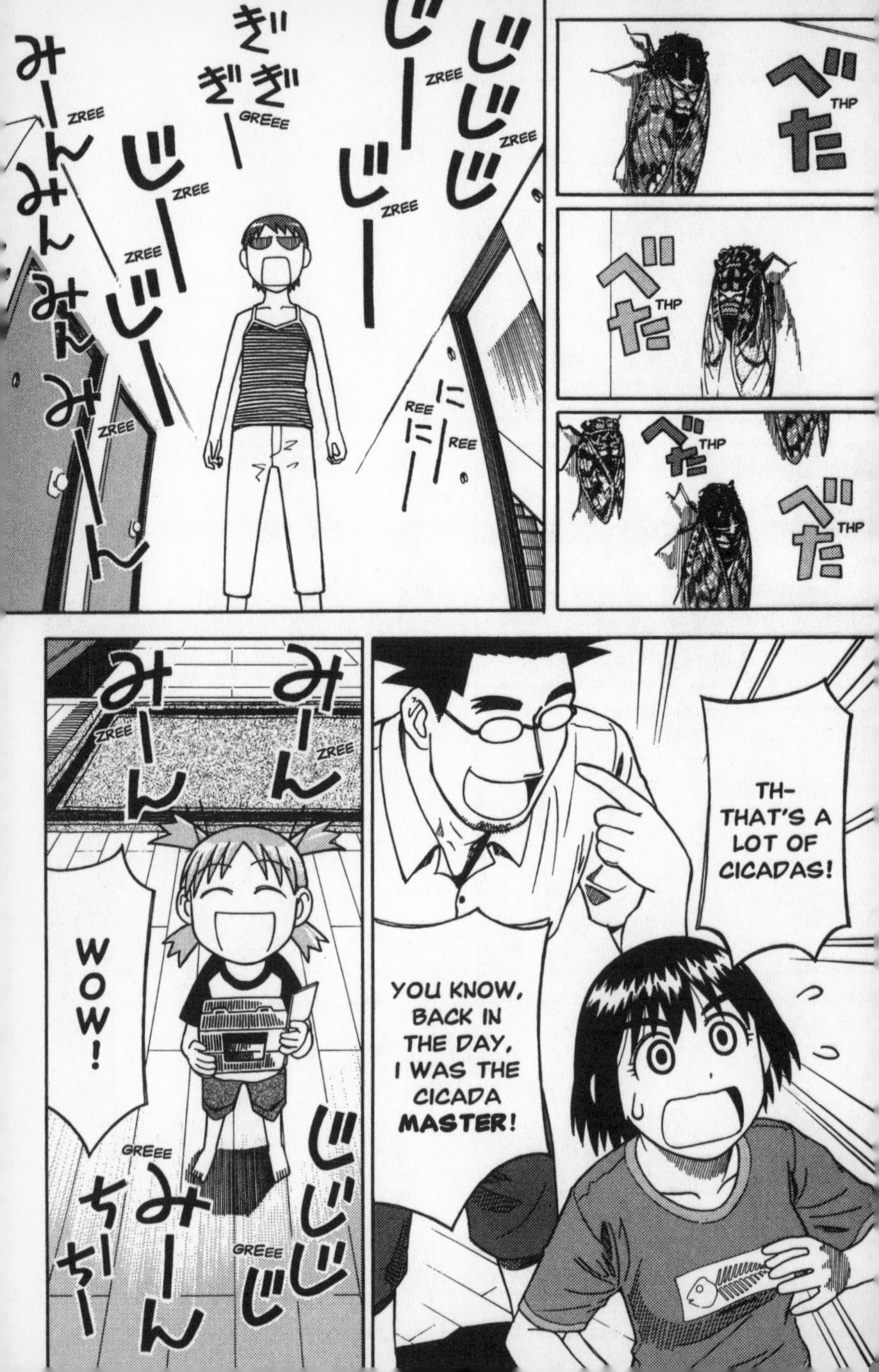

べた
THP
べた
THP
べた
THP
べた
THP
じじじ
ZREE
じーじー
ZREE
ZREE
ぎぎぎー
GREEE
じーじー
ZREE
ZREE
みーんみんみんみーん
ZREE
ZREE
にーにー
REE
REE
TH- THAT'S A LOT OF CICADAS!
YOU KNOW, BACK IN THE DAY, I WAS THE CICADA MASTER!
みーん
ZREE
みーん
ZREE
WOW!
じじじじ
GREEE
みーん
GREEE
ちーちー

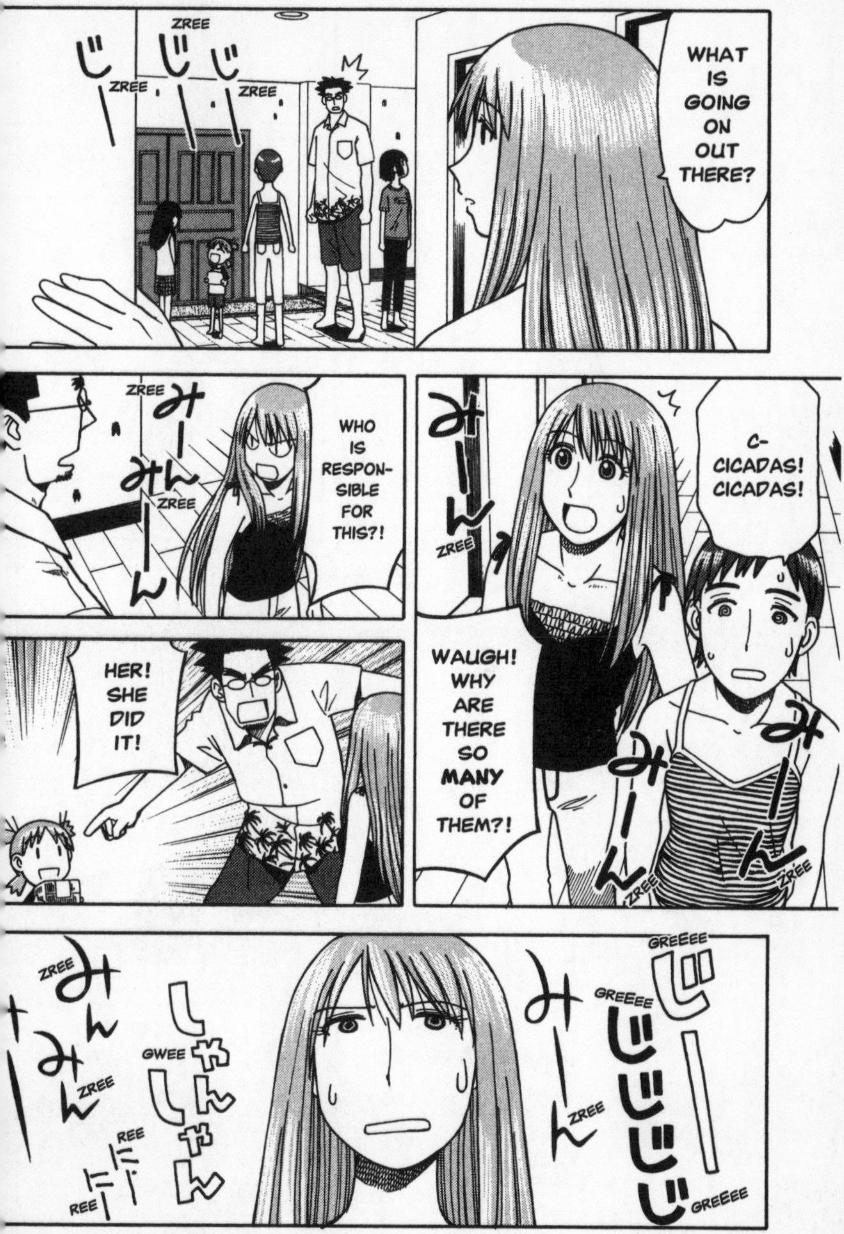
WHAT IS GOING ON OUT THERE?
ZREE
ZREE
ZREE
C-CICADAS! CICADAS!
WAUGH! WHY ARE THERE SO MANY OF THEM?!
ZREE
ZREE
ZREE
WHO IS RESPONSIBLE FOR THIS?!
ZREE
ZREE
HER! SHE DID IT!
GREEEE
GREEEE
GREEEE
ZREE
GWEE
ZREE
ZREE
REE
REE

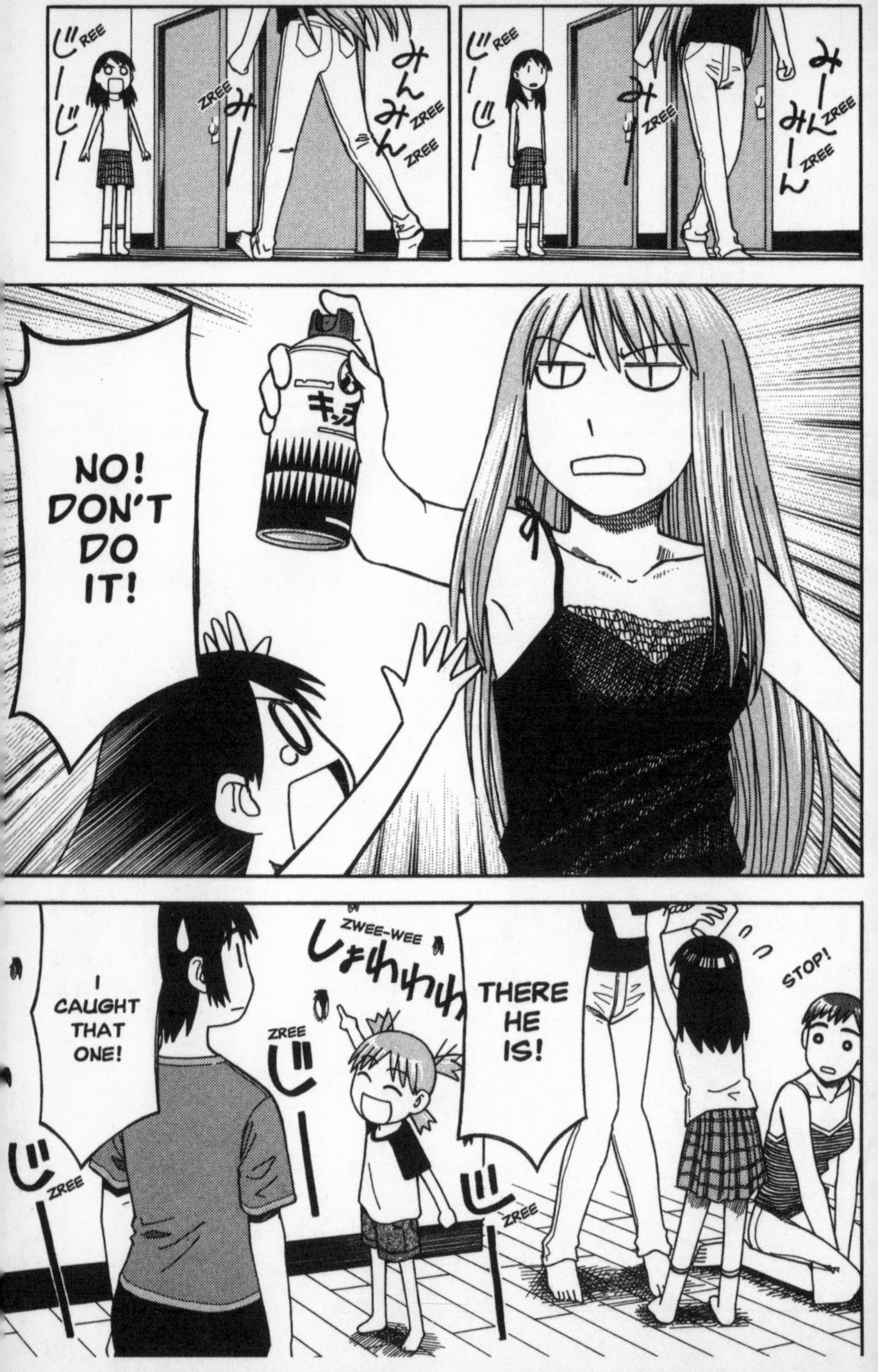

みーみんみーん
ZREE
ZREE
み
ZREE
じーじー
REE
みんみん
ZREE
ZREE
み
ZREE
じーじー
REE
NO! DON'T DO IT!
STOP!
THERE HE IS!
しょわわわ
ZWEE-WEE
じー
ZREE
じー
ZREE
I CAUGHT THAT ONE!
じー
ZREE

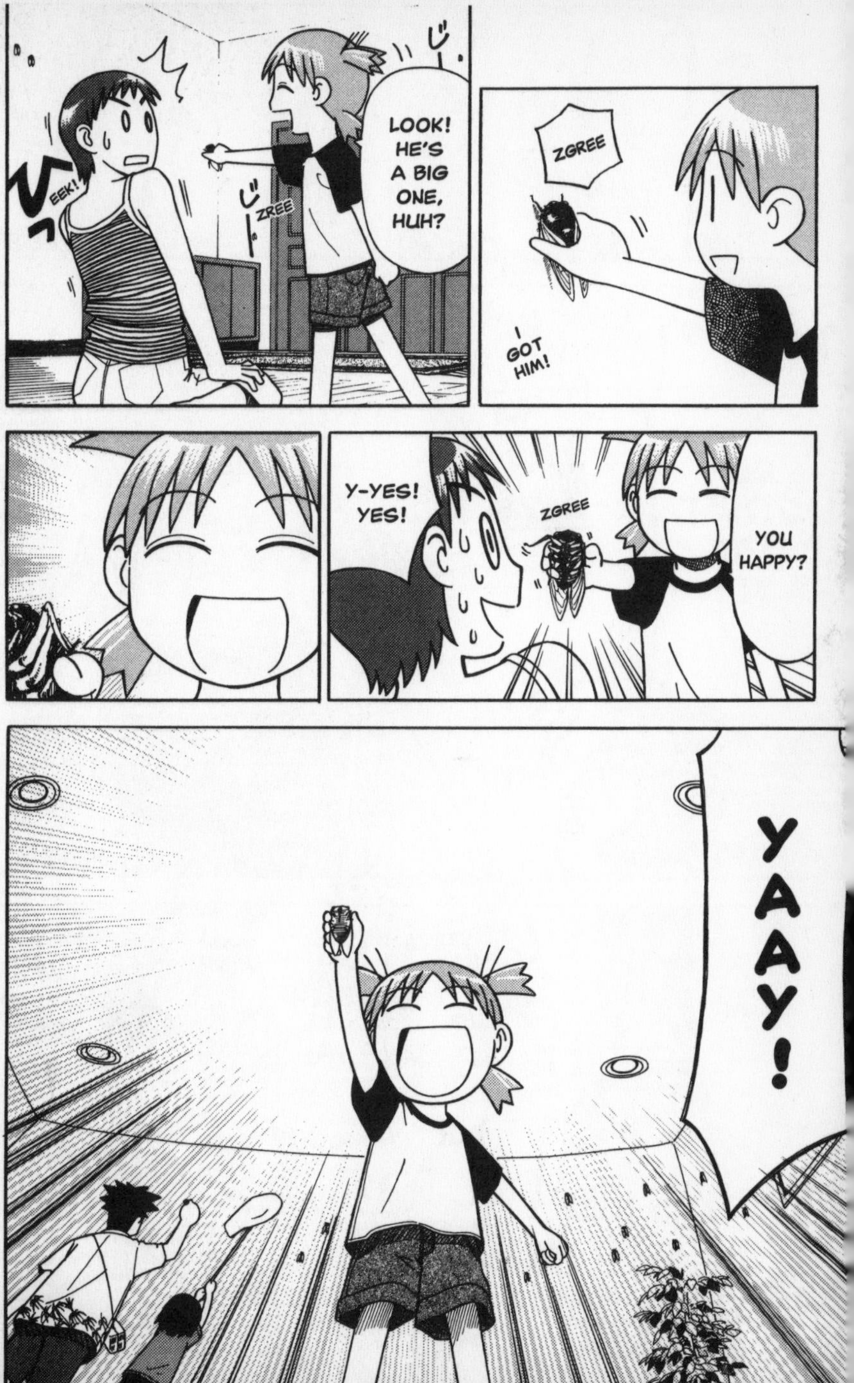
ZGREE
I GOT HIM!
LOOK! HE'S A BIG ONE, HUH?
EEK!
ZREE
YOU HAPPY?
ZGREE
Y-YES! YES!
YAAY!

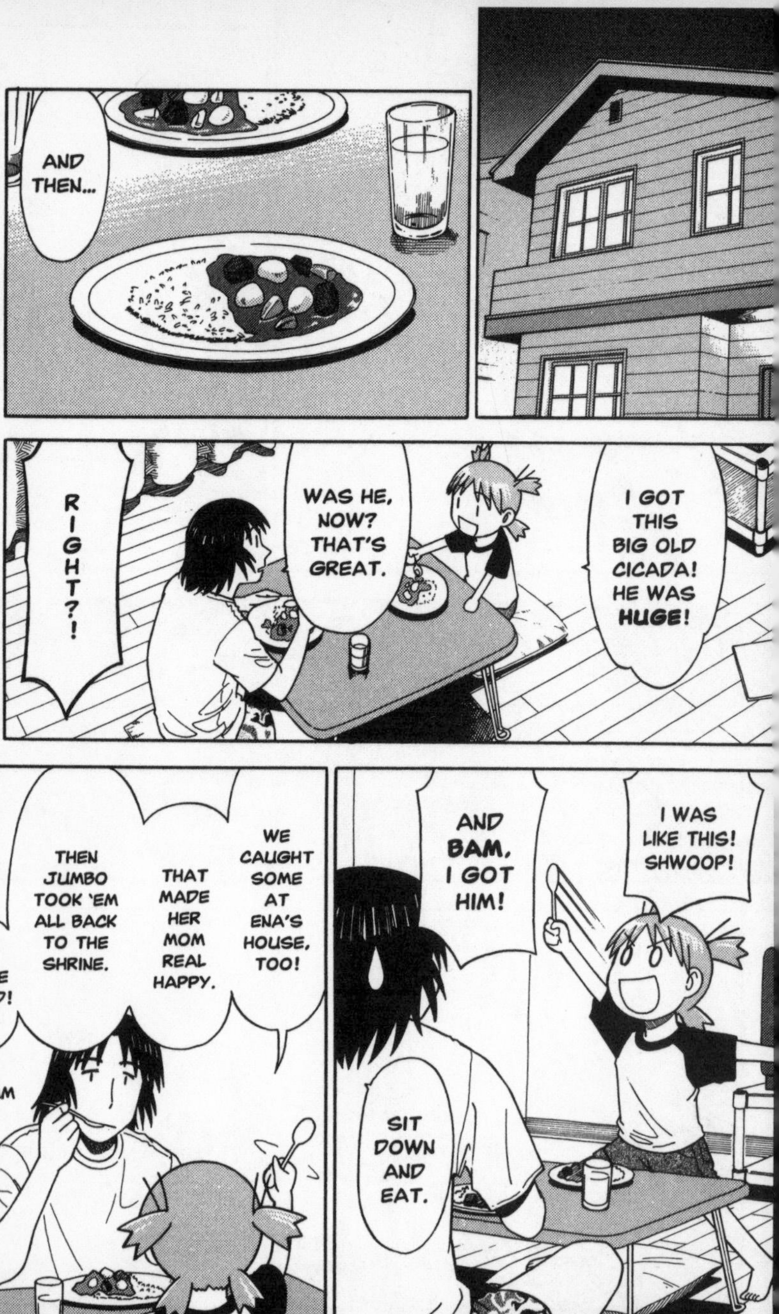
AND THEN...
I GOT THIS BIG OLD CICADA! HE WAS HUGE!
WAS HE, NOW? THAT'S GREAT.
RIGHT?!
I WAS LIKE THIS! SHWOOP!
AND BAM, I GOT HIM!
SIT DOWN AND EAT.
WE CAUGHT SOME AT ENA'S HOUSE, TOO!
THAT MADE HER MOM REAL HAPPY.
THEN JUMBO TOOK 'EM ALL BACK TO THE SHRINE.
THE END!
HMM

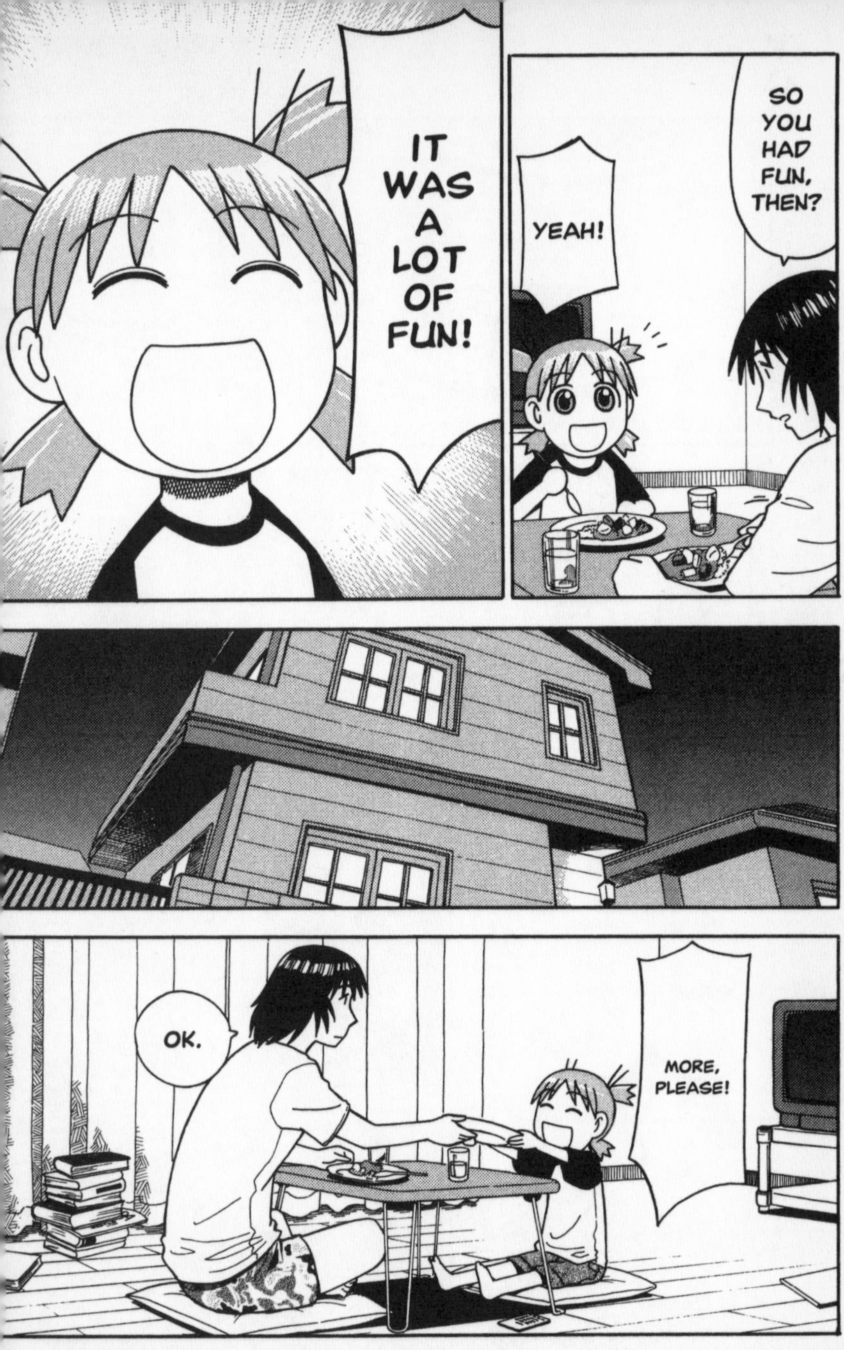
SO YOU HAD FUN, THEN?
YEAH!
IT WAS A LOT OF FUN!
MORE, PLEASE!
OK.

CHAPTER 7

YOTSUBA & RAIN!

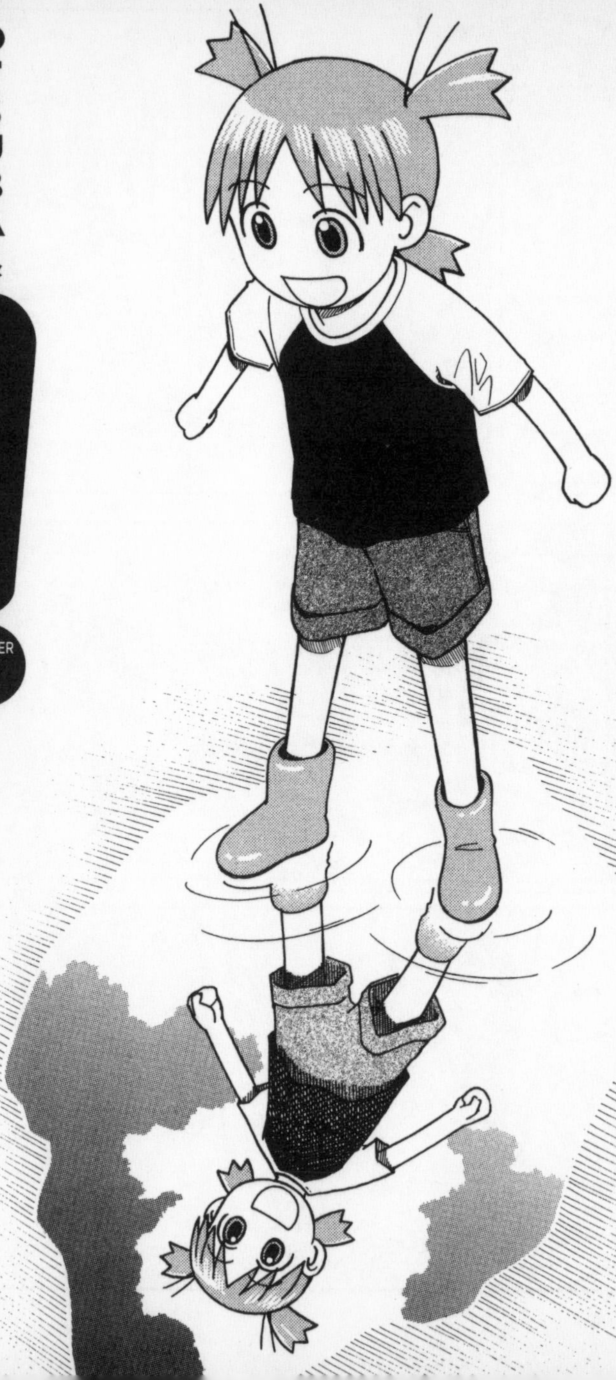

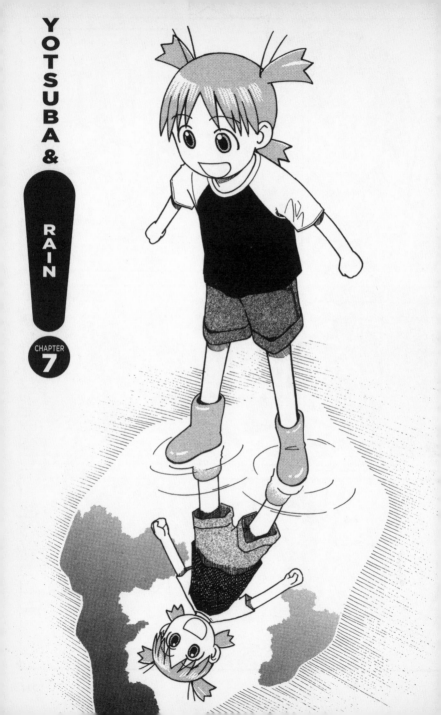

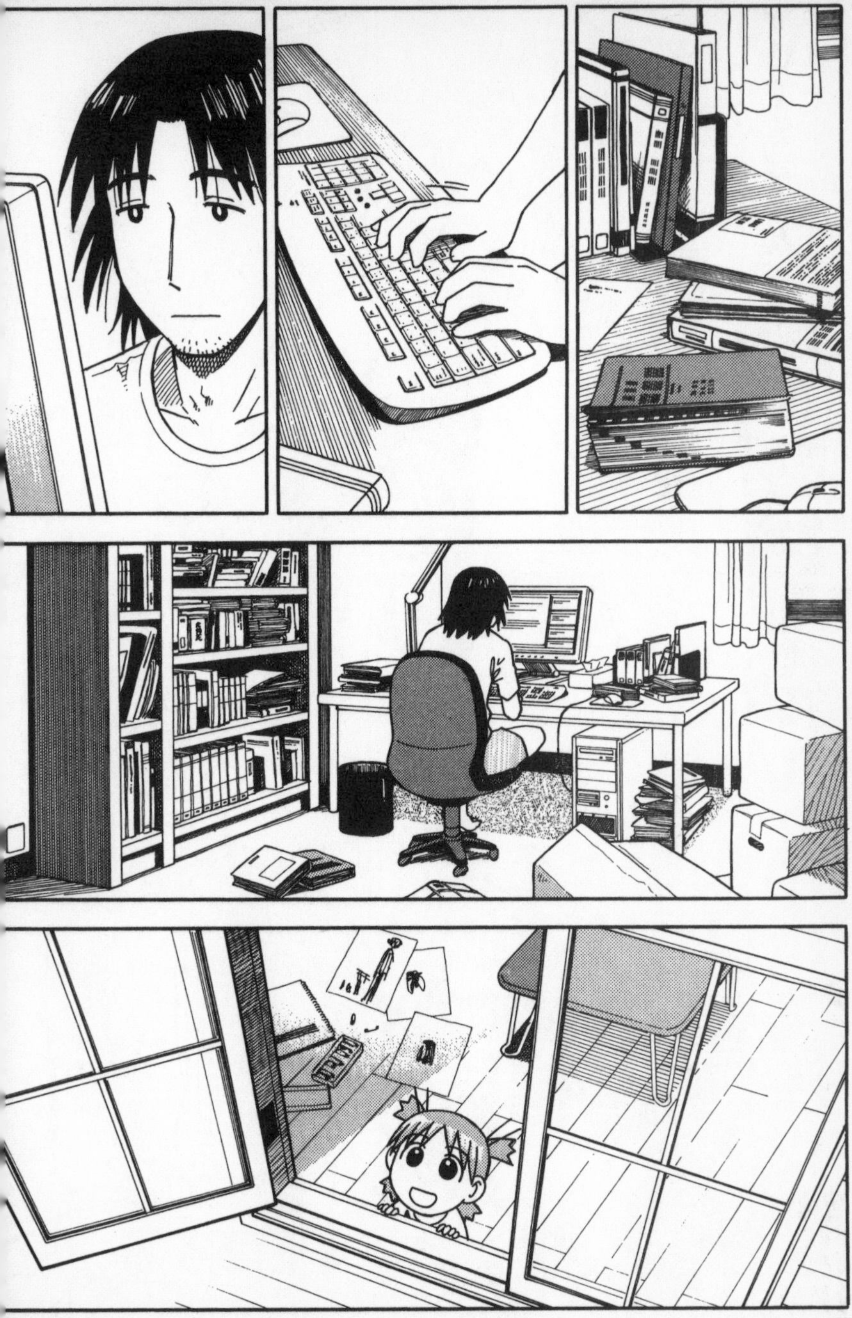

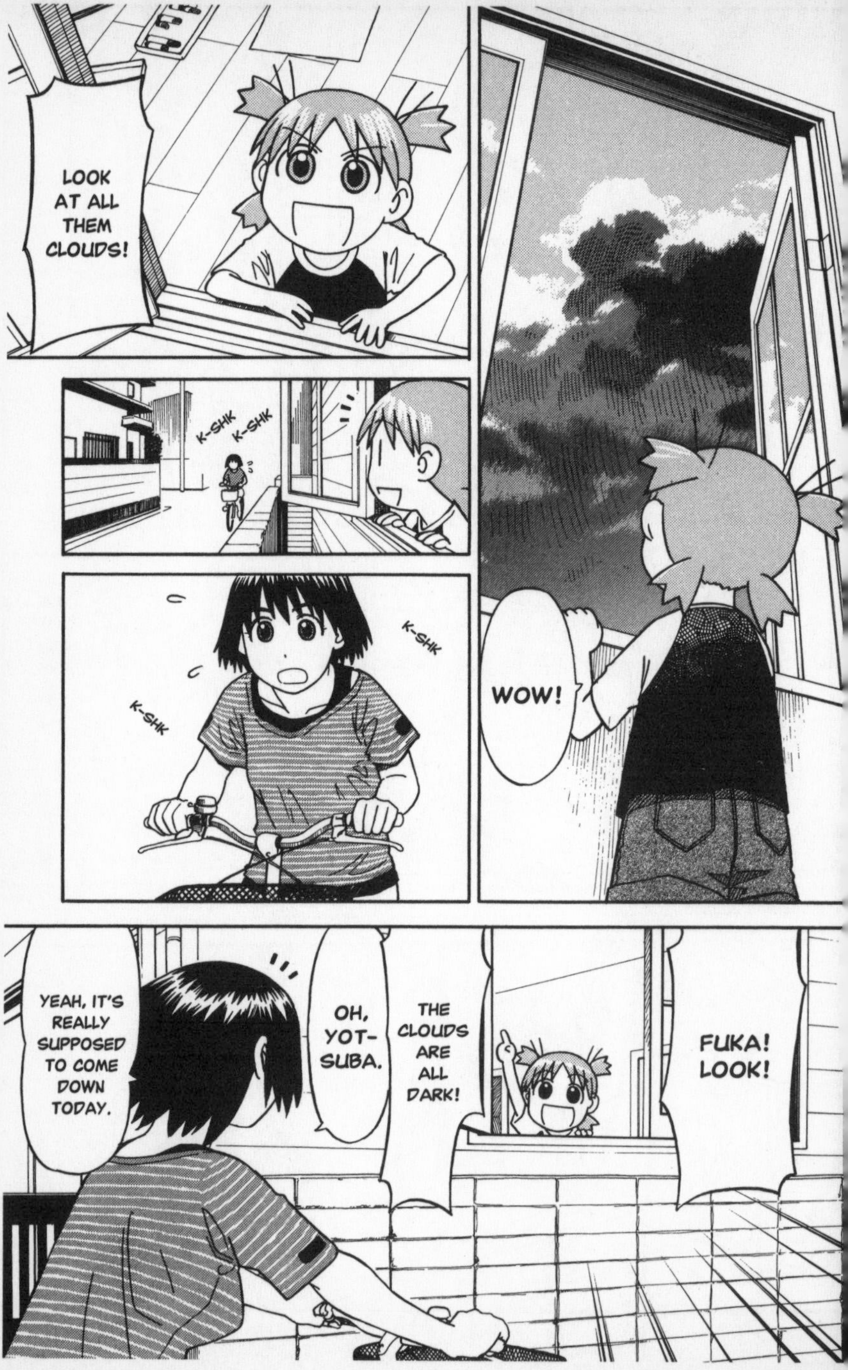
WOW!
LOOK AT ALL THEM CLOUDS!
K-SHK
K-SHK
K-SHK
K-SHK
FUKA! LOOK!
THE CLOUDS ARE ALL DARK!
OH, YOT-SUBA.
YEAH, IT'S REALLY SUPPOSED TO COME DOWN TODAY.

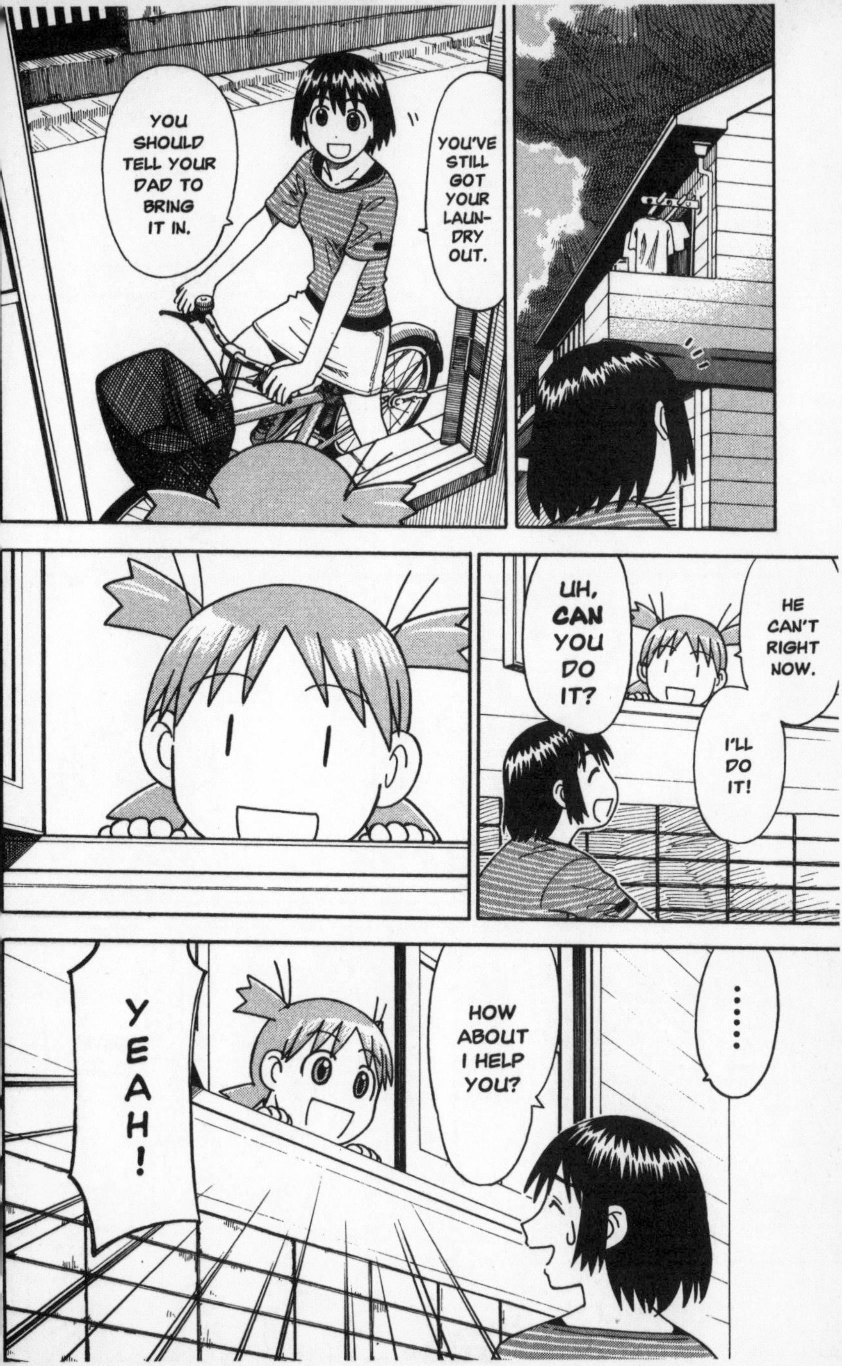
YOU'VE STILL GOT YOUR LAUNDRY OUT.
YOU SHOULD TELL YOUR DAD TO BRING IT IN.
HE CAN'T RIGHT NOW.
I'LL DO IT!
UH, CAN YOU DO IT?
......
HOW ABOUT I HELP YOU?
YEAH!

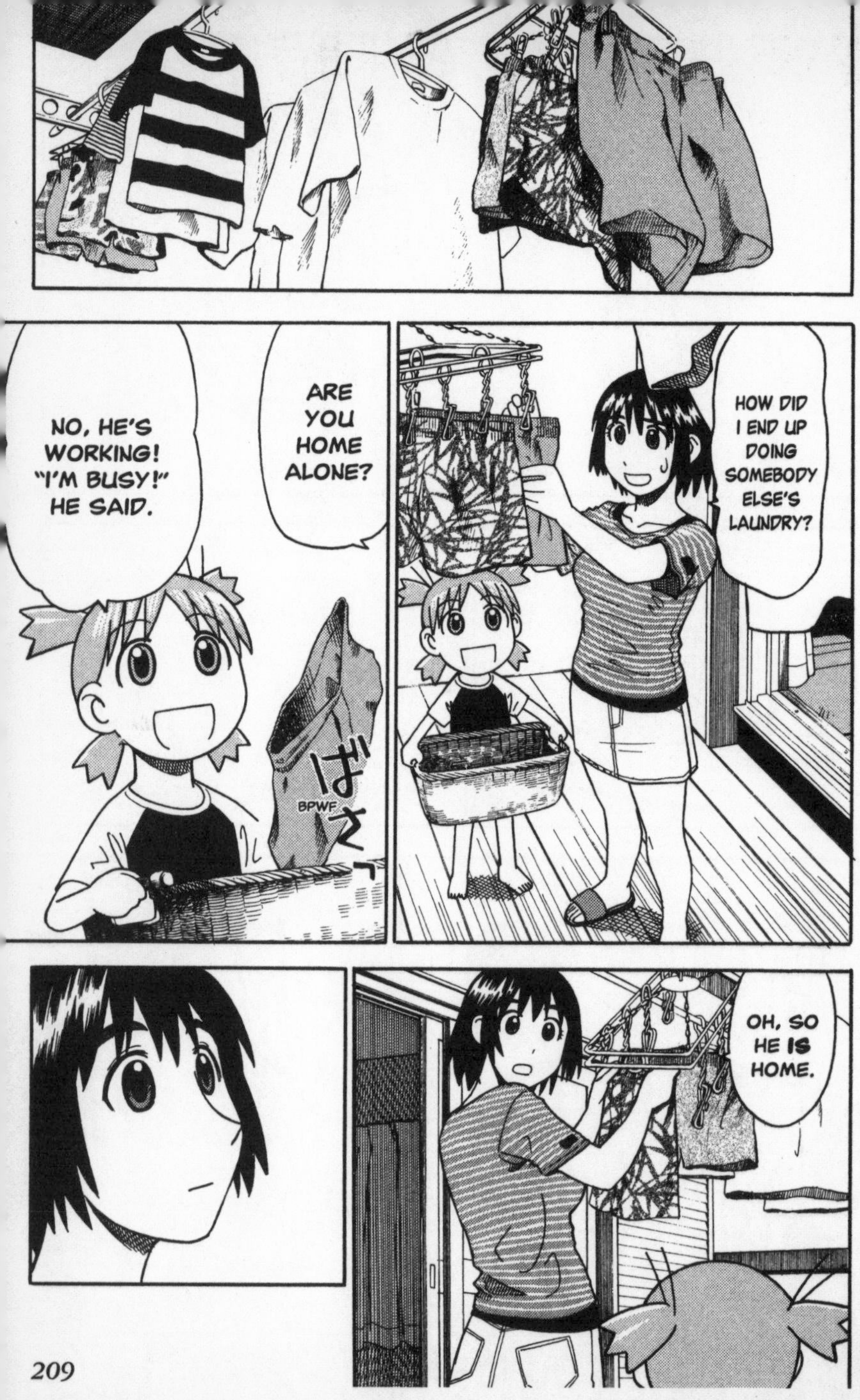
HOW DID I END UP DOING SOMEBODY ELSE'S LAUNDRY?
ARE YOU HOME ALONE?
NO, HE'S WORKING! "I'M BUSY!" HE SAID.
ばさ
BPWF
OH, SO HE **IS** HOME.

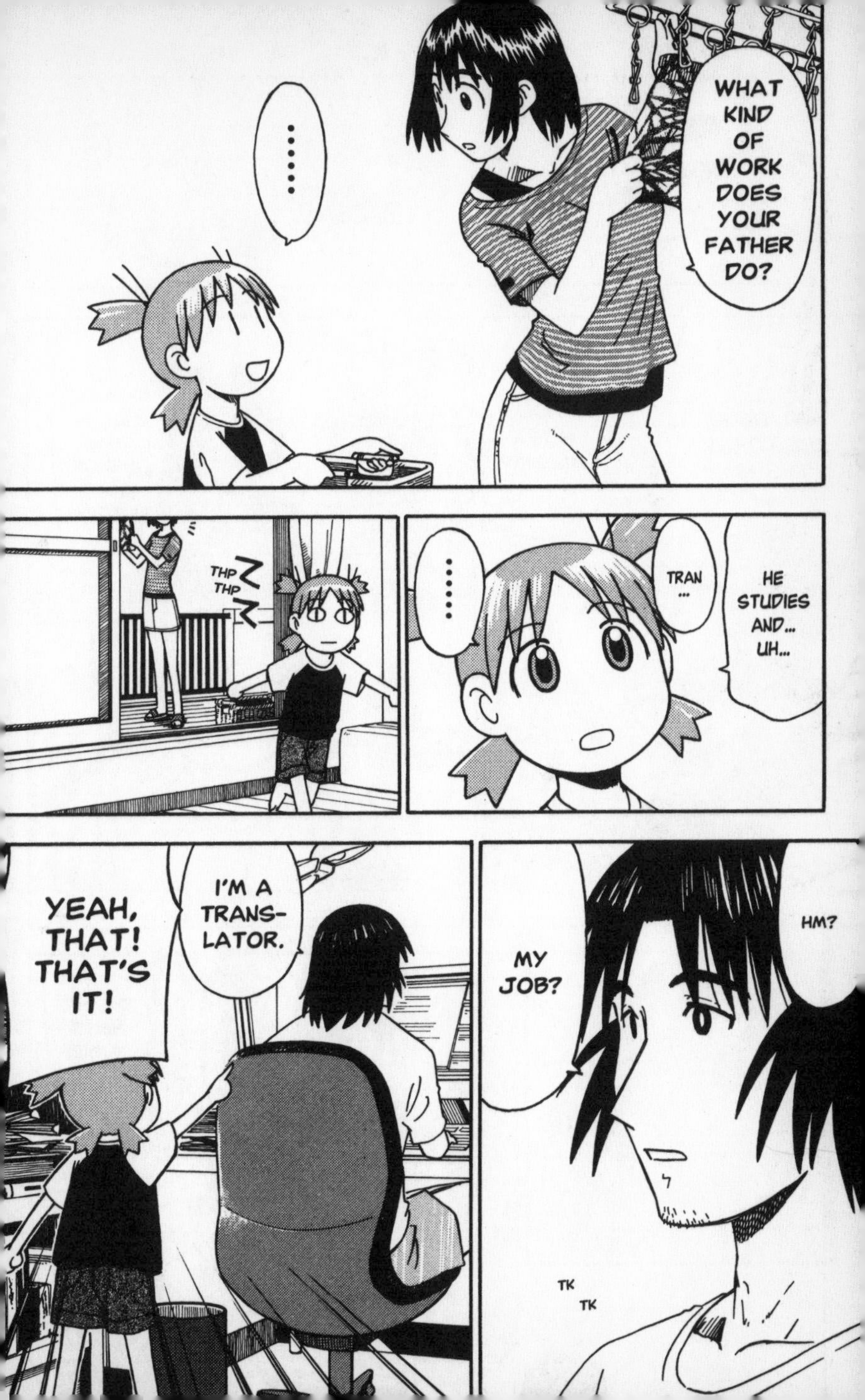
WHAT KIND OF WORK DOES YOUR FATHER DO?
......
HE STUDIES AND... UH...
TRAN ...
......
THP THP
HM?
MY JOB?
TK TK
I'M A TRANS-LATOR.
YEAH, THAT! THAT'S IT!

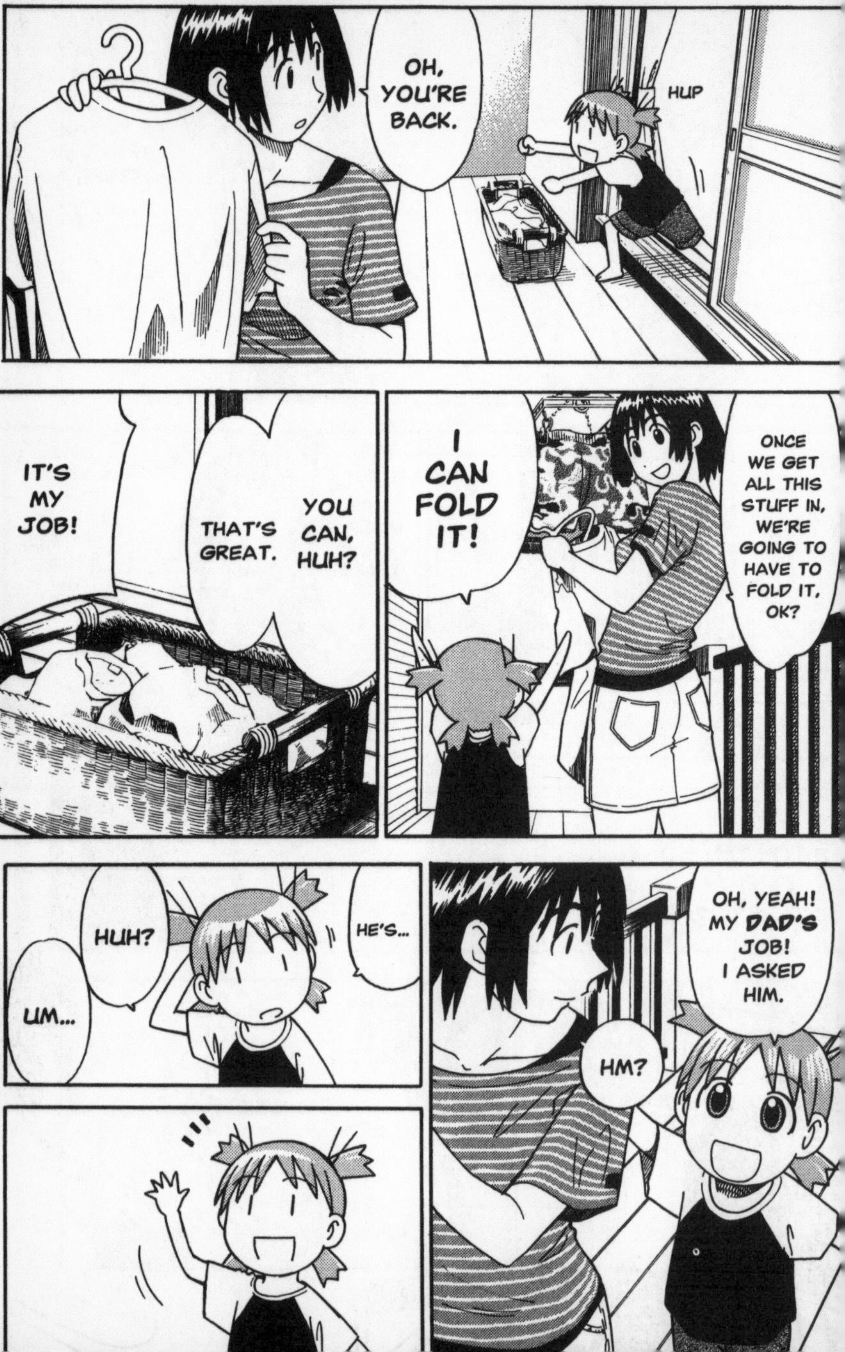
HUP
OH, YOU'RE BACK.
ONCE WE GET ALL THIS STUFF IN, WE'RE GOING TO HAVE TO FOLD IT, OK?
I CAN FOLD IT!
YOU CAN, HUH?
THAT'S GREAT.
IT'S MY JOB!
OH, YEAH! MY **DAD'S** JOB! I ASKED HIM.
HM?
HE'S...
HUH?
UM...

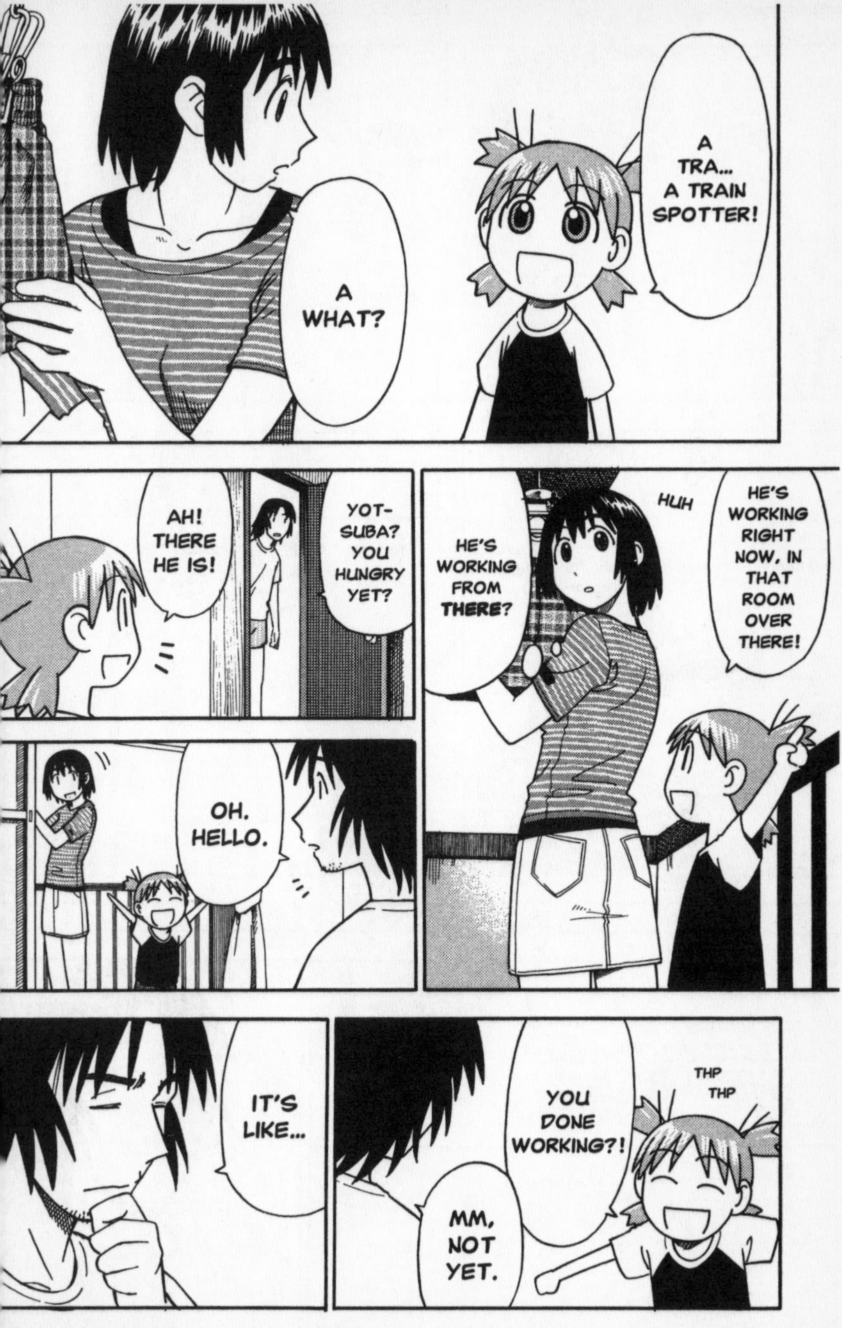
A TRA... A TRAIN SPOTTER!
A WHAT?
HE'S WORKING RIGHT NOW, IN THAT ROOM OVER THERE!
HUH
HE'S WORKING FROM THERE?
YOT-SUBA? YOU HUNGRY YET?
AH! THERE HE IS!
OH. HELLO.
THP THP
YOU DONE WORKING?!
MM, NOT YET.
IT'S LIKE...

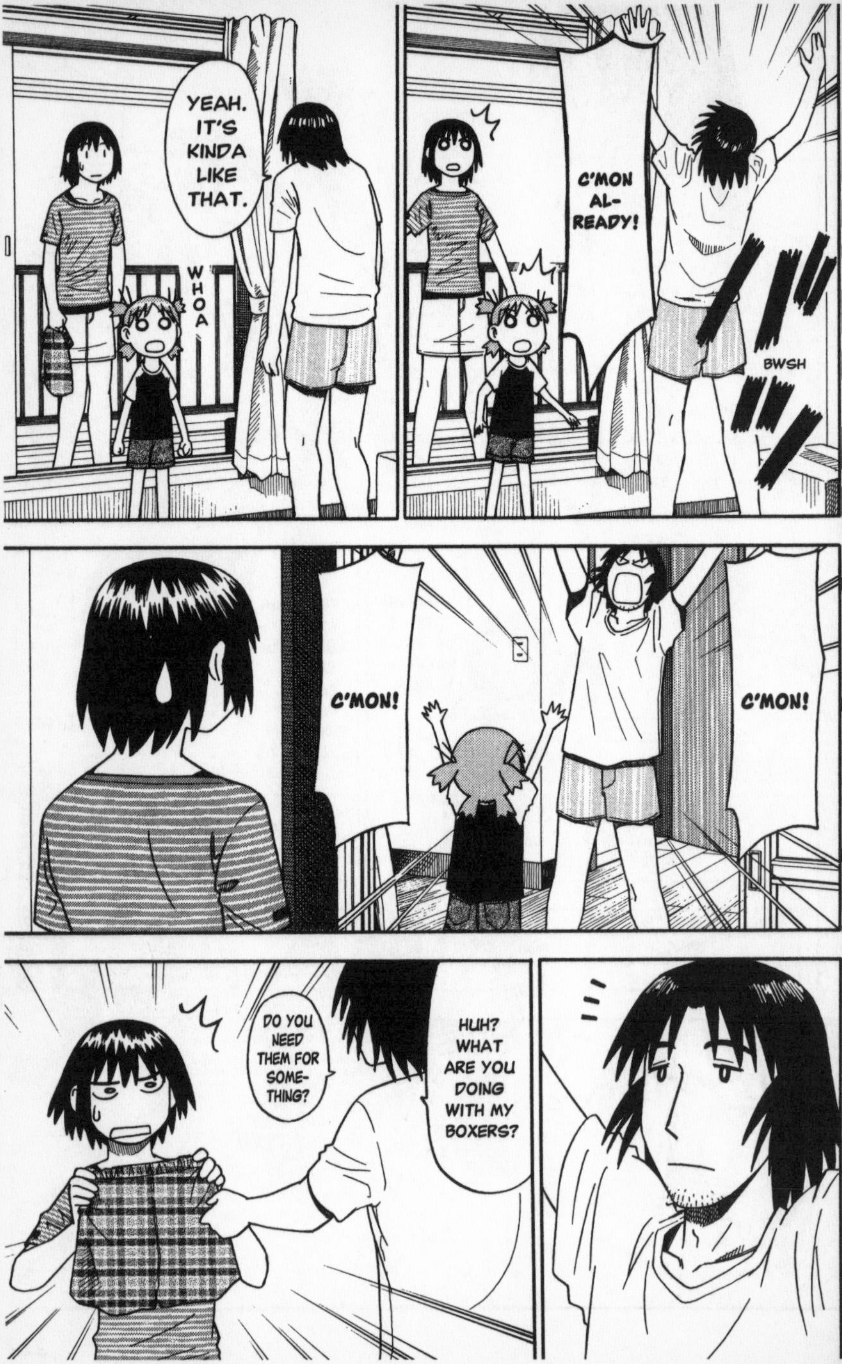
C'MON AL-READY!
BWSH
YEAH. IT'S KINDA LIKE THAT.
WHOA
C'MON!
C'MON!
HUH? WHAT ARE YOU DOING WITH MY BOXERS?
DO YOU NEED THEM FOR SOME-THING?

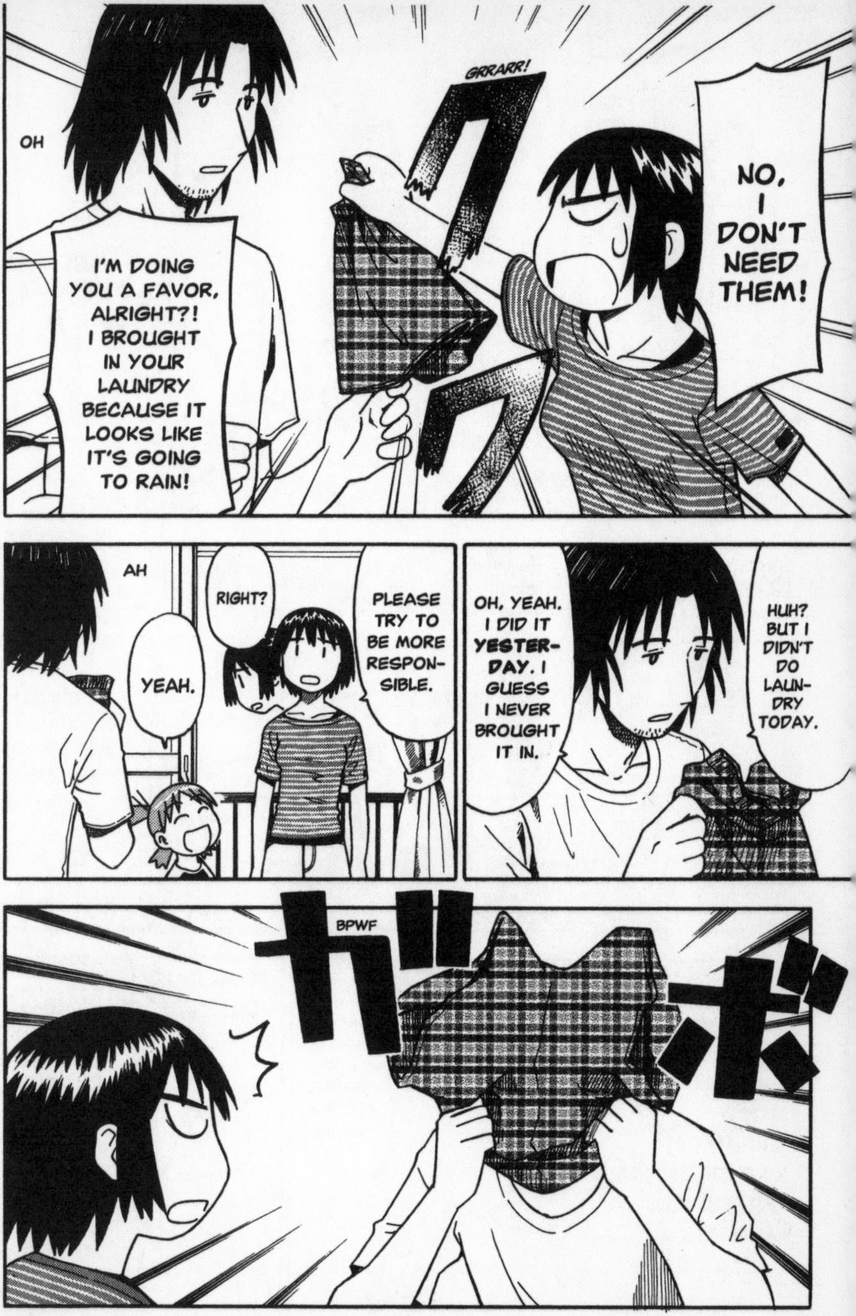
NO, I DON'T NEED THEM!
GRRRARR!
OH
I'M DOING YOU A FAVOR, ALRIGHT?! I BROUGHT IN YOUR LAUNDRY BECAUSE IT LOOKS LIKE IT'S GOING TO RAIN!
HUH? BUT I DIDN'T DO LAUNDRY TODAY.
OH, YEAH. I DID IT YESTERDAY. I GUESS I NEVER BROUGHT IT IN.
PLEASE TRY TO BE MORE RESPONSIBLE.
RIGHT?
AH
YEAH.
BPWF

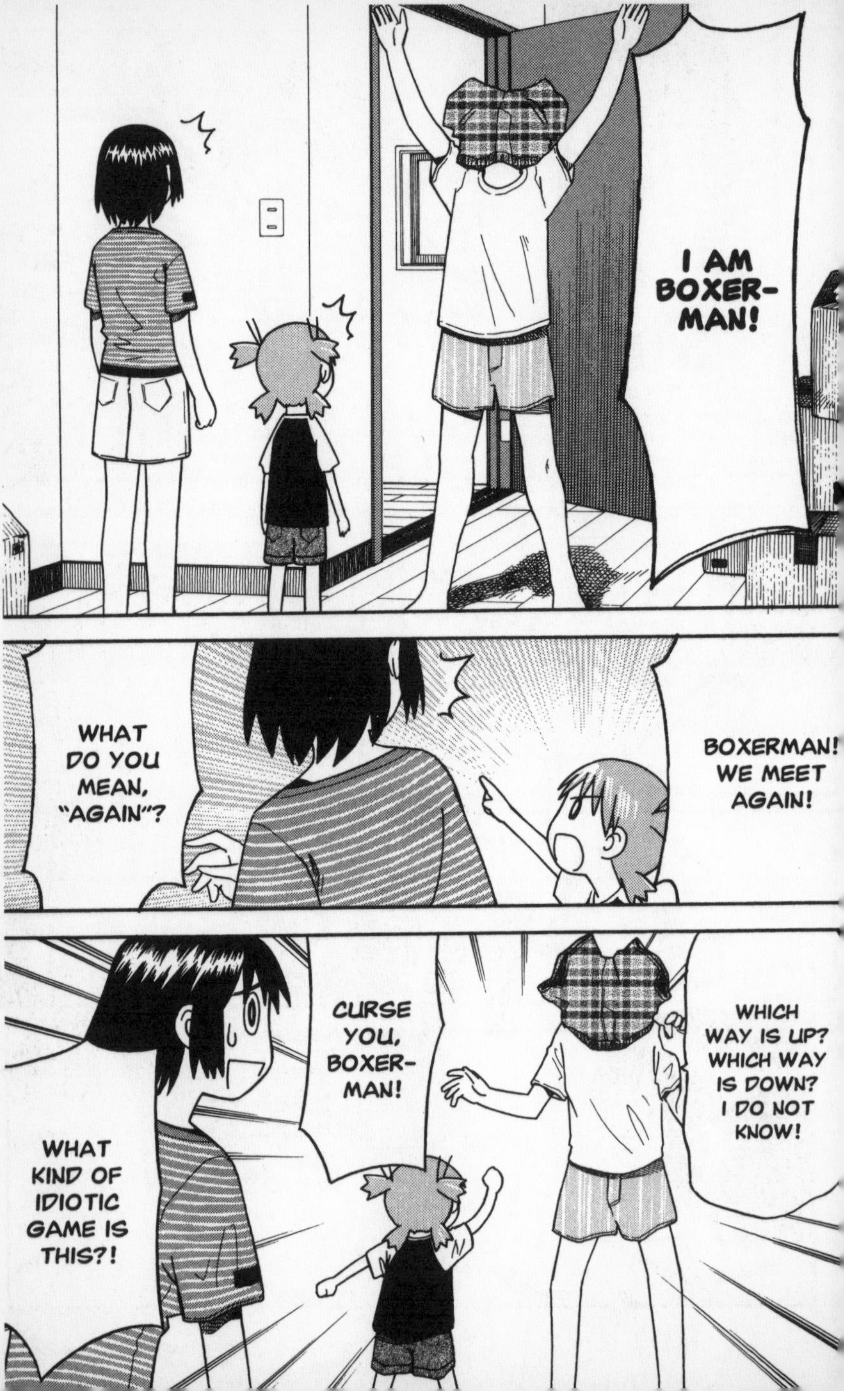
I AM BOXER-MAN!
BOXERMAN! WE MEET AGAIN!
WHAT DO YOU MEAN, "AGAIN"?
WHICH WAY IS UP? WHICH WAY IS DOWN? I DO NOT KNOW!
CURSE YOU, BOXER-MAN!
WHAT KIND OF IDIOTIC GAME IS THIS?!

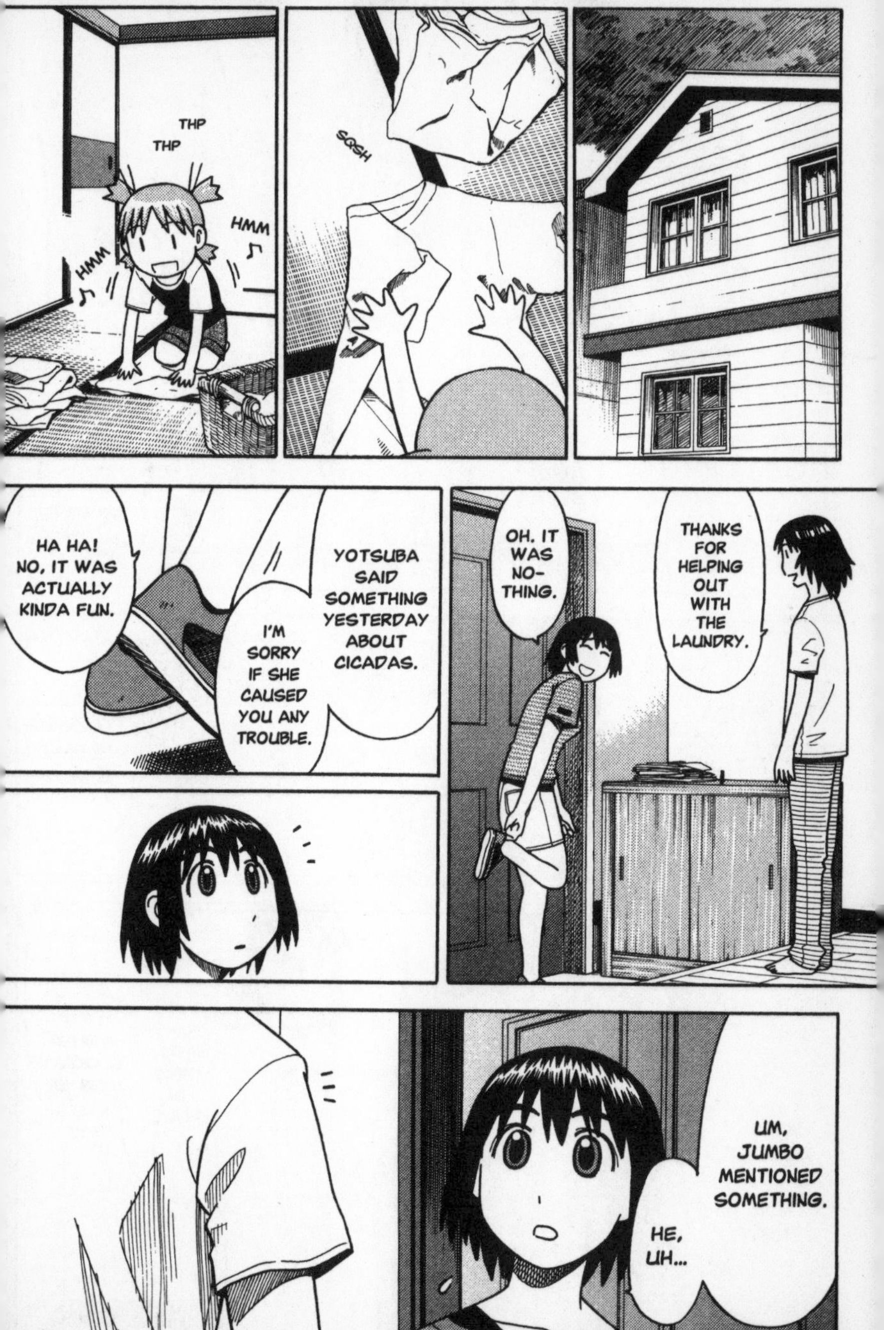
SQSH
THP
THP
HMM
HMM
THANKS FOR HELPING OUT WITH THE LAUNDRY.
OH. IT WAS NO-THING.
YOTSUBA SAID SOMETHING YESTERDAY ABOUT CICADAS.
I'M SORRY IF SHE CAUSED YOU ANY TROUBLE.
HA HA! NO, IT WAS ACTUALLY KINDA FUN.
UM, JUMBO MENTIONED SOMETHING.
HE, UH...

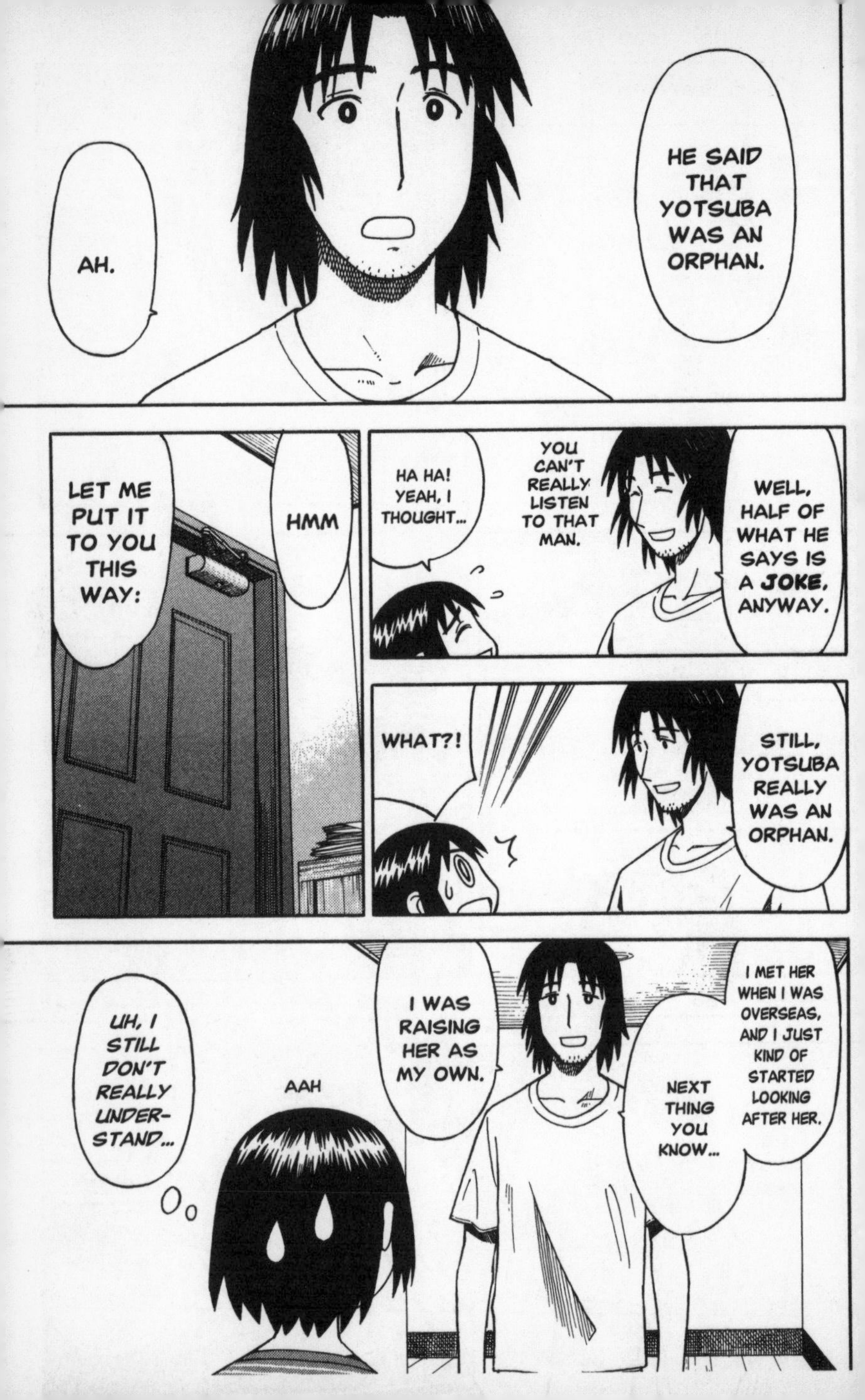
HE SAID THAT YOTSUBA WAS AN ORPHAN.
AH.
WELL, HALF OF WHAT HE SAYS IS A JOKE, ANYWAY.
YOU CAN'T REALLY LISTEN TO THAT MAN.
HA HA! YEAH, I THOUGHT...
STILL, YOTSUBA REALLY WAS AN ORPHAN.
WHAT?!
HMM
LET ME PUT IT TO YOU THIS WAY:
I MET HER WHEN I WAS OVERSEAS, AND I JUST KIND OF STARTED LOOKING AFTER HER.
NEXT THING YOU KNOW...
I WAS RAISING HER AS MY OWN.
AAH
UH, I STILL DON'T REALLY UNDERSTAND...

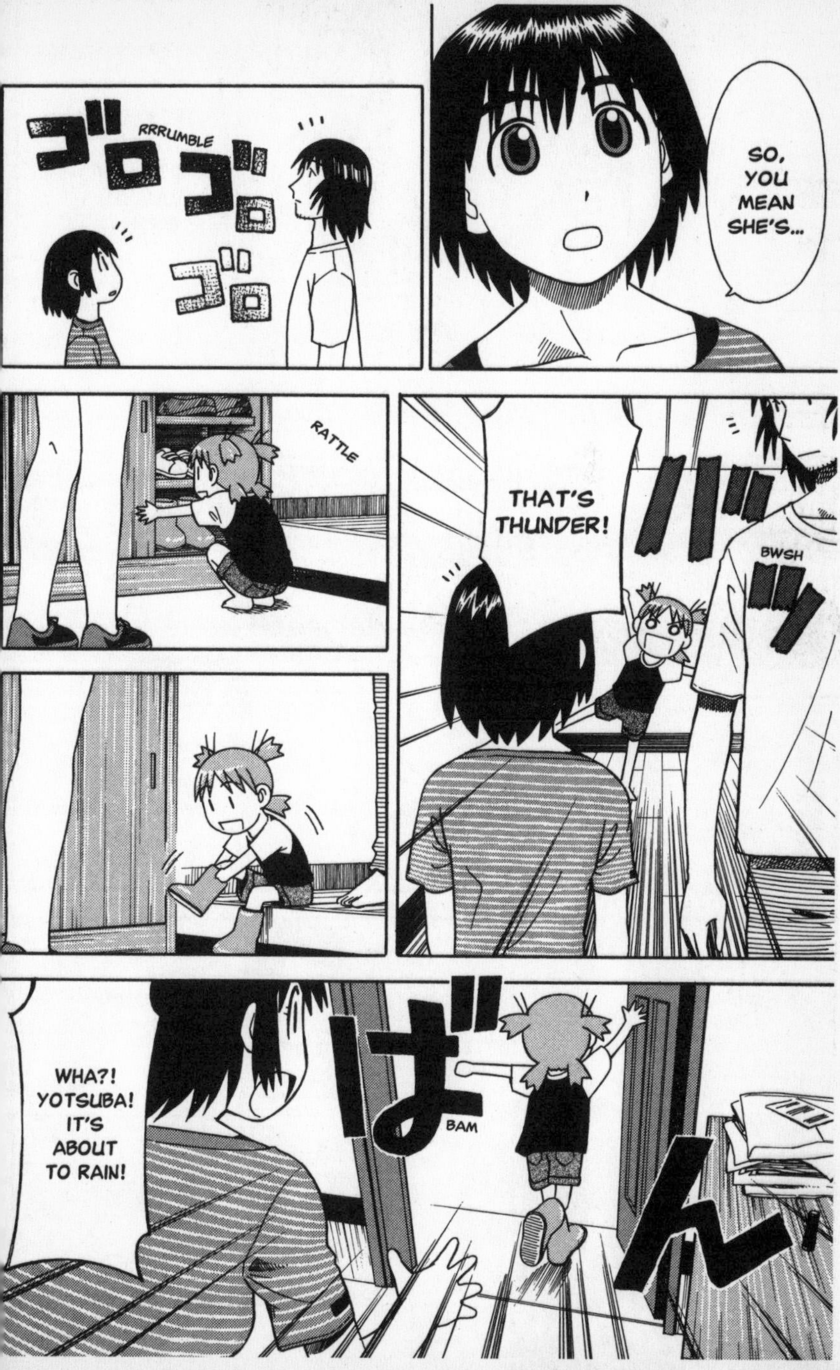
SO, YOU MEAN SHE'S...
ゴロゴロゴロ
RRRUMBLE
THAT'S THUNDER!
バッ
BWSH
RATTLE
ばん
BAM
WHA?! YOTSUBA! IT'S ABOUT TO RAIN!

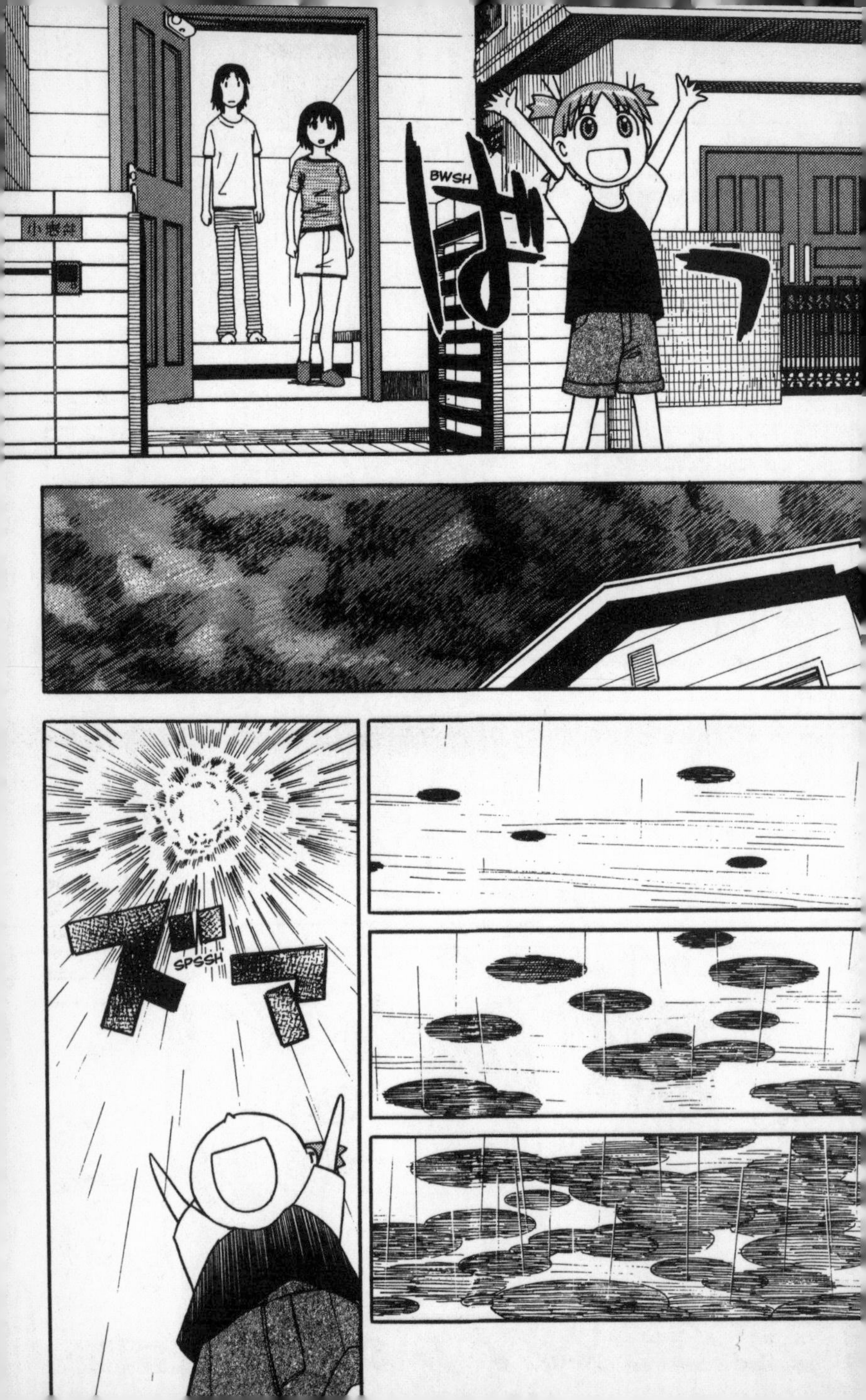
BWSH
SPSSH

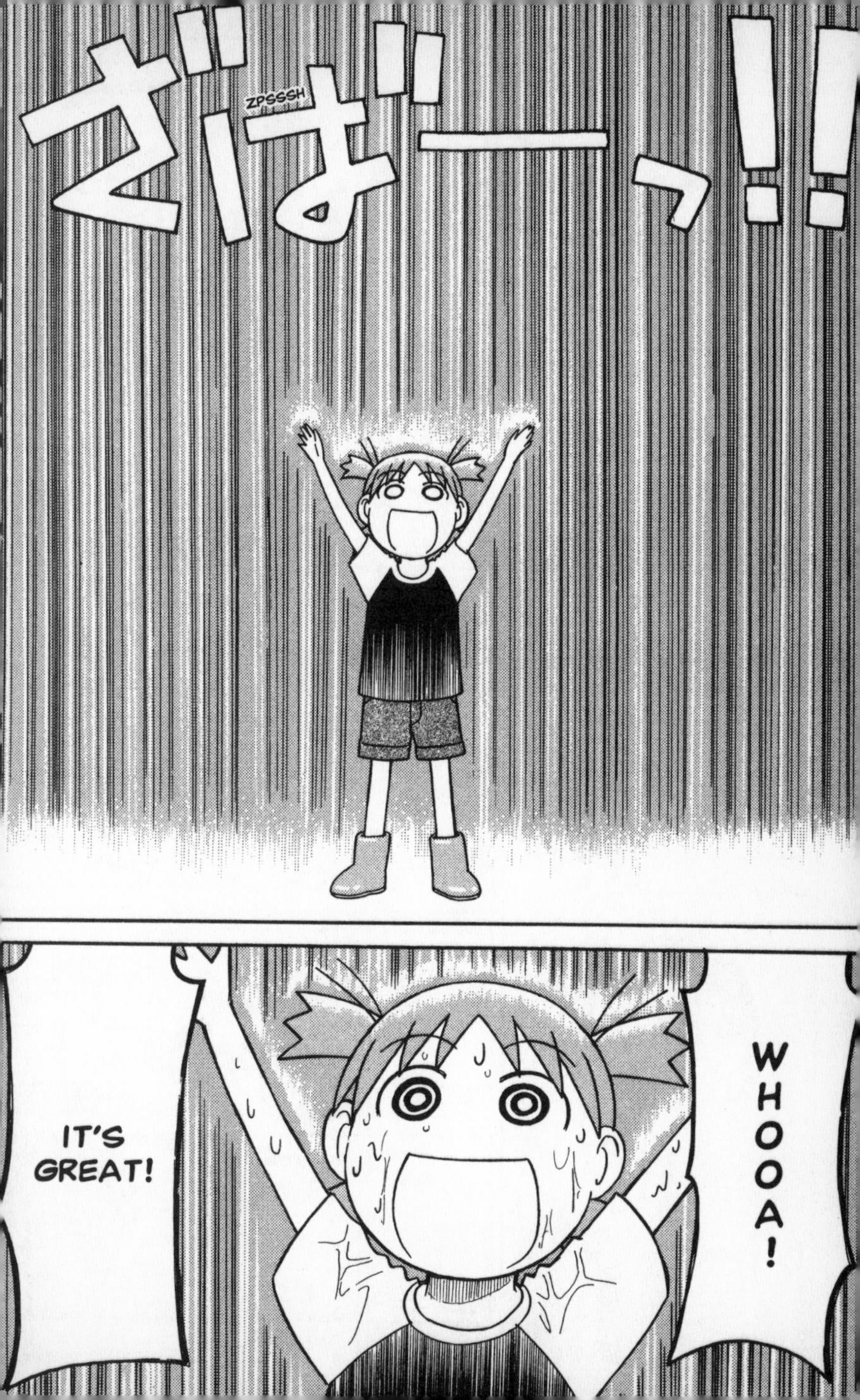
ざばーっ!!
ZPSSSH
WHOOOA!
IT'S GREAT!

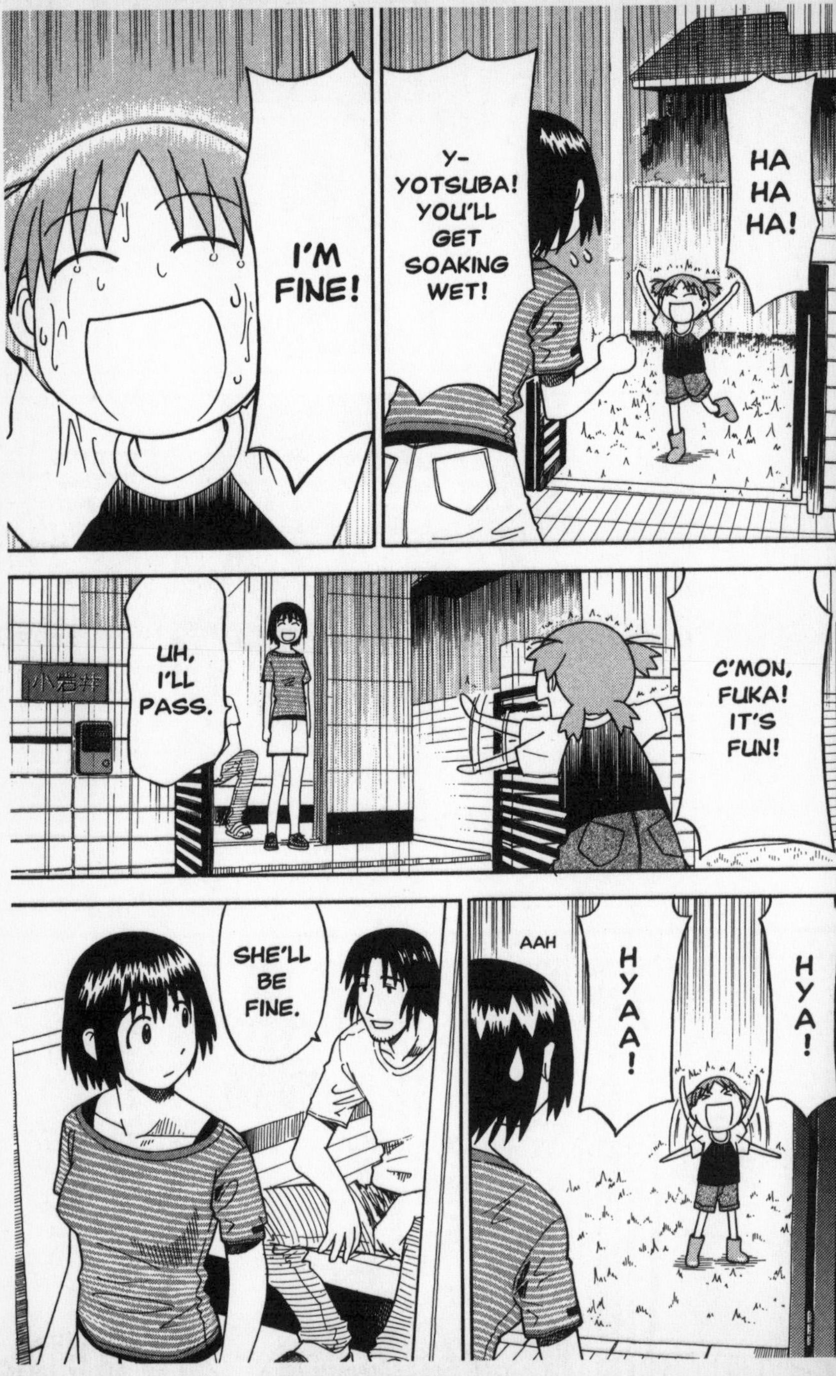
HA HA HA!
Y-YOTSUBA! YOU'LL GET SOAKING WET!
I'M FINE!
C'MON, FUKA! IT'S FUN!
UH, I'LL PASS.
小岩井
HYA!
HYAA!
AAH
SHE'LL BE FINE.

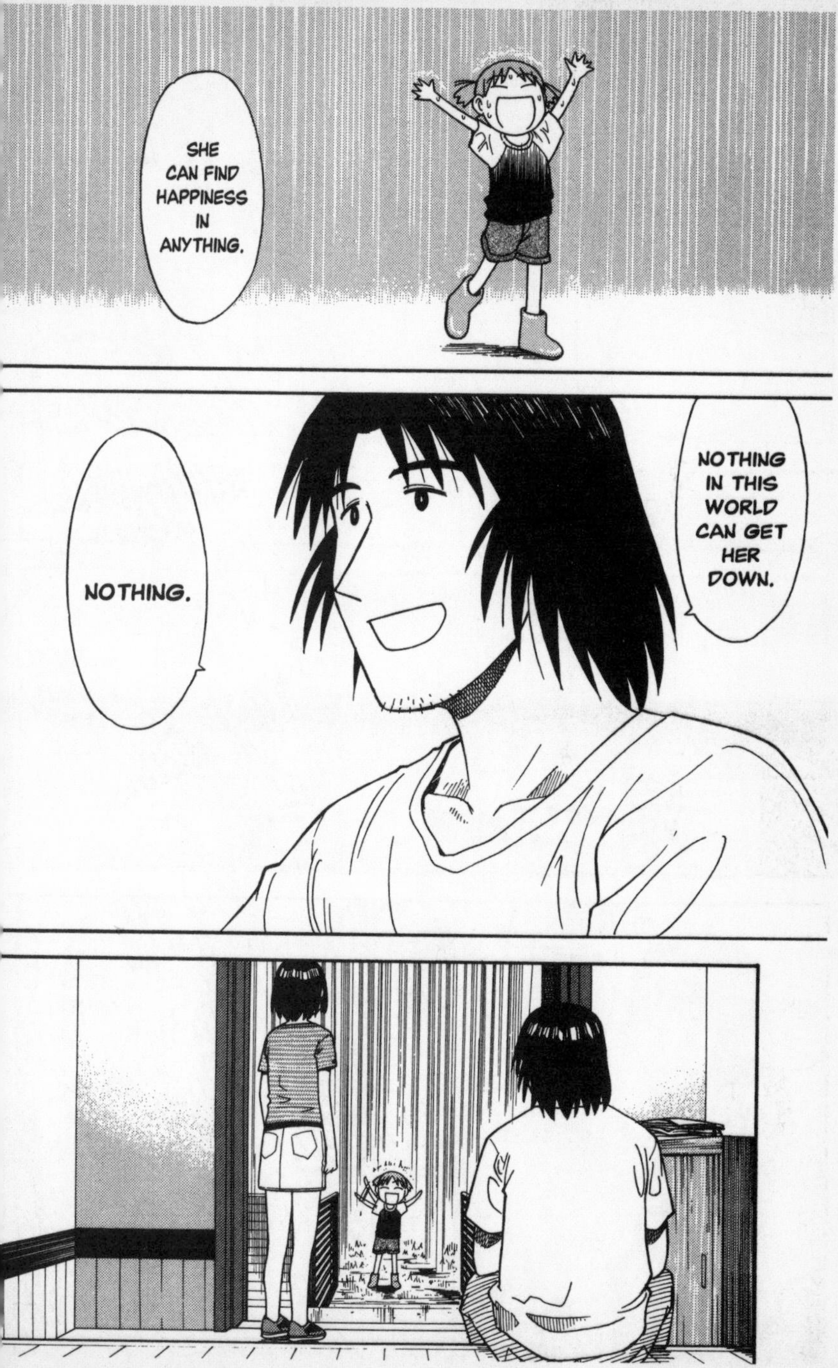
SHE CAN FIND HAPPINESS IN ANYTHING.
NOTHING IN THIS WORLD CAN GET HER DOWN.
NOTHING.

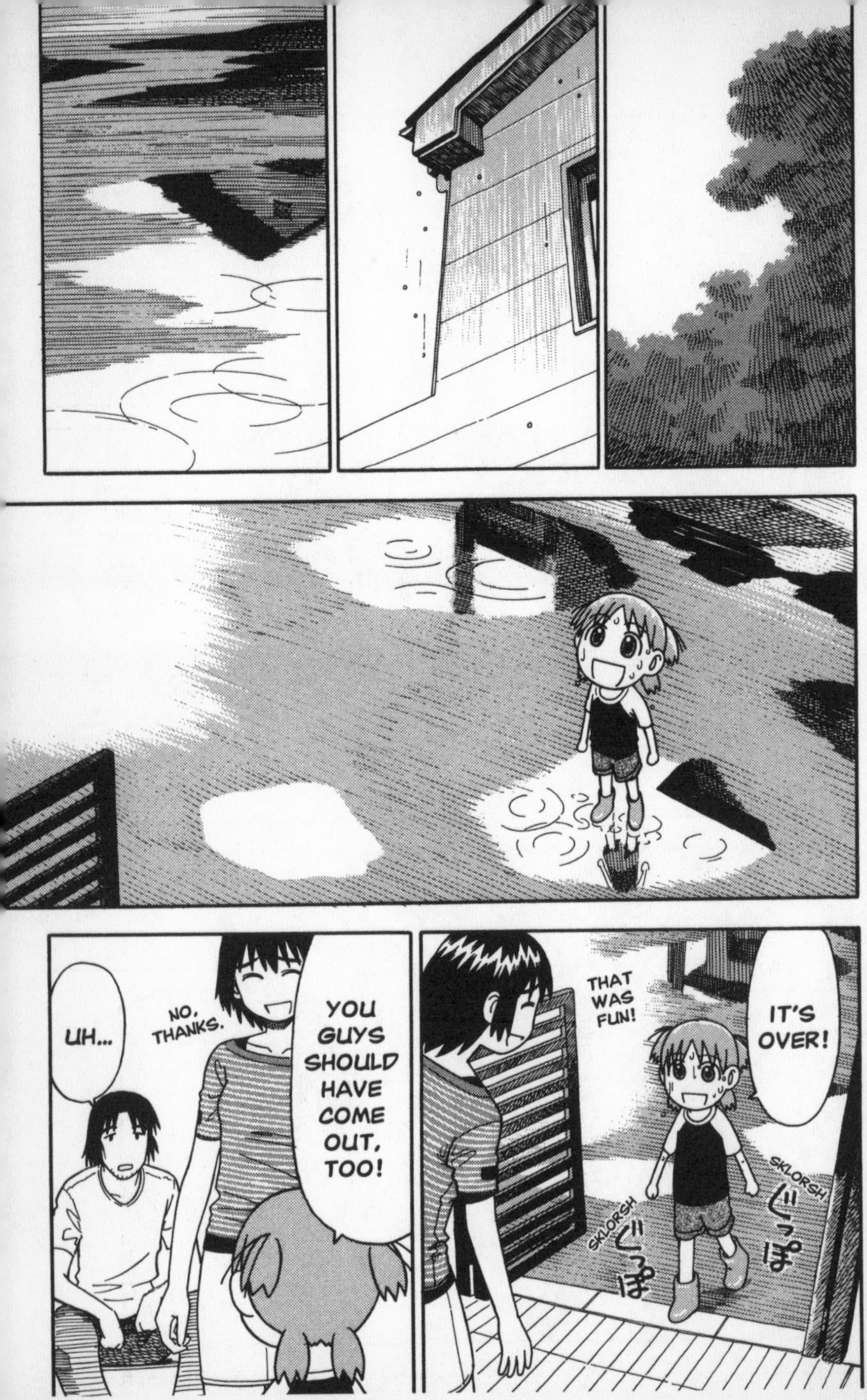
IT'S OVER!
THAT WAS FUN!
SKLORSH
ぐっぽ
SKLORSH
ぐっぽ
YOU GUYS SHOULD HAVE COME OUT, TOO!
NO, THANKS.
UH...

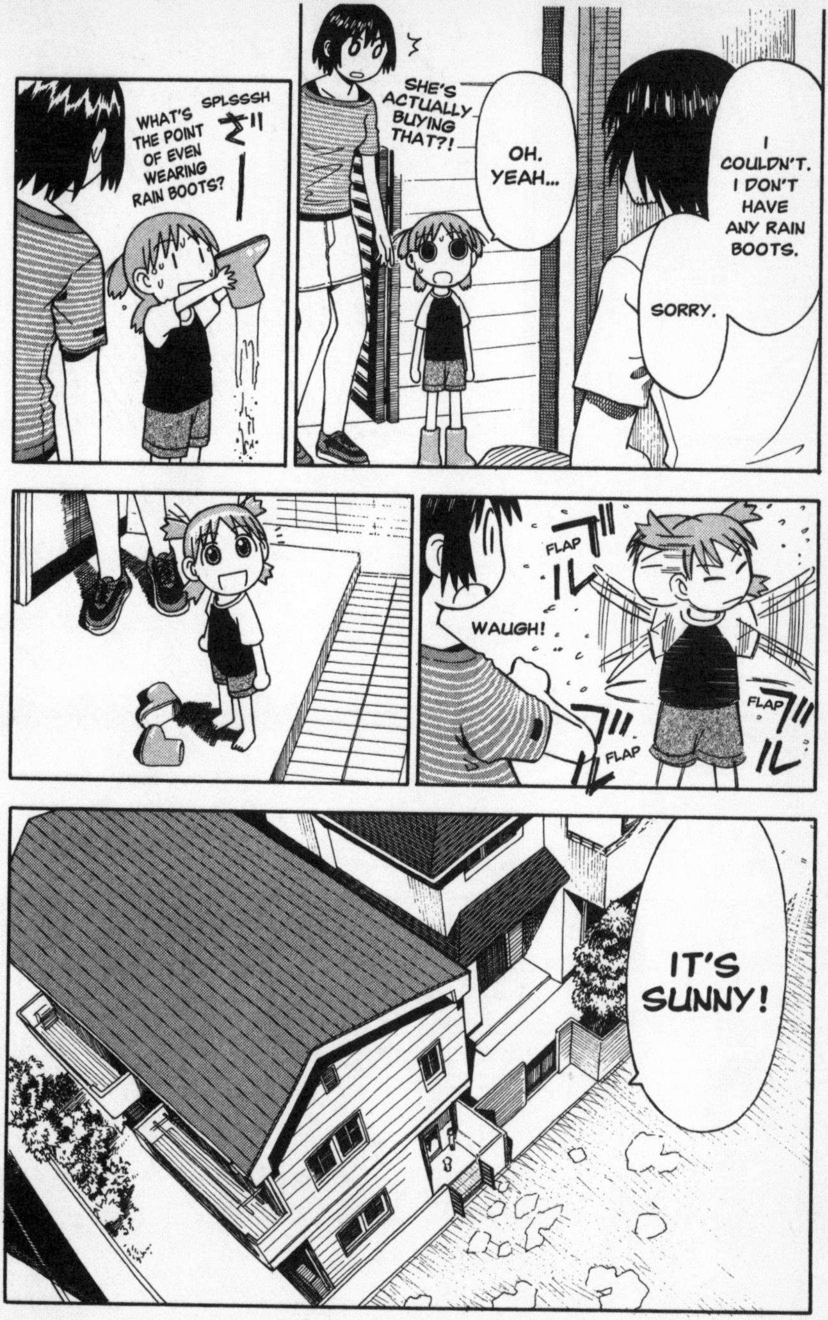
I COULDN'T. I DON'T HAVE ANY RAIN BOOTS.
SORRY.
OH. YEAH...
SHE'S ACTUALLY BUYING THAT?!
SPLSSSH
WHAT'S THE POINT OF EVEN WEARING RAIN BOOTS?
FLAP
WAUGH!
FLAP
FLAP
IT'S SUNNY!

© KIYOHIKO AZUMA/YOTUBA SUTAZIO 2003
First published in 2003 by Media Works Inc., Tokyo, Japan.
English translation rights arranged with Media Works Inc.

Translator **JAVIER LOPEZ**
Translation Staff **KAY BERTRAND, AMY FORSYTH AND BRENDAN FRAYNE**
Editor **JAVIER LOPEZ**
Assistant Editor **SHERIDAN JACOBS**
Graphic Artists **HEATHER GARY AND NATALIA MORALES**
Graphic Intern **MARK MEZA**

Editorial Director **GARY STEINMAN**
Creative Director **JASON BABLER**
Sales and Marketing **CHRIS OARR**
Print Production Manager **BRIDGETT JANOTA**
Pre-press Manager **KLYS REEDYK**

International Coordinators **TORU IWAKAMI, ATSUSHI KANBAYASHI,
KYOKO DRUMHELLER AND AI TAKAI**

President, CEO & Publisher **JOHN LEDFORD**

Email: editor@adv-manga.com
www.adv-manga.com
www.advfilms.com

For sales and distribution inquiries please call 1.800.282.7202

ADV MANGA™ is a division of A.D. Vision, Inc.
10114 W. Sam Houston Parkway, Suite 200, Houston, Texas 77099

English text © 2005 published by A.D. Vision, Inc. under exclusive license.
ADV MANGA is a trademark of A.D. Vision, Inc.

ISBN: 1-4139-0317-7
First printing, June 2005
10 9 8 7 6 5 4 3 2 1
Printed in Canada

TO BE CONTINUED...

YOTSUBA&! Vol. 01

COVER **YOTSUBA&!**
While the title of this manga could also be transcribed as *Yotsubato*, the official rendering is in fact *YOTSUBA&!*, which is the spelling used in the original Japanese editions. *Yotsuba* actually means "four leaf," as in a four-leaf clover (note the green hair and four pigtails of the manga's titular character), while *to* means "with" or "and." Transpose *to* with an ampersand, add an exclamation mark, and voilá—YOTSUBA&!

PG. 16 **Garbage days**
Japan has a system of rigidly-defined schedules for garbage collection, with specific days reserved for the disposal of certain wastes (as we saw in Fuka's explanation). These schedules will vary from area to area, hence Mr. Koiwai's confusion.

PG. 118 **Neighborhood association**
Called *chonaikai* in Japanese, these independent organizations deal primarily with sanitation and crime prevention. Expenses are covered through the collection of membership fees.

PG. 139 **Salt**
Here, Fuka is tossing salt in a mock "purification ceremony" to rid herself of Jumbo and Koiwai's presence.

PG. 148 **Shrines and festivals**
As noted, shrines are home to a number of region-specific festivals throughout the year. During this time, the shrine grounds are choked with vendors offering everything from toys to fortunes to a variety of snacks.

PG. 165 **Namu**
This is the first part of *Namu Amida Butsu*, a Buddhist supplication.

Yotsuba is trying her hand at **drawing**, but a few ruthless art critics could **squash** her crayon-wielding dreams.

A new love for **gangster** movies will tear her away from her artistic endeavors, when this **pigtailed** girl-turned-good-fella uses her trigger-happy tactics for the greater good—to find **cake**!

It's a **gun-toting** tyke on a desperate hunt for **sweets** in *YOTSUBA&!* Volume 2!

YOTSUBA&!

2

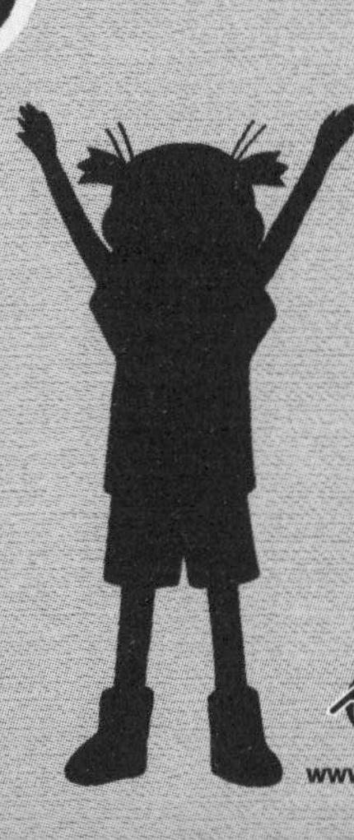

ADV Manga™

www.adv-manga.com

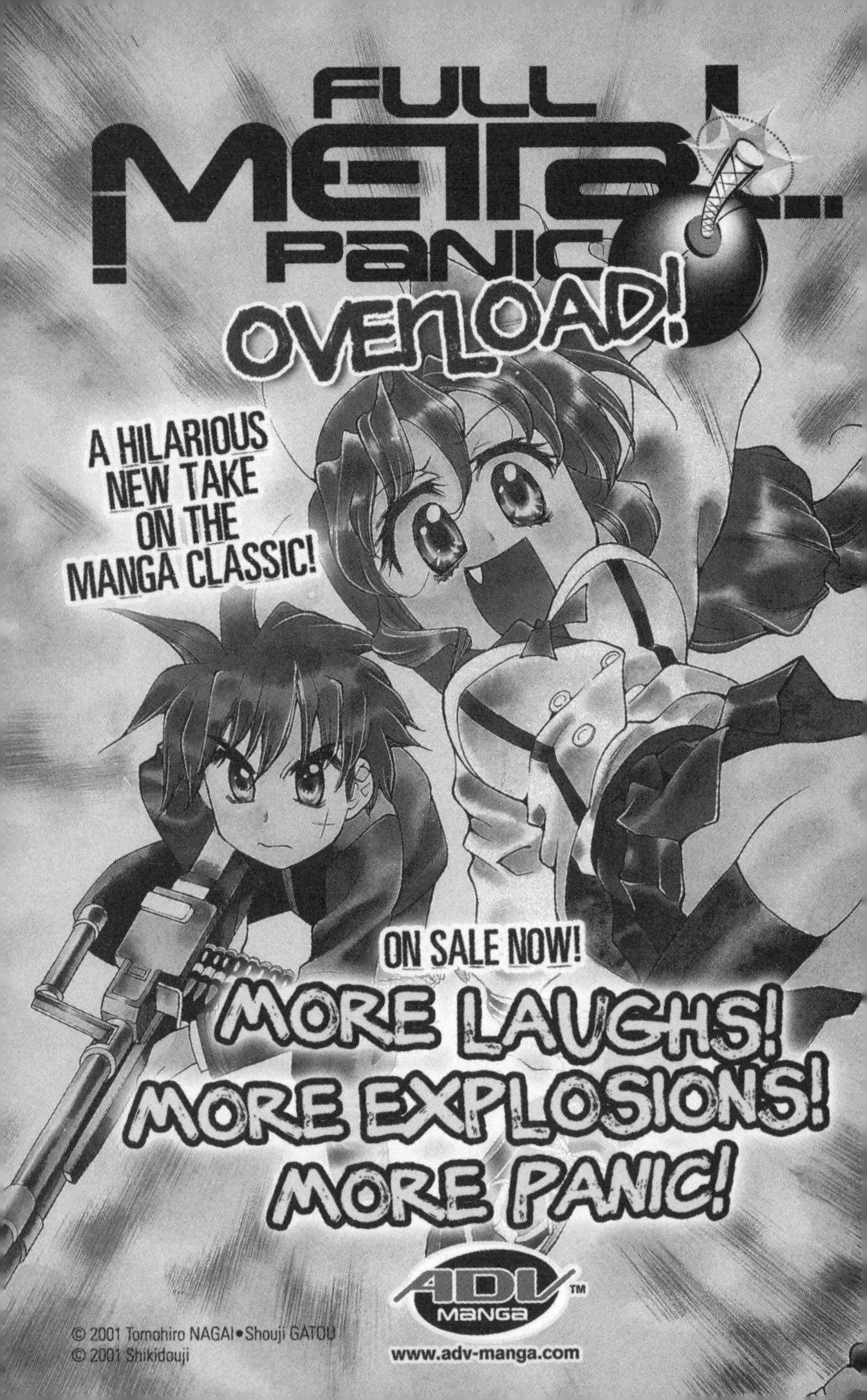

FULL METAL PANIC
OVERLOAD!
A HILARIOUS NEW TAKE ON THE MANGA CLASSIC!
ON SALE NOW!
MORE LAUGHS!
MORE EXPLOSIONS!
MORE PANIC!
ADV Manga ™
© 2001 Tomohiro NAGAI • Shouji GATOU
© 2001 Shikidouji
www.adv-manga.com

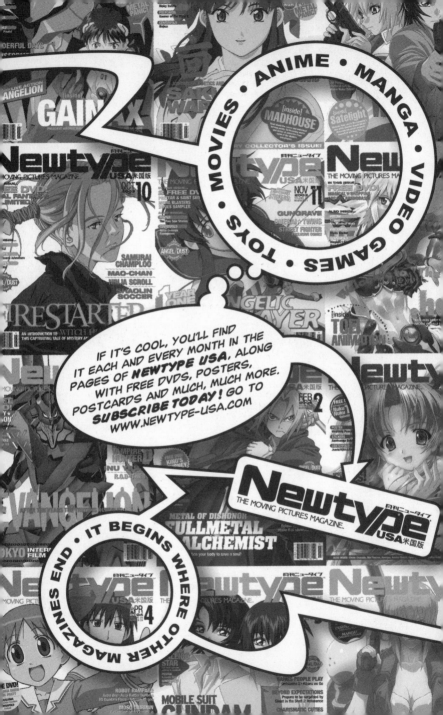

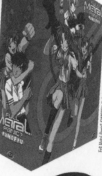